VISTAS

Introducción a la lengua española | FIFTH EDITION

Student Activities Manual

VISTA®
HIGHER LEARNING

ISBN: 978-1-62680-640-5

6 7 8 9 PP 19 18

Table of Contents

VIDEO MANUAL

Fotonovela Activities

Panorama cultural Activities

LAB MANUAL

Introduction

The VISTAS 5/e Student Activities Manual

Completely coordinated with the **VISTAS** student textbook, the Student Activities Manual (SAM) for **VISTAS** provides you with additional practice of the vocabulary, grammar, and language functions presented in each of the textbook's eighteen lessons. The Workbook and Video Manual sections will help you continue building your reading and writing skills in Spanish. The Lab Manual section will help you continue building your listening and speaking skills in Spanish. Icons and page references in the **recursos** boxes of the **VISTAS** student textbook correlate the Workbook, Video Manual, and Lab Manual sections to your textbook, letting you know when activities are available for use. Answers to the Workbook, Video Manual, and Lab Manual activities are located in a separate SAM Answer Key.

The Workbook

Each lesson's workbook activities focus on developing your reading and writing skills as they recycle the language of the corresponding textbook lesson. Exercise formats include, but are not limited to, true/false, multiple choice, fill-in-the-blanks, sentence completions, fleshing out sentences from key elements, and answering questions. You will also find activities based on drawings, photographs, and maps.

Reflecting the overall organization of the textbook lessons, each workbook lesson consists of **Contextos, Estructura,** and **Panorama** sections. After every three lessons, there is a **Repaso** section, providing cumulative practice of the grammar and vocabulary you learned over previous lessons.

The Video Manual
Fotonovela

The **VISTAS Fotonovela** video offers 6–9 minutes of footage for each of the textbook's lessons. Each episode tells the continuing story of a group of college students from various Spanish-speaking countries who are studying in Mexico. The video, shot in a variety of locations throughout Mexico, follows them through an academic year.

The video activities will guide you through the video episodes. **Antes de ver el video** offers previewing activities to prepare you for successful video viewing experiences. **Mientras ves el video** contains while-viewing activities. Lastly, **Después de ver el video** provides post-viewing questions that check your comprehension of the video. These are followed by some questions that ask you to apply what you have learned to your own life or offer your own opinions.

Panorama cultural

The **Panorama cultural** video is integrated with the **Panorama** section in each lesson of **VISTAS**. Each video is 2–3 minutes long and consists of documentary footage from the countries of focus. The images were specially chosen for interest level and visual appeal, while the all-Spanish narrations were carefully written to reflect the vocabulary and grammar covered in the text.

As you watch the videos, you will experience a diversity of images and topics: cities, monuments, traditions, festivals, archeological sites, geographical wonders, and more. You will be transported to each Spanish-speaking country, including the United States and Canada, thereby having the opportunity to expand your cultural perspectives with information directly related to the content of your textbook.

The video activities that accompany the **Panorama cultural** video will prepare you for viewing and guide you through the video modules using the same pre-, while-, and post-viewing activity structure as the **Fotonovela** video activities.

Flash cultura

The dynamic **Flash cultura** video is integrated with the **Adelante** section of each lesson. The video was filmed in eight countries. **Flash cultura**'s reporters take you on a tour of the sites and customs of the Spanish-speaking world. Along the way, they conduct impromptu interviews with the people they meet, who in turn share their own perspectives on their country and culture.

The segments will provide you with valuable cultural insights as well as authentic linguistic input as they gradually move into Spanish. Be prepared to listen to a wide variety of accents and vocabulary from the Spanish-speaking world!

Lab Manual

The Lab Manual activities are designed for use with the **VISTAS** Lab Audio Program MP3s on the Supersite (also available for purchase on CD). They focus on building your listening comprehension, speaking, and pronunciation skills in Spanish, as they reinforce the vocabulary and grammar of the corresponding textbook lesson. The Lab Manual guides you through the Lab Audio Program MP3 files, providing the written cues you will need in order to follow along easily. You will hear statements, questions, mini-dialogues, conversations, monologues, commercials, and many other kinds of listening passages, all recorded by native Spanish speakers. You will encounter a wide range of activities, such as listening-and-repeating exercises, listening-and-speaking practice, listening-and-writing activities, illustration-based work, and dictations.

Each lesson of the Lab Manual contains a **Contextos** section that practices the vocabulary taught in the corresponding textbook lesson. In **Lecciones 1–9**, a **Pronunciación** section follows; it parallels the one found in your textbook, and, in addition, offers a dictation exercise. In **Lecciones 10–18**, the **Pronunciación** sections are unique to the Lab Manual and the Lab MP3 files since, in those lessons, your textbook features **Ortografía** sections instead of **Pronunciación**. Each lesson then continues with an **Estructura** section and closes with a **Vocabulario** section that allows you to listen to and repeat the active vocabulary listed on the final page of the corresponding section in the student textbook.

We hope that you will find the **VISTAS 5/e** Student Activities Manual to be a useful language learning resource and that it will help you increase your Spanish language skills in a productive, enjoyable fashion.

*The **VISTAS** 5/e Authors and the Vista Higher Learning Editorial Staff*

Photography Credits

contextos

1 **Saludos** For each question or expression, write the appropriate answer from the box in each blank.

De nada.	Encantada.	Muy bien, gracias.	Nos vemos.
El gusto es mío.	Me llamo Pepe.	Nada.	Soy de Argentina.

1. ¿Cómo te llamas? _____

2. ¿Qué hay de nuevo? _____

3. ¿De dónde eres? _____

4. Adiós. _____

5. ¿Cómo está usted? _____

6. Mucho gusto. _____

7. Te presento a la señora Díaz. _____

8. Muchas gracias. _____

2 **Conversación** Complete this conversation by writing one word in each blank.

ANA Buenos días, señor González. ¿Cómo (1)_____ (2)_____?

SR. GONZÁLEZ (3)_____ bien, gracias. ¿Y tú, (4)_____ estás?

ANA Regular. (5)_____ presento a Antonio.

SR. GONZÁLEZ Mucho (6)_____, Antonio.

ANTONIO El gusto (7)_____ (8)_____.

SR. GONZÁLEZ ¿De dónde (9)_____, Antonio?

ANTONIO (10)_____ (11)_____ México.

ANA (12)_____ luego, señor González.

SR. GONZÁLEZ Nos (13)_____, Ana.

ANTONIO (14)_____, señor González.

3 **Saludos, despedidas y presentaciones** Complete these phrases with the missing words. Then write each phrase in the correct column of the chart.

1. ¿_____ pasa?

2. _____ luego.

3. _____ gusto.

4. Te _____ a Irene.

5. ¿_____ estás?

6. _____ días.

7. El _____ es mío.

8. Nos _____.

Saludos	Despedidas	Presentaciones

4 **Diferente** Write the word or phrase that does not belong in each group.

1. Hasta mañana.
   Nos vemos.
   Buenos días.
   Hasta pronto.

   _____

2. ¿Qué tal?
   Regular.
   ¿Qué pasa?
   ¿Cómo estás?

   _____

3. Igualmente.
   De nada.
   Mucho gusto.
   Encantada.

   _____

4. Muchas gracias.
   Muy bien, gracias.
   No muy bien.
   Regular.

   _____

5. ¿De dónde eres?
   ¿Cómo está usted?
   ¿De dónde es usted?
   ¿Cómo se llama usted?

   _____

6. Chau.
   Buenos días.
   Hola.
   ¿Qué tal?

   _____

estructura

1.1 Nouns and articles

1 **¿Masculino o femenino?** Write the correct definite article before each noun. Then write each article and noun in the correct column.

_____ hombre   _____ pasajero   _____ chico

_____ profesora   _____ mujer   _____ pasajera

_____ chica   _____ conductora   _____ profesor

Masculino   **Femenino**

_____   _____

_____   _____

_____   _____

_____   _____

_____   _____

2 **¿El, la, los o las?** Write the correct definite article before each noun.

1. _____ autobús   6. _____ mano

2. _____ maleta   7. _____ país

3. _____ lápices   8. _____ problema

4. _____ diccionario   9. _____ cosas

5. _____ palabras   10. _____ diarios

3 **Singular y plural** Give the plural form of each singular article and noun and the singular form of each plural article and noun.

1. unas fotografías _____   6. unas escuelas _____

2. un día _____   7. unos videos _____

3. un cuaderno _____   8. un programa _____

4. unos pasajeros _____   9. unos autobuses _____

5. una computadora _____   10. una palabra _____

4 **Las cosas** For each picture, provide the noun with its corresponding definite and indefinite articles.

1. _____   2. _____   3. _____   4. _____

Lección 1 Workbook Activities   **3**

1.2 Numbers 0–30

1 **Los números** Solve the math problems to complete the crossword puzzle.

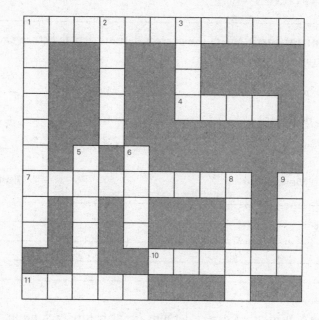

Horizontales

1. veinte más cinco
4. veintiséis menos quince
7. treinta menos catorce
10. veinticinco menos veintiuno
11. once más dos

Verticales

1. once más once
2. seis más tres
3. trece menos trece
5. doce más ocho

6. veintinueve menos diecinueve
8. veintitrés menos dieciséis
9. siete más uno

2 **¿Cuántos hay?** Write questions that ask how many items there are. Then write the answers. Write out the numbers.

> **modelo**
> 2 cuadernos
> ¿Cuántos cuadernos hay? Hay *dos cuadernos*.

1. 3 diccionarios _____

2. 12 estudiantes _____

3. 10 lápices _____

4. 7 maletas _____

5. 25 palabras _____

6. 21 países _____

7. 13 escuelas _____

8. 18 pasajeros _____

9. 15 computadoras _____

10. 27 fotografías _____

1.3 Present tense of **ser**

1 **Los pronombres** In the second column, write the subject pronouns that you would use when addressing the people listed in the first column. In the third column, write the pronouns you would use when talking about them. The first item has been done for you.

Personas	Addressing them	Talking about them
1. el señor Díaz	usted	él
2. Jimena y Marissa		
3. Maru y Miguel		
4. la profesora		
5. un estudiante		
6. el director de una escuela		
7. tres chicas		
8. un pasajero de autobús		
9. Juan Carlos y Felipe		
10. una turista		

2 **Nosotros somos...** Rewrite each sentence with the new subject. Change the verb **ser** as necessary.

> modelo
> Ustedes son profesores.
> Nosotros *somos profesores*.

1. Nosotros somos estudiantes. Ustedes _____.
2. Usted es de Puerto Rico. Ella _____.
3. Nosotros somos conductores. Ellos _____.
4. Yo soy turista. Tú _____.
5. Ustedes son de México. Nosotras _____.
6. Ella es profesora. Yo _____.
7. Tú eres de España. Él _____.
8. Ellos son pasajeros. Ellas _____.

3 **¡Todos a bordo! (All aboard!)** Complete Jorge's introduction of his travelling companions with the correct forms of **ser**.

Hola, me llamo Jorge y (1)_____ de Cuba. Pilar y Nati (2)_____ de España. Pedro, Juan y Paco (3)_____ de México. Todos nosotros (4)_____ estudiantes. La señorita Blasco (5)_____ de San Antonio. Ella (6)_____ la profesora. Luis (7)_____ el conductor. Él (8)_____ de Puerto Rico. Ellos (9)_____ de los Estados Unidos. El autobús (10)_____ de la agencia Marazul. Todos nosotros (11)_____ pasajeros de la agencia de viajes Marazul. Perdón, ¿de dónde (12)_____ tú, quién (13)_____ ella y de quién (14)_____ las maletas?

Lección 1 Workbook Activities **5**

Workbook

4 **¿De quién es?** Use **ser** + **de** (or **del**) to indicate that the object belongs to the person or people listed.

modelo

nombre / el pasajero
Es el nombre del pasajero.

1. diccionario / el estudiante _____

2. cuadernos / las chicas _____

3. mano / Sara _____

4. maletas / la turista _____

5. computadoras / los profesores _____

6. autobús / el conductor _____

7. lápices / la joven _____

8. fotografía / los chicos _____

9. computadora / la directora _____

10. país / David _____

5 **¿De dónde son?** Use **ser** + **de** to indicate where the people are from.

modelo

Ustedes / Costa Rica
Ustedes son de Costa Rica.

1. Lina y María / Colombia _____

2. El profesor / México _____

3. Tú y los jóvenes / Argentina _____

4. Las estudiantes / Estados Unidos _____

5. Ellos / Canadá _____

6. La mujer / Puerto Rico _____

7. Los turistas / España _____

8. Él y yo / Chile _____

9. Nosotras / Cuba _____

10. Usted / Venezuela _____

6 **¿De quién?** Write questions for these answers using the correct interrogative words from the list.

modelo

¿De dónde son ellos?
Ellos son de España.

| cómo | dónde | de quién(es) | por qué |
| cuándo | de dónde | qué | quién(es) |

1. _____

Los lápices son de Alejandro.

2. _____

Daniela es de Ecuador.

3. _____

Es una foto.

4. _____

Ellas son Claudia y Marta.

1.4 Telling time

1 **La hora** Give the time shown on each clock using complete sentences.

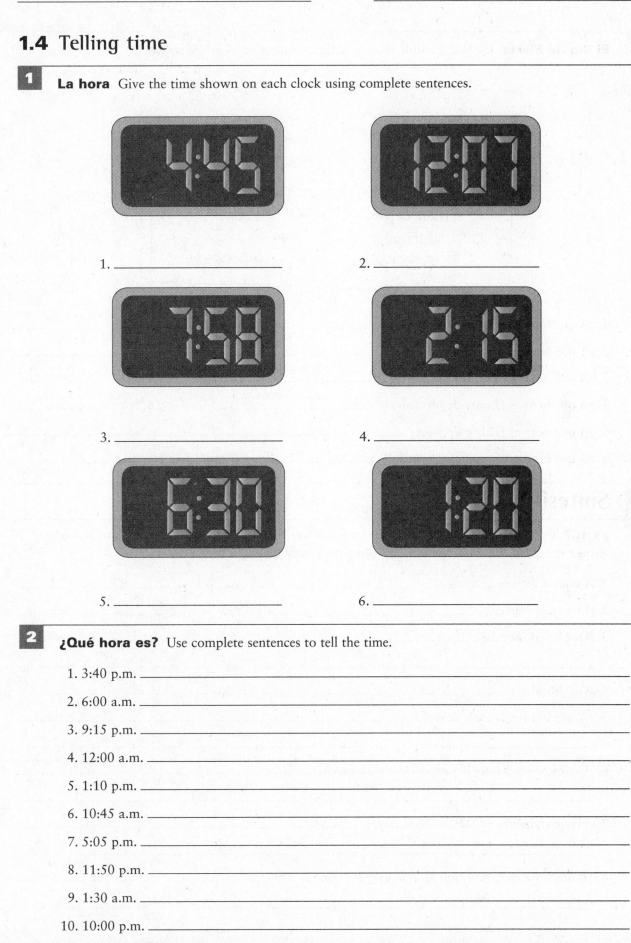

1. _____

2. _____

3. _____

4. _____

5. _____

6. _____

2 **¿Qué hora es?** Use complete sentences to tell the time.

1. 3:40 p.m. _____

2. 6:00 a.m. _____

3. 9:15 p.m. _____

4. 12:00 a.m. _____

5. 1:10 p.m. _____

6. 10:45 a.m. _____

7. 5:05 p.m. _____

8. 11:50 p.m. _____

9. 1:30 a.m. _____

10. 10:00 p.m. _____

Lección 1 Workbook Activities

3   **El día de Marta** Use the schedule to answer the questions in complete sentences.

8:45 a.m.	Biología
11:00 a.m.	Cálculo
12:00 p.m.	Almuerzo
2:00 p.m.	Literatura
4:15 p.m.	Yoga
10:30 p.m.	Programa especial

1. ¿A qué hora es la clase de biología? _____

2. ¿A qué hora es la clase de cálculo? _____

3. ¿A qué hora es el almuerzo (*lunch*)? _____

4. ¿A qué hora es la clase de literatura? _____

5. ¿A qué hora es la clase de yoga? _____

6. ¿A qué hora es el programa especial? _____

Síntesis

¿Y tú? Use lesson vocabulary, the present tense of **ser**, expressions for telling time, and numbers to answer the questions about yourself and your class using complete sentences.

1. ¿Cómo te llamas? _____

2. ¿De dónde eres? _____

3. ¿Qué hay de nuevo? _____

_____

4. ¿Qué hora es? _____

5. ¿A qué hora es la clase de español? _____

_____

6. ¿Cuántos estudiantes hay en la clase de español? _____

_____

7. ¿Hay estudiantes de México en la clase? _____

8. ¿A qué hora es tu (*your*) programa de televisión favorito? _____

panorama

Estados Unidos y Canadá

1 **¿Cierto o falso?** Indicate if each statement is **cierto** (*true*) or **falso** (*false*). Then correct the false statements.

1. La mayor parte de la población hispana de los Estados Unidos es de origen mexicano.

_____

2. Hay más (*more*) hispanos en Illinois que (*than*) en Texas.

_____

3. El estado con la mayor población hispana de los Estados Unidos es California.

_____

4. Muchos hispanos en Canadá tienen estudios universitarios.

_____

5. Muchos hispanos en Canadá hablan una de las lenguas oficiales: inglés o portugués.

_____

6. Hoy, uno de cada cuatro niños en los Estados Unidos es de origen hispano.

_____

7. Los tacos, las enchiladas y las quesadillas son platos cubanos.

_____

8. Las ciudades con más población hispana en Canadá son Montreal, Toronto y Vancouver.

_____

9. Un barrio cubanoamericano importante de Miami se llama la Pequeña Cuba.

_____

10. Los puertorriqueños de Nueva York celebran su origen con un desfile.

_____

2 **Completar** Complete the sentences with the correct information from **Panorama** about the Hispanic communities in Canada and the United States.

1. Se estima que en el año 2034 uno de cada tres _____ va a ser de origen hispano.

2. Los hispanos _____ activamente en la vida cotidiana y profesional de Canadá.

3. La Pequeña Habana es una _____ de Cuba en los Estados Unidos.

4. El desfile puertorriqueño es un gran espectáculo con carrozas y música _____, _____ y hip-hop.

5. La comida mexicana es muy _____ en los Estados Unidos.

Lección 1 Workbook Activities   **9**

3   **Un mapa**   Write the name of each state numbered on the map and provide its Hispanic population (rounded to the nearest million).

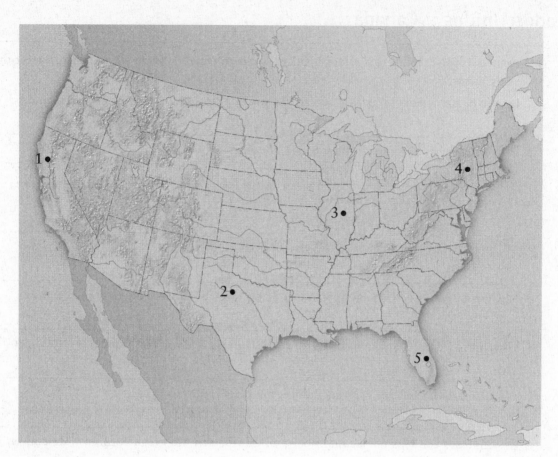

1. _____   (_____ millones de hispanos)

2. _____   (_____ millones de hispanos)

3. _____   (_____ millones de hispanos)

4. _____   (_____ millones de hispanos)

5. _____   (_____ millones de hispanos)

4   **¿De dónde es?**   Write the origin of each item listed (**estadounidense, mexicano, cubano,** or **puertorriqueño**).

                                                            Origen

1. desfile en Nueva York   _____

2. enchiladas, tacos y quesadillas   _____

3. Pequeña Habana   _____

4. comida tex-mex y cali-mex   _____

5. mayor población hispana de EE.UU.   _____

contextos

Lección 2

1 **Categorías** Read each group of items. Then write the word from the list that describes a category for the group.

cafetería	clase	laboratorio
ciencias	geografía	materias

1. sándwiches, tacos, sodas, bananas _____

2. mapas, capitales, países, nacionalidades _____

3. literatura, matemáticas, geografía, lenguas extranjeras _____

4. microscopios, experimentos, ciencias, elementos _____

5. física, química, biología, astronomía _____

6. pizarras, tiza, borrador, papelera, escritorios _____

2 **Buscar (To search)** Find school-related words in the grid, looking horizontally and vertically. Circle them in the puzzle, and write the words in the blanks with the correct accents.

S	P	F	Í	S	I	C	A	B	Q	G	Ñ	E
O	E	S	P	A	Ñ	O	L	E	U	S	B	R
C	X	B	E	C	O	N	O	M	Í	A	I	M
I	A	R	T	E	G	Q	F	A	M	F	O	I
O	M	C	A	C	L	O	U	R	I	V	L	N
L	E	P	R	U	E	B	A	A	C	D	O	G
O	N	U	E	O	N	E	Z	H	A	U	G	L
G	Ñ	D	A	M	C	L	A	S	E	T	Í	É
Í	E	J	I	L	C	I	E	N	C	I	A	S
A	P	E	R	I	O	D	I	S	M	O	P	I
D	S	T	H	O	R	A	R	I	O	Q	X	A
H	U	M	A	N	I	D	A	D	E	S	M	O

_____   _____

_____   _____

_____   _____

_____   _____

3 **El calendario** Use the calendar to answer these questions with complete sentences.

marzo

L	M	M	J	V	S	D
		1	2	3	4	5
6	7	8	9	10	11	12
13	14	15	16	17	18	19
20	21	22	23	24	25	26
27	28	29	30	31		

abril

L	M	M	J	V	S	D
					1	2
3	4	5	6	7	8	9
10	11	12	13	14	15	16
17	18	19	20	21	22	23
24	25	26	27	28	29	30

modelo

¿Qué día de la semana es el 8 de abril (*April*)?
El *8 de abril es sábado./Es sábado.*

1. ¿Qué día de la semana es el 21 de marzo (*March*)? _____

2. ¿Qué día de la semana es el 7 de abril? _____

3. ¿Qué día de la semana es el 2 de marzo? _____

4. ¿Qué día de la semana es el 28 de marzo? _____

5. ¿Qué día de la semana es el 19 de abril? _____

6. ¿Qué día de la semana es el 12 de marzo? _____

7. ¿Qué día de la semana es el 3 de abril? _____

8. ¿Qué día de la semana es el 22 de abril? _____

9. ¿Qué día de la semana es el 31 de marzo? _____

10. ¿Qué día de la semana es el 9 de abril? _____

4 **Completar** Complete these sentences using words from the word bank.

arte	ciencias	examen	horario	tarea
biblioteca	matemáticas	geografía	laboratorio	universidad

1. La biología, la química y la física son _____.

2. El _____ dice (*says*) a qué hora son las clases.

3. A las once hay un _____ de biología.

4. Martín es artista y toma (*takes*) una clase de _____.

5. Hay veinte calculadoras en la clase de _____.

6. Los experimentos se hacen (*are made*) en el _____.

7. Hay muchos libros en la _____.

8. Los mapas son importantes en el curso de _____.

Nombre _____ Fecha _____

estructura

2.1 Present tense of **-ar** verbs

1 **Tabla (*Chart*) de verbos** Write the missing forms of each verb.

Present tense					
Infinitivo	yo	tú	Ud., él, ella	nosotros/as	Uds., ellos
1. cantar					
2. _____	pregunto				
3. _____		contestas			
4. _____			practica		
5. _____				deseamos	
6. _____					llevan

2 **Completar** Complete these sentences using the correct form of the verb in parentheses.

1. Los turistas _____ (viajar) en un autobús.

2. Elena y yo _____ (hablar) español en clase.

3. Los estudiantes _____ (llegar) a la residencia estudiantil.

4. Yo _____ (dibujar) un reloj en la pizarra.

5. La señora García _____ (comprar) libros en la librería de la universidad.

6. Francisco y tú _____ (regresar) de la biblioteca.

7. El semestre _____ (terminar) en mayo (*May*).

8. Tú _____ (buscar) a tus (*your*) compañeros de clase en la cafetería.

3 **¿Quién es?** Complete these sentences with the correct verb form so that the sentence makes sense.

| busco | conversas | esperan | regresamos | trabaja |
| compran | enseña | necesitas | toman | viajan |

1. Nosotras _____ a las seis de la tarde.

2. Muchos estudiantes _____ el curso de periodismo.

3. Rosa y Laura no _____ a Manuel.

4. Tú _____ con los chicos en la residencia estudiantil.

5. El compañero de cuarto de Jaime _____ en el laboratorio.

6. Yo _____ un libro en la biblioteca.

7. Rebeca y tú _____ unas maletas para viajar.

8. La profesora Reyes _____ el curso de español.

4 **Usar los verbos** Form sentences using the words provided. Use the correct present tense or infinitive form of each verb.

1. una estudiante / desear / hablar / con su profesora de biología

_____

2. Mateo / desayunar / en la cafetería de la universidad

_____

3. (mí) / gustar / cantar y bailar

_____

4. los profesores / contestar / las preguntas (*questions*) de los estudiantes

_____

5. ¿(ti) / gustar / la clase de música?

_____

6. (nosotros) / esperar / viajar / a Madrid

_____

7. (yo) / necesitar / practicar / los verbos en español

_____

8. (mí) / no / gustar / los exámenes

_____

5 **¿Y tú?** Use complete sentences to answer these yes/no questions.

> *modelo*
> ¿Bailas el tango?
> Sí, bailo el tango./No, no bailo el tango.

1. ¿Estudias ciencias en la universidad?

_____

2. ¿Conversas mucho con los compañeros de clase?

_____

3. ¿Esperas estudiar administración de empresas?

_____

4. ¿Necesitas descansar después de (*after*) los exámenes?

_____

5. ¿Compras los libros en la librería?

_____

6. ¿Te gusta viajar?

_____

2.2 Forming questions in Spanish

1   **Las preguntas** Make questions out of these statements by inverting the word order.

1. Ustedes son de Puerto Rico.

   _____

2. El estudiante dibuja un mapa.

   _____

3. Los turistas llegan en autobús.

   _____

4. La clase termina a las dos de la tarde.

   _____

5. Samuel trabaja en la biblioteca.

   _____

6. Los chicos miran un programa.

   _____

7. El profesor Miranda enseña la clase de humanidades.

   _____

8. Isabel compra cinco libros de historia.

   _____

9. Mariana y Javier preparan la tarea.

   _____

10. Ellas conversan en la cafetería de la universidad.

   _____

2   **Seleccionar** Choose an interrogative word from the list to write a question that corresponds with each response.

adónde	cuándo	de dónde	por qué	quién
cuáles	cuántos	dónde	qué	quiénes

1. _____

   Ellos caminan a la biblioteca.

2. _____

   El profesor de español es de México.

3. _____

   Hay quince estudiantes en la clase.

4. _____

   El compañero de cuarto de Jaime es Manuel.

5. _____

   La clase de física es en el laboratorio.

6. _____

   Julia lleva una computadora portátil.

7. _____

   El programa de televisión termina en dos horas.

8. _____

   Estudio biología porque hay un examen mañana.

Lección 2 Workbook Activities

3 **Muchas preguntas** Form four different questions from each statement.

1. Mariana canta en el coro (*choir*) de la universidad.

_____

_____

_____

_____

2. Carlos busca el libro de arte.

_____

_____

_____

_____

3. La profesora Gutiérrez enseña contabilidad.

_____

_____

_____

_____

4. Ustedes necesitan hablar con el profesor de economía.

_____

_____

_____

_____

4 **¿Qué palabra?** Write the interrogative word or phrase that makes sense in each question.

1. ¿_____ es la clase de administración de empresas?
   Es en la biblioteca.

2. ¿_____ preparas la tarea de matemáticas?
   Preparo la tarea de matemáticas el lunes.

3. ¿_____ es el profesor de inglés?
   Es de los Estados Unidos.

4. ¿_____ libros hay en la clase de biología?
   Hay diez libros.

5. ¿_____ caminas con (*with*) Olga?
   Camino a la clase de biología con Olga.

6. ¿_____ enseña el profesor Hernández en la universidad?
   Enseña literatura.

7. ¿_____ llevas cinco libros en la mochila?
   Porque regreso de la biblioteca.

8. ¿_____ es la profesora de física?
   Es la señora Caballero.

2.3 Present tense of **estar**

1 **Están en...** Answer the questions based on the pictures. Write complete sentences.

1. ¿Dónde están Cristina y
   Bruno? _____

2. ¿Dónde están la profesora
   y el estudiante? _____

3. ¿Dónde está la puerta?
   _____

4. ¿Dónde está la mochila?
   _____
   _____

5. ¿Dónde está el pasajero?
   _____
   _____

6. ¿Dónde está José Miguel?
   _____
   _____

2 **¿Dónde están?** Use these cues and the correct form of **estar** to write complete sentences. Add any missing words.

1. libros / cerca / escritorio

   _____

2. ustedes / al lado / puerta

   _____

3. calculadora / entre / computadoras

   _____

4. lápices / sobre / cuaderno

   _____

5. estadio / lejos / residencias

   _____

6. mochilas / debajo / mesa

   _____

7. tú / en / clase de psicología

   _____

8. reloj / a la derecha / ventana

   _____

9. Rita / a la izquierda / Julio

   _____

3 **¿Ser o estar?** Complete these sentences with the correct present-tense form of the verb **ser** or **estar**.

1. Sonia _____ muy bien hoy.

2. Las sillas _____ delante del escritorio.

3. Ellos _____ estudiantes de sociología.

4. Alma _____ de la capital de España.

5. _____ las diez y media de la mañana.

6. Nosotras _____ en la biblioteca.

4 **El libro** Complete this cell phone conversation with the correct forms of **estar**.

GUSTAVO Hola, Pablo. ¿(1)_____ en la residencia estudiantil?

PABLO Sí, (2)_____ en la residencia.

GUSTAVO Necesito el libro de física.

PABLO ¿Dónde (3)_____ el libro?

GUSTAVO El libro (4)_____ en mi cuarto (*room*), al lado de la computadora.

PABLO ¿Dónde (5)_____ la computadora?

GUSTAVO La computadora (6)_____ encima del escritorio.

PABLO ¡Aquí (*Here*) (7)_____ la computadora y... el libro de física!

5 **Conversación** Complete this conversation with the correct forms of **ser** and **estar**.

PILAR Hola, Irene. ¿Cómo (1)_____?

IRENE Muy bien, ¿y tú? ¿Qué tal?

PILAR Bien, gracias. Te presento a Pablo.

IRENE Encantada, Pablo.

PILAR Pablo (2)_____ de México.

IRENE ¿De qué parte de (*where in*) México (3)_____?

PABLO (4)_____ de Monterrey. Y tú, ¿de dónde (5)_____?

IRENE (6)_____ de San Juan, Puerto Rico.

PILAR ¿Dónde (7)_____ Claudia, tu (*your*) compañera de cuarto?

IRENE (8)_____ en la residencia estudiantil.

PABLO Nosotros vamos a (*are going to*) la librería ahora.

PILAR Necesitamos comprar el manual del laboratorio de física.

IRENE ¿A qué hora (9)_____ la clase de física?

PABLO (10)_____ a las doce del día. ¿Qué hora (11)_____ ahora?

PILAR (12)_____ las once y media.

IRENE ¡Menos mal que (*Fortunately*) la librería (13)_____ cerca del laboratorio!

PILAR Sí, no (14)_____ muy lejos de la clase. Nos vemos.

IRENE Hasta luego.

PABLO Chau.

2.4 Numbers 31 and higher

1 **Números de teléfono** Provide the words for these telephone numbers.

> **modelo**
> 968-3659
> nueve, sesenta y ocho, treinta y seis, cincuenta y nueve

1. 776-7799

_____

2. 543-3162

_____

3. 483-4745

_____

4. 352-5073

_____

5. 888-7540

_____

6. 566-3857

_____

2 **¿Cuántos hay?** Use the inventory list to answer these questions about the amount of items in stock at the school bookstore. Use complete sentences and write out the Spanish words for numbers.

Inventario			
libros	320	mochilas	31
cuadernos	276	diccionarios	43
plumas	125	mapas	66

1. ¿Cuántos mapas hay? _____

2. ¿Cuántas mochilas hay? _____

3. ¿Cuántos diccionarios hay? _____

4. ¿Cuántos cuadernos hay? _____

5. ¿Cuántas plumas hay? _____

6. ¿Cuántos libros hay? _____

3 **Mi universidad** Use the information provided to complete the paragraph about your university. Write out the Spanish words for numbers.

> 25.000 estudiantes en total   44 nacionalidades diferentes   1.432 computadoras
> 350 españoles   10.500 libros   126 especialidades

Mi universidad es muy grande, hay (1)_____ estudiantes en el campus. Hay personas de (2)_____ países diferentes y (3)_____ son estudiantes de España. La biblioteca tiene (4)_____ libros de (5)_____ especialidades diferentes. Hay mucha tecnología; hay (6)_____ computadoras en el campus. ¡Me encanta mi universidad!

4 **Por ciento** Use the pie chart to complete these sentences. Write out the Spanish numbers in words.

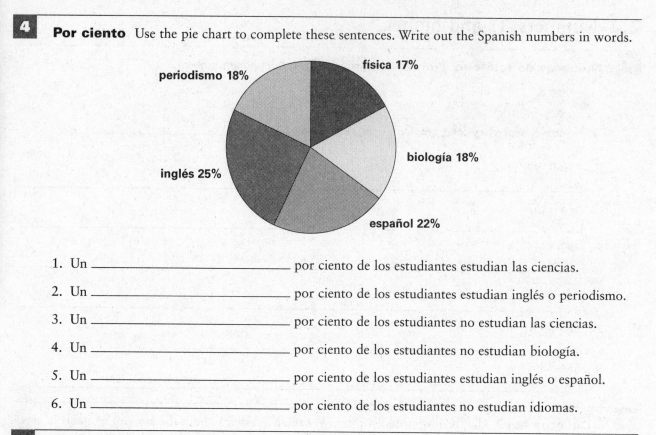

1. Un _____ por ciento de los estudiantes estudian las ciencias.

2. Un _____ por ciento de los estudiantes estudian inglés o periodismo.

3. Un _____ por ciento de los estudiantes no estudian las ciencias.

4. Un _____ por ciento de los estudiantes no estudian biología.

5. Un _____ por ciento de los estudiantes estudian inglés o español.

6. Un _____ por ciento de los estudiantes no estudian idiomas.

Síntesis

La universidad Imagine that a parent calls a college student during the second week of courses. Write questions that the parent might ask about the son or daughter's schedule, courses, and campus life. Use the cues provided. Then write possible answers. Use question words, the present tense of **estar**, the present tense of **-ar** verbs, and lesson vocabulary.

> **modelo**
>
> ¿A qué hora termina la clase de español?
> La clase de español termina a las tres.

- ¿A qué hora...?
- ¿Dónde está...?
- ¿Qué cursos...?
- ¿Trabajas...?

- ¿Estudias...?
- ¿Qué días de la semana...?
- ¿Hay...?
- ¿Cuántos...?

_____

_____

_____

_____

_____

_____

_____

panorama

España

1 **¿De qué ciudad es?** Write the city or town in Spain associated with each item.

1. el Museo del Prado _____
2. el baile flamenco _____
3. la Sagrada Familia _____
4. La Tomatina _____
5. segunda (*second*) ciudad en población _____

2 **¿Cierto o falso?** Indicate whether each statement is **cierto** or **falso**. Then correct the false statements.

1. Las islas Canarias y las islas Baleares son de España.
_____

2. Zaragoza es una de las ciudades principales de España.
_____

3. La moneda de España es el peso.
_____

4. En España hay más de un idioma.
_____

5. La Tomatina es uno de los platos más deliciosos de España.
_____

6. El chef José Andrés vive en Washington, D.C.
_____

3 **El mapa de España** Fill in the blanks with the name of the city or geographical feature.

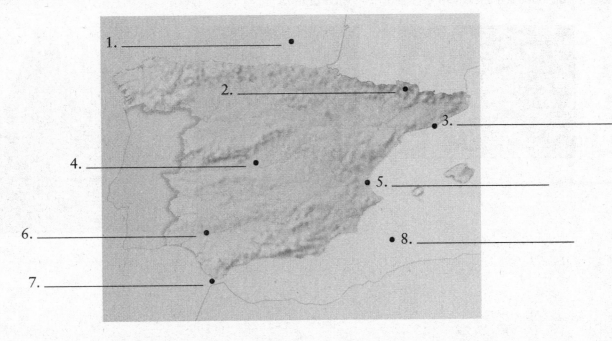

1. _____
2. _____
3. _____
4. _____
5. _____
6. _____
7. _____
8. _____

4   **Profesiones**   Complete these sentences with the person's occupation.

1. Fernando Alonso es _____.

2. Rosa Montero es _____.

3. Pedro Almodóvar es _____.

4. Miguel de Cervantes es _____.

5. Paz Vega es _____.

6. Diego Velázquez es _____.

5   **Palabras cruzadas (*crossed*)**   Write one letter on each blank. Then answer the final question, using the new word that is formed.

1. Islas españolas del mar Mediterráneo

2. Español, catalán, gallego, valenciano y euskera

3. José Andrés es dueño (*owner*) de varios

4. Museo español famoso

5. Pintor español famoso

6. Obra más conocida de Diego Velázquez

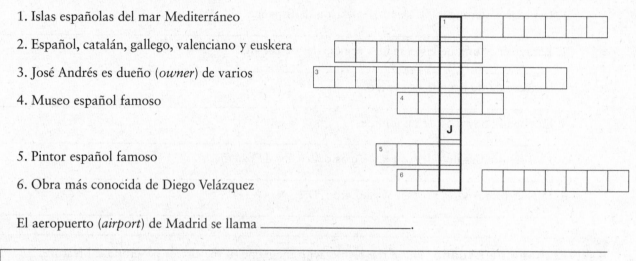

El aeropuerto (*airport*) de Madrid se llama _____.

6   **Las fotos**   Label the object shown in each photo.

1. _____

2. _____

3. _____

contextos

Workbook

1 **La familia** Look at the family tree and describe the relationships between these people.

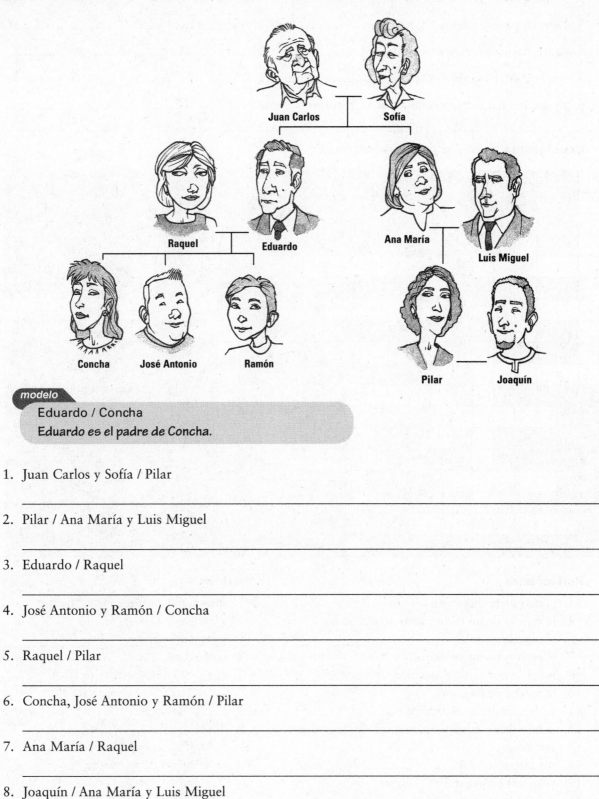

modelo

Eduardo / Concha
Eduardo es el padre de Concha.

1. Juan Carlos y Sofía / Pilar

_____

2. Pilar / Ana María y Luis Miguel

_____

3. Eduardo / Raquel

_____

4. José Antonio y Ramón / Concha

_____

5. Raquel / Pilar

_____

6. Concha, José Antonio y Ramón / Pilar

_____

7. Ana María / Raquel

_____

8. Joaquín / Ana María y Luis Miguel

_____

2 **Diferente** Write the word that does not belong in each group.

1. ingeniera, médica, programadora, periodista, hijastra _____

2. cuñado, nieto, yerno, suegra, nuera _____

3. sobrina, prima, artista, tía, hermana _____

4. padre, hermano, hijo, novio, abuelo _____

5. muchachos, tíos, niños, chicos, hijos _____

6. amiga, hermanastra, media hermana, madrastra _____

3 **Crucigrama** Complete this crossword puzzle.

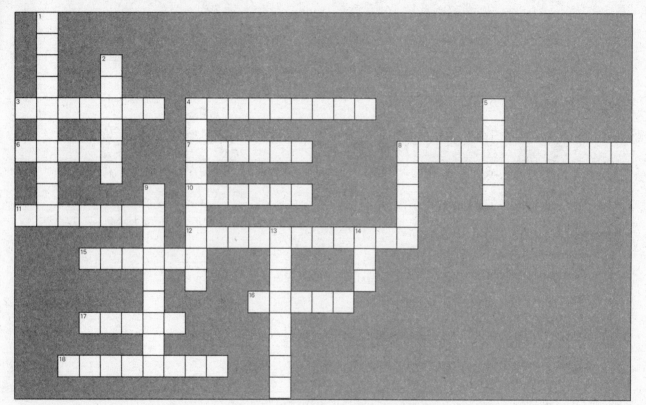

Horizontales

3. el hijo de mi hermano
4. la esposa de mi padre, pero no soy su hijo
6. el hijo de mi hija
7. el esposo de mi hermana
8. hombre que estudió (*studied*) computación
10. la madre de mi padre
11. padre, madre e (*and*) hijos
12. el hijo de mi madrastra, pero no de mi padre
15. doctor
16. tus nietos son los _____ de tus hijos
17. personas en general
18. la hija de mi esposa, pero no es mi hija

Verticales

1. mujer que escribe (*writes*) para el *New York Times*
2. compañeros inseparables
4. chicos
5. el esposo de mi madre es el _____ de mis abuelos
8. el hijo de mi tía
9. abuelos, primos, tíos, etc.
13. Pablo Picasso y Diego Velázquez
14. el hermano de mi madre

estructura

3.1 Descriptive adjectives

1 **¿Cómo son?** Use the adjective in parentheses that agrees with each subject to write descriptive sentences about them.

> **modelo**
> **(gordo, delgada)**
> Lidia: Lidia *es delgada.*
> el novio de Olga: *El novio de Olga es gordo.*

(simpático, guapos, alta)

1. la profesora de historia: _____

2. David y Simón: _____

3. el artista: _____

(trabajadora, viejo, delgadas)

4. esas (*those*) muchachas: _____

5. el abuelo de Alberto: _____

6. la programadora: _____

2 **Descripciones** Complete each sentence with the correct form of the adjective in parentheses.

1. Lupe, Rosa y Tomás son _____ (bueno) amigos.

2. Ignacio es _____ (alto) y _____ (guapo).

3. Laura y Virginia son _____ (bajo) y _____ (delgado).

4. Pedro y Vanessa son _____ (moreno), pero Diana es _____ (pelirrojo).

5. Nosotras somos _____ (inteligente) y _____ (trabajador).

6. Esos (*Those*) chicos son _____ (simpático), pero son _____ (tonto).

3 **No** Answer these questions using the adjective with the opposite meaning.

> **modelo**
> ¿Es alta Manuela?
> No, *es baja.*

1. ¿Es antipático don Antonio? _____

2. ¿Son morenas las hermanas de Lupe? _____

3. ¿Es fea la mamá de Carlos? _____

4. ¿Son viejos los primos de Sofía? _____

5. ¿Son malos los padres de Alejandro? _____

6. ¿Es guapo el tío de Andrés? _____

Lección 3 Workbook Activities **25**

4 **Origen y nacionalidad** Read the names and origins of the people in this tour group. Then write sentences saying what city they are from and what their nationalities are.

> modelo
>
> Álvaro Estrada / Miami, Estados Unidos
> Álvaro Estrada *es de Miami. Es estadounidense.*

1. Lucy y Lee Hung / Pekín, China _____

2. Pierre y Marie Lebrun / Montreal, Canadá _____

3. Luigi Mazzini / Roma, Italia _____

4. Elizabeth Mitchell / Londres, Inglaterra (*England*) _____

5. Roberto Morales / Madrid, España _____

6. Andrés y Patricia Padilla / La Habana, Cuba _____

7. Paula y Cecilia Robles / San José, Costa Rica _____

8. Arnold Schmidt / Berlín, Alemania (*Germany*) _____

9. Antoinette y Marie Valois / París, Francia _____

10. Marta Zedillo / Guadalajara, México _____

5 **Completar** Complete each sentence with the correct form of the adjective in parentheses.

(bueno)

1. La clase de matemáticas es muy _____ .

2. Rogelio es un _____ compañero de cuarto.

3. Agustina compra una _____ mochila para (*for*) los libros.

4. Andrés y Guillermo son muy _____ estudiantes.

(malo)

5. Federico es antipático y una _____ persona.

6. Ahora es un _____ momento para descansar.

7. La comida (*food*) de la cafetería es _____ .

8. Son unas semanas _____ para viajar.

(grande)

9. Hay un _____ evento en el estadio hoy.

10. Los problemas en esa (*that*) familia son muy _____ .

11. La biblioteca de la universidad es _____ .

12. La prima de Irma es una _____ amiga.

3.2 Possessive adjectives

1 **¿De quién es?** Answer each question affirmatively using the correct possessive adjective.

> **modelo**
> ¿Es tu maleta?
> Sí, *es mi maleta.*

1. ¿Es la calculadora de Adela? _____

2. ¿Es mi clase de español? _____

3. ¿Son los papeles de la profesora? _____

4. ¿Es el diccionario de tu compañera de cuarto? _____

5. ¿Es tu novia? _____

6. ¿Son los lápices de ustedes? _____

2 **Familia** Write the appropriate forms of the possessive adjectives indicated in parentheses.

1. _____ (*My*) cuñada, Christine, es francesa.

2. _____ (*Their*) parientes están en Costa Rica.

3. ¿Quién es _____ (*your* fam.) tío?

4. _____ (*Our*) padres regresan a las diez.

5. Es _____ (*his*) tarea de matemáticas.

6. Linda y María son _____ (*my*) hijas.

7. ¿Dónde trabaja _____ (*your* form.) esposa?

8. _____ (*Our*) familia es grande.

3 **Clarificar** Add a prepositional phrase that clarifies to whom the item(s) belongs.

> **modelo**
> ¿Es su libro? (ellos)
> *¿Es el libro de ellos?*

1. ¿Cuál es su problema? (ella)

   _____

2. Trabajamos con su madre. (ellos)

   _____

3. ¿Dónde están sus papeles? (ustedes)

   _____

4. ¿Son sus plumas? (ella)

   _____

5. ¿Quiénes son sus compañeros de cuarto? (él)

   _____

6. ¿Cómo se llaman sus sobrinos? (usted)

   _____

Lección 3 Workbook Activities   **27**

4 **Posesiones** Write sentences using possessive adjectives to indicate who owns these items.

> modelo
>
> Yo compro un escritorio.
> **Es mi escritorio.**

1. Ustedes compran cuatro sillas. _____

2. Tú compras una mochila. _____

3. Nosotros compramos una mesa. _____

4. Yo compro una maleta. _____

5. Él compra unos lápices. _____

6. Ellos compran una calculadora. _____

5 **Mi familia** Paula is talking about her family. Complete her description with the correct possessive adjectives.

Somos cinco hermanos. Ricardo, José Luis y Alejandro son (1)_____
hermanos. Francisco es (2)_____ cuñado. Es el esposo de (3)_____
hermana mayor, Mercedes. Francisco es argentino. (4)_____ papás viven en
Mar del Plata. Vicente es el hijo de (5)_____ hermano mayor, Ricardo. Él es
(6)_____ sobrino favorito. (7)_____ mamá se llama Isabel y es española.
Ellos viven con (8)_____ familia en Sevilla. José Luis estudia en Monterrey y vive
con la tía Remedios y (9)_____ dos hijos, Carlos y Raquel, (10)_____
primos. Alejandro y yo vivimos con (11)_____ papás en Guadalajara. Los papás
de (12)_____ mamá viven también con nosotros. Alejandro y yo compartimos
(13)_____ problemas con (14)_____ abuelos. Ellos son muy buenos.
Y tú, ¿cómo es (15)_____ familia?

6 **Preguntas** Answer these questions using possessive adjectives and the words in parentheses.

> modelo
>
> ¿Dónde está tu amiga? (Barcelona)
> **Mi amiga está en Barcelona.**

1. ¿Cómo es tu padre? (alto y moreno)

_____

2. José, ¿dónde están mis papeles? (en el escritorio)

_____

3. ¿Cómo es la escuela de Felipe? (pequeña y vieja)

_____

4. ¿Son mexicanos los amigos de ustedes? (puertorriqueños)

_____

5. Mami, ¿dónde está mi tarea? (en la mesa)

_____

6. ¿Cómo son los hermanos de Pilar? (simpáticos)

_____

Workbook

3.3 Present tense of **-er** and **-ir** verbs

1 **Conversaciones** Complete these conversations with the correct forms of the verbs in parentheses.

(leer)

1. —¿Qué _____, Ana?

2. —_____ un libro de historia.

(vivir)

3. —¿Dónde _____ ustedes?

4. —Nosotros _____ en Nueva York. ¿Y tú?

(comer)

5. —¿Qué _____ ustedes?

6. —Yo _____ un sándwich y Eduardo _____ pizza.

(deber)

7. —Profesora, ¿_____ abrir nuestros libros ahora?

8. —Sí, ustedes _____ abrir los libros en la página (*page*) 87.

(escribir)

9. —¿_____ un libro, Melinda?

10. —Sí, _____ un libro de ciencia ficción.

2 **Frases** Write complete sentences using the correct forms of the verbs in parentheses.

1. (nosotros) (Escribir) muchas composiciones en la clase de literatura.

_____

2. Esteban y Luisa (aprender) a bailar el tango.

_____

3. ¿Quién no (comprender) la lección de hoy?

_____

4. (tú) (Deber) comprar un mapa de Quito.

_____

5. Ellos no (recibir) muchos mensajes electrónicos (*e-mails*) de sus padres.

_____

6. (yo) (Buscar) unas fotos de mis primos.

_____

3 **¿Qué verbo es?** Choose the most logical verb to complete each sentence, and write the correct form.

1. Tú _____ (abrir, correr, decidir) en el parque (*park*), ¿no?

2. Yo _____ (asistir, compartir, leer) a conciertos de Juanes.

3. ¿_____ (aprender, creer, deber) a leer tu sobrino?

4. Yo no _____ (beber, vivir, comprender) la tarea de física.

5. Los estudiantes _____ (escribir, beber, comer) hamburguesas en la cafetería.

6. Mi esposo y yo _____ (decidir, leer, deber) el *Miami Herald*.

Workbook

4   **Tú y ellos** Rewrite each sentence using the subject in parentheses. Change the verb form and possessive adjectives as needed.

> **modelo**
>
> Carolina no lee sus libros. (nosotros)
> *Nosotros no leemos nuestros libros.*

1. Rubén cree que la lección 3 es fácil. (ellos)

_____

2. Mis hermanos aprenden alemán en la universidad. (mi tía)

_____

3. Aprendemos a hablar, leer y escribir en la clase de español. (yo)

_____

4. Sandra escribe en su diario todos los días (*every day*). (tú)

_____

5. Comparto mis problemas con mis padres. (Víctor)

_____

6. Vives en una residencia interesante y bonita. (nosotras)

_____

5   **Descripciones** Look at the drawings and use these verbs to describe what the people are doing.

abrir	aprender	comer	leer

1. Nosotros _____   2. Yo _____

3. Mirta _____   4. Los estudiantes _____

3.4 Present tense of **tener** and **venir**

1   **Completar** Complete these sentences with the correct forms of **tener** and **venir**.

1. ¿A qué hora _____ ustedes al estadio?

2. ¿_____ tú a la universidad en autobús?

3. Nosotros _____ una prueba de psicología mañana.

4. ¿Por qué no _____ Juan a la clase de literatura?

5. Yo _____ dos hermanos y mi prima _____ tres.

6. ¿_____ ustedes fotos de sus parientes?

7. Mis padres _____ unos amigos japoneses.

8. Inés _____ con su esposo y yo _____ con Ernesto.

9. Marta y yo no _____ al laboratorio los sábados.

10. ¿Cuántos nietos _____ tú?

11. Yo _____ una clase de contabilidad a las once de la mañana.

12. Mis amigos _____ a comer a la cafetería hoy.

2   **¿Qué tienen?** Rewrite each sentence, using the logical expression with **tener**.

1. Los estudiantes (tienen hambre, tienen miedo de) tomar el examen de química.

_____

2. Las turistas (tienen sueño, tienen prisa) por llegar al autobús.

_____

3. Mi madre (tiene cincuenta años, tiene razón) siempre (*always*).

_____

4. Vienes a la cafetería cuando (*when*) (tienes hambre, tienes frío).

_____

5. (Tengo razón, Tengo frío) en la biblioteca porque abren las ventanas.

_____

6. Rosaura y María (tienen calor, tienen ganas) de mirar la televisión.

_____

7. Nosotras (tenemos cuidado, no tenemos razón) con el sol (*sun*).

_____

8. David toma mucha agua cuando (*when*) (tiene miedo, tiene sed).

_____

Workbook

3   **Expresiones con *tener***   Complete each sentence with the correct expression and the appropriate form of **tener**.

tener cuidado	tener miedo	tener mucha suerte	tener que
tener ganas	tener mucha hambre	tener prisa	tener razón

1. Mis sobrinos _____ del perro (*dog*) de mis abuelos.

2. Necesitas _____ con la computadora portátil (*laptop*).

3. Yo _____ practicar el vocabulario de español.

4. Lola y yo _____ de escuchar música latina.

5. Anita cree que (*that*) dos más dos son cinco. Ella no _____.

6. Ganas (*You win*) cien dólares en la lotería. Tú _____.

Síntesis

Tus parientes   Choose an interesting relative of yours and write a description of that person. Use possessive adjectives, descriptive adjectives, the present tense of **tener** and **venir**, the present tense of **-er** and **-ir** verbs, and lesson vocabulary to answer these questions in your description.

- ¿Quién es?
- ¿Cómo es?
- ¿De dónde viene?
- ¿Cuántos hermanos/primos/hijos... tiene?

- ¿Cómo es su familia?
- ¿Dónde vive?
- ¿Cuántos años tiene?
- ¿De qué tiene miedo?

_____

_____

_____

_____

_____

_____

_____

_____

_____

_____

_____

panorama

Ecuador

1 **¿Cierto o falso?** Indicate whether the statements are **cierto** or **falso**. Correct the false statements.

1. Ecuador tiene aproximadamente el área de Rhode Island.

_____

2. Panamá y Chile limitan con (*border*) Ecuador.

_____

3. Las islas Galápagos están en el océano Pacífico.

_____

4. Quito está en la cordillera de los Andes.

_____

5. Todos (*All*) los ecuatorianos hablan lenguas indígenas.

_____

6. Rosalía Arteaga es novelista y pintora.

_____

7. Hay volcanes activos en Ecuador.

_____

8. Oswaldo Guayasamín fue un novelista ecuatoriano famoso.

_____

2 **El mapa de Ecuador** Fill in the blanks on this map with the correct geographical names.

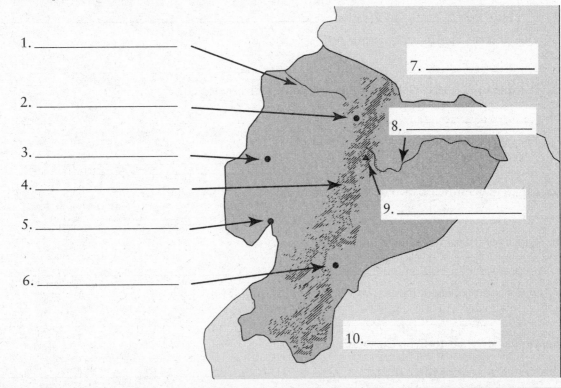

1. _____

2. _____

3. _____

4. _____

5. _____

6. _____

7. _____

8. _____

9. _____

10. _____

3 **Fotos de Ecuador** Label the place shown in each photograph.

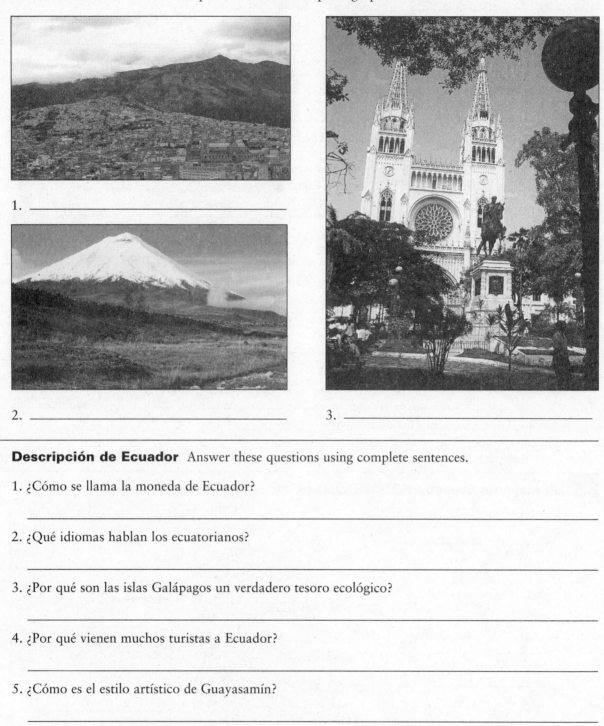

1. _____

2. _____   3. _____

4 **Descripción de Ecuador** Answer these questions using complete sentences.

1. ¿Cómo se llama la moneda de Ecuador?

_____

2. ¿Qué idiomas hablan los ecuatorianos?

_____

3. ¿Por qué son las islas Galápagos un verdadero tesoro ecológico?

_____

4. ¿Por qué vienen muchos turistas a Ecuador?

_____

5. ¿Cómo es el estilo artístico de Guayasamín?

_____

6. ¿Qué es la Mitad del Mundo?

_____

7. ¿Qué deportes puedes hacer (*can you do*) en los Andes?

_____

8. ¿Dónde viven las tortugas gigantes?

_____

repaso   **Lecciones 1–3**

1 **¿Ser o estar?** Complete each sentence with the correct form of **ser** or **estar**.

1. Los abuelos de Maricarmen _____ de España.

2. La cafetería de la universidad _____ cerca del estadio.

3. Gerónimo y Daniel _____ estudiantes de sociología.

4. —Hola, Gabriel. _____ María. ¿Cómo _____?

5. El cuaderno de español _____ debajo del libro de química.

6. Victoria no viene a clase hoy porque _____ enferma.

2 **¿Quiénes son?** Read the clues and complete the chart. Write out the numbers.

1. La persona de los Estados Unidos tiene 32 años.
2. David es de Canadá.
3. La programadora no es la persona de Cuba.
4. El conductor tiene 45 años.
5. Gloria es artista.
6. La médica tiene 51 años.
7. La persona de España tiene ocho años menos que el conductor.
8. Ana es programadora.

Nombre	Profesión	Edad (*Age*)	Nacionalidad
Raúl	estudiante	diecinueve	mexicano
Carmen			
			estadounidense
David			
	programadora		

3 **Oraciones** Form complete sentences using the words provided. Write out the words for numbers.

1. ¿cómo / estar / usted, / señora Rodríguez?

_____

2. estudiante / llegar / grande / biblioteca / 5:30 p.m.

_____

3. hay / 15 / cuadernos / sobre / escritorio

_____

4. nieto / Inés / aprender / español / escuela

_____

5. conductora / autobús / no / ser / antipático

_____

6. abuelo / Lisa / tener / 72 / años

_____

4   **Preguntas** Write sentences with the words provided. Then make each statement into a question.

1. clase de contabilidad / ser / 11:45 a.m.

_____

_____

2. su tía / favorito / tener / 35 años

_____

_____

3. tu profesor / biología / ser / México

_____

_____

4. biblioteca / estar / cerca / residencia estudiantil

_____

_____

5   **Los países** Complete these sentences with information from the **Panorama** sections.

1. En Miami, hay un barrio cubano que se llama la _____.

2. Las personas de origen _____ son el grupo hispano más grande en los EE.UU.

3. Las islas Baleares y las islas Canarias son parte de _____.

4. La lengua indígena que más se habla en Ecuador es el _____.

6   **Tu familia** Imagine that these people are your relatives. Choose one and write several sentences about that person. First, say where the person is located in the photo. Include this information: name, relationship to you, profession, age, and place of origin. Describe the person and his or her activities using the adjectives and verbs you have learned.

_____

_____

_____

_____

_____

contextos

1 **Los deportes** Name the sport associated with each object. Include the definite article.

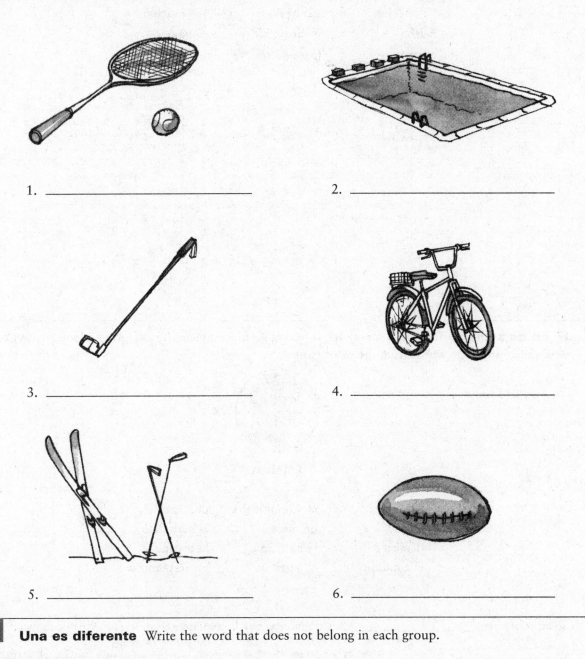

1. _____

2. _____

3. _____

4. _____

5. _____

6. _____

2 **Una es diferente** Write the word that does not belong in each group.

1. pasatiempo, diversión, ratos libres, trabajar _____

2. patinar, descansar, esquiar, nadar, bucear _____

3. baloncesto, películas, fútbol, tenis, vóleibol _____

4. museo, equipo, jugador, partido, pelota _____

5. correo electrónico, revista, periódico, tenis _____

6. cine, deportivo, gimnasio, piscina, restaurante _____

3 **¿Qué son?** Write each of these words in the appropriate column in the chart.

andar en patineta	fútbol	montaña
baloncesto	gimnasio	natación
béisbol	jugar un videojuego	pasear
centro	leer una revista	restaurante

Deportes	Lugares	Actividades

4 **El fin de semana** Esteban is a very active young man. Complete the paragraph about his weekend with the appropriate words from the word bank.

Esteban

el centro	el monumento	una pelota
el cine	un museo	el periódico
deportes	la natación	la piscina
el gimnasio	el partido	un restaurante

Siempre leo (1)_____ los domingos por la mañana. Después, me gusta practicar

(2)_____. A veces, nado en (3)_____ que hay en el parque.

Cuando no nado, hago ejercicio (*exercise*) en (4)_____. Cuando hay mucho

tráfico en (5)_____, voy al gimnasio en bicicleta.

Cuando no como en casa, como en (6)_____ con mis amigos, y luego nosotros

podemos ver (7)_____ de béisbol. Algunos días, veo películas. Me gusta más ver

películas en (8)_____ que en mi casa.

estructura

4.1 Present tense of **ir**

1 **Vamos a la universidad** Complete the paragraph with the correct forms of **ir**.

Alina, Cristina y yo somos buenas amigas. (Nosotras) (1)_____ a la universidad a las

ocho de la mañana todos los días (*every day*). Ellas y yo (2)_____ al centro de

computación y leemos el correo electrónico. A las nueve Alina y Cristina (3)_____

a su clase de psicología y yo (4)_____ a mi clase de historia. A las diez y media yo

(5)_____ a la biblioteca a estudiar. A las doce (yo) (6)_____ a

la cafetería y como con ellas. Luego (*Afterwards*), Alina y yo (7)_____ a

practicar deportes. Yo (8)_____ a practicar fútbol y Alina (9)_____

a la piscina. Cristina (10)_____ a trabajar en la librería. Los fines de semana Alina,

Cristina y yo (11)_____ al cine.

2 **Los planes** Mr. Díaz wants to make sure he knows about everything that is going on. Answer his questions in complete sentences using the words in parentheses.

1. ¿Adónde van Marissa y Felipe? (pasear por la ciudad)

_____

2. ¿Cuándo van a correr los chicos? (noche)

_____

3. ¿A qué hora van al Bosque de Chapultepec? (a las dos y media)

_____

4. ¿Cuándo van a ir a la playa? (martes)

_____

5. ¿Qué va a hacer Jimena en el parque? (leer un libro)

_____

6. ¿Qué va a hacer Felipe en el parque? (jugar al fútbol)

_____

3 Conversación Complete this conversation with the correct forms of **ir**.

ELENA ¡Hola, Daniel! ¿Qué tal?

DANIEL Muy bien, gracias. ¿Y tú?

ELENA Muy bien. ¿Adónde (1)_____ ahora?

DANIEL (2)_____ al cine a ver una película. ¿Quieres (3)_____ conmigo?

ELENA No, gracias. Tengo mucha prisa ahora. (4)_____ al museo de arte.

DANIEL ¿Y adónde (5)_____ hoy por la noche?

ELENA Mi compañera de cuarto y yo (6)_____ a comer en un restaurante

italiano. ¿Quieres (7)_____ con nosotras?

DANIEL ¡Sí! ¿Cómo (8)_____ ustedes al restaurante?

ELENA (9)_____ en autobús. Hay un autobús que (10)_____

directamente al barrio (*neighborhood*) italiano.

DANIEL ¿A qué hora (11)_____ ustedes?

ELENA Creo que (12)_____ a llegar al restaurante a las nueve.

DANIEL ¿Desean (13)_____ a bailar luego (*afterwards*)?

ELENA ¡Sí!

DANIEL (14)_____ a invitar a nuestro amigo Pablo también. ¡Nos vemos a las nueve!

ELENA ¡Chau, Daniel!

4 ¡Vamos! Víctor is planning a weekend out with his friends. Combine elements from each column to describe what everyone is going to do. Use the correct verb forms.

ustedes	ver películas	el domingo
nosotros	ir al estadio de fútbol	el fin de semana
Víctor	tomar el sol	al mediodía
Claudio y su primo	visitar monumentos	a las tres
tú	pasear por el parque	por la noche
yo	comer en el restaurante	por la mañana

_____

_____

_____

_____

_____

_____

_____

_____

4.2 Stem-changing verbs: e→ie, o→ue

1 **¿Qué hacen?** Write complete sentences using the cues provided.

1. Vicente y Francisco / jugar / al vóleibol los domingos

_____

2. Adela y yo / empezar / a tomar clases de tenis

_____

3. ustedes / volver / de Cancún el viernes

_____

4. los jugadores de béisbol / recordar / el partido importante

_____

5. la profesora / mostrar / las palabras del vocabulario

_____

6. Adán / preferir / escalar la montaña de noche

_____

7. (yo) / entender / el plan de estudios

_____

8. (tú) / cerrar / los libros y te vas a dormir

_____

2 **Quiero ir** Alejandro wants to go on a hike with his friends, but Gabriela says he doesn't have time. Write the correct forms of the verbs in parentheses.

ALEJANDRO ¿(1)_____ (poder) ir a la excursión con ustedes? Aunque (*Although*) tengo que volver a mi casa a las tres.

GABRIELA No, no (2)_____ (poder) venir. Nosotros (3)_____(pensar) salir a las doce.

ALEJANDRO Yo (4)_____ (querer) ir. ¿(5)_____ (poder) ustedes volver a las dos?

GABRIELA No, tú tienes que comprender: Nosotros no (6)_____ (volver) a las dos. Nosotros (7)_____ (preferir) estar más tiempo en el pueblo.

ALEJANDRO Bueno, ¿a qué hora (8)_____ (pensar) regresar?

GABRIELA Yo no (9)_____ (pensar) volver hasta las nueve o las diez de la noche.

3 **No, no quiero** Answer these questions negatively, using complete sentences.

> **modelo**
>
> ¿Puedes ir a la biblioteca a las once?
> No, no puedo ir a la biblioteca a las once.

1. ¿Quieren ustedes patinar en línea con nosotros?

   _____

2. ¿Recuerdan ellas los libros que necesitan?

   _____

3. ¿Prefieres jugar al fútbol a nadar en la piscina?

   _____

4. ¿Duermen tus sobrinos en casa de tu abuela?

   _____

5. ¿Juegan ustedes al baloncesto en la universidad?

   _____

6. ¿Piensas que la clase de química orgánica es difícil?

   _____

7. ¿Encuentras el programa de computadoras en la librería?

   _____

8. ¿Vuelven ustedes a casa los fines de semana?

   _____

9. ¿Puedo tomar el autobús a las once de la noche?

   _____

10. ¿Entendemos la tarea de psicología?

    _____

4 **Mensaje electrónico** Complete this e-mail message with the correct form of the logical verb. Use each verb once.

dormir
empezar
entender
jugar
pensar
poder
preferir
querer
volver

Para Daniel Moncada	De Paco	Asunto Saludo

Hola, Daniel. Estoy con Mario en la biblioteca. Los exámenes
(1)_____ mañana. Por las noches Mario y yo no (2)_____
mucho porque tenemos que estudiar. Tú (3)_____ cómo estamos,
¿no? Yo (4)_____ que los exámenes serán (will be) muy difíciles.
Tengo muchas ganas de volver al pueblo. Cuando (5)_____ al
pueblo puedo descansar. Yo (6)_____ el pueblo a la ciudad.
(7)_____ volver pronto.
Si (If) Mario y yo compramos pasajes (tickets) de autobús, (8)_____
pasar el fin de semana contigo. En casa (At home) mis hermanos y yo
(9)_____ al fútbol en nuestros ratos libres.

Nos vemos,
Paco

4.3 Stem-changing verbs: e→i

1 **En el cine** Amalia and her brothers are going to the movies. Complete the story using the correct form of the verb provided.

1. Al entrar al cine, mis hermanos _____ (pedir) una soda.

2. Mis hermanos _____ (decir) que prefieren las películas de acción.

3. Nosotros _____ (pedir) ver la película de las seis y media.

4. Mis hermanos y yo _____ (conseguir) entradas (*tickets*) para estudiantes.

5. Yo _____ (repetir) el diálogo para mis hermanos.

6. Mis hermanos son pequeños y no _____ (seguir) bien la trama (*plot*) de la película.

2 **Conversaciones** Complete these conversations with the correct form of the verbs in parentheses.

(pedir)

1. —¿Qué _____ en la biblioteca, José?

2. — _____ un libro que necesito para el examen.

(conseguir)

3. —¿Dónde _____ ustedes las entradas (*tickets*) para los partidos de fútbol?

4. —Nosotros _____ las entradas en una oficina de la escuela.

(repetir)

5. —¿Quién _____ la excursión?

6. —Yo _____, me gusta mucho ese pueblo.

(seguir)

7. —¿Qué equipo _____ Manuel y Pedro?

8. —Pedro _____ a los Red Sox y Manuel _____ a los Yankees de Nueva York.

3 **¿Qué haces?** Imagine that you are writing in your diary. Choose at least five of these phrases and describe what you do on any given day. You should add any details you feel are necessary.

conseguir hablar español	pedir una pizza
conseguir el periódico	repetir una pregunta
pedir un libro	seguir las instrucciones

_____

_____

_____

_____

_____

Lección 4 Workbook Activities   **43**

Workbook

4   **La película** Read the paragraph. Then answer the questions using complete sentences.

Gastón y Lucía leen el periódico y deciden ir al cine. Un crítico dice que *Una noche en el centro* es buena. Ellos siguen la recomendación. Quieren conseguir entradas (*tickets*) para estudiantes, que son más baratas. Para conseguir entradas para estudiantes, deben ir a la oficina de la escuela antes de las seis de la tarde. La oficina cierra a las seis. Ellos corren para llegar a tiempo. Cuando ellos llegan, la oficina está cerrada y la secretaria está afuera (*outside*). Ellos le piden un favor a la secretaria. Explican que no tienen mucho dinero y necesitan entradas para estudiantes. La secretaria sonríe (*smiles*) y dice: "Está bien, pero es la última vez (*last time*)".

1. ¿Qué deciden hacer Gastón y Lucía?

_____

2. ¿Siguen la recomendación de quién?

_____

3. ¿Por qué Gastón y Lucía quieren conseguir entradas para estudiantes?

_____

4. ¿Cómo y cuándo pueden conseguir entradas para estudiantes?

_____

5. ¿Qué ocurre cuando llegan a la oficina de la escuela?

_____

_____

6. ¿Qué le piden a la secretaria? ¿Crees que ellos consiguen las entradas?

_____

_____

_____

5   **Preguntas** Answer these questions, using complete sentences.

1. ¿Cómo consigues buenas calificaciones (*grades*)?

_____

2. ¿Dónde pides pizza?

_____

3. ¿Sigues a algún (*any*) equipo deportivo?

_____

4. ¿Qué dicen tus padres si no consigues buenas calificaciones?

_____

5. ¿Qué programas repiten en la televisión?

_____

4.4 Verbs with irregular **yo** forms

 1 **Hago muchas cosas** Complete each sentence by choosing the best verb and writing its correct form.

1. (Yo) _____ un disco de música latina. (oír, suponer, salir)

2. (Yo) _____ la hamburguesa y la soda sobre la mesa. (poner, oír, suponer)

3. (Yo) _____ la tarea porque hay un examen mañana. (salir, hacer, suponer)

4. (Yo) _____ a mi sobrina a mi clase de baile. (traer, salir, hacer)

5. (Yo) _____ una película sobre un gran equipo de béisbol. (salir, suponer, ver)

6. (Yo) _____ a bailar los jueves por la noche. (ver, salir, traer)

7. (Yo) _____ que la película es buena, pero no estoy seguro (*sure*). (hacer, poner, suponer)

8. (Yo) _____ mi computadora portátil (*laptop*) a clase en la mochila. (traer, salir, hacer)

2 **Completar** Complete these sentences with the correct verb. Use each verb in the **yo** form once.

hacer	suponer
oír	traer
salir	ver

1. _____ para la clase a las dos.

2. Los fines de semana _____ mi computadora a casa.

3. _____ que me gusta trabajar los sábados por la mañana.

4. Por las mañanas, _____ música en la radio.

5. Cuando tengo hambre, _____ un sándwich.

6. Para descansar, _____ películas en la televisión.

3 **Preguntas** Answer these questions, using complete sentences.

1. ¿Adónde sales a bailar con tus amigos?

_____

2. ¿Ves partidos de béisbol todos los fines de semana?

_____

3. ¿Oyes música clásica?

_____

4. ¿Traes una computadora portátil (*laptop*) a clase?

_____

5. ¿Cómo supones que va a ser el examen de español?

_____

6. ¿Cuándo sales a comer?

_____

Workbook

4 **La descripción** Read this description of Marisol. Then imagine that you are Marisol, and write a description of yourself based on the information you read. The first sentence has been done for you.

Marisol es estudiante de biología en la universidad. Hace sus tareas todas (*every*) las tardes y sale por las noches a bailar o a comer en un restaurante cerca de la universidad. Los fines de semana, Marisol va a su casa a descansar, pero (*but*) trae sus libros. En los ratos libres, oye música o ve una película en el cine. Si hay un partido de fútbol, Marisol pone la televisión y ve los partidos con su papá. Hace algo (*something*) de comer y pone la mesa (*sets the table*).

Soy estudiante de biología en la universidad. _____

_____

_____

_____

_____

_____

_____

_____

Síntesis

Interview a classmate about his or her pastimes, weekend activities, and favorite sports. Use these questions as guidelines, and prepare several more before the interview. Then, write up the interview in a question-and-answer format, faithfully reporting your classmate's responses. Use lesson vocabulary, stem-changing verbs, and the present tense of **ir**.

- ¿Cuáles son tus pasatiempos? ¿Dónde los practicas?

- ¿Cuál es tu deporte favorito? ¿Practicas ese (*that*) deporte? ¿Eres un(a) gran aficionado/a? ¿Tu equipo favorito pierde muchas veces? ¿Quién es tu jugador(a) favorito/a?

- ¿Adónde vas los fines de semana? ¿Qué piensas hacer este (*this*) viernes?

- ¿Duermes mucho los fines de semana? ¿Vuelves a casa muy tarde (*late*)?

_____

_____

_____

_____

_____

_____

panorama

México

1 **Palabras** Use the clues to put the letters in order, spelling words in **Panorama**.

1. MGEÓINARIC _____
   resultado de la proximidad geográfica de México y los EE.UU.

2. ÍAD ED RMOTESU _____
   celebración en honor a las personas muertas

3. ALUJDAAAGRA _____
   ciudad número dos de México en población

4. ONETBI RZUEÁJ _____
   héroe nacional de México

5. CÁUNYAT _____
   península mexicana

6. ARSISTUT _____
   el D.F. atrae a miles de ellos

7. RADIF OKLAH _____
   la esposa de Diego Rivera

8. NGADORU _____
   estado mexicano que produce mucha plata

2 **¿Cierto o falso?** Indicate if each statement is **cierto** or **falso**. Then correct the false statements.

1. El área de México es casi dos veces el área de Texas.
   _____

2. Octavio Paz era un célebre periodista y narrador mexicano.
   _____

3. La geografía de México influye en aspectos económicos y sociales.
   _____

4. No hay mucho crecimiento en la población del D.F.
   _____

5. Frida Kahlo y Diego Rivera eran escritores.
   _____

6. El fin del imperio azteca comenzó (*started*) con la llegada (*arrival*) de los españoles en 1519.
   _____

7. Los turistas van a Guadalajara a ver las ruinas de Tenochtitlán.
   _____

8. México es el mayor productor de plata en el mundo.
   _____

Lección 4 Workbook Activities   **47**

3 **Completar** Complete these sentences with the correct words.

1. México está localizado geográficamente al _____ de los Estados Unidos.

2. Hoy en día hay _____ de personas de ascendencia mexicana en los Estados Unidos.

3. Los idiomas que se hablan en México son el español, el _____ y _____.

4. Frida Kahlo, esposa del artista _____, es conocida por sus autorretratos (*self-portraits*).

5. El imperio _____ dominó México del siglo XIV al siglo XVI.

6. Se celebra el Día de Muertos en los _____.

4 **¿Qué hacen?** Write sentences using these cues and adding what you learned in **Panorama**.

1. la tercera (*third*) ciudad de México en población / ser

_____

2. la moneda mexicana / ser

_____

3. el Distrito Federal / atraer (*to attract*)

_____

4. muchos turistas / ir a ver las ruinas de

_____

5. el D.F. / tener una población mayor que las de

_____

6. tú / poder / ver / las obras de Diego Rivera y Frida Kahlo en

_____

5 **Preguntas** Answer these questions in complete sentences.

1. ¿Cuáles son las cinco ciudades más importantes de México?

_____

2. ¿Quiénes son seis mexicanos célebres?

_____

3. ¿Qué países hacen frontera (*border*) con México?

_____

4. ¿Cuál es un río importante de México?

_____

5. ¿Cuáles son dos sierras importantes de México?

_____

6. ¿Qué ciudad mexicana importante está en la frontera con los EE.UU.?

_____

7. ¿En qué siglo (*century*) fue (*was*) fundada la Ciudad de México?

_____

contextos

1 **Viajes** Complete these sentences with the logical words.

1. Una persona que tiene una habitación en un hotel es _____.

2. El lugar donde los pasajeros esperan el tren es _____.

3. Para viajar en avión, tienes que ir _____.

4. Antes de entrar (*enter*) en el avión, tienes que mostrar _____.

5. La persona que trabaja en la recepción del hotel es _____.

6. Para planear (*plan*) tus vacaciones, puedes ir a _____.

7. El/la agente de viajes puede confirmar _____.

8. Para subir a tu habitación, tomas _____.

9. Para abrir la puerta de la habitación, necesitas _____.

10. Cuando una persona entra a otro país, tiene que mostrar _____.

2 **De vacaciones** Complete this conversation with the logical words.

aeropuerto	equipaje	llegada	playa
agente de viajes	habitación	pasajes	sacar fotos
cama	hotel	pasaportes	salida
confirmar	llave	pasear	taxi

ANTONIO ¿Llevas todo (*everything*) lo que vamos a necesitar para el viaje, Ana?

ANA Sí. Llevo los (1)_____ de avión. También llevo

los (2)_____ para entrar (*enter*) a Costa Rica.

ANTONIO Y yo tengo el (3)_____ con todas (*all*) nuestras cosas.

ANA ¿Tienes la cámara para (4)_____?

ANTONIO Sí, está en mi mochila.

ANA ¿Vamos al (5)_____ en metro?

ANTONIO No, vamos a llamar un (6)_____. Nos lleva directamente al aeropuerto.

ANA Voy a llamar al aeropuerto para (7)_____ la reservación.

ANTONIO La (8)_____ dice que está confirmada ya (*already*).

ANA Muy bien. Tengo muchas ganas de (9)_____ por Puntarenas.

ANTONIO Yo también. Quiero ir a la (10)_____ y nadar en el mar.

ANA ¿Cuál es la hora de (11)_____ al aeropuerto de San José?

ANTONIO Llegamos a las tres de la tarde y vamos directamente al (12)_____.

3   **Los meses** Write the appropriate month next to each description or event.

1. el Día de San Valentín _____
2. el tercer mes del año _____
3. Hannukah _____

4. el Día de las Madres _____
5. el séptimo mes del año _____
6. el Día de Año Nuevo (*New*) _____

4   **Las estaciones** Answer these questions using complete sentences.

1. ¿Qué estación sigue al invierno? _____

2. ¿En qué estación va mucha gente a la playa? _____

3. ¿En qué estación empiezan las clases? _____

5   **El tiempo** Answer these questions with complete sentences based on the weather map.

EL TIEMPO ESPAÑA HOY

Soleado
Variable
Nublado
Llueve
Tormenta
Viento
Nieva

Soria
Salamanca
Lleida
Girona
Barcelona
Madrid
Teruel
Cáceres
Castellón
Palma de Mallorca
Murcia
Almería
Las Palmas

1. ¿Hace buen tiempo en Soria? _____

2. ¿Llueve en Teruel? _____

3. ¿Hace sol en Girona? _____

4. ¿Está nublado en Murcia? _____

5. ¿Nieva en Cáceres? _____

6. ¿Qué tiempo hace en Salamanca? _____

7. ¿Hace viento cerca de Castellón? _____

8. ¿Qué tiempo hace en Almería? _____

9. ¿Está nublado en Las Palmas? _____

10. ¿Hace buen tiempo en Lleida? _____

estructura

5.1 Estar with conditions and emotions

1 **¿Por qué?** Choose the best phrase to complete each sentence.

1. José Miguel está cansado porque...
   a. trabaja mucho.
   b. su familia lo quiere.
   c. quiere ir al cine.

2. Los viajeros están preocupados porque...
   a. es la hora de comer.
   b. va a pasar un huracán (*hurricane*).
   c. estudian matemáticas.

3. Maribel y Claudia están tristes porque...
   a. nieva mucho y no pueden salir.
   b. van a salir a bailar.
   c. sus amigos son simpáticos.

4. Los estudiantes están equivocados porque...
   a. estudian mucho.
   b. pasean en bicicleta.
   c. su respuesta es incorrecta.

5. Laura está enamorada porque...
   a. tiene que ir a la biblioteca.
   b. su novio es simpático, inteligente y guapo.
   c. sus amigas ven una película.

6. Mis abuelos están felices porque...
   a. vamos a pasar el verano con ellos.
   b. mucha gente toma el sol.
   c. el autobús no llega.

2 **Completar** Complete these sentences with the correct forms of **estar** and the conditions or emotions from the list.

abierto	cerrado	desordenado	sucio
aburrido	cómodo	equivocado	triste
cansado	contento	feliz	

1. No tenemos nada que hacer; _____ muy _____.

2. Humberto _____ muy _____ en su gran cama nueva (*new*).

3. Los estudiantes de filosofía no _____ _____; ellos tienen razón.

4. Cuando Estela llega a casa a las tres de la mañana, _____ muy _____.

5. La habitación _____ _____ porque no tengo tiempo (*time*) de organizar los libros y papeles.

6. Son las once de la noche; no puedo ir a la biblioteca ahora porque _____ _____.

7. El auto de mi tío _____ muy _____ por la nieve y el lodo (*mud*) de esta semana.

8. Mi papá canta en la casa cuando _____ _____.

9. Alberto _____ _____ porque sus amigos están muy lejos.

10. Las ventanas _____ _____ porque hace calor.

Lección 5 Workbook Activities

3 **Marta y Juan** Complete this letter using **estar** + the correct forms of the emotions and conditions. Do not use terms more than once.

abierto	cómodo	enamorado	nervioso
aburrido	confundido	enojado	ocupado
avergonzado	contento	equivocado	seguro
cansado	desordenado	feliz	triste

Querida Marta:

¿Cómo estás? Yo (1)_____ porque mañana vuelvo a Puerto Rico y te voy a ver. Sé (I know) que tú (2)_____ porque tenemos que estar separados durante el semestre, pero (3)_____ de que (that) te van a aceptar en la universidad y que vas a venir en septiembre. La habitación en la residencia estudiantil no es grande, pero mi compañero de cuarto y yo (4)_____ aquí. Las ventanas son grandes y (5)_____ porque el tiempo es muy bueno en California. El cuarto no (6)_____ porque mi compañero de cuarto es muy ordenado. En la semana mis amigos y yo (7)_____ porque trabajamos y estudiamos muchas horas al día. Cuando llego a la residencia estudiantil por la noche, (8)_____ y me voy a dormir. Los fines de semana no (9)_____ porque hay muchas cosas que hacer en San Diego. Ahora (10)_____ porque mañana tengo que llegar al aeropuerto a las cinco de la mañana y está lejos de la universidad. Pero tengo ganas de estar contigo porque (11)_____ de ti (you) y (12)_____ porque te voy a ver mañana.

Te quiero mucho,
Juan

4 **¿Cómo están?** Read each sentence, then write a new one for each, using **estar** + an emotion or condition to tell how these people are doing or feeling.

> **modelo**
> Pepe tiene que trabajar muchas horas.
> *Pepe está ocupado.*

1. Vicente y Mónica tienen sueño. _____

2. No tenemos razón. _____

3. El pasajero tiene miedo. _____

4. Paloma se quiere casar con (*marry*) su novio. _____

5. Los abuelos de Irene van de vacaciones a Puerto Rico. _____

6. No sé (*I don't know*) si el examen va a ser fácil o difícil. _____

5.2 The present progressive

1 **Completar** Complete these sentences with the correct form of **estar** + the present participle of the verbs in parentheses.

1. Ana _____ (buscar) un apartamento en el centro de la ciudad.

2. Vamos a ver a mis primos que _____ (comer) en el café de la esquina.

3. (Yo) _____ (empezar) a entender muy bien el español.

4. Miguel y Elena _____ (vivir) en un apartamento en la playa.

5. El amigo de Antonio _____ (trabajar) en la oficina hoy.

6. (Tú) _____ (jugar) al *Monopolio* con tu sobrina y su amiga.

7. Las familias _____ (tener) muchos problemas con los hijos adolescentes.

8. El inspector de aduanas _____ (abrir) las maletas de Ramón.

9. (Nosotros) _____ (pensar) en ir de vacaciones a Costa Rica.

10. Mi compañera de cuarto _____ (estudiar) en la biblioteca esta tarde.

2 **Están haciendo muchas cosas** Look at the illustration and label what each person is doing. Use the present progressive.

1. El señor Rodríguez _____

_____.

2. Pepe y Martita _____

_____.

3. Paquito _____

_____.

4. Kim _____

5. Tus abuelos _____

_____.

6. (Yo) _____

_____.

7. La madre de David _____

_____.

8. (Tú) _____

_____.

5.3 Ser and estar

1

Usos de *ser* y *estar* Complete these sentences with **ser** and **estar**. Then write the letter that corresponds to the correct use of the verb in the blank at the end of each sentence.

Uses of *ser*	Uses of *estar*
a. Nationality and place of origin	i. Location or spatial relationships
b. Profession or occupation	j. Health
c. Characteristics of people and things	k. Physical states or conditions
d. Generalizations	l. Emotional states
e. Possession	m. Certain weather expressions
f. What something is made of	n. Ongoing actions (progressive tenses)
g. Time and date	
h. Where an event takes place	

1. El concierto de jazz _____ a las ocho de la noche. _____

2. Inés y Pancho _____ preocupados porque el examen va a ser difícil. _____

3. La playa _____ sucia porque hay muchos turistas. _____

4. No puedo salir a tomar el sol porque _____ nublado. _____

5. En el verano, Tito _____ empleado del hotel Brisas de Loíza. _____

6. Rita no puede venir al trabajo hoy porque _____ enferma. _____

7. La motocicleta nueva _____ de David. _____

8. (Yo) _____ estudiando en la biblioteca porque tengo un examen mañana. _____

9. La piscina del hotel _____ grande y bonita. _____

10. _____ importante estudiar, pero también tienes que descansar. _____

2

¿Ser o estar? In each of the following pairs, complete one sentence with the correct form of **ser** and the other with the correct form of **estar**.

1. Irene todavía no _____ lista para salir.

   Ricardo _____ el chico más listo de la clase.

2. Tomás no es un buen amigo porque _____ muy aburrido.

   Quiero ir al cine porque _____ muy aburrida.

3. Mi mamá está en cama porque _____ mala del estómago (*stomach*).

   El restaurante chino que está cerca del laboratorio _____ muy malo.

4. La mochila de Javier _____ verde (*green*).

   No me gustan las bananas cuando _____ verdes.

5. Elena _____ más rubia por tomar el sol.

   La hija de mi profesor _____ rubia.

6. Gabriela _____ muy delgada porque está enferma (*sick*).

   Mi hermano _____ muy delgado.

3 **En el hotel** Describe the Hotel San Juan using these cues and either **ser** or **estar** as appropriate.

1. la habitación / limpio y ordenado

_____

2. el restaurante del hotel / excelente

_____

3. la puerta del ascensor / abierta

_____

4. los otros huéspedes / franceses

_____

5. (yo) / cansada de viajar

_____

6. Paula y yo / buscando al botones

_____

7. la empleada / muy simpática

_____

8. el botones / ocupado

_____

9. ustedes / en la ciudad de San Juan

_____

10. (tú) / José Javier Fernández

_____

4 **La familia Piñero** Complete this paragraph with the correct forms of **ser** and **estar**.

Los Piñero (1)_____ de Nueva York, pero (2)_____ de vacaciones

en Puerto Rico. (3)_____ en un hotel grande en el pueblo de Dorado. Los padres

(4)_____ Elena y Manuel, y ahora (5)_____ comiendo en el

restaurante del hotel. Los hijos (6)_____ Cristina y Luis, y (7)_____

nadando en la piscina. Ahora mismo (8)_____ lloviendo, pero el sol va a salir

muy pronto (soon). Hoy (9)_____ lunes y la familia (10)_____

muy contenta porque puede descansar. El señor Piñero (11)_____ profesor

y la señora Piñero (12)_____ doctora. Los Piñero dicen: "¡Cuando

no (13)_____ de vacaciones, (14)_____ todo el tiempo

muy ocupados!".

Lección 5 Workbook Activities **55**

5.4 Direct object nouns and pronouns

1 **Monólogo de un viajero** Complete this monologue with the correct direct object pronouns.

Hoy es lunes. El sábado voy de viaje. Tengo cinco días, ¿no? Sí, (1)_____ tengo. Tengo que conseguir un pasaje de ida y vuelta. ¡Imprescindible! Mi hermano trabaja en una agencia de viajes; él me (2)_____ consigue fácilmente. Tengo que buscar un buen mapa de la ciudad. En Internet (3)_____ puedo encontrar. Y en la biblioteca puedo encontrar libros sobre el país; libros sobre su historia, su arquitectura, su geografía, su gente... (4)_____ voy a leer en el avión. También quiero comprar una mochila nueva. Pero (5)_____ quiero muy grande. ¿Y dónde está mi vieja cámara de fotos? (6)_____ tengo que buscar esta noche. Voy a tomar muchas fotos; mi familia (7)_____ quiere ver. Y... ¿cuándo voy a hacer las maletas? (8)_____ tengo que hacer el miércoles. Y eso es todo, ¿verdad? No, no es todo. Necesito encontrar un compañero o una compañera de viaje. Pero, hay un pequeño problema: ¿dónde (9)_____ encuentro o (10)_____ encuentro?

Síntesis

On another sheet of paper, describe the room and the people in the illustration. Use complete sentences. Explain what the people are doing and feeling, and why. Then choose one of the groups of people and write a conversation that they could be having. They should discuss a vacation that they are planning, the arrangements they are making for it, and the things that they will need to take. Use **ser** and **estar**, the present progressive, **estar** with conditions and emotions, direct object nouns and pronouns, and lesson vocabulary.

panorama

Puerto Rico

1 **¿Cierto o falso?** Indicate if each statement is **cierto** or **falso**. Then correct the false statements.

1. El área de Puerto Rico es menor que (*smaller than*) la de Connecticut.

   _____

2. Todos (*All*) los puertorriqueños hablan inglés y español.

   _____

3. La fortaleza del Morro protegía (*protected*) la bahía de Mayagüez.

   _____

4. La música salsa tiene raíces españolas.

   _____

5. Los científicos detectan emisiones de radio desde (*from*) el Observatorio de Arecibo.

   _____

6. Los puertorriqueños no votan en las elecciones presidenciales de los Estados Unidos.

   _____

2 **Datos de Puerto Rico** Complete these sentences with words and expressions from **Panorama**.

1. Aproximadamente la mitad de la población de Puerto Rico vive en _____.

2. El uso del inglés es obligatorio en los documentos _____.

3. _____ fue (*was*) un beisbolista puertorriqueño famoso.

4. Hoy día _____ es el centro internacional de la salsa.

5. El Observatorio de Arecibo tiene uno de los _____ más grandes del mundo.

6. Puerto Rico se hizo parte de los EE.UU. en 1898 y se hizo un _____ en 1952.

3 **Cosas puertorriqueñas** Fill in each category with information from **Panorama**.

	Ciudades puertorriqueñas	Ríos puertorriqueños	Islas puertorriqueñas	Puertorriqueños célebres

Lección 5 Workbook Activities   **57**

4 **¿Lo hacen?** Answer these questions correctly using a direct object pronoun in each answer.

> **modelo**
> ¿Lees el artículo de Puerto Rico?
> Sí, lo leo./ No, no lo leo.

1. ¿Usan los pesos como moneda los puertorriqueños?

_____

2. ¿Habla el idioma inglés la cuarta parte de la población puertorriqueña?

_____

3. ¿Sacan fotografías del Morro muchas personas?

_____

4. ¿Tocan música salsa Felipe Rodríguez, El Gran Combo y Héctor Lavoe?

_____

5. ¿Estudian las montañas los científicos del Observatorio de Arecibo?

_____

6. ¿Pagan impuestos federales los puertorriqueños?

_____

5 **Fotos de Puerto Rico** Write the name of what is shown in each picture.

1. _____

2. _____

3. _____

4. _____

contextos

1 **El almacén** Look at the department store directory. Then complete the sentences with terms from the word list.

Almacén Gema

PRIMER PISO	Departamento de caballeros
SEGUNDO PISO	Ropa de invierno y zapatos
TERCER PISO	Departamento de damas y óptica
CUARTO PISO	Ropa interior, ropa de verano y trajes de baño

abrigos	corbatas	sandalias
blusas	faldas	trajes de baño
bolsas	gafas de sol	trajes de hombre
botas	guantes	vestidos
calcetines	medias	zapatos de tenis
cinturones	pantalones de hombre	

1. En el primer piso puedes encontrar _____

_____

2. En el segundo piso puedes encontrar _____

_____

3. En el tercer piso puedes encontrar _____

_____

4. En el cuarto piso puedes encontrar _____

_____

5. Quiero unos pantalones cortos. Voy al _____ piso.

6. Buscas unos lentes. Vas al _____ piso.

7. Arturo ve una chaqueta en el _____ piso.

8. Ana ve los jeans en el _____ piso.

2 **Necesito muchas cosas** Complete these sentences with the correct terms.

1. Voy a nadar en la piscina. Necesito _____.

2. Está lloviendo mucho. Necesito _____.

3. No puedo ver bien porque hace sol. Necesito _____.

4. Voy a correr por el parque. Necesito _____.

5. Queremos entrar en muchas tiendas diferentes. Vamos al _____.

6. No tengo dinero en la cartera. Voy a pagar con la _____.

3   **Los colores** Answer these questions in complete sentences.

1. ¿De qué color es el chocolate?

_____

2. ¿De qué color son las bananas?

_____

3. ¿De qué color son las naranjas (*oranges*)?

_____

4. ¿De qué colores es la bandera (*flag*) de los Estados Unidos?

_____

5. ¿De qué color son las nubes (*clouds*) cuando está nublado?

_____

6. ¿De qué color son los bluejeans?

_____

7. ¿De qué color son muchos aviones?

_____

8. ¿De qué color son las palabras de este libro?

_____

4   **¿Qué lleva?** Look at the illustration and fill in the blanks with the names of the numbered items.

estructura

6.1 Saber and conocer

1 **¿Saber o conocer?** Complete the sentences, using **saber** and **conocer**.

1. (yo) No _____ a los padres de Juan Carlos.

2. Marissa _____ las ciudades de Canadá.

3. Maru, ¿(tú) _____ dónde estamos?

4. Yo _____ hablar italiano y francés.

5. La señora Díaz _____ bien la capital de México.

6. Jimena y yo no _____ a los otros turistas.

2 **¿Qué hacen?** Complete the sentences, using the verbs from the word bank. Use each verb only once.

| conducir | ofrecer | saber |
| conocer | parecer | traducir |

1. El señor Díaz _____ su automóvil todos los días.

2. Miguel _____ usar su computadora muy bien.

3. Jimena _____ ser una estudiante excelente.

4. Miguel y Maru no _____ bien al vendedor.

5. La Universidad del Mar _____ cursos muy interesantes.

6. Nosotros _____ libros a diferentes lenguas extranjeras.

3 **Oraciones completas** Create sentences, using the elements and **saber** or **conocer**.

1. Eugenia / mi amiga Frances

_____

2. Pamela / hablar español muy bien

_____

3. el sobrino de Rosa / leer y escribir

_____

4. José y Laura / la ciudad de Barcelona

_____

5. nosotros no / llegar a la residencia estudiantil

_____

6. yo / el profesor de literatura

_____

7. Elena y María Victoria / patinar en línea

_____

6.2 Indirect object pronouns

1 **¿A quién?** Complete these sentences with the correct indirect object pronouns.

1. _____ pido a la profesora los libros de español.

2. Amelia _____ pregunta a nosotras adónde queremos ir.

3. El empleado _____ busca trabajo a sus primas en el almacén.

4. Julio _____ quiere dar un televisor nuevo a sus padres.

5. Los clientes _____ piden rebajas a nosotros todos los años.

6. Tu hermano no _____ presta la ropa a ti (*you*).

7. La empleada de la tienda _____ cerró la puerta a mi tía.

8. La mamá no _____ hace la tarea a sus hijos.

9. _____ deben pagar mucho dinero a ti, porque llevas ropa muy cara.

10. Las dependientas _____ traen el vestido rosado a mí.

2 **Planes** Complete this paragraph with the correct indirect object pronouns and find out Sara's plans for this summer.

Mis amigos Loles, Antonio y Karen (1)_____ preguntan a mí si quiero ir a Italia con ellos este verano. Yo (2)_____ digo: "¡Sí, sííí, síííííí!" Ellos (3)_____ quieren pedir un libro o dos a la profesora de historia del arte. Yo (4)_____ quiero dar a ellos un álbum de fotos muy interesante. El novio de mi hermana es italiano. Él tiene una colección con dos mil cuatrocientas sesenta y tres fotos de muchas ciudades y museos de su país. (5)_____ voy a preguntar a mi hermana dónde lo tiene y a mis padres (6)_____ voy a decir: "¡Mamá, papá, en agosto voy a Italia con unos amigos! La señorita Casanova (7)_____ va a prestar un par de libros y el novio de Ángeles (8)_____ va a prestar su maravilloso álbum de fotos".

Loles tiene suerte. Su tía (9)_____ va a pagar el pasaje. Antonio y Karen van a trabajar en el centro comercial los meses de junio y julio. ¿Y yo qué hago? ¿Quién (10)_____ va a pagar el pasaje a mí? ¿A quién (11)_____ pido dinero yo? ¿A papá?... Pero él (12)_____ dice: "Sarita, hija, lo siento, pero yo no (13)_____ puedo pagar tu pasaje. Tu prima (14)_____ puede dar trabajo de dependienta en su tienda de ropa". ¡¡¿Trabajo?!!

3 **Delante o detrás** Rewrite these sentences, using an alternate placement for the indirect object pronouns.

> *modelo*
> Me quiero comprar un coche nuevo.
> *Quiero comprarme un coche nuevo.*

1. Les vas a dar muchos regalos a tus padres.

_____

2. Quiero comprarles unos guantes a mis sobrinos.

_____

3. Clara va a venderle sus libros de literatura francesa a su amiga.

_____

4. Los clientes nos pueden pagar con tarjeta de crédito.

_____

4 **De compras** Complete the paragraph with the correct indirect object pronouns.

Isabel y yo vamos de compras al centro comercial. Yo (1)_____ tengo que comprar unas cosas a mis parientes porque voy a viajar a mi ciudad este fin de semana. A mi hermana Laura (2)_____ quiero comprar unas gafas de sol, pero ella (3)_____ tiene que comprar un traje de baño a mí. A mis dos sobrinos (4)_____ voy a comprar una pelota de béisbol. A mi padre (5)_____ llevo un libro y a mi madre (6)_____ tengo que conseguir una blusa. (7)_____ quiero llevar camisetas con el nombre de mi universidad a todos.

5 **Respuestas** Answer these questions negatively. Use indirect object pronouns in the answer.

> *modelo*
> ¿Le compras una camisa a tu novio?
> *No, no le compro una camisa.*

1. ¿Le escribe Rolando un mensaje electrónico a Miguel?

_____

2. ¿Nos trae el botones las maletas a la habitación?

_____

3. ¿Les dan gafas de sol los vendedores a los turistas?

_____

4. ¿Te compra botas en el invierno tu mamá?

_____

5. ¿Les muestra el traje a ustedes el dependiente?

_____

6. ¿Me vas a buscar la revista en la librería?

_____

6.3 Preterite tense of regular verbs

1 **El pretérito** Complete these sentences with the preterite tense of the indicated verb.

1. Marcela _____ (encontrar) las sandalias debajo de la cama.

2. Gustavo _____ (recibir) un regalo muy bonito.

3. Sara y Viviana _____ (terminar) el libro al mismo tiempo.

4. La agente de viajes _____ (preparar) un itinerario muy interesante.

5. (yo) _____ (visitar) la ciudad en invierno.

6. Los dependientes _____ (escuchar) el partido por la radio.

7. Patricia y tú _____ (viajar) a México el verano pasado.

8. (nosotras) _____ (escribir) una carta al empleado del almacén.

9. (tú) _____ (regresar) del centro comercial a las cinco de la tarde.

10. Ustedes _____ (vivir) en casa de sus padres.

2 **Ahora y en el pasado** Rewrite these sentences in the preterite tense.

1. Ramón escribe una carta al director del programa.

_____

2. Mi tía trabaja de dependienta en un gran almacén.

_____

3. Comprendo el trabajo de la clase de biología.

_____

4. La familia de Daniel vive en Argentina.

_____

5. Virginia y sus amigos comen en el café de la librería.

_____

6. Los ingenieros terminan la construcción de la tienda en junio.

_____

7. Cada día llevas ropa muy elegante.

_____

8. Los turistas caminan, compran y descansan.

_____

9. Corremos cada día en el parque.

_____

3 **Confundido** Your friend Mario has a terrible memory. Answer his questions negatively, indicating that what he asks already happened.

> modelo
>
> ¿Va a comprar ropa Silvia en el centro comercial?
> No, Silvia ya *compró ropa en el centro comercial.*

1. ¿Va a viajar a Perú tu primo Andrés?

_____

2. ¿Vas a buscar una tienda de computadoras en el centro comercial?

_____

3. ¿Vamos a encontrar muchas rebajas en el centro?

_____

4. ¿Va María a pagar las sandalias en la caja?

_____

5. ¿Van a regatear con el vendedor Mónica y Carlos?

_____

6. ¿Va a pasear por la playa tu abuela?

_____

4 **La semana pasada** Now Mario wants to know what you did last week. Write his question, then answer it affirmatively or negatively.

> modelo
>
> sacar fotos de los amigos
> —¿Sacaste fotos de los amigos?
> —Sí, saqué fotos de los amigos./No, no saqué fotos de los amigos.

1. pagar el abrigo con la tarjeta de crédito

_____

_____

2. jugar al tenis

_____

_____

3. buscar un libro en la biblioteca

_____

_____

4. llegar tarde a clase

_____

_____

5. empezar a escribir una carta

_____

_____

Lección 6 Workbook Activities

6.4 Demonstrative adjectives and pronouns

1 **De compras** Complete these sentences with the correct form of the adjective in parentheses.

1. Me quiero comprar _____ (*these*) zapatos porque me gustan mucho.

2. Comimos en _____ (*that*) centro comercial la semana pasada.

3. _____ (*that over there*) tienda vende las gafas de sol a un precio muy alto.

4. Las rebajas en _____ (*this*) almacén son legendarias.

5. _____ (*those*) botas hacen juego con tus pantalones negros.

6. Voy a llevar _____ (*these*) pantalones con la blusa roja.

2 **Claro que no** Your friend Mario hates shopping, and can't keep anything straight. Answer his questions negatively, using the cues in parentheses and the corresponding demonstrative adjectives.

> **modelo**
>
> ¿Compró esas medias Sonia? (cartera)
> *No, compró esa cartera.*

1. ¿Va a comprar ese suéter Gloria? (pantalones)

_____

2. ¿Llevaste estas sandalias? (zapatos de tenis)

_____

3. ¿Quieres ver esta ropa interior? (medias)

_____

4. ¿Usa aquel traje David? (chaqueta negra)

_____

5. ¿Decidió Silvia comprar esas gafas de sol? (sombrero)

_____

6. ¿Te mostró el vestido aquella vendedora? (dependiente)

_____

3 **Ésos no** Complete these sentences using demonstrative pronouns. Choose a pronoun for each sentence, paying attention to agreement.

1. Aquellas sandalias son muy cómodas, pero _____ son más elegantes.

2. Esos vestidos largos son muy caros; voy a comprar _____.

3. No puedo usar esta tarjeta de crédito; tengo que usar _____.

4. Esos zapatos tienen buen precio, pero _____ no.

5. Prefiero este sombrero porque _____ es muy grande.

6. Estas medias son buenas; las prefiero a _____.

4 **Éstas y aquéllas** Look at the illustration and complete this conversation with the appropriate demonstrative adjectives and pronouns. Use the correct forms of **este**, **ese**, and **aquel**.

CLAUDIA ¿Quieres comprar (1)_____ corbata, Gerardo?

GERARDO No, no quiero comprar (2)_____. Prefiero (3)_____ del escaparate (*display case*).

CLAUDIA (4)_____ es bonita, pero no hace juego con tu chaqueta.

GERARDO Mira (5)_____ chaqueta. Es muy elegante y está a buen precio. Sí, puedo usar (6)_____ y darle a mi hermano ésta.

CLAUDIA ¿Y (7)_____ cinturón?

GERARDO (8)_____ es muy elegante. ¿Es caro?

CLAUDIA Es más barato que (9)_____ tres del escaparate.

5 **Más compras** Pilar and Marta are at the mall trying to get a new outfit for a special occasion. Write the conversation in which they talk about different clothing. Use at least six expressions from the list.

aquel vendedor	esa camisa	esos colores	esta falda
aquellas botas	ese precio	esos zapatos	este vestido

_____

_____

_____

_____

_____

_____

Síntesis

Imagine that you went with your brother to an open-air market last weekend. This weekend you take a friend there. Write a conversation between you and your friend, using as many different verbs as you can from those you have learned.

• Indicate to your friend the items you saw last weekend, what you liked and didn't like, the items that you bought, how much you paid for them, and for whom you bought the items.

• Suggest items that your friend might buy and for whom he or she might buy them. Use the preterite tense of regular verbs, indirect object pronouns, and lesson vocabulary.

_____

_____

_____

_____

_____

_____

_____

_____

_____

_____

_____

_____

_____

_____

_____

_____

_____

_____

_____

_____

_____

_____

_____

panorama

Cuba

1 **Crucigrama (*Crossword*)** Complete this crossword puzzle with the correct terms.

Horizontales

4. Nombre de la bailarina que fundó el Ballet Nacional de Cuba
5. Especie cubana de colibrí
6. Calle de la Habana Vieja frecuentada por Hemingway
9. Apellido de una escritora cubana célebre
10. Uno de los productos agrícolas más importantes en Cuba

Verticales

1. Esta organización declaró a la Habana Vieja Patrimonio Cultural de la Humanidad.
2. Apellido del ex líder del gobierno de Cuba
3. El azúcar se saca (*is extracted*) de esta planta.
7. Alicia Alonso practicaba (*practiced*) este baile.
8. Moneda cubana

2 **Preguntas de Cuba** Answer these questions about Cuba in complete sentences.

1. ¿De dónde son los antepasados de muchos cubanos de hoy en día?

_____

2. ¿De qué colores es la bandera cubana?

_____

3. ¿Cuál es un medio de transporte muy popular en Cuba?

_____

4. ¿Qué es *Buena Vista Social Club*?

_____

3 **Datos de Cuba** Complete these sentences with information from **Panorama**.

1. El _____ en la Plaza de Armas de la Habana Vieja es ahora un museo.

2. En Cuba se encuentran la Cordillera de los _____ y la Sierra _____.

3. Una isla que forma parte de Cuba es la _____.

4. Alicia Alonso fundó el _____ en 1948.

5. La _____ es un producto de exportación muy importante para Cuba.

6. El tabaco se usa para fabricar los famosos _____.

7. La inmigración fue muy importante en Cuba desde la _____ hasta mediados del siglo XX.

8. *Buena Vista Social Club* interpreta canciones clásicas del _____.

4 **Cubanos célebres** Write the name of the famous Cuban who might have said each of these quotations.

1. "Nací en 1927 y mi música es famosa."

_____

2. "Me convertí en una estrella internacional con el Ballet de Nueva York en 1943."

_____

3. "Soy el ex jefe de las fuerzas armadas de Cuba."

_____

4. "Viví en el siglo (*century*) diecinueve y escribí poemas."

_____

5. "Tengo más de cincuenta años, soy cubana y escribo libros."

_____

6. "Curé a muchas personas enfermas y estudié las ciencias."

_____

5 **Números cubanos** Write out the numbers in Spanish that complete these sentences about Cuba.

1. Hay _____ habitantes en la isla de Cuba.

2. Hay _____ habitantes en La Habana.

3. En el año _____ la Habana Vieja fue declarada Patrimonio Cultural de la Humanidad.

4. El área de Cuba es de _____ millas cuadradas.

5. El colibrí abeja de Cuba es una de las más de _____ especies de colibrí del mundo.

6. En el año _____ nació Fidel Castro.

repaso

1 **No lo hago** Answer these questions affirmatively or negatively as indicated, replacing the direct object with a direct object pronoun.

> **modelo**
> ¿Traes la computadora a clase? (no)
> No, no la traigo.

1. ¿Haces la tarea de economía en tu habitación? (sí) _____

2. ¿Pones esos libros sobre el escritorio? (no) _____

3. ¿Traes los pasajes y el pasaporte al aeropuerto? (sí) _____

4. ¿Oyes ese programa de radio a veces (*sometimes*)? (no) _____

5. ¿Conoces a aquellas chicas que están tomando el sol? (sí) _____

6. ¿Pones la televisión mientras (*while*) estudias? (no) _____

2 **El tiempo** Complete these sentences with the most logical verbs from the list. Use each verb once.

cerrar	pedir	poder	querer
comenzar	pensar	preferir	volver

1. Está empezando a hacer frío. Mi mamá _____ comprar un abrigo.

2. Hace mucho sol. (Tú) _____ a buscar tus gafas de sol.

3. Hace fresco. Melissa _____ salir a pasear en bicicleta.

4. Está nevando. (Yo) _____ estar en casa hoy.

5. Está lloviendo. Luis y Pilar _____ las ventanas del auto.

6. Hace mucho calor. Ustedes _____ ir a nadar en la piscina.

7. Está nublado. Los chicos _____ temprano de la playa.

8. Llueve. Los turistas _____ un impermeable en el hotel.

3 **No son éstos** Answer these questions negatively using demonstrative pronouns.

> **modelo**
> ¿Les vas a prestar esos programas a ellos? (*those over there*)
> No, les voy a prestar aquéllos./No, voy a prestarles aquéllos.

1. ¿Me vas a vender esa calculadora? (*this one*)

_____

2. ¿Van ustedes a abrirle ese auto al cliente? (*that one over there*)

_____

3. ¿Va a llevarles estas maletas Marisol? (*those ones*)

_____

4. ¿Les van a enseñar esos verbos a los estudiantes? (*these ones*)

_____

4 **¿Son o están?** Form complete sentences using the words provided and **ser** or **estar**.

1. Paloma y Carlos / inteligentes y trabajadores

_____

2. Mariela / cantando una canción bonita

_____

3. (tú) / conductor de taxi en la ciudad

_____

4. (nosotros) / en un hotel en la playa

_____

5. Gilberto / preocupado porque tiene mucho trabajo

_____

6. Roberto y yo / puertorriqueños, de San Juan

_____

5 **La compra** Look at the photo and imagine everything that led up to the woman's purchase. What did she need? Why did she need it? What kind of weather is it for? Where did she decide to go buy it? Where did she go looking for it? Who helped her, and what did she ask them? Did she bargain with anyone? Was she undecided about anything? How did she pay for the purchase? Who did she pay? Answer these questions in a paragraph, using the preterite of the verbs that you know.

_____

_____

_____

_____

_____

_____

_____

_____

_____

contextos

Lección 7

1 **Las rutinas** Complete each sentence with a word from **Contextos**.

1. Susana se lava el pelo con _____.

2. La ducha y el lavabo están en el _____.

3. Manuel se lava las manos con _____.

4. Después de lavarse las manos, usa la _____.

5. Luis tiene un _____ para levantarse temprano.

6. Elena usa el _____ para maquillarse.

2 **¿En el baño o en la habitación?** Write **en el baño** or **en la habitación** to indicate where each activity takes place.

1. bañarse _____

2. levantarse _____

3. ducharse _____

4. lavarse la cara _____

5. acostarse _____

6. afeitarse _____

7. cepillarse los dientes _____

8. dormirse _____

3 **Ángel y Lupita** Look at the drawings, and choose the appropriate phrase to describe what Ángel and Lupita are doing.

afeitarse por la mañana   cepillarse los dientes después de comer
bañarse por la tarde   ducharse antes de salir

1. _____

2. _____

Lección 7 Workbook Activities **73**

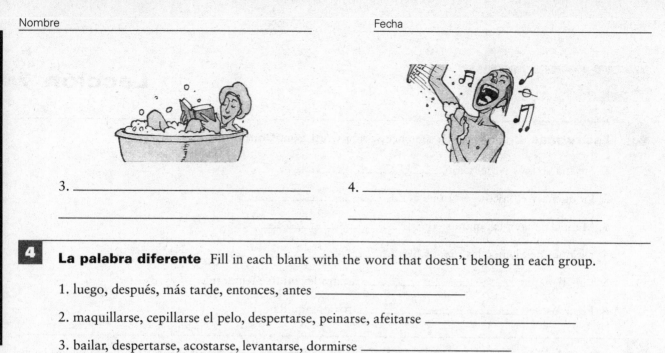

3. _____   4. _____

_____   _____

4 **La palabra diferente** Fill in each blank with the word that doesn't belong in each group.

1. luego, después, más tarde, entonces, antes _____

2. maquillarse, cepillarse el pelo, despertarse, peinarse, afeitarse _____

3. bailar, despertarse, acostarse, levantarse, dormirse _____

4. champú, despertador, jabón, maquillaje, crema de afeitar _____

5. entonces, bañarse, lavarse las manos, cepillarse los dientes, ducharse _____

6. pelo, vestirse, dientes, manos, cara _____

5 **La rutina de Silvia** Rewrite this paragraph, selecting the correct sequencing words from the parentheses.

(Por la mañana, Durante el día) Silvia se prepara para salir. (Primero, Antes de) se levanta y se ducha. (Después, Antes) de ducharse, se viste. (Entonces, Durante) se maquilla. (Primero, Antes) de salir, come algo y bebe un café. (Durante, Por último) se peina y se pone una chaqueta. (Durante el día, Antes de) Silvia no tiene tiempo (*time*) de volver a su casa. (Más tarde, Antes de) come algo en la cafetería de la universidad y estudia en la biblioteca. (Por la tarde, Por último), Silvia trabaja en el centro comercial. (Por la noche, Primero) llega a su casa y está cansada. (Más tarde, Después de) prepara algo de comer y mira la televisión un rato. (Antes de, Después de) acostarse a dormir siempre estudia un rato.

_____

_____

_____

_____

_____

_____

_____

_____

_____

_____

estructura

7.1 Reflexive verbs

1 **Completar** Complete each sentence with the correct present tense form of the verb in parentheses.

1. Marcos y Gustavo _____ (enojarse) con Javier.

2. Mariela _____ (sentirse) feliz.

3. (yo) _____ (acostarse) temprano porque tengo clase por la mañana.

4. Los jugadores _____ (secarse) con toallas nuevas.

5. (tú) _____ (preocuparse) por tu novio porque siempre pierde las cosas.

6. Usted _____ (lavarse) la cara con un jabón especial.

7. Mi mamá _____ (ponerse) muy contenta cuando llego temprano a casa.

2 **Lo hiciste** Answer the questions affirmatively, using complete sentences.

1. ¿Te cepillaste los dientes después de comer?

_____

2. ¿Se maquilla Julia antes de salir a bailar?

_____

3. ¿Se duchan ustedes antes de nadar en la piscina?

_____

4. ¿Se ponen sombreros los turistas cuando van a la playa?

_____

5. ¿Nos ponemos las pantuflas cuando llegamos a casa?

_____

3 **Terminar** Complete each sentence with the correct reflexive verbs. You will use some verbs more than once.

acordarse	cepillarse	enojarse	maquillarse
acostarse	dormirse	levantarse	quedarse

1. Mi mamá _____ porque no queremos _____ temprano.

2. La profesora _____ con nosotros cuando no _____ de los verbos.

3. Mi hermano _____ los dientes cuando _____.

4. Mis amigas y yo _____ estudiando en la biblioteca por la noche y por la mañana yo _____ muy cansada.

5. Muchas noches _____ delante del televisor, porque no quiero _____.

Lección 7 Workbook Activities

4 **Escoger** Choose the correct verb from the parentheses, then fill in the blank with its correct form.

1. (lavar/lavarse)

Josefina _____ las manos en el lavabo.

Josefina _____ la ropa en casa de su madre.

2. (peinar/peinarse)

(yo) _____ a mi hermana todas las mañanas.

(yo) _____ en el baño, delante del espejo.

3. (poner/ponerse)

(nosotros) _____ nerviosos antes de un examen.

(nosotros) _____ la toalla al lado de la ducha.

4. (levantar/levantarse)

Los estudiantes _____ muy temprano.

Los estudiantes _____ la mano y hacen preguntas.

5 **El incidente** Fill in the blanks with the infinitive or the conjugated forms of the reflexive verbs in the list. Use each verb only once.

acordarse	enojarse	levantarse	preocuparse
afeitarse	irse	maquillarse	quedarse
despertarse	lavarse	ponerse	vestirse

Luis (1) _____ todos los días a las seis de la mañana. Luego entra en la

ducha y (2) _____ el pelo con champú. Cuando sale de la ducha, usa la crema de

afeitar para (3) _____ delante del espejo. Come algo con su familia y él y sus

hermanos (4) _____ hablando un rato.

Cuando sale tarde, Luis (5) _____ porque no quiere llegar tarde a la clase de

español. Los estudiantes (6) _____ nerviosos porque a veces (*sometimes*) tienen

pruebas sorpresa en la clase.

Ayer por la mañana, Luis (7) _____ con su hermana Marina porque ella

(8) _____ tarde y pasó mucho tiempo en el cuarto de baño con la puerta cerrada.

—¿Cuándo sales, Marina? —le preguntó Luis.

—¡Tengo que (9) _____ porque voy a salir con mi novio y quiero estar bonita!

—dijo Marina.

—¡Tengo que (10) _____ ya, Marina! ¿Cuándo terminas?

—Ahora salgo, Luis. Tengo que (11) _____. Me voy a poner mi vestido favorito.

—Tienes que (12) _____ de que viven muchas personas en esta casa, Marina.

7.2 Indefinite and negative words

1 **Alguno o ninguno** Complete the sentences with indefinite and negative words from the word bank.

alguien	algunas	ninguna
alguna	ningún	tampoco

1. No tengo ganas de ir a _____ lugar hoy.

2. ¿Tienes _____ ideas para mejorar (*to improve*) la economía?

3. ¿Viene _____ a la fiesta de mañana?

4. No voy a _____ estadio nunca.

5. ¿Te gusta _____ de estas corbatas?

6. Jorge, tú no eres el único. Yo _____ puedo ir de vacaciones.

2 **Estoy de mal humor** Your classmate Jaime is in a terrible mood. Complete his complaints with negative words.

1. No me gustan estas gafas. _____ quiero comprar _____ de ellas.

2. Estoy muy cansado. _____ quiero ir a _____ restaurante.

3. No tengo hambre. _____ quiero comer _____.

4. A mí no me gusta la playa. _____ quiero ir a la playa _____.

5. Soy muy tímido. _____ hablo con _____ _____.

6. No me gusta el color rojo, _____ el color rosado _____.

3 **¡Amalia!** Your friend Amalia is chronically mistaken. Change her statements as necessary to correct her; each statement should be negative.

> **modelo**
> Buscaste algunos vestidos en la tienda.
> No busqué ningún vestido en la tienda.

1. Las dependientas venden algunas blusas.

_____

2. Alguien va de compras al centro comercial.

_____

3. Siempre me cepillo los dientes antes de salir.

_____

4. Te voy a traer algún programa de computadora.

_____

5. Mi hermano prepara algo de comer.

_____

6. Quiero tomar algo en el café de la librería.

_____

4 **No, no es cierto** Now your friend Amalia realizes that she's usually wrong and is asking you for the correct information. Answer her questions negatively.

> modelo
> ¿Comes siempre en casa?
> No, nunca como en casa./No, no como en casa nunca.

1. ¿Tienes alguna falda?

_____

2. ¿Sales siempre los fines de semana?

_____

3. ¿Quieres comer algo ahora?

_____

4. ¿Le prestaste algunos discos de jazz a César?

_____

5. ¿Podemos ir a la playa o nadar en la piscina?

_____

6. ¿Encontraste algún cinturón barato en la tienda?

_____

7. ¿Buscaron ustedes a alguien en la playa?

_____

8. ¿Te gusta alguno de estos trajes?

_____

5 **Lo opuesto** Rodrigo's good reading habits have changed since this description was written. Rewrite the paragraph, changing the indefinite words to negative ones.

Rodrigo siempre está leyendo algún libro. También lee el periódico. Siempre lee algo. Alguien le pregunta si leyó una novela de Mario Vargas Llosa. Leyó algunos libros de Vargas Llosa el año pasado. También leyó algunas novelas de Gabriel García Márquez. Siempre quiere leer o libros de misterio o novelas fantásticas.

_____

_____

_____

_____

_____

_____

_____

7.3 Preterite of **ser** and **ir**

1 **¿Ser o ir?** Complete the sentences with the preterite of **ser** or **ir**. Then write the infinitive form of the verb you used.

1. Ayer María y Javier _____ a la playa con sus amigos. _____

2. La película del sábado por la tarde _____ muy bonita. _____

3. El fin de semana pasado (nosotros) _____ al centro comercial. _____

4. La abuela y la tía de Maricarmen _____ doctoras. _____

5. (nosotros) _____ muy simpáticos con la familia de Claribel. _____

6. Manuel _____ a la universidad en septiembre. _____

7. Los vendedores _____ al almacén muy temprano. _____

8. Lima _____ la primera parada (*stop*) de nuestro viaje. _____

9. (yo) _____ a buscarte a la cafetería, pero no te encontré. _____

10. Mi compañera de cuarto _____ a la tienda a comprar champú. _____

2 **Viaje a Perú** Complete the paragraph with the preterite of **ser** and **ir**. Then write the infinitive form of the verbs you used.

El mes pasado mi amiga Clara y yo (1) _____ de vacaciones a Perú. El vuelo

(*flight*) (2) _____ un miércoles por la mañana y (3) _____

cómodo. Primero Clara y yo (4) _____ a Lima y (5) _____

a comer a un restaurante de comida peruana. La comida (6) _____ muy buena.

Luego (7) _____ al hotel y nos (8) _____ a dormir. El

jueves (9) _____ un día nublado. Nos (10) _____ a Cuzco,

y el viaje en autobús (11) _____ largo. Yo (12) _____

la primera en despertarse y ver la ciudad de Cuzco. Aquella mañana, el paisaje

(13) _____ impresionante. Luego Clara y yo (14) _____

de excursión a Machu Picchu. El cuarto día nos levantamos muy temprano y

(15) _____ a la ciudad inca. El amanecer sobre Machu Picchu

(16) _____ hermoso. La excursión (17) _____ una

experiencia inolvidable (*unforgettable*). ¿(18) _____ tú a Perú el año pasado?

1. _____	7. _____	13. _____
2. _____	8. _____	14. _____
3. _____	9. _____	15. _____
4. _____	10. _____	16. _____
5. _____	11. _____	17. _____
6. _____	12. _____	18. _____

Lección 7 Workbook Activities **79**

7.4 Verbs like **gustar**

1 **La fotonovela** Rewrite each sentence, choosing the correct form of the verb in parentheses.

1. Maru, te (quedan, queda) bien las faldas y los vestidos.

_____

2. A Jimena y a Juan Carlos no les (molesta, molestan) la lluvia.

_____

3. A los chicos no les (importa, importan) ir de compras.

_____

4. A don Diego y a Felipe les (aburre, aburren) probarse ropa en las tiendas.

_____

5. A Jimena le (fascina, fascinan) las tiendas y los almacenes.

_____

6. A Felipe le (falta, faltan) dos años para terminar la carrera (*degree*).

_____

7. A los chicos les (encanta, encantan) pescar y nadar en el mar.

_____

8. A Miguel le (interesan, interesa) el arte.

_____

2 **Nos gusta el fútbol** Complete the paragraph with the correct forms of the verbs in parentheses.

A mi familia le (1) _____ (fascinar) el fútbol. A mis hermanas les

(2) _____ (encantar) los jugadores porque son muy guapos. También les

(3) _____ (gustar) la emoción (*excitement*) de los partidos. A mi papá le

(4) _____ (interesar) mucho los partidos y, cuando puede, los ve por

Internet. A mi mamá le (5) _____ (molestar) nuestra afición porque no hacemos

las tareas de la casa cuando hay partidos. A ella generalmente le (6) _____

(aburrir) los partidos. Pero cuando al equipo argentino le (7) _____ (faltar) un

gol para ganar, le (8) _____ (encantar) los minutos finales del partido.

3   **El viaje** You and your friend are packing and planning your upcoming vacation to the Caribbean. Rewrite her sentences, replacing the subject with the one in parentheses. Make all the necessary changes.

> **modelo**
>
> A mis amigos les fascinan los partidos de béisbol. (la comida peruana)
> A mis amigos les fascina la *comida peruana*.

1. Te quedan bien los vestidos largos. (la blusa cara)

   _____

2. Les molesta la música estadounidense. (las canciones populares)

   _____

3. ¿No te interesa aprender a bailar salsa? (nadar)

   _____

4. Les encantan las tiendas. (el centro comercial)

   _____

5. Nos falta practicar el español. (unas semanas de clase)

   _____

6. No les importa esperar un rato. (buscar unos libros nuestros)

   _____

   _____

4   **¿Qué piensan?** Complete the sentences with the correct pronouns and forms of the verbs in parentheses.

1. A mí _____ (encantar) las películas de misterio.

2. A Gregorio _____ (molestar) mucho la nieve y el frío.

3. A ustedes _____ (faltar) un libro de esa colección.

4. ¿_____ (quedar) bien los sombreros a ti?

5. A ella no _____ (importar) las apariencias (*appearances*).

6. A mí los deportes por televisión _____ (aburrir) mucho.

5   **Mi rutina diaria** Answer these questions using verbs like **gustar** in complete sentences.

1. ¿Te molesta levantarte temprano durante la semana?

   _____

2. ¿Qué te interesa hacer por las mañanas?

   _____

3. ¿Te importa despertarte temprano los fines de semana?

   _____

4. ¿Qué te encanta hacer los domingos?

   _____

Síntesis

Interview a friend or relative about an interesting vacation he or she took. Then gather the answers into a report. Use verbs like **gustar**, reflexive verbs, the preterite of **ser** and **ir**, and lesson vocabulary to answer the following questions:

- What did he or she like or love about the vacation? What interested him or her?
- Where did he or she stay, what were the accommodations like, and what was his or her daily routine like during the trip?
- Where did he or she go, what were the tours like, what were the tour guides like, and what were his or her travelling companions like?
- What bothered or angered him or her? What bored him or her during the vacation?

Be sure to address both the negative and positive aspects of the vacation.

_____

_____

_____

_____

_____

_____

_____

_____

_____

_____

_____

_____

_____

_____

_____

_____

_____

_____

_____

_____

_____

_____

panorama

Perú

1 **Datos de Perú** Complete the sentences with the correct words.

1. _____ es la capital de Perú y _____ es la segunda ciudad más poblada.

2. _____ es un puerto muy importante en el río Amazonas.

3. El barrio bohemio de la ciudad de Lima se llama _____.

4. Hiram Bingham redescubrió las ruinas de _____ en los Andes.

5. Las llamas, alpacas, guanacos y vicuñas son parientes del _____.

6. Las Líneas de _____ son uno de los grandes misterios de la humanidad.

2 **Perú** Fill in the blanks with the names and places described. Then use the words formed by the highlighted boxes to answer the final question.

1. barrio bohemio de Lima
2. animales que se usan para carga y transporte
3. en Perú se habla este idioma
4. capital de Perú
5. montañas de Perú
6. dirección de Machu Picchu desde Cuzco

7. puerto en el río Amazonas
8. animales que dan lana
9. esta civilización peruana dibujó líneas
10. profesión de César Vallejo

¿Por dónde se llega caminando a Machu Picchu?

Se llega por el _____.

3 **Ciudades peruanas** Fill in the blanks with the names of the appropriate cities in Peru.

1. ciudad al sureste (*southeast*) de Cuzco _____

2. se envían productos por el Amazonas _____

3. Museo Oro del Perú _____

4. está a 80 km de Machu Picchu _____

5. ciudad antigua del Imperio inca _____

4 **¿Cierto o falso?** Indicate whether each statement is **cierto** or **falso**. Correct the false statements.

1. Trujillo es un destino popular para los ecoturistas que visitan la selva.

_____

2. Mario Vargas Llosa es un novelista peruano famoso.

_____

3. La Iglesia de San Francisco es notable por la influencia de la arquitectura árabe.

_____

4. Las ruinas de Machu Picchu están en la cordillera de los Andes.

_____

5. Las llamas se usan para la carga y el transporte en Perú.

_____

6. La civilización inca hizo dibujos que sólo son descifrables desde el aire.

_____

5 **El mapa de Perú** Label the map of Peru.

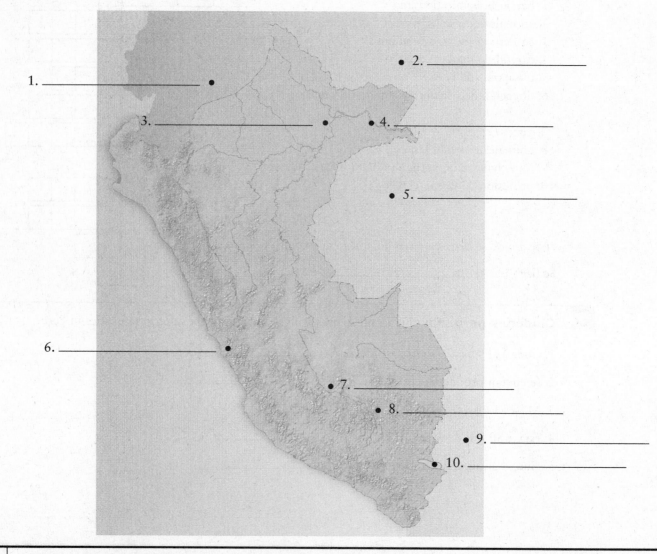

1. _____

2. _____

3. _____

4. _____

5. _____

6. _____

7. _____

8. _____

9. _____

10. _____

contextos

1 **¿Qué comida es?** Read the descriptions and write the names of the food in the blanks.

1. Son rojos y se sirven (*they are served*) en las ensaladas. _____

2. Se come (*It is eaten*) antes del plato principal; es líquida y caliente (*hot*). _____

3. Son unas verduras anaranjadas, largas y delgadas. _____

4. Hay de naranja y de manzana; se bebe en el desayuno. _____

5. Son dos rebanadas (*slices*) de pan con queso y jamón. _____

6. Es comida rápida; se sirven con hamburguesas y se les pone sal. _____

7. Son pequeños y rosados; viven en el mar. _____

8. Son frutas amarillas; con ellas, agua y azúcar se hace una bebida de verano. _____

2 **Categorías** Categorize the foods listed in the word bank.

aceite	cebollas	langosta	mayonesa	pollo	vinagre
atún	chuletas de	leche	melocotones	queso	yogur
azúcar	cerdo	lechuga	naranjas	sal	zanahorias
bananas	espárragos	limones	papas	salchichas	
bistec	hamburguesas	mantequilla	peras	salmón	
camarones	jamón	manzanas	pimienta	uvas	

Verduras	Productos lácteos (*dairy*)	Condimentos	Carnes y aves (*poultry*)	Pescados y mariscos	Frutas

3 **¿Qué es?** Label the food item shown in each drawing.

1. _____

2. _____

3. _____

4. _____

4 **¿Cuándo lo comes?** Read the lists of meals, then categorize when the meals would be eaten.

1. un sándwich de jamón y queso, unas chuletas de cerdo con arroz y frijoles, un yogur y un café con leche

Desayuno _____

Almuerzo _____

Cena _____

2. una langosta con papas y espárragos, huevos fritos y jugo de naranja, una hamburguesa y un refresco

Desayuno _____

Almuerzo _____

Cena _____

3. pan tostado con mantequilla, un sándwich de atún y un té helado, un bistec con cebolla y arroz

Desayuno _____

Almuerzo _____

Cena _____

4. una sopa y una ensalada, cereales con leche, pollo asado con ajo y champiñones

Desayuno _____

Almuerzo _____

Cena _____

estructura

8.1 Preterite of stem-changing verbs

1 **En el pasado** Rewrite each sentence, conjugating the verbs into the preterite tense.

1. Ana y Enrique piden unos refrescos fríos.

_____

2. Mi mamá nos sirve arroz con frijoles y carne.

_____

3. Tina y Linda duermen en un hotel de Lima.

_____

4. Las flores (*flowers*) de mi tía mueren durante el otoño.

_____

5. Ustedes se sienten bien porque ayudan a las personas.

_____

2 **¿Qué hicieron?** For each sentence, choose the correct verb from those in parentheses. Then complete the sentence by writing the preterite form of the verb.

1. Rosana y Héctor _____ las palabras del profesor. (repetir, dormir, morir)

2. El abuelo de Luis _____ el año pasado. (pedir, morir, servir)

3. (yo) _____ camarones y salmón de cena en mi casa. (morir, conseguir, servir)

4. Lisa y tú _____ pan tostado con queso y huevos. (sentirse, seguir, pedir)

5. Elena _____ en casa de su prima el sábado. (dormir, pedir, repetir)

6. Gilberto y su familia _____ ir al restaurante francés. (servir, preferir, vestirse)

3 **No pasó así** Your brother is very confused today. Correct his mistakes by rewriting each sentence, replacing the subject with the one given in parentheses.

1. Anoche nos sentimos alegres. (mis primos)

_____

2. Melinda y Juan siguieron a Camelia por la ciudad en el auto. (yo)

_____

3. Alejandro prefirió quedarse en casa. (ustedes)

_____

4. Pedí un plato de langosta con salsa de mantequilla. (ellas)

_____

5. Los camareros les sirvieron una ensalada con atún y espárragos. (tu esposo)

_____

Lección 8 Workbook Activities

4 **En el restaurante** Create sentences from the elements provided. Use the preterite form of the verbs.

1. (nosotros) / preferir / este restaurante al restaurante italiano

_____

2. mis amigos / seguir / a Gustavo para encontrar el restaurante

_____

3. la camarera / servirte / huevos fritos y café con leche

_____

4. ustedes / pedir / ensalada de mariscos y vino blanco

_____

5. Carlos / preferir / las papas fritas

_____

6. (yo) / conseguir / el menú del restaurante

_____

5 **La planta de la abuela** Complete this message with the preterite form of the verbs from the word bank. Use each verb only once.

conseguir	morir	preferir	seguir	servir
dormir	pedir	repetir	sentirse	vestirse

Querida mamá:

El fin de semana pasado fui a visitar a mi abuela Lilia en el campo. (Yo) Le
(1)_____ unos libros en la librería de la universidad porque ella me
los (2)_____. Cuando llegué, mi abuela me (3)_____
un plato sabroso de arroz con frijoles. La encontré triste porque la semana pasada su
planta de tomates (4)_____ y ahora tiene que comprar los tomates en el
mercado. Me invitó a quedarme, y yo (5)_____ en su casa. Por la
mañana, abuela Lilia se despertó temprano, (6)_____ y salió a
comprar huevos para el desayuno. Me levanté inmediatamente y la
(7)_____ porque quería ir con ella al mercado. En el mercado, ella me
(8)_____ que estaba triste por la planta de tomates. Le pregunté:
¿Debemos comprar otra planta de tomates?, pero ella (9)_____
esperar hasta el verano. Después del desayuno yo (10)_____ triste
cuando volví a la universidad. Quiero mucho a la abuela. ¿Cuándo la vas a visitar?

Chau,

Mónica

8.2 Double object pronouns

1 **Buena gente** Rewrite each sentence, replacing the direct objects with direct object pronouns.

1. La camarera te sirvió el plato de pasta con mariscos.

_____

2. Isabel nos llevó la sal y la pimienta a la mesa.

_____

3. Javier me pidió el aceite y el vinagre anoche.

_____

4. El dueño nos busca una mesa para seis personas.

_____

5. Tu madre me consigue unos melocotones deliciosos.

_____

6. ¿Te recomendaron este restaurante Lola y Paco?

_____

2 **En el restaurante** Last night, you and some friends ate in a popular new restaurant. Rewrite what happened there, using double object pronouns in each sentence.

1. La dueña nos abrió la sección de no fumar.

_____

2. Le pidieron los menús al camarero.

_____

3. Nos buscaron un lugar cómodo y nos sentamos.

_____

4. Les sirvieron papas fritas con el pescado a los clientes.

_____

5. Le llevaron unos entremeses a la mesa a Marcos.

_____

6. Me sirvieron una ensalada de lechuga y tomate.

_____

7. El dueño le compró la carne al señor Gutiérrez.

_____

8. Ellos te mostraron los vinos antes de servirlos.

_____

3 **¿Quiénes son?** Answer the questions, using double object pronouns.

1. ¿A quiénes les escribiste las postales? (a ellos) _____

2. ¿Quién le recomendó ese plato? (su tío) _____

3. ¿Quién nos va a abrir la puerta a esta hora? (Sonia) _____

4. ¿Quién les sirvió el pescado asado? (Miguel) _____

5. ¿Quién te llevó los entremeses? (mis amigas) _____

6. ¿A quién le ofrece frutas Roberto? (a su familia) _____

4 **La cena** Read the two conversations. Then answer the questions, using double object pronouns.

CELIA	*(A Tito)* Rosalía me recomendó este restaurante.
DUEÑO	Buenas noches, señores. Les traigo unos entremeses, cortesía del restaurante.
CAMARERO	Buenas noches. ¿Quieren ver el menú?
TITO	Sí, por favor. ¿Está buena la langosta?
CAMARERO	Sí, es la especialidad del restaurante.
CELIA	¿Cuánto vale la langosta?
CAMARERO	Vale treinta dólares.
TITO	Entonces queremos pedir dos.
CELIA	Y yo quiero una copa *(glass)* de vino tinto, por favor.

CAMARERO	Tenemos flan y fruta de postre *(for dessert)*.
CELIA	Perdón, ¿me lo puede repetir?
CAMARERO	Tenemos flan y fruta.
CELIA	Yo no quiero nada de postre, gracias.
DUEÑO	¿Les gustó la cena?
TITO	Sí, nos encantó. Muchas gracias. Fue una cena deliciosa.

1. ¿Quién le recomendó el restaurante a Celia? _____

2. ¿Quién les sirvió los entremeses a Celia y a Tito? _____

3. ¿Quién les llevó los menús a Celia y a Tito? _____

4. ¿A quién le preguntó Celia el precio de la langosta? _____

5. ¿Quién le pidió las langostas al camarero? _____

6. ¿Quién le pidió un vino tinto al camarero? _____

7. ¿Quién le repitió a Celia la lista de postres? _____

8. ¿A quién le dio las gracias Tito cuando se fueron? _____

8.3 Comparisons

1 **¿Cómo se comparan?** Complete the sentences with the Spanish of the comparison in parentheses.

1. Puerto Rico es _____ (*smaller than*) Guatemala.

2. Felipe corre _____ (*faster than*) su amigo Juan Carlos.

3. Los champiñones son _____ (*as tasty as*) los espárragos.

4. Los jugadores de baloncesto son _____ (*taller than*) los otros estudiantes.

5. Laura es _____ (*more hard-working than*) su novio Pablo.

6. Marisol es _____ (*less intelligent than*) su hermana mayor.

7. La nueva novela de ese escritor es _____ (*as bad as*) su primera novela.

8. Agustín y Mario están _____ (*less fat than*) antes.

2 **Lo obvio** Your friend Francisco is always sharing his opinions with you, even though his comparisons are always painfully obvious. Write sentences that express his opinions, using the adjectives in parentheses.

> **modelo**
> (inteligente) Albert Einstein / Homer Simpson
> Albert Einstein es más inteligente que Homer Simpson.

1. (famoso) Adele / mi hermana

_____

2. (difícil) estudiar química orgánica / leer una novela

_____

3. (malo) el tiempo en Boston / el tiempo en Florida

_____

4. (barato) los restaurantes elegantes / los restaurantes de comida rápida

_____

5. (viejo) mi abuelo / mi sobrino

_____

3 **¿Por qué?** Complete the sentences with the correct comparisons.

> **modelo**
> Darío juega mejor al fútbol que tú.
> Es porque Darío *practica más que tú.*

1. Mi hermano es más gordo que mi padre. Es porque mi hermano come _____.

2. Natalia conoce más países que tú. Es porque Natalia viaja _____.

3. Estoy más cansado que David. Es porque duermo _____.

4. Rolando tiene más hambre que yo. Va a comer _____.

5. Mi vestido favorito es más barato que el tuyo. Voy a pagar _____.

6. Julia gana más dinero que Lorna. Es porque Julia trabaja _____.

Lección 8 Workbook Activities   **91**

4 Comparaciones Form complete sentences using one word from each column.

la carne	bueno	el aceite
la comida rápida	caro	el almuerzo
el desayuno	malo	las chuletas de cerdo
la fruta	pequeño	la ensalada
la mantequilla	rico	los entremeses
el pollo	sabroso	el pescado

modelo
La carne es más cara que el pescado.

1. _____   4. _____
2. _____   5. _____
3. _____   6. _____

5 Tan... como Compare Jorge and Marcos using comparisons of equality and the following words. Be creative in your answers.

alto	delgado	inteligente
bueno	guapo	joven

Marcos

Jorge

modelo
Marcos no es tan inteligente como Jorge.

1. _____   4. _____
2. _____   5. _____
3. _____   6. _____

6 ¿Más o menos? Read the pairs of sentences. Then write a new sentence comparing the first item to the second one.

modelo
Ese hotel tiene cien habitaciones. El otro hotel tiene cuarenta habitaciones.
Ese hotel tiene más habitaciones que el otro.

1. La biblioteca tiene ciento cincuenta sillas. El laboratorio de lenguas tiene treinta sillas.

_____

2. Ramón compró tres corbatas. Roberto compró tres corbatas.

_____

3. Yo comí un plato de pasta. Mi hermano comió dos platos de pasta.

_____

4. Anabel durmió ocho horas. Amelia durmió ocho horas.

_____

5. Mi primo toma seis clases. Mi amiga Tere toma ocho clases.

_____

8.4 Superlatives

1 **El mejor...** Complete with the appropriate information in each case. Form complete sentences using the superlatives.

> **modelo**
> el restaurante _____ / bueno / ciudad
> El restaurante Dalí es el mejor restaurante de la ciudad.

1. la película _____ / mala / la historia del cine

_____

2. la comida _____ / sabrosa / todas

_____

3. mi _____ / joven / mi familia

_____

4. el libro _____ / interesante / biblioteca

_____

5. las vacaciones de _____ / buenas / año

_____

2 **Facilísimo** Rewrite each sentence, using absolute superlatives.

1. Miguel y Maru están muy cansados. _____

2. Felipe es muy joven. _____

3. Jimena es muy inteligente. _____

4. La madre de Marissa está muy contenta. _____

5. Estoy muy aburrido. _____

3 **Compárate** Compare yourself with the members of your family and the students in your class. Write at least two complete sentences using comparisons of equality and inequality, superlatives, and absolute superlatives.

> **modelo**
> En mi familia, yo soy más bajo que mi hermano.

_____

_____

_____

> **modelo**
> En mi clase, mi amigo Evan es tan inteligente como yo.

_____

_____

_____

Síntesis

Interview a friend or a relative and ask him or her to describe two restaurants where he or she recently ate.

- How was the quality of the food at each restaurant?
- How was the quality of the service at each restaurant?
- How did the prices of the two restaurants compare?
- What did his or her dining companions think about the restaurants?
- How was the ambience different at each restaurant?
- How convenient are the restaurants? Are they centrally located? Are they accessible by public transportation? Do they have parking?

When you are finished with the interview, write up a comparison of the two restaurants based on the information you collected. Use lesson vocabulary and as many different types of comparisons and superlative phrases as possible in your report.

_____

_____

_____

_____

_____

_____

_____

_____

_____

_____

_____

_____

_____

_____

_____

_____

_____

_____

panorama

Guatemala

1 **Guatemala** Complete the sentences with the correct words.

1. La _____ de Guatemala recibe su nombre de un pájaro que simboliza la libertad.

2. Un _____ por ciento de la población guatemalteca tiene una lengua materna diferente del español.

3. El _____ y los colores de cada *huipil* indican el pueblo de origen de la persona que lo lleva.

4. El _____ es un pájaro en peligro de extinción.

5. La civilización maya inventó un _____ complejo y preciso.

6. La ropa tradicional refleja el amor de la cultura maya por la _____.

2 **Preguntas** Answer the questions with complete sentences.

1. ¿Cuál es un cultivo de mucha importancia en la cultura maya? _____

_____

2. ¿Quién es Miguel Ángel Asturias? _____

_____

3. ¿Qué países limitan con (*border*) Guatemala? _____

_____

4. ¿Hasta cuándo fue la Antigua Guatemala una capital importante? ¿Qué pasó? _____

_____

5. ¿Por qué simbolizó el quetzal la libertad para los mayas? _____

_____

6. ¿Qué hace el gobierno para proteger al quetzal? _____

_____

3 **Fotos de Guatemala** Label each photo.

1. _____   2. _____

4 **Comparar** Read the sentences about Guatemala. Then rewrite them, using comparisons and superlatives. Do not change the meaning.

> **modelo**
>
> La Ciudad de Guatemala no es una ciudad pequeña.
> La Ciudad de Guatemala es la más grande del país.

1. El área de Guatemala no es más grande que la de Tennessee.

_____

2. Un componente muy interesante de las telas (*fabrics*) de Guatemala es el mosquito.

_____

3. Las lenguas mayas no se hablan tanto como el español.

_____

4. Rigoberta Menchú no es mayor que Margarita Carrera.

_____

5. La celebración de la Semana Santa en la Antigua Guatemala es importantísima para muchas personas.

_____

_____

5 **¿Cierto o falso?** Indicate whether the statements about Guatemala are **cierto** or **falso**. Correct the false statements.

1. Rigoberta Menchú ganó el Premio Nobel de la Paz en 1992.

_____

2. La lengua materna de muchos guatemaltecos es una lengua inca.

_____

3. La civilización de los mayas no era avanzada.

_____

4. Guatemala es un país que tiene costas en dos océanos.

_____

5. Hay muchísimos quetzales en los bosques de Guatemala.

_____

6. La civilización maya descubrió y usó el cero antes que los europeos.

_____

contextos

1 **Identificar** Label the following terms as **estado civil**, **fiesta**, or **etapa de la vida**.

1. casada _____

2. adolescencia _____

3. viudo _____

4. juventud _____

5. Navidad _____

6. niñez _____

7. vejez _____

8. aniversario de bodas _____

9. divorciado _____

10. madurez _____

11. cumpleaños _____

12. soltera _____

2 **Las etapas de la vida** Label the stages of life on the timeline.

```
    0   5  10  15  20  25  30  35  40  45  50  55  60  65  70  75  80  85  90  100
```

4. _____

1. _____   3. _____   5. _____   6. _____

2. _____

3 **Escribir** Fill in the blanks with the stage of life in which these events would normally occur.

1. jubilarse _____

2. graduarse de la universidad _____

3. cumplir nueve años _____

4. conseguir el primer trabajo _____

5. graduarse de la escuela secundaria _____

6. morir o quedar viudo _____

7. casarse (por primera vez) _____

8. tener un hijo _____

9. celebrar el aniversario de bodas número cincuenta _____

10. tener la primera cita _____

4 **Información personal** Read the descriptions and answer the questions.

"Me llamo Jorge Rosas. Nací el 26 de enero de 1952. Mi esposa murió el año pasado. Tengo dos hijos: Marina y Daniel. Terminé mis estudios de sociología en la Universidad Interamericana en 1974. Me voy a jubilar este año. Voy a celebrar este evento con una botella de champán."

1. ¿Cuál es la fecha de nacimiento de Jorge? _____

2. ¿Cuál es el estado civil de Jorge? _____

3. ¿En qué etapa de la vida está Jorge? _____

4. ¿Cuándo es el cumpleaños de Jorge? _____

5. ¿Cuándo se graduó Jorge? _____

6. ¿Cómo va a celebrar la jubilación (*retirement*) Jorge? _____

"Soy Julia Jiménez. Nací el 11 de marzo de 1990. Me comprometí a los veinte años, pero rompí con mi novio antes de casarme. Ahora estoy saliendo con un músico cubano. Soy historiadora del arte desde que terminé mi carrera (*degree*) en la Universidad de Salamanca en 2012. Mi postre favorito es el flan de caramelo."

7. ¿Cuál es la fecha de nacimiento de Julia? _____

8. ¿Cuál es el estado civil de Julia? _____

9. ¿En qué etapa de la vida está Julia? _____

10. ¿Cuándo es el cumpleaños de Julia? _____

11. ¿Cuándo se graduó Julia? _____

12. ¿Qué postre le gusta a Julia? _____

"Me llamo Manuel Blanco y vivo en Caracas. Mi esposa y yo nos comprometimos a los veintiséis años, y la boda fue dos años después. Pasaron quince años y tuvimos tres hijos. Me gustan mucho los dulces."

13. ¿Dónde vive Manuel? _____

14. ¿En qué etapa de la vida se comprometió Manuel? _____

15. ¿A qué edad se casó Manuel? _____

16. ¿Cuál es el estado civil de Manuel? _____

17. ¿Cuántos hijos tiene Manuel? _____

18. ¿Qué postre le gusta a Manuel? _____

estructura

9.1 Irregular preterites

1 **¿Hay o hubo?** Complete these sentences with the correct tense of **haber**.

1. Ahora _____ una fiesta de graduación en el patio de la universidad.

2. _____ muchos invitados en la fiesta de aniversario anoche.

3. Ya _____ una muerte en su familia el año pasado.

4. Siempre _____ galletas y dulces en esas conferencias.

5. _____ varios entremeses en la cena de ayer.

6. Por las mañanas _____ unos postres deliciosos en esa tienda.

2 **¿Cómo fue?** Complete these sentences with the preterite of the verb in parentheses.

1. Cristina y Lara _____ (estar) en la fiesta anoche.

2. (yo) _____ (tener) un problema con mi pasaporte y lo pasé mal en la aduana.

3. Rafaela _____ (venir) temprano a la fiesta y conoció a Humberto.

4. El padre de la novia _____ (hacer) un brindis por los novios.

5. Román _____ (poner) las maletas en el auto antes de salir.

3 **¿Qué hicieron?** Complete these sentences, using the preterite of **decir**, **conducir**, **traducir**, and **traer**.

1. Felipe y Silvia _____ que no les gusta ir a la playa.

2. Claudia le _____ unos papeles al inglés a su hermano.

3. David _____ su motocicleta nueva durante el fin de semana.

4. Rosario y Pepe me _____ un pastel de chocolate de regalo.

5. Cristina y yo les _____ a nuestras amigas que vamos a bailar.

4 **Es mejor dar...** Rewrite these sentences in the preterite tense.

1. Antonio le da un beso a su madre.

_____

2. Los invitados le dan las gracias a la familia.

_____

3. Tú les traes una sorpresa a tus padres.

_____

4. Rosa y yo le damos un regalo al profesor.

_____

5. Carla nos trae mucha comida para el viaje.

_____

5 **Combinar** Create logical sentences in the preterite using one element from each column. Notice that, using each word once, there is only one correct match between second and third columns.

Rita y Sara	decir	una cámara
ellos	estar	a este lugar
tú	hacer	un examen
mi tía	poner	galletas
ustedes	producir	una película
Rosa	tener	en Perú
nosotras	traer	la televisión
yo	venir	la verdad

1. _____

2. _____

3. _____

4. _____

5. _____

6. _____

7. _____

8. _____

6 **Ya lo hizo** Your friend Miguel is very forgetful. Answer his questions negatively, indicating that the action has already occurred. Use the phrases or words in parentheses.

> **modelo**
> ¿Quiere Pepe cenar en el restaurante japonés? (restaurante chino)
> No, Pepe ya cenó en el restaurante chino.

1. ¿Vas a estar en la biblioteca hoy? (ayer)

_____

2. ¿Quieren dar una fiesta Elena y Sergio este fin de semana? (el sábado pasado)

_____

3. ¿Debe la profesora traducir esa novela este semestre? (el año pasado)

_____

4. ¿Va a haber pastel de limón en la cena de hoy? (anoche)

_____

5. ¿Deseas poner los abrigos en la silla? (sobre la cama)

_____

6. ¿Van ustedes a tener un hijo? (tres hijos)

_____

9.2 Verbs that change meaning in the preterite

1 **Completar** Complete these sentences with the preterite tense of the verbs in parentheses.

1. Liliana no _____ (poder) llegar a la fiesta de cumpleaños de Esteban.

2. Las chicas _____ (conocer) a muchos estudiantes en la biblioteca.

3. Raúl y Marta no _____ (querer) invitar al padre de Raúl a la boda.

4. Lina _____ (saber) ayer que sus tíos se van a divorciar.

5. (nosotros) _____ (poder) regalarle una bicicleta a Marina.

6. María _____ (querer) romper con su novio antes del verano.

2 **Traducir** Use these verbs to translate the sentences into Spanish.

> conocer   querer
> poder   saber

1. I failed to finish the book on Wednesday.

_____

2. Inés found out last week that Vicente is divorced.

_____

3. Her girlfriends tried to call her, but they failed to.

_____

4. Susana met Alberto's parents last night.

_____

5. The waiters managed to serve dinner at eight.

_____

6. Your mother refused to go to your brother's house.

_____

3 **Raquel y Ronaldo** Complete the paragraph with the preterite of the verbs in the word bank.

> conocer   querer
> poder   saber

El año pasado Raquel (1) _____ al muchacho que ahora es su esposo, Ronaldo.

Primero, Raquel no (2) _____ salir con él porque él vivía (*was living*) en una ciudad

muy lejos de ella. Ronaldo (3) _____ convencerla durante muchos meses, pero no

(4) _____ hacerlo. Finalmente, Raquel decidió darle una oportunidad a Ronaldo.

Cuando empezaron a salir, Raquel y Ronaldo (5) _____ inmediatamente que eran el

uno para el otro (*they were made for each other*). Raquel y Ronaldo (6) _____ comprar

una casa en la misma ciudad y se casaron ese verano.

Lección 9 Workbook Activities   **101**

9.3 ¿Qué? and ¿cuál?

1 **¿Qué o cuál?** Complete these sentences with **qué**, **cuál**, or **cuáles**.

1. ¿_____ estás haciendo ahora?

2. ¿_____ gafas te gustan más?

3. ¿_____ prefieres, el vestido largo o el corto?

4. ¿Sabes _____ de éstos es mi disco favorito?

5. ¿_____ es un departamento de hacienda?

6. ¿_____ trajiste, las de chocolate o las de limón?

7. ¿_____ auto compraste este año?

8. ¿_____ es la tienda más elegante del centro?

2 **¿Cuál es la pregunta?** Write questions that correspond to these responses. Use each word or phrase from the word bank only once.

¿a qué hora?	¿cuál?	¿cuándo?	¿de dónde?	¿qué?
¿adónde?	¿cuáles?	¿cuántos?	¿dónde?	¿quién?

1. _____

La camisa que más me gusta es ésa.

2. _____

Hoy quiero descansar durante el día.

3. _____

Mi profesora de matemáticas es la señora Aponte.

4. _____

Soy de Buenos Aires, Argentina.

5. _____

Mis gafas favoritas son las azules.

6. _____

El pastel de cumpleaños está en el refrigerador.

7. _____

La fiesta sorpresa empieza a las ocho en punto de la noche.

8. _____

El restaurante cierra los lunes.

9. _____

Hay ciento cincuenta invitados en la lista.

10. _____

Vamos a la fiesta de cumpleaños de Inés.

9.4 Pronouns after prepositions

1 **Antes de la fiesta** Choose and write the correct pronouns to complete the paragraph.

Hoy voy al mercado al aire libre cerca de mi casa con mi tía Carmen. Me gusta ir con

(1) _____ (usted, ella) porque sabe escoger las mejores frutas y verduras del mercado.

Y a ella le gusta ir (2) _____ (contigo, conmigo) porque sé regatear mejor que nadie.

—Entre (3) _____ (tú, ellas) y yo, debes saber que a (4) _____ (ella, mí) no me

gusta gastar mucho dinero. Me gusta venir (5) _____ (con usted, contigo) porque me ayudas a

ahorrar (*save*) dinero —me confesó un día en el mercado. Hoy la vienen a visitar sus hijos porque es su

cumpleaños, y ella quiere hacer una ensalada de frutas para (6) _____ (ellos, nosotros).

—Estas peras son para (7) _____ (mí, ti), por venir conmigo al mercado. También me

llevo unos hermosos melocotones para el novio de Verónica, que viene con (8) _____

(ella, nosotras). Siempre compro frutas para (9) _____ (mí, él) porque le encantan y no

consigue muchas frutas en el lugar donde vive —dice mi tía.

—¿Voy a conocer al novio de Verónica?

—Sí, ¡queremos invitarte a (10) _____ (ti, él) a la fiesta de cumpleaños!

2 **El pastel de Carlota** Some friends are having Carlota's birthday cake. Complete the conversation with the correct pronouns.

SR. MARTÍNEZ Chicos, voy a buscar a mi esposa, en un momento estoy con

(1) _____.

TOMÁS Sí, señor Martínez, no se preocupe por (2) _____.

YOLANDA ¡Qué rico está el pastel! A (3) _____ me encantan los pasteles.

Tomás, ¿quieres compartir un pedazo (*slice*) (4) _____?

TOMÁS ¡Claro! Para (5) _____ el chocolate es lo más delicioso.

CARLOTA Pero no se lo terminen... Víctor, quiero compartir el último (*last*) pedazo

(6) _____.

VÍCTOR Mmmh, está bien; sólo por (7) _____ hago este sacrificio.

CARLOTA Toma, Víctor, este pedazo es especial para (8) _____.

TOMÁS ¡Oh, no! Mira, Yolanda, ¡hay más miel (*honey*) en (9) _____

que en cien pasteles!

Síntesis

Research the life of a famous person who has had a stormy personal life, such as Elizabeth Taylor or Henry VIII. Write a brief biography of the person, including the following information:

- When was the person born?
- What was that person's childhood like?
- With whom did the person fall in love?
- Whom did the person marry?
- Did he or she have children?

- Did the person get divorced?
- Did the person go to school, and did he or she graduate?
- How did his or her career or lifestyle vary as the person went through different stages in life?

Use lesson vocabulary, irregular preterites, and verbs that change meaning in the preterite in your biography.

_____

_____

_____

_____

_____

_____

_____

_____

_____

_____

_____

_____

_____

_____

_____

_____

_____

_____

panorama

Chile

1 **Datos chilenos** Complete the chart with the correct information about Chile.

Ciudades principales	Deportes de invierno	Países fronterizos (*bordering*)	Escritores

2 **¿Cierto o falso?** Indicate whether the sentences are **cierto** or **falso.** Correct the false sentences.

1. Una quinta parte de los chilenos vive en Santiago de Chile.

_____

2. En Chile se hablan el idioma español y el mapuche.

_____

3. La mayoría (*most*) de las playas de Chile están en la costa del océano Atlántico.

_____

4. El desierto de Atacama es el más seco del mundo.

_____

5. La isla de Pascua es famosa por sus observatorios astronómicos.

_____

6. El Parque Nacional Villarrica está situado al pie de un volcán y junto a un lago.

_____

7. Se practican deportes de invierno en los Andes chilenos.

_____

8. La exportación de vinos chilenos se redujo (*decreased*) en los últimos años.

_____

3 **Información de Chile** Complete the sentences with the correct words.

1. La moneda de Chile es el _____.

2. Bernardo O'Higgins fue un militar y _____ nacional de Chile.

3. Los exploradores _____ descubrieron la isla de Pascua.

4. Desde los _____ chilenos de los Andes, los científicos estudian las estrellas.

5. La producción de _____ es una parte importante de la actividad agrícola de Chile.

6. El país al este de Chile es _____.

4 **Fotos de Chile** Label the photos.

1. _____

2. _____

5 **El pasado de Chile** Complete the sentences with the preterite of the correct verbs from the word bank.

> comenzar   escribir
> decidir   recibir

1. Pablo Neruda _____ muchos poemas románticos durante su vida.

2. La isla de Pascua _____ su nombre porque la descubrieron el día de Pascua.

3. No se sabe por qué los *rapa nui* _____ abandonar la isla de Pascua.

4. La producción de vino en Chile _____ en el siglo XVI.

6 **Preguntas chilenas** Write questions that correspond to the answers below. Vary the interrogative words you use.

1. _____

Hay más de diecisiete millones de habitantes en Chile.

2. _____

Santiago de Chile es la capital chilena.

3. _____

Los idiomas que se hablan en Chile son el español y el mapuche.

4. _____

Los exploradores holandeses descubrieron la isla de Pascua.

5. _____

El centro de esquí Valle Nevado organiza excursiones de heliesquí.

6. _____

La producción de vino en Chile comenzó en el siglo XVI.

Workbook

repaso — Lecciones 7–9

1 **¿Te importa?** Complete the sentences with the correct indirect object pronoun and the form of the verb in parentheses.

1. A nosotros _____ (gustar) ir de excursión y acampar.

2. A mí _____ (encantar) las novelas históricas.

3. A mi hermano _____ (molestar) la radio cuando está estudiando.

4. A ustedes no _____ (importar) esperar un rato para sentarse, ¿no?

5. Ese vestido largo _____ (quedar) muy bien (a ti) con las sandalias.

6. A ellos _____ (faltar) dos clases para graduarse de la universidad.

2 **No quiero nada** Answer the questions negatively, using negative words.

1. ¿Debo ponerme algo elegante esta noche?

_____

2. ¿Te enojaste con alguien en el restaurante?

_____

3. ¿Se probó algún vestido Ana en la tienda?

_____

4. ¿Quiere Raúl quedarse en las fiestas siempre?

_____

3 **La fiesta** Complete the paragraph with the correct preterite forms of the verbs in parentheses.

Ignacio y yo (1) _____ (ir) a la fiesta de cumpleaños de un amigo el sábado.

(2) _____ (Ir) juntos en mi auto, pero Ignacio (3) _____ (conducir). La fiesta

(4) _____ (ser) en el salón de fiestas del Hotel Condado. En la fiesta (5) _____

(haber) un pastel enorme y muchísimos invitados. (Yo) (6) _____ (saber) en la fiesta que mi

amiga Dora (7) _____ (romper) con su novio. Ignacio y yo (8) _____ (querer)

hacerla sentir mejor, pero no (9) _____ (ser) fácil. Primero Ignacio (10) _____ (pedir)

una botella de vino. Luego le (11) _____ (decir) a su amigo Marc: "Ven (*Come*) a sentarte

con nosotros". Ignacio le (12) _____ (servir) algo de vino a Marc y todos (13) _____

(brindar). Nosotros les (14) _____ (dar) la oportunidad a Dora y a Marc de conocerse. Marc

es francés, y por mucho rato ellos no (15) _____ (poder) entenderse. Luego yo (16) _____

(traducir) sus palabras un rato. Dora (17) _____ (repetir) las palabras hasta decirlas bien. Dora

y Marc (18) _____ (estar) hablando toda (*all*) la noche. Ignacio les (19) _____ (traer)

entremeses y él y yo nos (20) _____ (ir) a bailar. Marc le (21) _____ (pedir) el número

a Dora. Ella (22) _____ (ponerse) feliz.

4 Te lo dije Rewrite these sentences in the preterite. Use double object pronouns in the new sentences.

modelo

> Carlos le traduce los documentos a su hermano. *Carlos se los tradujo.*

1. Rebeca quiere comprarle un regalo a Jorge. _____

2. Les hago una cena deliciosa. _____

3. Los López le dicen unos chistes (*jokes*). _____

4. Francisco no puede prestarnos el auto. _____

5. Les debes decir tu apellido a los dueños. _____

6. Te traigo unas cosas importantes. _____

5 Los países Compare the items listed, using information from the **Panorama** sections.

1. Guatemala / pequeño / Perú

_____

2. Líneas de Nazca / misteriosas / los *moái* de la isla de Pascua

_____

3. habitantes de Guatemala / hablar idiomas / habitantes de Chile

_____

4. Ciudad de Guatemala / grande / puerto de Iquitos

_____

5. peruanos / usar las llamas / chilenos

_____

6 La boda Imagine that you know the couple in the photo. Write some background about their wedding. How and when did the couple meet? When did they become engaged? Do they get along well? Do they really love each other? Next, talk about the food and drinks served at the wedding and whether you enjoyed the event.

_____

_____

_____

_____

_____

_____

_____

_____

_____

contextos

1 **El cuerpo humano** Label the parts of the body.

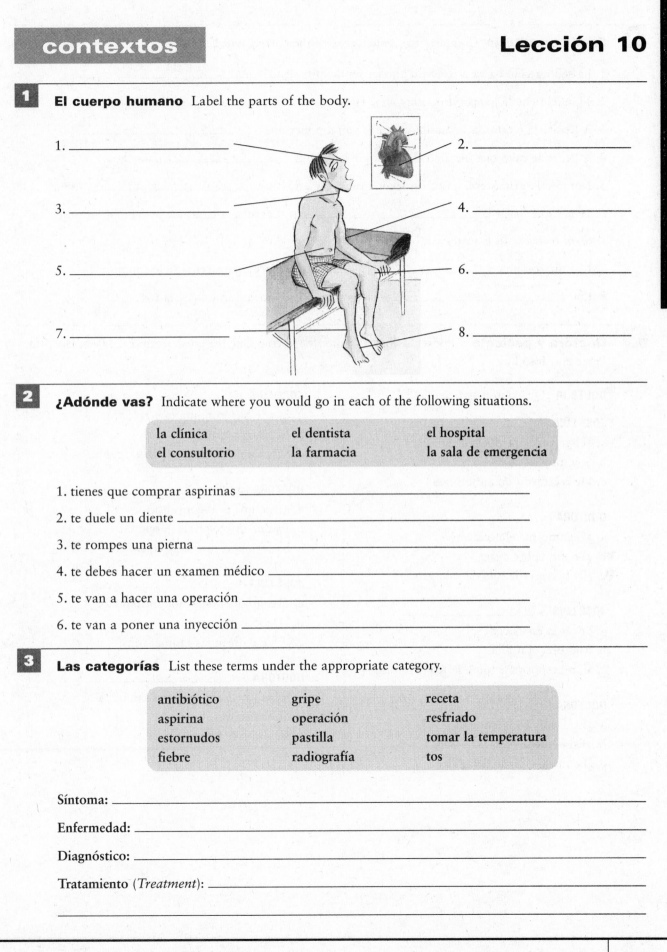

1. _____

2. _____

3. _____

4. _____

5. _____

6. _____

7. _____

8. _____

2 **¿Adónde vas?** Indicate where you would go in each of the following situations.

la clínica	el dentista	el hospital
el consultorio	la farmacia	la sala de emergencia

1. tienes que comprar aspirinas _____

2. te duele un diente _____

3. te rompes una pierna _____

4. te debes hacer un examen médico _____

5. te van a hacer una operación _____

6. te van a poner una inyección _____

3 **Las categorías** List these terms under the appropriate category.

antibiótico	gripe	receta
aspirina	operación	resfriado
estornudos	pastilla	tomar la temperatura
fiebre	radiografía	tos

Síntoma: _____

Enfermedad: _____

Diagnóstico: _____

Tratamiento (*Treatment*): _____

_____

4   **En el consultorio** Complete the sentences with the correct words.

1. La señora Gandía va a tener un hijo en septiembre. Está _____.

2. Manuel tiene la temperatura muy alta. Tiene _____.

3. A Rosita le recetaron un antibiótico y le van a poner una _____.

4. A Pedro le cayó una mesa en el pie. El pie le _____ mucho.

5. Durante la primavera, mi tía estornuda mucho y está muy _____.

6. Tienes que llevar la _____ a la farmacia para que te vendan (*in order for them to sell you*) la medicina.

7. Le tomaron una _____ de la pierna para ver si se le rompió.

8. Los _____ de un resfriado son los estornudos y la tos.

5   **Doctora y paciente** Choose the logical sentences to complete the conversation between Doctora Pérez and José Luis.

DOCTORA ¿Qué síntomas tiene?

JOSÉ LUIS (1) _____
a. Tengo tos y me duele la cabeza.
b. Soy muy saludable.
c. Me recetaron un antibiótico.

DOCTORA (2) _____
a. ¿Cuándo fue el accidente?
b. ¿Le dio fiebre ayer?
c. ¿Dónde está la sala de emergencia?

JOSÉ LUIS (3) _____
a. Fue a la farmacia.
b. Me torcí el tobillo.
c. Sí, mi esposa me tomó la temperatura.

DOCTORA (4) _____
a. ¿Está muy congestionado?
b. ¿Está embarazada?
c. ¿Le duele el dedo del pie?

JOSÉ LUIS (5) _____
a. Sí, me hicieron una operación.
b. Sí, estoy mareado.
c. Sí, y también me duele la garganta.

DOCTORA (6) _____
a. Tiene que ir al consultorio.
b. Es una infección de garganta.
c. La farmacia está muy cerca.

JOSÉ LUIS (7) _____
a. ¿Tengo que tomar un antibiótico?
b. ¿Debo ir al dentista?
c. ¿Qué indican las radiografías?

DOCTORA (8) _____
a. Sí, es usted una persona saludable.
b. Sí, se lastimó el pie.
c. Sí, ahora se lo voy a recetar.

estructura

10.1 The imperfect tense

1 **¿Cómo eran las cosas?** Complete the sentences with the imperfect forms of the verbs in parentheses.

1. Antes, la familia Álvarez _____ (cenar) a las ocho de la noche.

2. De niña, yo _____ (cantar) en el Coro de Niños de San Juan.

3. Cuando vivían en la costa, ustedes _____ (nadar) por las mañanas.

4. Mis hermanas y yo _____ (jugar) en un equipo de béisbol.

5. La novia de Raúl _____ (tener) el pelo rubio en ese tiempo.

6. Antes de tener la computadora, (tú) _____ (escribir) a mano (*by hand*).

7. (nosotros) _____ (creer) que el concierto era el miércoles.

8. Mientras ellos lo _____ (buscar) en su casa, él se fue a la universidad.

2 **Oraciones imperfectas** Create sentences with the elements provided and the imperfect tense.

1. mi abuela / ser / muy trabajadora y amable

_____

2. tú / ir / al teatro / cuando vivías en Nueva York

_____

3. ayer / haber / muchísimos pacientes en el consultorio

_____

4. (nosotros) / ver / tu casa desde allí

_____

5. ser / las cinco de la tarde / cuando llegamos a San José

_____

6. ella / estar / muy nerviosa durante la operación

_____

3 **No, pero antes...** Your nosy friend Cristina is asking you many questions. Answer her questions negatively, using the imperfect tense.

> **modelo**
> ¿Juega Daniel al fútbol?
> No, pero antes jugaba.

1. ¿Hablas por teléfono? _____

2. ¿Fue a la playa Susana? _____

3. ¿Come carne Benito? _____

4. ¿Te trajo muchos regalos tu novio? _____

5. ¿Conduce tu mamá? _____

Lección 10 Workbook Activities **111**

Workbook

4 **¿Qué hacían?** Write sentences that describe what the people in the drawings were doing yesterday at three o'clock in the afternoon. Use the subjects provided and the imperfect tense.

1. Tú

_____

_____

_____

2. Rolando

_____

_____

_____

3. Pablo y Elena

_____

_____

_____

4. Lilia y yo

_____

_____

_____

5 **Antes y ahora** Javier is thinking about his childhood—how things were then and how they are now. Write two sentences comparing what Javier used to do and what he does now.

> **modelo**
>
> vivir en casa / vivir en la residencia estudiantil
>
> Antes vivía en casa.
>
> Ahora vivo en la residencia estudiantil.

1. jugar al fútbol con mis primos / jugar en el equipo de la universidad

_____

_____

2. escribir las cartas a mano / escribir el correo electrónico con la computadora

_____

_____

3. ser gordito (*chubby*) / ser delgado

_____

_____

4. tener a mi familia cerca / tener a mi familia lejos

_____

_____

5. estudiar en mi habitación / estudiar en la biblioteca

_____

_____

6. conocer a personas de mi ciudad / conocer a personas de todo el (*the whole*) país

_____

_____

10.2 The preterite and the imperfect

1 **Los accidentes** Complete the sentences correctly with imperfect or preterite forms of the verbs in parentheses.

1. Claudia _____ (celebrar) su cumpleaños cuando se torció el tobillo.

2. Ramiro tenía fiebre cuando _____ (llegar) a la clínica.

3. Mientras el doctor _____ (mirar) la radiografía, yo llamé por teléfono a mi novia.

4. (yo) _____ (estar) mirando la televisión cuando mi mamá se lastimó la mano con la puerta.

5. Cuando Sandra llegó a la universidad, _____ (tener) un dolor de cabeza terrible.

6. ¿De niño (tú) _____ (enfermarse) con frecuencia?

7. El verano pasado, Luis y Olivia _____ (sufrir) una enfermedad exótica.

8. Anoche, mi primo y yo _____ (perder) la receta de mi tía.

2 **Antes y ayer** Complete each pair of sentences by using the imperfect and preterite forms of the verbs in parentheses.

(bailar)

1. Cuando era pequeña, Sara _____ ballet todos los lunes y miércoles.

2. Ayer Sara _____ ballet en el recital de la universidad.

(escribir)

3. La semana pasada, (yo) le _____ un mensaje electrónico a mi papá.

4. Antes (yo) _____ las cartas a mano o con una máquina de escribir (*typewriter*).

(ser)

5. El novio de María _____ delgado y deportista.

6. El viaje de novios _____ una experiencia inolvidable (*unforgettable*).

(haber)

7. _____ una fiesta en casa de Maritere el viernes pasado.

8. Cuando llegamos a la fiesta, _____ mucha gente.

(ver)

9. El lunes (yo) _____ a mi prima Lisa en el centro comercial.

10. De niña, yo _____ a Lisa todos los días.

3   **¿Qué pasaba?** Look at the drawings, then complete the sentences, using the preterite or imperfect.

1. Cuando llegué a casa anoche, las

niñas _____

_____.

2. Cuando empezó a llover, Sara

_____

_____.

3. Antes de irse de vacaciones, la señora

García _____

_____.

4. Cada verano, las chicas

_____

_____.

4   **El pasado** Decide whether the verbs in parentheses should be in the preterite or the imperfect. Then rewrite the sentences.

1. Ayer Clara (ir) a casa de sus primos, (saludar) a su tía y (comer) con ellos.

_____

2. Cuando Manuel (vivir) en San José, (conducir) muchos kilómetros todos los días.

_____

3. Mientras Carlos (leer) las traducciones (*translations*), Blanca (traducir) otros textos.

_____

4. El doctor (terminar) el examen médico y me (recetar) un antibiótico.

_____

5. La niña (tener) ocho años y (ser) inteligente y alegre.

_____

6. Rafael (cerrar) todos los programas, (apagar) la computadora y (irse).

_____

5 **¡Qué diferencia!** Complete this paragraph with the preterite or the imperfect of the verbs in parentheses.

La semana pasada (yo) (1) _____ (llegar) a la universidad y me di cuenta (*realized*) de que este año iba a ser muy diferente a los anteriores. Todos los años Laura y yo

(2) _____ (vivir) con Regina, pero la semana pasada (nosotras)

(3) _____ (conocer) a nuestra nueva compañera de cuarto, Gisela. Antes Laura,

Regina y yo (4) _____ (tener) un apartamento muy pequeño, pero al llegar la

semana pasada, (nosotras) (5) _____ (ver) el apartamento nuevo: es enorme y

tiene mucha luz. Antes de vivir con Gisela, Laura y yo no (6) _____ (poder) leer

el correo electrónico desde la casa, pero ayer Gisela (7) _____ (conectar) su

computadora a Internet y todas (8) _____ (mirar) nuestros mensajes. Antes

(nosotras) siempre (9) _____ (caminar) hasta la biblioteca para ver el correo,

pero anoche Gisela nos (10) _____ (decir) que podemos compartir su

computadora. ¡Qué diferencia!

6 **¿Dónde estabas?** Write questions and answers with the words provided. Ask where these people were when something happened.

> **modelo**
>
> Jimena ⟶ Marissa / salir a bailar // cuarto / dormir la siesta
> ¿Dónde estaba Jimena cuando Marissa salió a bailar?
> Jimena estaba en el cuarto. Dormía la siesta.

1. Miguel ⟶ (yo) / llamar por teléfono // cocina / lavar los platos

   _____

   _____

2. (tú) ⟶ Juan Carlos y yo / ir al cine // casa / leer una revista

   _____

   _____

3. tu hermano ⟶ empezar a llover // calle / pasear en bicicleta

   _____

   _____

4. ustedes ⟶ Felipe / venir a casa // estadio / jugar al fútbol

   _____

   _____

5. Jimena y Felipe ⟶ (tú) / saludarlos // supermercado / hacer la compra

   _____

   _____

Workbook

7 **El diario de Laura** Laura has just found a page from her old diary. Rewrite the page in the past tense, using the preterite and imperfect forms of the verbs as appropriate.

Querido diario:

Estoy pasando el verano en Alajuela, y es un lugar muy divertido. Salgo con mis amigas todas las noches hasta tarde. Bailamos con nuestros amigos y nos divertimos mucho. Durante la semana trabajo: doy clases de inglés. Los estudiantes son alegres y se interesan mucho por aprender. El día de mi cumpleaños conocí a un chico muy simpático que se llama Francisco. Me llamó al día siguiente (next) y nos vemos todos los días. Me siento enamorada de él.

_____

_____

_____

_____

_____

_____

_____

_____

_____

_____

8 **Un día en la playa** Laura is still reading her old diary. Rewrite this paragraph, using the preterite or imperfect forms of the verbs in parentheses as appropriate.

Querido diario:

Ayer mi hermana y yo (ir) a la playa. Cuando llegamos, (ser) un día despejado con mucho sol, y nosotras (estar) muy contentas. A las doce (comer) unos sándwiches de almuerzo. Los sándwiches (ser) de jamón y queso. Luego (descansar) y entonces (nadar) en el mar. Mientras (nadar), (ver) a las personas que (practicar) el esquí acuático. (Parecer) muy divertido, así que (decidir) probarlo. Mi hermana (ir) primero, mientras yo la (mirar). Luego (ser) mi turno. Las dos (divertirse) mucho esa tarde.

_____

_____

_____

_____

_____

_____

_____

_____

10.3 Constructions with **se**

1   **¿Qué se hace?** Complete the sentences with verbs from the word bank. Use impersonal constructions with **se** in the present tense.

caer	hablar	recetar	vender
dañar	poder	servir	vivir

1. En Costa Rica _____ español.

2. En las librerías _____ libros y revistas.

3. En los restaurantes _____ comida.

4. En los consultorios _____ medicinas.

5. En el campo _____ muy bien.

6. En el mar _____ nadar y pescar.

2   **Los anuncios** Write advertisements or signs for the situations described. Use impersonal constructions with **se**.

1. "Está prohibido fumar."

2. "Vendemos periódicos."

3. "Hablamos español."

4. "Necesitamos enfermeras."

5. "No debes nadar."

6. "Estamos buscando un auto usado."

3   **¿Qué les pasó?** Complete the sentences with the correct indirect object pronouns.

1. Se _____ perdieron las maletas a Roberto.

2. A mis hermanas se _____ cayó la mesa.

3. A ti se _____ olvidó venir a buscarme ayer.

4. A mí se _____ quedó la ropa nueva en mi casa.

5. A las tías de Ana se _____ rompieron los vasos.

6. A Isabel y a mí se _____ dañó el auto.

   Lección 10 Workbook Activities

4 **Los accidentes** Your classmates are very unlucky. Rewrite what happened to them, using the correct form of the verb in parentheses.

1. A Marina se le (cayó, cayeron) la bolsa.

_____

2. A ti se te (olvidó, olvidaron) comprarme la medicina.

_____

3. A nosotros se nos (quedó, quedaron) los libros en el auto.

_____

4. A Ramón y a Pedro se les (dañó, dañaron) el proyecto.

_____

5 **Mala suerte** You and your friends are trying to go on vacation, but everything is going wrong. Use the elements provided, the preterite tense, and constructions with **se** to write sentences.

> modelo
>
> (a Raquel) / olvidar / traer su pasaporte
> *Se le olvidó traer su pasaporte.*

1. (a nosotros) / perder / las llaves del auto

_____

2. (a ustedes) / olvidar / ponerse las inyecciones

_____

3. (a ti) / caer / los papeles del médico

_____

4. (a Marcos) / romper / la pierna cuando esquiaba

_____

5. (a mí) / dañar / la cámara durante el viaje

_____

6 **¿Qué pasó?** As the vacation goes on, you and your friends have more bad luck. Answer the questions, using the phrases in parentheses and the preterite tense.

> modelo
>
> ¿Qué le pasó a Roberto? (quedar la cámara nueva en casa)
> *Se le quedó la cámara nueva en casa.*

1. ¿Qué les pasó a Pilar y a Luis? (dañar el coche)

_____

2. ¿Qué les pasó a los padres de Sara? (romper la botella de vino)

_____

3. ¿Qué te pasó a ti? (perder las llaves del hotel)

_____

4. ¿Qué les pasó a ustedes? (quedar las toallas en la playa)

_____

5. ¿Qué le pasó a Hugo? (olvidar estudiar para el examen en el avión)

10.4 Adverbs

1 **En mi ciudad** Complete the sentences by changing the adjectives in the first sentences into adverbs in the second.

1. Los conductores son lentos. Conducen _____.

2. Esa doctora es amable. Siempre nos saluda _____.

3. Los autobuses de mi ciudad son frecuentes. Pasan por la parada _____.

4. Rosa y Julia son chicas muy alegres. Les encanta bailar y cantar _____.

5. Mario y tú hablan un español perfecto. Hablan español _____.

6. Los pacientes visitan al doctor de manera constante. Lo visitan _____.

7. Llegar tarde es normal para David. Llega tarde _____.

8. Me gusta trabajar de manera independiente. Trabajo _____.

2 **Completar** Complete the sentences with adverbs and adverbial expressions from the word bank. Do not use a term more than once.

a menudo	así	por lo menos
a tiempo	bastante	pronto
apenas	casi	

1. Tito no es un niño muy sano. Se enferma _____.

2. El doctor Garrido es muy puntual. Siempre llega al consultorio _____.

3. Mi madre visita al doctor con frecuencia. Se chequea _____ una vez cada año.

4. Fui al doctor el año pasado. Tengo que volver _____.

5. Llegué tarde al autobús; _____ tengo que ir al centro caminando.

6. El examen fue _____ difícil.

3 **Traducir** Complete the sentences with the adverbs or adverbial phrases that correspond to the words in parentheses.

1. Llegaron temprano al concierto; _____ (*so*), consiguieron asientos muy buenos.

2. El accidente fue _____ (*rather*) grave, pero al conductor no se le rompió ningún hueso.

3. Irene y Vicente van a comer _____ (*less*) porque quieren estar más delgados.

4. Silvia y David _____ (*almost*) se cayeron de la motocicleta cerca de su casa.

5. Para aprobar (*pass*) el examen, tienes que contestar _____ (*at least*) el 75 por

   ciento de las preguntas.

6. Mi mamá _____ (*sometimes*) se tuerce el tobillo cuando camina mucho.

Lección 10 Workbook Activities **119**

4 **Háblame de ti** Answer the questions using the adverbs and adverbial phrases that you learned in this lesson. Do not repeat the adverb or adverbial phrase of the question. Then, say how long it's been since you last did each activity.

> **modelo**
> ¿Vas a la playa siempre?
> No, voy a la playa a veces. Hace cuatro meses que no voy a la playa.

1. ¿Tú y tus amigos van al cine con frecuencia?

   _____

2. ¿Comes comida china?

   _____

3. ¿Llegas tarde a tu clase de español?

   _____

4. ¿Te enfermas con frecuencia?

   _____

5. ¿Comes carne?

   _____

Síntesis

Think of a summer in which you did a lot of different things on vacation or at home. Use the preterite to state exceptional situations or activities that you did just once. Then use the imperfect tense to state the activities that you used to do during that summer; mention which of those things you still do in the present. Use adverbs to answer these questions: How often did you do those activities then? How often do you do them now? Create a "photo album" of that summer, using actual photographs if you have them, or drawings that you make. Use your writing about the summer as captions for the photo album.

_____

_____

_____

_____

_____

_____

_____

_____

_____

_____

panorama

Costa Rica

1 **El mapa de Costa Rica** Label the map of Costa Rica.

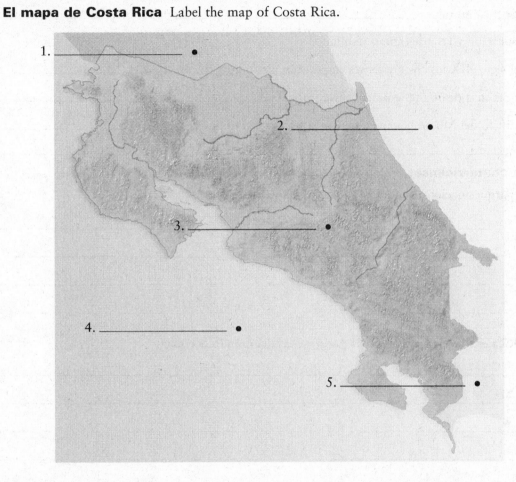

1. _____
2. _____
3. _____
4. _____
5. _____

2 **¿Cierto o falso?** Indicate whether the statements are **cierto** or **falso**. Correct the false statements.

1. Los parques nacionales costarricenses se establecieron para el turismo.

_____

2. Costa Rica fue el primer país centroamericano en desarrollar la industria del café.

_____

3. El café representa más del 50% de las exportaciones anuales de Costa Rica.

_____

4. Costa Rica tiene un nivel de alfabetización del 96%.

_____

5. El ejército de Costa Rica es uno de los más grandes y preparados de Latinoamérica.

_____

6. En Costa Rica se eliminó la educación gratuita para los costarricenses.

_____

3 Costa Rica Complete the sentences with the correct words.

1. Costa Rica es el país de Centroamérica con la población más _____.

2. La moneda que se usa en Costa Rica es _____.

3. Costa Rica no tiene _____; puede invertir más dinero en

   la educación y las artes como resultado.

4. En el siglo XIX los costarricenses empezaron a exportar su café a _____.

5. Hoy día más de 50.000 costarricenses trabajan _____ café.

6. El edificio del Museo Nacional de Costa Rica es el antiguo _____.

4 Datos costarricenses Fill in the blanks with the correct information.

En los parques nacionales de Costa Rica los ecoturistas pueden ver:

1. _____   5. _____

2. _____   6. _____

3. _____   7. _____

4. _____   8. _____

Costa Rica es uno de los países más progresistas del mundo porque:

9. _____

10. _____

11. _____

12. _____

5 Completar Use impersonal constructions with **se** to complete the sentences. Be sure to use the
correct tense of the verbs in the word bank.

> *modelo*
>
> En Costa Rica ahora *se pone* más dinero en la educación y las artes.

comprar	establecer	eliminar	poder
empezar	invertir	ofrecer	proveer

1. En Costa Rica _____ y se vende en colones.

2. El sistema de parques nacionales _____ para la protección de los ecosistemas.

3. En los parques, los animales _____ ver en su hábitat natural.

4. En el siglo XIX _____ a exportar el café costarricense.

5. En Costa Rica _____ educación gratuita a todos los ciudadanos.

6. En 1871 _____ la pena de muerte en Costa Rica.

contextos

1 **La tecnología** Fill in the blanks with the correct terms.

1. Para navegar en la red sin cables (*wires*) necesitas _____.

2. Para hacer videos de tu familia puedes usar _____.

3. Cuando vas a un sitio web, lo primero (*the first thing*) que ves es _____.

4. Si alguien te llama a tu celular y no respondes, te puede dejar un mensaje en _____.

5. La red de computadoras y servidores más importante del mundo es _____.

6. Para encontrar información en la red, usas un _____.

2 **Eso hacían** Match a subject from the word bank to each verb phrase. Then write complete sentences for the pairs using the imperfect.

muchos jóvenes estadounidenses	el conductor del autobús	el mecánico de Jorge
el carro viejo	la impresora nueva	el teléfono celular

1. manejar lentamente por la nieve

_____

2. imprimir los documentos muy rápido

_____

3. revisarle el aceite al auto todos los meses

_____

4. sonar insistentemente, pero nadie responder

_____

5. no arrancar cuando llover

_____

6. navegar en Internet cuando eran niños

_____

3 **La computadora** Label the drawing with the correct terms.

1. _____

2. _____

5. _____

3. _____

4. _____

6. _____

7. _____

4   **Preguntas** Answer the questions with complete sentences.

1. ¿Para qué se usa la impresora?

_____

2. ¿Para qué se usan los frenos (*brakes*) del coche?

_____

3. ¿Qué se usa para conducir por carreteras que no conoces?

_____

4. ¿Qué se usa para llevar el carro a la derecha o a la izquierda?

_____

5. ¿Qué se usa para cambiar los canales del televisor?

_____

6. ¿Para qué se usa la llave del carro?

_____

_____

5   **Mi primer día en la carretera** Complete the paragraph with terms from the word bank.

accidente	estacionar	policía
aceite	lento	revisar
arrancar	licencia de conducir	subir
autopista	llanta	taller mecánico
calle	lleno	tráfico
descargar	parar	velocidad máxima

Después de dos exámenes, conseguí mi (1) _____ para poder manejar legalmente

por primera vez. Estaba muy emocionado cuando (2) _____ al carro de mi papá.

El tanque estaba (3) _____ y el (4) _____ lo revisaron el día

anterior (*previous*) en el (5) _____. El carro y yo estábamos listos para

(6) _____. Primero salí por la (7) _____ en donde está mi

casa. Luego llegué a un área de la ciudad donde había mucha gente y también mucho

(8) _____. Se me olvidó (9) _____ en el semáforo (*light*), que

estaba amarillo, y estuve cerca de tener un (10) _____. Sin saberlo, entré en la

(11) _____ interestatal (*interstate*). La (12) _____ era de 70

millas (*miles*) por hora, pero yo estaba tan nervioso que iba mucho más (13) _____,

a 10 millas por hora. Vi un carro de la (14) _____ y tuve miedo. Por eso volví a

casa y (15) _____ el carro en la calle. ¡Qué aventura!

estructura

11.1 Familiar commands

1 **Cosas por hacer** Read the list of things to do. Then use familiar commands to finish the e-mail from Ana to her husband, Eduardo, about the things that he has to do before their vacation.

comprar un paquete de papel para la impresora	revisar el aceite del carro
ir al sitio web de la agencia de viajes y pedir la información sobre nuestro hotel	comprobar que tenemos una llanta extra
	limpiar el parabrisas
imprimir la información	llenar el tanque de gasolina
terminar de hacer las maletas	venir a buscarme a la oficina

```
Para Eduardo    De Ana      Asunto Cosas por hacer

  Hola mi amor, éstas son las cosas por hacer antes de salir para Mar del Plata:
  _____
  _____
  _____
  _____
  _____
  _____
```

2 **Díselo** You are feeling bossy today. Give your friends instructions based on the cues provided using familiar commands.

> **modelo**
> Ramón / comprarte un disco compacto en Mendoza
> Ramón, *cómprame un disco compacto en Mendoza.*

1. Mario / traerte la cámara digital que le regaló Gema

   _____

2. Natalia / escribirle un mensaje de texto a su hermana

   _____

3. Martín / llamarlos por teléfono celular

   _____

4. Gloria / hacer la cama antes de salir

   _____

5. Carmen / no revisar el aceite hasta la semana que viene

   _____

6. Lilia / enseñarte a manejar

   _____

3 **Planes para el invierno** Rewrite this paragraph from a travel website. Use familiar commands instead of the infinitives you see.

Este invierno, (decirles) adiós al frío y a la nieve. (Descubrir) una de las más grandes maravillas (*marvels*) naturales del mundo (*world*). (Ir) al Parque Nacional Iguazú en Argentina y (visitar) las hermosas cascadas. (Explorar) el parque y (mirar) las más de 400 especies de pájaros y animales que viven ahí. (Visitar) este santuario de la naturaleza en los meses de enero a marzo y (disfrutar) de una temperatura promedio de 77° F. Para unas vacaciones de aventura, (hacer) un safari por la selva (*jungle*) o (reservar) una excursión por el río Iguazú. De noche, (dormir) en uno de nuestros exclusivos hoteles en medio de la selva. (Respirar) el aire puro y (probar) la deliciosa comida de la región.

Invierno en Argentina

_____

_____

_____

_____

_____

_____

_____

_____

4 **¿Qué hago?** Clara's brother Manuel is giving her a driving lesson, and Clara has a lot of questions. Write Manuel's answers to her questions in the form of affirmative or negative familiar commands.

> **modelo**
> ¿Tengo que comprar gasolina?
> Sí, compra gasolina./No, no compres gasolina.

1. ¿Puedo hablar por teléfono celular con mis amigos?

_____

2. ¿Puedo manejar en la autopista?

_____

3. ¿Debo estacionar por aquí?

_____

4. ¿Debo sacar mi licencia de conducir?

_____

5. ¿Puedo bajar por esta calle?

_____

6. ¿Tengo que seguir el tráfico?

_____

11.2 Por and para

1 **Para éste o por aquello** Complete the sentences with **por** or **para** as appropriate.

1. Pudieron terminar el trabajo _____ haber empezado (*having begun*) a tiempo.

2. Ese control remoto es _____ prender y apagar el televisor.

3. Elsa vivió en esa ciudad _____ algunos meses hace diez años.

4. Mi mamá compró esta computadora portátil _____ mi papá.

5. Sales _____ Argentina mañana a las ocho y media.

6. Rosaura cambió el estéreo _____ el reproductor de MP3.

7. El señor López necesita el informe _____ el 2 de agosto.

8. Estuve estudiando toda la noche _____ el examen.

9. Los turistas fueron de excursión _____ las montañas.

10. Mis amigos siempre me escriben _____ correo electrónico.

2 **Por muchas razones** Complete the sentences with the expressions in the word bank. Note that you will use two of them twice.

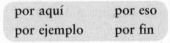

por aquí	por eso
por ejemplo	por fin

1. Ramón y Sara no pudieron ir a la fiesta anoche; _____ no los viste.

2. Buscaron el vestido perfecto por mucho tiempo, y _____ lo encontraron en esa tienda.

3. Creo que va a ser difícil encontrar un teclado y un monitor _____.

4. Pídele ayuda a uno de tus amigos, _____, Miguel, Carlos o Francisco.

5. Miguel y David no saben si podemos pasar _____ en bicicleta.

6. El monitor no está conectado, _____ no funciona.

3 **Por y para** Complete the sentences with **por** or **para**.

1. Fui a comprar frutas _____ (*instead of*) mi madre.

2. Fui a comprar frutas _____ (*to give to*) mi madre.

3. Rita le dio dinero _____ (*in order to buy*) la computadora portátil.

4. Rita le dio dinero _____ (*in exchange for*) la computadora portátil.

5. La familia los llevó _____ (*through*) los Andes.

6. La familia los llevó _____ (*to*) los Andes.

Lección 11 Workbook Activities   **127**

4 **Escribir oraciones** Write sentences in the preterite, using the elements provided and **por** or **para**.

> **modelo**
> (tú) / salir en el auto / ¿? / Córdoba
> *Saliste en el auto para Córdoba.*

1. Ricardo y Emilia / traer un pastel / ¿? / su prima

_____

2. los turistas / llegar a las ruinas / ¿? / barco

_____

3. (yo) / tener un resfriado / ¿? / el frío

_____

4. mis amigas / ganar dinero / ¿? / viajar a Suramérica

_____

5. ustedes / buscar a Teresa / ¿? / toda la playa

_____

6. el avión / salir a las doce / ¿? / Buenos Aires

_____

5 **Para Silvia** Complete the paragraph with **por** and **para**.

Fui a la agencia de viajes porque quería ir (1) _____ Mendoza

(2) _____ visitar a mi novia, Silvia. Entré (3) _____ la

puerta y Marta, la agente de viajes, me dijo: "¡Tengo una oferta excelente (4) _____

ti!". Me explicó que podía viajar en avión (5) _____ Buenos Aires

(6) _____ seiscientos dólares. Podía salir un día de semana,

(7) _____ ejemplo lunes o martes. Me podía quedar en un hotel en Buenos Aires

(8) _____ quince dólares (9) _____ noche. Luego viajaría

(10) _____ tren a Mendoza (11) _____ encontrarme con

Silvia. "Debes comprar el pasaje (12) _____ el fin de mes", me recomendó

Marta. Fue la oferta perfecta (13) _____ mí. Llegué a Mendoza y Silvia fue a la

estación (14) _____ mí. Llevé unas flores (15) _____ ella.

Estuve en Mendoza (16) _____ un mes y (17) _____ fin

Silvia y yo nos comprometimos. Estoy loco (18) _____ ella.

11.3 Reciprocal reflexives

1 **Se conocen** Complete the sentences with the reciprocal reflexives of the verbs in parentheses. Use the present tense.

1. Andrea y Daniel _____ (ver) todos los días.

2. Los amigos _____ (encontrar) en el centro de la ciudad.

3. El padre y la madre de Lisa _____ (querer) mucho.

4. Javier y yo _____ (saludar) por las mañanas.

5. Los compañeros de clase _____ (ayudar) con las tareas.

6. Paula y su mamá _____ (llamar) por teléfono todos los días.

2 **Nos vemos** Complete the sentences with the reciprocal reflexives of the verbs in the word bank.

abrazar	besar	escribir	mirar	saludar
ayudar	encontrar	llamar	querer	ver

1. Cuando los estudiantes llegan a clase, todos _____.

2. Hace seis meses que Ricardo no ve a su padre. Cuando se ven, _____.

3. Los buenos amigos _____ cuando tienen problemas.

4. Es el final de la boda. El novio y la novia _____.

5. Mi novia y yo nos vamos a casar porque _____ mucho.

6. Irene y Vicente _____ muchos mensajes electrónicos cuando no se ven.

7. Hablo todos los días con mi hermana. Nosotras _____ todos los días.

8. Cuando Sandra sale a comer con sus amigas, ellas _____ en el restaurante.

3 **Así fue** Write sentences from the elements provided. Use reciprocal reflexives and the preterite of the verbs.

1. ayer / Felipe y Lola / enviar / mensajes por correo electrónico

_____

2. Raúl y yo / encontrar / en el centro de computación

_____

3. mis abuelos / querer / mucho toda la vida

_____

4. los protagonistas de la película / abrazar y besar / al final

_____

5. esos hermanos / ayudar / a conseguir trabajo

_____

4 **Noticias (News) de Alma** Read the letter from Alma, then complete the sentences about the letter with reciprocal reflexive forms of the correct verbs.

> Querida Claudia:
>
> Conocí a Manolo el mes pasado en Buenos Aires. Desde el día en que lo conocí, lo veo todos los días. Cuando salgo de la universidad me encuentro con él en algún lugar de la ciudad. Nuestro primer beso fue en el parque. Anoche Manolo me dijo que me quiere a mí y yo le dije que lo quiero mucho a él. Siempre nos ayudamos mucho con las tareas de la universidad. Llamo mucho a mi hermana y ella me llama a mí para hablar de nuestras cosas. Mi hermana me entiende muy bien y viceversa.
>
> Hasta luego,
> Alma

1. Manolo y Alma _____ el mes pasado en Buenos Aires.

2. Ellos _____ todos los días desde que se conocieron.

3. Manolo y Alma _____ después de clase en algún lugar de la ciudad.

4. La primera vez que _____, Manolo y Alma estaban en el parque.

5. Anoche Manolo y Alma _____ que se quieren mucho.

6. Manolo y Alma siempre _____ mucho con las tareas de la universidad.

7. Alma y su hermana _____ mucho para hablar de sus cosas.

8. Alma y su hermana _____ muy bien.

5 **Completar** Complete each pair of sentences with the preterite of the verbs in parentheses. Use the reciprocal reflexive verb in only one sentence in each pair.

(conocer)

1. Ricardo y Juan _____ a Cristina el año pasado.

2. Los González _____ en un viaje por Europa.

(saludar)

3. Los chicos _____ cuando llegaron al restaurante.

4. La camarera _____ a los chicos cuando les trajo el menú.

(ayudar)

5. Las enfermeras _____ al paciente a levantarse.

6. Los niños _____ para terminar la tarea más temprano.

(ver)

7. Los mecánicos _____ los coches descompuestos.

8. El profesor y los estudiantes _____ por primera vez en clase.

11.4 Stressed possessive adjectives and pronouns

1 **Esas cosas tuyas** Fill in the blanks with the possessive adjectives as indicated.

1. Ana nos quiere mostrar unas fotos _____ (of hers).

2. A Lorena le encanta la ropa _____ (of ours).

3. Los turistas traen las toallas _____ (of theirs).

4. El mecánico te muestra unos autos _____ (of his).

5. El sitio web _____ (of his) es espectacular.

6. ¿Quieres probar el programa de computación _____ (of ours)?

7. Roberto prefiere usar la computadora _____ (of mine).

8. Ese ratón _____ (of yours, fam.) es el más moderno que existe.

2 **¿De quién es?** Complete the sentences with possessive adjectives.

1. Ésa es mi computadora. Es la computadora _____.

2. Vamos a ver su sitio web. Vamos a ver el sitio web _____.

3. Aquéllos son mis archivos. Son los archivos _____.

4. Quiero usar el programa de él. Quiero usar el programa _____.

5. Buscamos la impresora de nosotros. Buscamos la impresora _____.

6. Ésos son los discos compactos de ella. Son los discos compactos _____.

7. Tienen que arreglar tu teclado. Tienen que arreglar el teclado _____.

8. Voy a usar el teléfono celular de ustedes. Voy a usar el teléfono celular _____.

3 **Los suyos** Answer the questions. Follow the model.

> **modelo**
> ¿Vas a llevar tu cámara de video?
> *Sí, voy a llevar la mía.*

1. ¿Prefieres usar tu cámara digital? _____

2. ¿Quieres usar nuestra conexión inalámbrica? _____

3. ¿Guardaste mis archivos? _____

4. ¿Llenaste el tanque de su carro? _____

5. ¿Manejó Sonia nuestro carro? _____

6. ¿Vas a comprar mi televisor? _____

7. ¿Tomaste los teclados de ellos? _____

8. ¿Tienes un blog de viajes? _____

Lección 11 Workbook Activities

4 **¿De quién son?** Replace the question with one using **de** to clarify the possession. Then answer the question affirmatively, using a possessive pronoun.

> **modelo**
>
> ¿Es suyo el teléfono celular? (de ella)
> ¿Es de ella el teléfono celular? Sí, es suyo.

1. ¿Son suyas las gafas? (de usted)

_____

2. ¿Es suyo el estéreo? (de Joaquín)

_____

3. ¿Es suya la impresora? (de ellos)

_____

4. ¿Son suyos esos reproductores de DVD? (de Susana)

_____

5. ¿Es suyo el coche? (de tu mamá)

_____

6. ¿Son suyas estas cámaras de video? (de ustedes)

_____

Síntesis

Tell the story of a romantic couple you know. Use reciprocal reflexive forms of verbs to tell what happened between them and when. Use stressed possessive adjectives and pronouns as needed to talk about their families and their difficulties. Use familiar commands to give examples of advice you give to each member of the couple on important issues.

_____

_____

_____

_____

_____

_____

_____

_____

_____

_____

_____

_____

panorama

Argentina

1 **Argentina** Fill in the blanks with the correct terms.

1. La ciudad de Buenos Aires se conoce como el _____.

2. Se dice que Argentina es el país más _____ de toda Latinoamérica.

3. Después de 1880, muchos _____ se establecieron en Argentina.

4. Los sonidos y ritmos del tango tienen raíces _____,

   _____ y _____.

5. A los habitantes de Buenos Aires se les llama _____.

6. El nombre de la Avenida 9 de Julio conmemora la _____ de Argentina.

2 **Palabras desordenadas** Unscramble the words about Argentina, using the clues.

1. DMAEZON _____
(una de las ciudades principales argentinas)

2. ESEDREMC _____
(nombre de una cantante argentina)

3. GAIOATNAP _____
(región fría que está en la parte sur (*south*) de Argentina)

4. INTAOLIA _____
(origen de muchos inmigrantes en Argentina)

5. OTÑSOERP _____
(personas de Buenos Aires)

6. TOORVPOAVCI _____
(una característica del baile del tango en un principio)

3 **Datos argentinos** Fill in the blanks with the aspects of Argentina described.

1. saxofonista argentino _____

2. las tres mayores ciudades de Argentina _____

3. países de origen de muchos inmigrantes argentinos _____

4. escritor argentino célebre _____

5. países que comparten las cataratas del Iguazú _____

6. primera dama argentina; nació en 1919 _____

4   **Fotos de Argentina**   Label the photographs from Argentina.

1. _____   2. _____

5   **¿Cierto o falso?**   Indicate whether the statements are **cierto** or **falso**. Correct the false statements.

1. Argentina es el país más grande del mundo.

_____

2. La Avenida 9 de Julio en Buenos Aires es una de las calles más anchas del mundo.

_____

3. Los idiomas que se hablan en Argentina son el español y el inglés.

_____

4. Los inmigrantes que llegaron a Argentina eran principalmente de Europa.

_____

5. El tango es un género musical con raíces indígenas y africanas.

_____

6. Las cataratas del Iguazú están cerca de la confluencia de los ríos Iguazú y Paraná.

_____

6   **Preguntas argentinas**   Answer the questions with complete sentences.

1. ¿Por qué se conoce a Buenos Aires como el "París de Suramérica"?

_____

2. ¿Quién fue la primera dama de Argentina hasta 1952?

_____

3. ¿Qué dejaron las diferentes culturas de los inmigrantes en Argentina?

_____

4. ¿Cómo cambió el baile del tango desde su origen hasta los años 30?

_____

contextos

Lección 12

1 **Los aparatos domésticos** Answer the questions with complete sentences.

> **modelo**
> Julieta quiere comer pan tostado. ¿Qué tiene que usar Julieta?
> Julieta tiene que usar una **tostadora**.

1. La ropa de Joaquín está sucia. ¿Qué necesita Joaquín?

_____

2. Clara lavó la ropa. ¿Qué necesita Clara ahora?

_____

3. Los platos de la cena están sucios. ¿Qué se necesita?

_____

4. Rita quiere hacer hielo (*ice*). ¿Dónde debe poner el agua?

_____

2 **¿En qué habitación?** Label these items as belonging to **la cocina**, **la sala**, or **el dormitorio**.

1. el lavaplatos _____

2. el sillón _____

3. la cama _____

4. el horno _____

5. la almohada _____

6. la cafetera _____

7. la mesita de noche _____

8. la cómoda _____

3 **¿Qué hacían?** Complete the sentences, describing the domestic activity in each drawing. Use the imperfect tense.

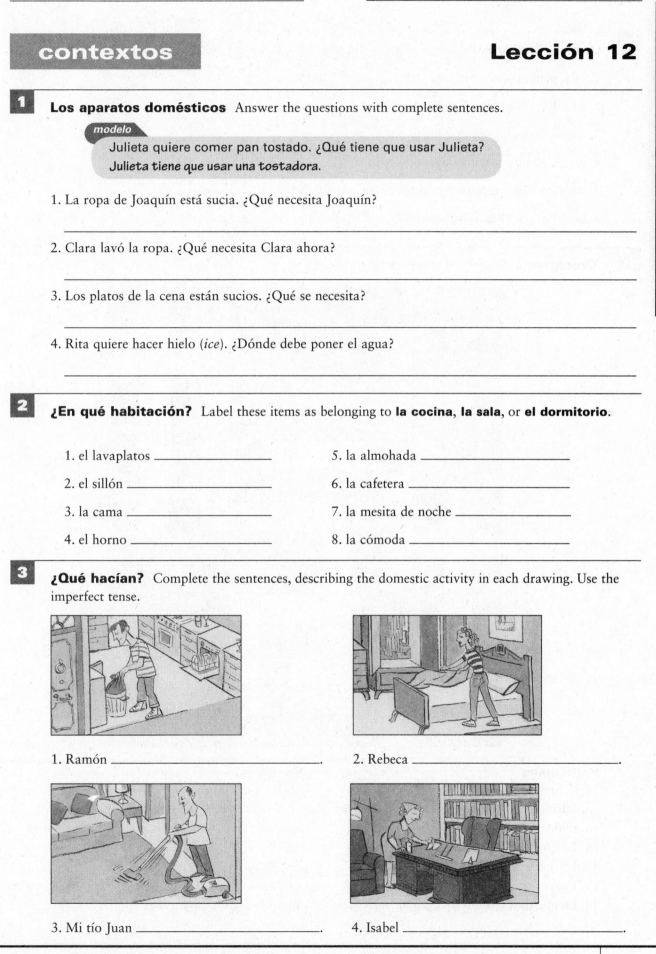

1. Ramón _____.

2. Rebeca _____.

3. Mi tío Juan _____.

4. Isabel _____.

4   **Una es diferente**   Fill in the blank with the word that doesn't belong in each group.

1. sala, plato, copa, vaso, taza _____

2. cuchillo, altillo, plato, copa, tenedor _____

3. cocina, balcón, patio, jardín, garaje _____

4. cartel, estante, pintura, lavadora, cuadro _____

5. dormitorio, sala, comedor, cafetera, oficina _____

6. lavadora, escalera, secadora, lavaplatos, tostadora _____

5   **Crucigrama**   Complete the crossword puzzle.

Horizontales

4. El hombre que vive al lado de tu casa.

5. Julieta habló con Romeo desde su _____.

6. sillón, mesa, cama o silla

8. Lo que prendes cuando necesitas luz.

10. Lo que se usa para tomar vino.

11. Usas estas cosas para tomar agua o soda.

14. Lo que usas cuando hace frío de noche.

Verticales

1. Lo que usas para ir de un piso a otro.

2. Obras (*works*) de Picasso, de Goya, etc.

3. pagar dinero cada mes por vivir en un lugar

7. _____ de microondas

9. Si vas a vivir en otro lugar, vas a _____.

12. Donde se pueden sentar tres o cuatro personas.

13. Lo que usas para tomar el café.

estructura

12.1 Relative pronouns

1 **Relativamente** Complete the sentences with **que**, **quien**, or **quienes**.

1. La persona a _____ debes conocer es Marta.

2. El restaurante _____ más me gusta es Il Forno.

3. Los amigos a _____ fue a visitar son Ana y Antonio.

4. Doña María, _____ me cuidaba cuando yo era niña, vino a verme.

5. El estudiante _____ mejor conozco de la clase es Gustavo.

6. La habitación _____ tiene las paredes azules es la tuya.

7. Los primos con _____ mejor me llevo son Pedro y Natalia.

8. El profesor _____ sabe la respuesta está en la biblioteca ahora.

2 **Conversación telefónica** You're talking on the phone with your mother, who wants to catch up on everything in your life. Answer her questions using the words in parentheses.

> **modelo**
> ¿Qué es lo que tienes en el altillo? (un álbum de fotos)
> *Lo que tengo en el altillo es un álbum de fotos.*

1. ¿Qué es lo que preparas en la cocina? (el almuerzo)

_____

2. ¿Qué es lo que buscas en el estante? (mi libro favorito)

_____

3. ¿Qué es lo que te gusta hacer en verano? (ir al campo)

_____

4. ¿Qué es lo que vas a poner en el balcón? (un sofá)

_____

5. ¿Qué es lo que tienes en el armario? (mucha ropa)

_____

6. ¿Qué es lo que le vas a regalar a tu hermana? (una cafetera)

_____

3 **¿Que o lo que?** Complete the sentences with **que** or **lo que**.

1. El pastel de cumpleaños _____ me trajo mi abuela estuvo delicioso.

2. _____ más les gusta a Pedro y Andrés es jugar al baloncesto.

3. Miguel perdió las llaves, _____ le hizo llegar tarde al dentista.

4. Ricardo y Ester querían los muebles _____ vieron en la tienda.

Lección 12 Workbook Activities   **137**

4 **Pronombres relativos** Complete the sentences with **que**, **quien**, **quienes**, or **lo que**.

1. Los vecinos _____ viven frente a mi casa son muy simpáticos.

2. Rosa y Pepe viajan mucho, _____ los expone a muchas culturas.

3. Las amigas con _____ estudias en la universidad son de varias ciudades.

4. El apartamento _____ Rebeca y Jorge alquilaron está cerca del centro.

5. Adrián y Daniel, _____ estudian física, son expertos en computación.

6. Rubén debe pedirle la aspiradora a Marcos, a _____ le regalaron una.

5 **Mi prima Natalia** Complete the paragraph with **que**, **quien**, **quienes**, or **lo que**.

Natalia, (1) _____ es mi prima, tiene un problema. Natalia es la prima

(2) _____ más quiero de todas las que tengo. (3) _____ le pasa a Natalia es

que siempre está muy ocupada. Su novio, a (4) _____ conoció hace dos años, quiere pasar

más tiempo con ella. La clase (5) _____ más le gusta a Natalia es la clase de francés.

Natalia, (6) _____ ya habla inglés y español, quiere aprender el francés muy bien. Tiene

dos amigos franceses con (7) _____ practica el idioma. Natalia también está en el equipo

de natación, (8) _____ le toma dos horas todas las mañanas. Las otras nadadoras

(9) _____ están en el equipo la necesitan siempre en las prácticas. Además, a Natalia le

gusta visitar a sus padres, a (10) _____ ve casi todos los fines de semana. También ve

con frecuencia a los parientes y amigos (11) _____ viven en su ciudad. ¡Este verano

(12) _____ Natalia necesita son unas vacaciones!

6 **Lo que me parece** Rewrite each sentence using **lo que**.

> **modelo**
> A mí me gusta comer en restaurantes.
> Lo que a mí me gusta es comer en restaurantes.

1. Raúl dijo una mentira.

_____

2. Conseguiste enojar a Victoria.

_____

3. Lilia va a comprar una falda.

_____

4. Ellos preparan una sorpresa.

_____

5. A Teo y a mí nos gusta la nieve.

_____

12.2 Formal (**usted/ustedes**) commands

1 **Háganlo así** Complete the commands, using the verbs in parentheses.

Usted

1. (lavar) _____ la ropa con el nuevo detergente.

2. (salir) _____ de su casa y disfrute del aire libre.

3. (decir) _____ todo lo que piensa hacer hoy.

4. (beber) No _____ demasiado en la fiesta.

5. (venir) _____ preparado para pasarlo bien.

6. (irse) No _____ sin probar la langosta de Maine.

Ustedes

7. (comer) No _____ con la boca abierta.

8. (oír) _____ música clásica en casa.

9. (poner) No _____ los codos (*elbows*) en la mesa.

10. (traer) _____ un regalo a la fiesta de cumpleaños.

11. (ver) _____ programas de televisión educativos.

12. (conducir) _____ con precaución (*caution*) por la ciudad.

2 **Por favor** Give instructions to the person cleaning a house by changing the verb phrases into formal commands.

modelo
sacudir la alfombra
Sacuda la alfombra, por favor.

1. traer la aspiradora

_____

2. arreglar el coche

_____

3. bajar al sótano

_____

4. apagar la cafetera

_____

5. venir a la casa

_____

3 Para emergencias Rewrite this hotel's emergency instructions, replacing each **debe** + (*infinitive*) with formal commands.

Querido huésped:

Debe leer estas instrucciones para casos de emergencia. Si ocurre (*occurs*) una emergencia, debe tocar la puerta antes de abrirla. Si la puerta no está caliente, debe salir de la habitación con cuidado (*carefully*). Al salir, debe doblar a la derecha por el pasillo y debe bajar por la escalera de emergencia. Debe mantener la calma y debe caminar lentamente. No debe usar el ascensor durante una emergencia. Debe dejar su equipaje en la habitación en caso de emergencia. Al llegar a la planta baja, debe salir al patio o a la calle. Luego debe pedir ayuda a un empleado del hotel.

Querido huésped:

_____

_____

_____

_____

_____

_____

_____

_____

_____

4 Lo opuesto Change each command to express the opposite sentiment.

> **modelo**
> Recéteselo a mi hija.
> *No se lo recete a mi hija.*

1. Siéntense en la cama. _____

2. No lo limpie ahora. _____

3. Lávenmelas mañana. _____

4. No nos los sirvan. _____

5. Sacúdalas antes de ponerlas. _____

6. No se las busquen. _____

7. Despiértenlo a las ocho. _____

8. Cámbiesela por otra. _____

9. Pídanselos a Martín. _____

10. No se lo digan hoy. _____

12.3 The present subjunctive

1   **Oraciones** Complete the sentences with the present subjunctive of the verb in parentheses.

1. Es bueno que ustedes _____ (comer) frutas, verduras y yogures.

2. Es importante que Laura y yo _____ (estudiar) para el examen de física.

3. Es urgente que el doctor te _____ (mirar) la rodilla y la pierna.

4. Es malo que los niños no _____ (leer) mucho de pequeños (*when they are little*).

5. Es mejor que (tú) les _____ (escribir) un mensaje antes de llamarlos.

6. Es necesario que (yo) _____ (pasar) por la casa de Mario por la mañana.

2   **El verbo correcto** Complete the sentences with the present subjunctive of the verbs from the word bank.

almorzar	hacer	oír	poner	traducir	venir
conducir	ofrecer	parecer	sacar	traer	ver

1. Es necesario que (yo) _____ a casa temprano para ayudar a mi mamá.

2. Es bueno que (la universidad) _____ muchos cursos por semestre.

3. Es malo que (ellos) _____ justo antes de ir a nadar a la piscina.

4. Es urgente que (Lara) _____ estos documentos legales.

5. Es mejor que (tú) _____ más lento para evitar (*avoid*) accidentes.

6. Es importante que (ella) no _____ la cafetera en la mesa.

7. Es bueno que (tú) _____ las fotos para verlas en la fiesta.

8. Es necesario que (él) _____ la casa antes de comprarla.

9. Es malo que (nosotros) no _____ la basura todas las noches.

10. Es importante que (ustedes) _____ los quehaceres domésticos.

3   **Opiniones** Rewrite these sentences using the present subjunctive of the verbs in parentheses.

1. Mi padre dice que es importante que yo (estar) contenta con mi trabajo.

_____

2. Rosario cree que es bueno que la gente (irse) de vacaciones más a menudo.

_____

3. Creo que es mejor que Elsa (ser) la encargada del proyecto.

_____

4. Es importante que les (dar) las gracias por el favor que te hicieron.

_____

5. Él piensa que es malo que muchos estudiantes no (saber) otras lenguas.

_____

6. El director dice que es necesario que (haber) una reunión de la facultad.

_____

Workbook

4 **Es necesario** Write sentences using the elements provided and the present subjunctive of the verbs.

modelo

malo / Roberto / no poder / irse de vacaciones
Es malo que Roberto no pueda irse de vacaciones.

1. importante / Nora / pensar / las cosas antes de tomar una decisión

_____

2. necesario / (tú) / entender / la situación de esas personas

_____

3. bueno / Clara / sentirse / cómoda en el apartamento nuevo

_____

4. urgente / mi madre / mostrarme / los papeles que llegaron

_____

5. mejor / David / dormir / antes de conducir la motocicleta

_____

6. malo / los niños / pedirles / tantos regalos a sus abuelos

_____

5 **Sí, es bueno** Answer the questions using the words in parentheses and the present subjunctive.

modelo

¿Tiene Álex que terminar ese trabajo hoy? (urgente)
Sí, es urgente que Álex termine ese trabajo hoy.

1. ¿Debemos traer el pasaporte al aeropuerto? (necesario)

_____

2. ¿Tienes que hablar con don Mario? (urgente)

_____

3. ¿Debe David ir a visitar a su abuela todas las semanas? (bueno)

_____

4. ¿Puede Mariana llamar a Isabel para darle las gracias? (importante)

_____

5. ¿Va Andrés a saber lo que le van a preguntar en el examen? (mejor)

_____

12.4 Subjunctive with verbs of will and influence

1 Preferencias Complete the sentences with the present subjunctive of the verbs in parentheses.

1. Rosa quiere que tú _____ (escoger) el sofá para la sala.

2. La mamá de Susana prefiere que ella _____ (estudiar) medicina.

3. Miranda insiste en que Luisa _____ (ser) la candidata a vicepresidenta.

4. Rita y yo deseamos que nuestros padres _____ (viajar) a Panamá.

5. A Eduardo no le importa que nosotros _____ (salir) esta noche.

6. La agente de viajes nos recomienda que _____ (quedarnos) en ese hotel.

2 Compra una casa Read the following suggestions for buying a house. Then write a note to a friend, repeating the advice and using the present subjunctive of the verbs.

Antes de comprar una casa:
- Se aconseja tener un agente inmobiliario (*real estate*).
- Se sugiere buscar una casa en un barrio seguro (*safe*).
- Se insiste en mirar los baños, la cocina y el sótano.
- Se recomienda comparar precios de varias casas antes de decidir.
- Se aconseja hablar con los vecinos del barrio.

Te aconsejo que tengas un agente inmobiliario. _____

_____

_____

_____

_____

_____

3 Instrucciones Write sentences using the elements provided and the present subjunctive. Replace the indirect objects with indirect object pronouns.

modelo
(a ti) / Simón / sugerir / terminar la tarea luego
Simón te sugiere que termines la tarea luego.

1. (a Daniela) / José / rogar / escribir esa carta de recomendación

_____

2. (a ustedes) / (yo) / aconsejar / vivir en las afueras de la ciudad

_____

3. (a ellos) / la directora / prohibir / estacionar frente a la escuela

_____

4. (a mí) / (tú) / sugerir / alquilar un apartamento en el barrio

_____

4 ¿Subjuntivo o infinitivo?

¿Subjuntivo o infinitivo? Write sentences using the elements provided. Use the subjunctive of the verbs when required.

1. Marina / querer / yo / traer / la compra a casa

_____

2. Sonia y yo / preferir / buscar / la información en Internet

_____

3. el profesor / desear / nosotros / usar / el diccionario

_____

4. ustedes / necesitar / escribir / una carta al consulado

_____

5. (yo) / preferir / Manuel / ir / al apartamento por mí

_____

6. Ramón / insistir en / buscar / las alfombras de la casa

_____

Síntesis

Imagine that you are going away for the weekend and you are letting some of your friends stay in your house. Write instructions for your houseguests asking them how to take care of the house. Use formal commands, the phrases **Es bueno**, **Es mejor**, **Es importante**, **Es necesario**, and **Es malo**, with the present subjunctive and the verbs **aconsejar**, **pedir**, **necesitar**, **prohibir**, **recomendar**, **rogar**, and **sugerir** in expressions of will and influence to describe how to make sure that your house is in perfect shape when you get home.

_____

_____

_____

_____

_____

_____

_____

_____

panorama

Panamá

1 **Datos panameños** Complete the sentences with the correct information.

1. _____ es un músico y político célebre de Panamá.

2. Una de las principales fuentes de ingresos de Panamá es _____.

3. Las _____ son una forma de arte textil de la tribu indígena kuna.

4. Algunos diseños de las molas se inspiran en las formas del _____.

2 **Relativamente** Rewrite each pair of sentences as one sentence. Use relative pronouns to combine the sentences.

> **modelo**
> La Ciudad de Panamá es la capital de Panamá. Tiene más de un millón de habitantes.
> *La Ciudad de Panamá, que tiene más de un millón de habitantes, es la capital de Panamá.*

1. La moneda de Panamá es equivalente al dólar estadounidense. Se llama el balboa.

_____

2. El Canal de Panamá se empezó a construir en 1903. Éste une los océanos Atlántico y Pacífico.

_____

3. La tribu indígena de los kuna vive principalmente en las islas San Blas. Ellos hacen molas.

_____

4. Panamá es un sitio excelente para el buceo. Panamá significa "lugar de muchos peces".

_____

3 **Geografía panameña** Fill in the blanks with the correct geographical name.

1. la capital de Panamá _____

2. ciudades principales de Panamá _____

3. países que limitan (*border*) con Panamá _____

4. mar al norte (*north*) de Panamá _____

5. océano al sur (*south*) de Panamá _____

6. por donde pasan más de 14.000 buques por año _____

7. en donde vive la tribu indígena de los kuna _____

8. parque donde se protege la fauna marina _____

Lección 12 Workbook Activities   **145**

4 **Viaje a Panamá** Complete the phrases with the correct information. Then write a paragraph of a tourist brochure about Panama. Use formal commands in the paragraph. The first sentence is done for you.

1. viajar en avión a la _____, capital de Panamá

2. visitar el país centroamericano, donde circulan los billetes de _____

3. conocer a los panameños; la lengua natal del 14% de ellos es _____

4. ir al Canal de Panamá, que une los océanos _____ y _____

5. ver las _____ que hace la tribu indígena kuna y decorar la casa con ellas

6. bucear en las playas de gran valor _____ por la riqueza y diversidad de su vida marina

> Viaje en avión a la Ciudad de Panamá, capital de Panamá. _____
>
> _____
>
> _____
>
> _____
>
> _____
>
> _____
>
> _____
>
> _____
>
> _____

5 **¿Cierto o falso?** Indicate whether the statements are **cierto** or **falso**. Correct the false statements.

1. Panamá tiene aproximadamente el tamaño de California.

_____

2. La moneda panameña, que se llama el balboa, es equivalente al dólar estadounidense.

_____

3. La lengua natal de todos los panameños es el inglés.

_____

4. El Canal de Panamá une los océanos Pacífico y Atlántico.

_____

5. Las molas tradicionales siempre se usaron para decorar las casas.

_____

repaso   ## Lecciones 10–12

---

1 **¿Cuánto tiempo hace?** Complete the answers with **por** or **para**. Then write questions that correspond to the answers.

1. _____

   Hace cuatro años que trabajo _____ mi padre en la tienda.

2. _____

   Pasamos _____ la casa de Javier y Olga hace dos horas.

3. _____

   Hace tres meses que compré una blusa _____ mi hermana.

4. _____

   Hace dos años que Ana estudia italiano _____ Internet.

---

2 **¿Pretérito o imperfecto?** Complete the sentences with the preterite or imperfect of the verbs in parentheses as appropriate.

1. De niña, Lina siempre _____ (usar) la ropa de sus primas.

2. El año pasado, Ricardo _____ (viajar) a Costa Rica durante las Navidades.

3. Cuando Gloria lo _____ (llamar) a su casa, él _____ (dormir) tranquilamente.

4. Mientras los niños _____ (jugar) en el parque, los padres _____ (hablar).

5. Yo _____ (ver) la televisión en casa cuando Carolina _____ (venir) a verme.

6. Mientras Lola _____ (saludar) a sus amigos, Rita _____ (estacionar) el coche.

---

3 **Hágalo ahora** Write sentences using the words provided. Use formal or informal commands and the subjects indicated.

1. (tú) / ayudarlos a traer la compra _____

2. (Uds.) / practicar el francés _____

3. (tú) / buscarme un reproductor de MP3 bueno _____

4. (Ud.) / decirle lo que desea _____

5. (Uds.) / no ser malas personas _____

6. (Ud.) / salir antes de las cinco _____

7. (tú) / comer frutas y verduras _____

8. (Ud.) / parar en la esquina _____

Lecciones 10–12 Workbook Activities

4 **El subjuntivo** Rewrite the sentences using the words in parentheses. Use the subjunctive of the verbs.

> **modelo**
>
> Ellos tienen muchos problemas. (ser malo)
> **Es malo que ellos tengan muchos problemas.**

1. El apartamento tiene dos baños. (Rita / preferir)

_____

2. Las mujeres ven al doctor todos los años. (ser importante)

_____

3. Los pacientes hacen ejercicio. (la enfermera / sugerir)

_____

5 **Los países** Complete the sentences with the verbs in the word bank and the pronoun **se**.

conocer	escuchar	hablar	ofrecer
empezar	establecer	hacer	ver

1. En los parques nacionales costarricenses _____ muchas plantas y animales.

2. El café costarricense _____ a exportar en el siglo XIX.

3. En Costa Rica _____ educación gratuita a todos los ciudadanos.

4. La ciudad de Buenos Aires _____ como el "París de Suramérica".

5. Después del año 1880, una gran cantidad de inmigrantes _____ en Argentina.

6. Hoy día el tango argentino _____ en todo el mundo.

7. En Panamá _____ español, lenguas indígenas e inglés.

8. Las molas panameñas _____ con fragmentos de tela de colores vivos.

6 **La vida de ayer y hoy** Describe what people's lives were like in the early 1800s and what they are like now. Mention the things that people used to do and the things they do now (you may want to use adverbs like **siempre, nunca,** and **a veces**). Then mention the things that people should do to ensure a better quality of life in the future (you may want to use phrases like **es importante que...** and **es necesario que...**).

_____

_____

_____

_____

_____

_____

contextos

1 **La naturaleza** Complete the sentences with the appropriate nature-related words.

1. La luna, las estrellas, el sol y las nubes están en el _____.

2. El _____ es un lugar donde no llueve y hace mucho calor.

3. Una montaña que tiene un cráter es un _____.

4. La región llana (*flat*) que hay entre dos montañas es un _____.

5. La _____ es un bosque tropical, lo que significa que está cerca del ecuador.

6. Para ir a pasear por las montañas, es importante seguir un _____.

2 **Problema y solución** Match each problem with its solution. Then write a sentence with each pair, providing a solution to the problem.

Problemas	Soluciones
1. la deforestación de los bosques	controlar las emisiones de los coches
2. la erosión de las montañas	plantar muchos árboles
3. la falta (*lack*) de recursos naturales	prohibir que se corten (*cut down*) los árboles en algunas regiones
4. la contaminación del aire en las ciudades	reciclar los envases y latas
5. la contaminación nuclear	desarrollar fuentes (*sources*) de energía renovable

modelo

la extinción de plantas y animales / proteger las especies en peligro
*Para resolver el problema de la extinción de plantas y animales,
tenemos que proteger las especies en peligro.*

1. _____

2. _____

3. _____

4. _____

5. _____

3 **Sinónimos y antónimos** Fill in the blanks with the correct verbs from the word bank.

conservar	contaminar	dejar de	mejorar	reducir

1. gastar ≠ _____ 4. continuar ≠ _____

2. hacerse mejor = _____ 5. limpiar ≠ _____

3. usar más ≠ _____

Lección 13 Workbook Activities

4 **Nuestra madre** Fill in the blanks with the correct terms. Then, read the word formed vertically to complete the final sentence.

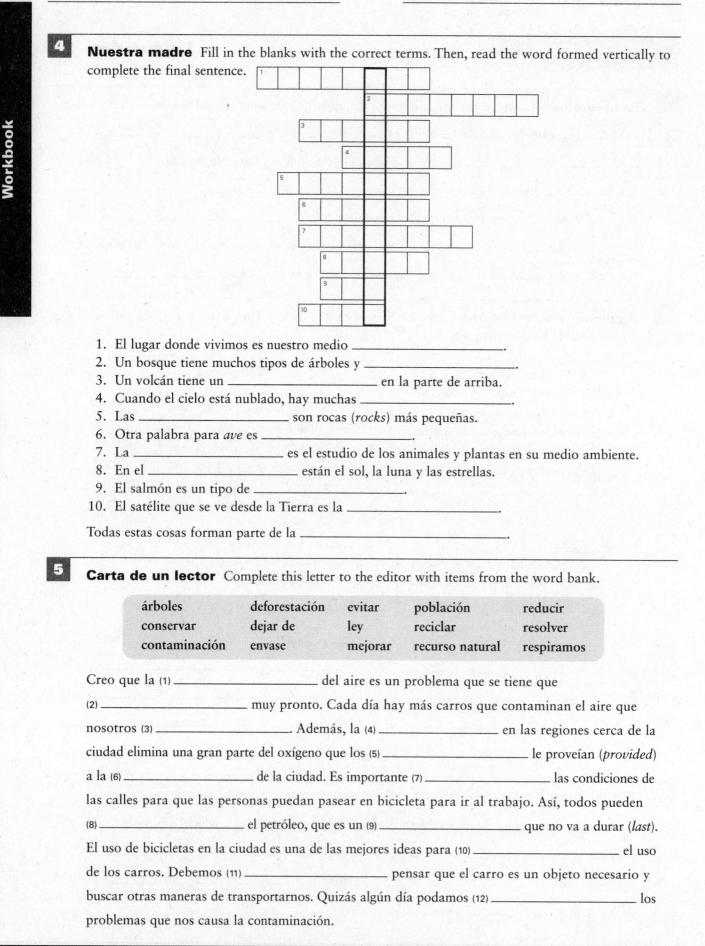

1. El lugar donde vivimos es nuestro medio _____.
2. Un bosque tiene muchos tipos de árboles y _____.
3. Un volcán tiene un _____ en la parte de arriba.
4. Cuando el cielo está nublado, hay muchas _____.
5. Las _____ son rocas (*rocks*) más pequeñas.
6. Otra palabra para *ave* es _____.
7. La _____ es el estudio de los animales y plantas en su medio ambiente.
8. En el _____ están el sol, la luna y las estrellas.
9. El salmón es un tipo de _____.
10. El satélite que se ve desde la Tierra es la _____.

Todas estas cosas forman parte de la _____.

5 **Carta de un lector** Complete this letter to the editor with items from the word bank.

árboles	deforestación	evitar	población	reducir
conservar	dejar de	ley	reciclar	resolver
contaminación	envase	mejorar	recurso natural	respiramos

Creo que la (1) _____ del aire es un problema que se tiene que

(2) _____ muy pronto. Cada día hay más carros que contaminan el aire que

nosotros (3) _____. Además, la (4) _____ en las regiones cerca de la

ciudad elimina una gran parte del oxígeno que los (5) _____ le proveían (*provided*)

a la (6) _____ de la ciudad. Es importante (7) _____ las condiciones de

las calles para que las personas puedan pasear en bicicleta para ir al trabajo. Así, todos pueden

(8) _____ el petróleo, que es un (9) _____ que no va a durar (*last*).

El uso de bicicletas en la ciudad es una de las mejores ideas para (10) _____ el uso

de los carros. Debemos (11) _____ pensar que el carro es un objeto necesario y

buscar otras maneras de transportarnos. Quizás algún día podamos (12) _____ los

problemas que nos causa la contaminación.

estructura

13.1 The subjunctive with verbs of emotion

1 **Emociones** Complete the sentences with the subjunctive of the verbs in parentheses.

1. A mis padres les molesta que los vecinos _____ (quitar) los árboles.

2. Julio se alegra de que _____ (haber) muchos pájaros en el jardín de su casa.

3. Siento que Teresa y Lola _____ (estar) enfermas.

4. Liliana tiene miedo de que sus padres _____ (decidir) mudarse a otra ciudad.

5. A ti te sorprende que la deforestación _____ (ser) un problema tan grande.

6. Rubén espera que el gobierno _____ (mejorar) las leyes que protegen la naturaleza.

2 **Comentarios de Manuel** Your friend Manuel is talking about his opinions on the environment. Combine his statements, using the subjunctive.

> **modelo**
> En algunos países cazan ballenas. Es terrible.
> Es terrible que en algunos países cacen ballenas.

1. Muchos ríos están contaminados. Es triste.

_____

2. Algunas personas evitan reciclar. Es ridículo.

_____

3. Los turistas no recogen la basura. Es una lástima.

_____

4. La gente destruye el medio ambiente. Es extraño.

_____

3 **Ojalá...** Manuel is still hopeful about the environment. Express his opinions using the elements provided. Start the sentences with **Ojalá que**.

1. los países / conservar sus recursos naturales

_____

2. este sendero / llevarnos al cráter del volcán

_____

3. la población / querer cambiar las leyes de deforestación

_____

4. las personas / reducir el uso de los carros en las ciudades

_____

5. todos nosotros / saber resolver el problema del calentamiento global

_____

Lección 13 Workbook Activities

4 **Lo que sea** Change the subject of the second verb in each sentence to the subject in parentheses. Then complete the new sentence with the new subject, using the subjunctive.

> **modelo**
>
> Pablo se alegra de ver a Ricardo. (su madre)
> *Pablo se alegra de que su madre vea a Ricardo.*

1. Me gusta salir los fines de semana. (mi hermana)

   Me gusta que _____.

2. José y tú esperan salir bien en el examen. (yo)

   José y tú esperan que _____.

3. Es ridículo contaminar el mundo en que vivimos. (la gente)

   Es ridículo que _____.

4. Carla y Patricia temen separarse del sendero. (sus amigos)

   Carla y Patricia temen que _____.

5. Te molesta esperar mucho al ir de compras. (tu novio)

   Te molesta que _____.

6. Es terrible usar más agua de la necesaria. (las personas)

   Es terrible que _____.

7. Es triste no saber leer. (Roberto)

   Es triste que _____.

8. Es una lástima encontrar animales abandonados. (los vecinos)

   Es una lástima que _____.

5 **Emociones** Describe the characters' feelings about the environment using the elements provided and the present subjunctive.

1. Miguel / alegrarse / sus amigos / reciclar los periódicos y los envases

   _____

2. a los turistas / sorprender / el país / proteger tanto los parques naturales

   _____

3. Maru / temer / algunas personas / cazar animales en peligro de extinción

   _____

4. don Diego / sentir / las playas de la ciudad / estar contaminadas

   _____

5. Felipe y sus amigos / esperar / el gobierno / desarrollar nuevos sistemas de energía

   _____

6. a Jimena / gustar / mi primo / recoger y cuidar animales abandonados

   _____

13.2 The subjunctive with doubt, disbelief, and denial

1 **No es probable** Complete the sentences with the subjunctive of the verbs in parentheses.

1. No es verdad que Luis _____ (ser) un mal científico.

2. Es probable que Carla y yo _____ (hacer) ecoturismo en el bosque nacional.

3. Lina no está segura de que el guía _____ (saber) dónde estamos.

4. No es seguro que Martín _____ (llegar) antes del viernes.

5. Es posible que Daniel y Nico _____ (venir) a visitarnos hoy.

6. No es probable que la agencia les _____ (pagar) mal a sus empleados.

2 **Es posible que pase** A group of hikers are asking their guide about the environment, but he isn't always sure what to tell them. Answer their questions, using the words in parentheses.

> **modelo**
> ¿Hay mucha contaminación en las ciudades? (probable)
> Es probable que haya mucha contaminación en las ciudades.

1. ¿Hay muchas vacas en los campos de la región? (probable)

_____

2. ¿El agua de esos ríos está contaminada? (posible)

_____

3. ¿Ese sendero nos lleva al lago? (quizás)

_____

4. ¿Protege el gobierno todos los peces del océano? (imposible)

_____

5. ¿La población reduce el uso de envases de plástico? (improbable)

_____

6. ¿El desierto es un lugar mejor para visitar en invierno? (tal vez)

_____

3 **¿Estás seguro?** Complete the sentences with the indicative or subjunctive form of the verbs in parentheses.

1. No dudo que Manuel _____ (ser) la mejor persona para hacer el trabajo.

2. El conductor no niega que _____ (tener) poca experiencia por estas carreteras.

3. Ricardo duda que Mirella _____ (decir) siempre toda la verdad.

4. Sé que es verdad que nosotros _____ (deber) cuidar el medio ambiente.

5. Lina no está segura de que sus amigos _____ (poder) venir a la fiesta.

6. Claudia y Julio niegan que tú _____ (querer) mudarte a otro barrio.

7. No es probable que ella _____ (buscar) un trabajo de secretaria.

Lección 13 Workbook Activities | **153**

4 **¿Es o no es?** Choose the correct phrase in parentheses to rewrite each sentence, based on the verb.

1. (Estoy seguro, No estoy seguro) de que a Mónica le gusten los perros.

_____

2. (Es verdad, No es verdad) que Ramón duerme muchas horas todos los días.

_____

3. Rita y Rosa (niegan, no niegan) que gaste mucho cuando voy de compras.

_____

4. (No cabe duda de, Dudas) que el aire que respiramos está contaminado.

_____

5. (No es cierto, Es obvio) que a Martín y a Viviana les encanta viajar.

_____

6. (Es probable, No hay duda de) que tengamos que reciclar todos los envases.

_____

5 **Desacuerdos** Your roommate often contradicts you. Write your roommate's responses to your statements, using the words in parentheses. Use the indicative or subjunctive form as appropriate.

1. Las matemáticas son muy difíciles. (no es cierto)

_____

2. El problema del cambio climático es bastante complicado. (el presidente no niega)

_____

3. Él va a terminar el trabajo a tiempo. (Ana duda)

_____

4. Esa película es excelente. (mis amigos están seguros de)

_____

5. El español se usa más y más cada día. (no cabe duda de)

_____

6. Lourdes y yo podemos ir a ayudarte esta tarde. (no es seguro)

_____

7. Marcos escribe muy bien en francés. (el maestro no cree)

_____

8. Pedro y Virginia nunca comen carne. (no es verdad)

_____

13.3 The subjunctive with conjunctions

1 **Las conjunciones** Complete the sentences with the subjunctive form of the verbs in parentheses.

1. Lucas debe terminar el trabajo antes de que su jefe (*boss*) _____ (llegar).

2. ¿Qué tenemos que hacer en caso de que _____ (haber) una emergencia?

3. Ellos van a pintar su casa con tal de que (tú) los _____ (ayudar).

4. No puedo ir al museo a menos que Juan _____ (venir) por mí.

5. Alejandro siempre va a casa de Carmen sin que ella lo _____ (invitar).

6. Tu madre te va a prestar dinero para que te _____ (comprar) un coche usado.

7. No quiero que ustedes se vayan sin que tu esposo _____ (ver) mi computadora nueva.

8. Pilar no puede irse de vacaciones a menos que (ellos) le _____ (dar) más días en el trabajo.

9. Andrés va a llegar antes de que Rocío y yo _____ (leer) el correo electrónico.

10. Miguel lo va a hacer con tal de que tú se lo _____ (sugerir).

2 **¿Hasta cuándo?** Your gossipy coworker is always in everyone else's business. Answer his questions in complete sentences, using the words in parentheses.

1. ¿Hasta cuándo vas a ponerte ese abrigo? (hasta que / el jefe / decirme algo)

_____

2. ¿Cuándo va Rubén a buscar a Marta? (tan pronto como / salir de clase)

_____

3. ¿Cuándo se van de viaje Juan y Susana? (en cuanto / tener vacaciones)

_____

4. ¿Cuándo van ellos a invitarnos a su casa? (después de que / nosotros / invitarlos)

_____

5. ¿Hasta cuándo va a trabajar aquí Ramón? (hasta que / su esposa / graduarse)

_____

6. ¿Cuándo puede mi hermana pasar por tu casa? (cuando / querer)

_____

7. ¿Hasta cuándo vas a tomar las pastillas? (hasta que / yo / sentirme mejor)

_____

8. ¿Cuándo va Julia a reciclar estos envases? (tan pronto como / regresar de vacaciones)

_____

3   **Siempre llegas tarde** Complete this conversation, using the subjunctive and the indicative as appropriate.

MARIO   Hola, Lilia. Ven a buscarme en cuanto (yo) (1) _____ (salir) de clase.

LILIA   Voy a buscarte tan pronto como la clase (2) _____ (terminar), pero no

quiero esperar como ayer.

MARIO   Cuando iba a salir, (yo) me (3) _____ (encontrar) con mi profesora de

química, y hablé con ella del examen.

LILIA   No quiero esperarte otra vez hasta que (4) _____ (ser) demasiado tarde

para almorzar.

MARIO   Hoy voy a estar esperándote en cuanto (tú) (5) _____ (llegar) a buscarme.

LILIA   Después de que (yo) te (6) _____ (recoger), podemos ir a comer

a la cafetería.

MARIO   En cuanto (tú) (7) _____ (entrar) en el estacionamiento, me vas a

ver allí, esperándote.

LILIA   No lo voy a creer hasta que (yo) lo (8) _____ (ver).

MARIO   Recuerda que cuando (yo) te (9) _____ (ir) a buscar al laboratorio la

semana pasada, te tuve que esperar media hora.

LILIA   Tienes razón. ¡Pero llega allí tan pronto como (tú) (10) _____ (poder)!

Síntesis

Write an opinion article about oil spills (**los derrames de petróleo**) and their impact on the environment. Use the subjunctive with verbs and expressions of emotion, doubt, disbelief, and denial, and use the indicative with expressions of certainty that you learned in this lesson to describe your own and other people's opinions about the effects of oil spills on the environment.

_____

_____

_____

_____

_____

_____

_____

_____

panorama

Colombia

1 **¿Cierto o falso?** Indicate whether each statement is **cierto** or **falso**. Then correct the false statements.

1. Más de la mitad de la superficie de Colombia está sin poblar.

_____

2. La moneda de Colombia es el dólar estadounidense.

_____

3. El Museo del Oro preserva orfebrería de la época de los españoles.

_____

4. El evento más importante del Carnaval de Barranquilla es la Batalla de Flores.

_____

5. El Castillo de San Felipe de Barajas es la fortaleza más grande de las Américas.

_____

6. Medellín se conoce por el Festival Internacional de Música y el Festival Internacional de Cine.

_____

2 **Consejos** Give advice to a friend who is going to visit Colombia by completing these sentences with the subjunctive of the verb in parentheses and information from **Panorama**.

1. Es importante que _____ (cambiar) los dólares a _____.

2. Ojalá que _____ (conducir) desde _____, la capital, hasta Cartagena.

3. En Cartagena, espero que _____ (nadar) en las playas del mar _____.

4. En Cartagena, también es posible que _____ (ver) edificios antiguos como _____ y _____.

5. Cuando _____ (volver) a Bogotá, vas a ver una parte de la cordillera de _____.

6. Te recomiendo que _____ (visitar) el Museo del Oro en Bogotá para ver las piezas de _____.

7. Me alegro de que _____ (conocer) las esculturas de Fernando _____.

8. Espero que _____ (leer) algún libro de Gabriel _____.

Lección 13 Workbook Activities

3 **Ciudades colombianas** Label each picture.

1. _____

2. _____

3. _____

4. _____

4 **Preguntas sobre Colombia** Answer the questions about Colombia with complete sentences.

1. ¿Cómo se compara el área de Colombia con el área de Montana?

_____

2. ¿Qué país conecta a Colombia con Centroamérica?

_____

3. Menciona a dos artistas colombianos que conozcas.

_____

4. ¿Qué creencia tenían las tribus indígenas sobre el oro?

_____

5. ¿Cuál es el libro más conocido de Gabriel García Márquez?

_____

6. ¿De qué época son las iglesias, monasterios, palacios y mansiones que se conservan en Cartagena?

_____

contextos

1   **El dinero** Complete the sentences with the correct banking-related words.

1. Necesito sacar dinero en efectivo. Voy al _____.

2. Quiero ahorrar para comprar una casa. Pongo el dinero en una _____.

3. Voy a pagar, pero no tengo efectivo ni tarjeta de crédito. Puedo usar un _____.

4. Cuando uso un cheque, el dinero sale de mi _____.

5. Para cobrar un cheque a mi nombre, lo tengo que _____ por detrás.

6. Para ahorrar, pienso _____ $200 en mi cuenta de ahorros todos los meses.

2   **¿Qué clase (kind) de tienda es ésta?** You are running errands, and you can't find the things you're looking for. Fill in the blanks with the names of the places you go.

1. ¿No tienen manzanas? ¿Qué clase de _____ es ésta?

2. ¿No tienen una chuleta de cerdo? ¿Qué clase de _____ es ésta?

3. ¿No tienen detergente? ¿Qué clase de _____ es ésta?

4. ¿No tienen dinero? ¿Qué clase de _____ es éste?

5. ¿No tienen diamantes (diamonds)? ¿Qué clase de _____ es ésta?

6. ¿No tienen estampillas? ¿Qué clase de _____ es éste?

7. ¿No tienen botas? ¿Qué clase de _____ es ésta?

8. ¿No tienen aceite vegetal? ¿Qué clase de _____ es éste?

3   **¿Cómo pagas?** Fill in the blank with the most likely form of payment for each item.

a plazos	con un préstamo
al contado	gratis

1. un refrigerador _____

2. una camisa _____

3. un coche nuevo _____

4. las servilletas en un restaurante _____

5. una computadora _____

6. un vaso de agua _____

7. una hamburguesa _____

8. una cámara digital _____

9. la universidad _____

10. unos sellos _____

4 **Tu empresa** Fill in the blanks with the type of store each slogan would promote.

1. "Compre aquí para toda la semana y ahorre en alimentos para toda la familia." _____

2. "Deliciosos filetes de salmón en oferta especial." _____

3. "Recién (*Just*) salido del horno." _____

4. "Naranjas y manzanas a dos dólares el kilo." _____

5. "Tráiganos su ropa más fina. ¡Va a quedar como nueva!" _____

6. "51 sabrosas variedades para el calor del verano." _____

7. "¡Reserva el pastel de cumpleaños de tu hijo hoy!" _____

8. "Un diamante es para siempre." _____

9. "Salchichas, jamón y chuletas de cerdo." _____

10. "Arréglese las uñas y péinese hoy por un precio económico." _____

5 **¿Cómo llego?** Identify the final destination for each set of directions.

1. De la Plaza Sucre, camine derecho en dirección oeste por la calle Comercio. Doble a la derecha en la calle La Paz hasta la calle Escalona. Doble a la izquierda y al final de la calle va a verlo.

_____

2. Del banco, camine en dirección este por la calle Escalona. Cuando llegue a la calle Sucre, doble a la derecha. Siga por dos cuadras hasta la calle Comercio. Doble a la izquierda. El lugar queda al cruzar la calle Bella Vista.

_____

3. Del estacionamiento de la calle Bella Vista, camine derecho por la calle Sta. Rosalía hasta la calle Bolívar. Cruce la calle Bolívar, y a la derecha en esa cuadra la va a encontrar.

_____

4. De la joyería, camine por la calle Comercio hasta la calle Bolívar. Doble a la derecha y cruce la calle Sta. Rosalía, la calle Escalona y la calle 2 de Mayo. Al norte en esa esquina la va a ver.

_____

El Hatillo

Plaza Bolívar	Farmacia	Joyería
Plaza Sucre	Iglesia	Zapatería
Banco	Terminal	Café Primavera
Casa de la Cultura	Escuela	Estacionamiento

estructura

14.1 The subjunctive in adjective clauses

1 **El futuro de las computadoras** Complete the paragraph with the subjunctive of the verbs in parentheses.

¿Alguna vez ha pensado en una computadora del tamaño de un celular que (1) _____ (tener) una imagen virtual que usted (2) _____ (poder) manipular? En nuestra compañía queremos desarrollar un programa que (3) _____ (mostrar) el contenido de una computadora en forma de holograma 3D sobre cualquier superficie (*surface*). Y que (4) _____ (funcionar) ¡sin necesidad de gafas especiales! Para desarrollar esta tecnología, se necesita una combinación de electrónica, óptica y un programa que (5) _____ (servir) para convertir una imagen de 2D en 3D. Es posible, por ejemplo, que se (6) _____ (usar) estas computadoras de manera cotidiana y que en el futuro (7) _____ (ser) normales los mensajes con las imágenes y la voz de la persona que los grabó, ¡justo como en la *Guerra de las Galaxias* (*Star Wars*)! Probablemente esta tecnología sea tan común que todos (nosotros) la (8) _____ (encontrar) en cualquier lugar de la ciudad.

2 **Completar** Complete the sentences with the indicative or the subjunctive of the verbs in parentheses.

(ser)

1. Inés quiere comprar una falda que _____ larga y elegante.

2. A María le gusta la falda que _____ verde y negra.

(estar)

3. Nunca estuvieron en el hotel que _____ al lado del aeropuerto.

4. No conocemos ningún hotel que _____ cerca de su casa.

(quedar)

5. Hay un banco en el edificio que _____ en la esquina.

6. Deben poner un banco en un edificio que _____ más cerca.

(tener)

7. Silvia quiere un apartamento que _____ balcón y piscina.

8. Ayer ellos vieron un apartamento que _____ tres baños.

(ir)

9. Hay muchas personas que _____ a Venezuela de vacaciones.

10. Raúl no conoce a nadie que _____ a Venezuela este verano.

Lección 14 Workbook Activities

3 **Fotonovela** Rewrite the sentences to make them negative, using the subjunctive where appropriate.

1. Maru conoce a un chico que estudia medicina.

_____

2. Los padres de Miguel cuidan a un perro que protege su casa.

_____

3. Juan Carlos tiene un pariente que escribe poemas.

_____

4. Los Díaz usan coches que son baratos.

_____

5. Don Diego trabaja con unas personas que conocen a su padre.

_____

6. Jimena hace un plato mexicano que es delicioso.

_____

4 **Paseando en Caracas** Answer these questions affirmatively or negatively, as indicated. Use the subjunctive where appropriate.

1. ¿Hay algún buzón que esté en la Plaza Bolívar?

Sí, _____.

2. ¿Conoces a alguien que sea abogado de inmigración?

No, _____.

3. ¿Ves a alguien aquí que estudie contigo en la universidad?

Sí, _____.

4. ¿Hay alguna panadería que venda pan caliente (*hot*) cerca de aquí?

No, _____.

5. ¿Tienes alguna compañera que vaya a ese gimnasio?

Sí, _____.

6. ¿Conoces a alguien en la oficina que haga envíos a otros países?

No, _____.

5 **Une las frases** Complete the sentences with the most logical endings from the word bank. Use the indicative or subjunctive forms of the verbs as appropriate.

abrir hasta las doce de la noche	gustarle mucho	siempre decirnos la verdad
no manejar en carretera	ser cómoda y barata	tener muchos museos

1. Rolando tiene un auto que _____.

2. Todos buscamos amigos que _____.

3. Irene y José viven en una ciudad que _____.

4. ¿Hay una farmacia que _____?

14.2 Nosotros/as commands

1

Hagamos eso Rewrite these sentences, using the **nosotros/as** command forms of the verbs in italics.

> **modelo**
>
> Tenemos que *terminar* el trabajo antes de las cinco.
> **Terminemos el trabajo antes de las cinco.**

1. Hay que *limpiar* la casa hoy.

   _____

2. Tenemos que *ir* al dentista esta semana.

   _____

3. Debemos *depositar* el dinero en el banco.

   _____

4. Podemos *viajar* a Venezuela este invierno.

   _____

5. Queremos *salir* a bailar este sábado.

   _____

6. Deseamos *invitar* a los amigos de Ana.

   _____

2

¡Sí! ¡No! You and your roommate disagree about everything. Write affirmative and negative **nosotros/as** commands for these actions.

> **modelo**
>
> abrir las ventanas
> tú: **Abramos las ventanas.**
> tu compañero/a: **No abramos las ventanas.**

1. pasar la aspiradora hoy

   tú: _____

   tu compañero/a: _____

2. poner la televisión

   tú: _____

   tu compañero/a: _____

3. compartir la comida

   tú: _____

   tu compañero/a: _____

4. hacer las camas todos los días

   tú: _____

   tu compañero/a: _____

Workbook

3 **Como Lina** Everyone likes Lina and wants to be like her. Using **nosotros/as** commands, write sentences telling your friends what you all should do to follow her lead.

1. Lina compra zapatos italianos en el centro.

_____

2. Lina conoce la historia del jazz.

_____

3. Lina se va de vacaciones a las montañas.

_____

4. Lina se relaja en casa por las tardes.

_____

5. Lina hace pasteles para los cumpleaños de sus amigas.

_____

6. Lina no sale de fiesta todas las noches.

_____

7. Lina corre al lado del río todas las mañanas.

_____

8. Lina no gasta demasiado dinero en la ropa.

_____

4 **El préstamo** Claudia is thinking of everything that she and her fiancé, Ramón, should do to buy an apartment. Write what she will tell Ramón, using **nosotros/as** commands for verbs in the infinitive. The first sentence has been done for you.

Podemos pedir un préstamo para comprar un apartamento. Debemos llenar este formulario cuando solicitemos el préstamo. Tenemos que ahorrar dinero todos los meses hasta que paguemos el préstamo. No debemos cobrar los cheques que nos lleguen; debemos depositarlos en la cuenta corriente. Podemos depositar el dinero que nos regalen cuando nos casemos. Le debemos pedir prestado a mi padre un libro sobre cómo comprar una vivienda. Queremos buscar un apartamento que esté cerca de nuestros trabajos. No debemos ir al trabajo mañana por la mañana; debemos ir al banco a hablar con un empleado.

Pidamos un préstamo para comprar un apartamento. _____

_____

_____

_____

_____

_____

_____

14.3 Past participles used as adjectives

1 **Completar** Complete the sentences with the correct past participle forms of these verbs.

1. Me voy de paseo junto al río en una bicicleta _____ (prestar).

2. Julián y yo tenemos las maletas _____ (abrir) por toda la sala.

3. Tu sobrino te regaló un barco _____ (hacer) de papel de periódico.

4. A la abuela de Gabriela le gusta recibir cartas _____ (escribir) a mano.

5. Para protegerse del sol, Rosa tiene un sombrero _____ (poner).

6. Lisa y David tienen bastante dinero _____ (ahorrar) en el banco.

7. Hay varios abrigos de invierno _____ (guardar) en el armario.

8. En Perú se descubrieron varias ciudades _____ (perder) cerca de Cuzco.

9. Natalia, José y Francisco son mis amigos _____ (preferir).

10. Miguel no puede caminar porque tiene el tobillo _____ (torcer).

2 **Las consecuencias** Complete the sentences with **estar** and the correct past participle.

> **modelo**
> La señora Gómez cerró la farmacia.
> La farmacia *está cerrada*.

1. Rafael resolvió los problemas. Los problemas _____.

2. Julia se preparó para el examen. Julia _____.

3. Le vendimos esa aspiradora a un cliente. Esa aspiradora _____.

4. Se prohíbe nadar en ese río. Nadar en ese río _____.

5. La agente de viajes confirmó la reservación. La reservación _____.

6. Carlos y Luis se aburrieron durante la película. Carlos y Luis _____.

3 **¿Cómo están?** Label each drawing with a complete sentence, using the nouns provided with **estar** and the past participle of the verbs.

1. pavo / servir _____

2. dormitorio / desordenar _____

_____

3. cama / hacer _____   4. niñas / dormir _____

_____ _____

4 **El misterio** Complete this paragraph with the correct past participle forms of the verbs in the word bank. Use each verb only once.

abrir	desordenar	hacer	poner	romper	ver
cubrir	escribir	morir	resolver	sorprender	volver

El detective llegó al hotel con el número de la habitación (1) _____ en un papel.

Entró en la habitación. La cama estaba (2) _____ y la puerta del baño estaba

(3) _____. Vio a un hombre que parecía estar (4) _____

porque no movía ni un dedo. El hombre tenía la cara (5) _____ con un periódico

y no tenía zapatos (6) _____. El espejo estaba (7) _____ y

el baño estaba (8) _____. De repente, el hombre se levantó y salió corriendo sin

sus zapatos. El detective se quedó muy (9) _____ y el misterio nunca fue

(10) _____.

Síntesis

Imagine you have a friend who lives in an exciting place you have never visited: New York City, Mexico, etc. You are about to visit your friend for the first time; you are very excited and have many things you want to do, but you also have a lot of questions. On a separate sheet of paper, write an e-mail to your friend to prepare for your trip. Your message should include the following:

• Statements about the preparations you have made for your trip, using past participles as adjectives.

• **Nosotros/as** commands that describe the preparations you need to complete in order to do certain activities.

• Questions about the logistics of banking, communications, shopping, etc. in the city or country, using the subjunctive in adjective clauses.

modelo

> Hola, Maribel. Estoy muy emocionada porque acabo de comprar el pasaje para visitarte en Madrid. ¡Las maletas ya están hechas! Intentemos planearlo todo esta semana: consigamos la reservación para la cena de Nochevieja (*New Year's Eve*), llamemos a tus amigos para quedar con (*meet up with*) ellos y compremos ropa nueva para ir a la disco. A propósito, ¿hay muchas tiendas que acepten tarjeta de crédito? ¿Y hay restaurantes que sirvan comida vegetariana? ¿Tienes algún amigo guapo que no tenga novia? ¡Hasta pronto!
> Sarah

panorama

Venezuela

1 **En Venezuela** Complete the sentences with information from **Panorama**.

1. Los _____ viven en comunidades de hasta 400 miembros.

2. El inmunólogo venezolano que ganó el Premio Nobel es _____.

3. La mayor concentración del petróleo en Venezuela se encuentra debajo del _____.

4. El principal país comprador del petróleo venezolano es _____.

5. El *boom* petrolero convirtió a Caracas en una ciudad _____.

6. El corazón de Caracas es la zona del _____.

7. A principios del siglo XIX, la actual Venezuela todavía estaba bajo el dominio de _____.

8. Simón Bolívar fue el líder del movimiento _____ suramericano.

2 **Datos venezolanos** Complete the chart with the indicated information.

Venezolanos famosos	Principales ciudades venezolanas	Idiomas que se hablan en Venezuela	Países del área liberada por Simón Bolívar

3 **¿Quién soy?** Identify the person or type of person who could make each statement.

1. "Soy parte de una tribu que vive en el sur de Venezuela."

_____

2. "Compuse música y toqué (*played*) el piano durante parte de los siglos XIX y XX."

_____

3. "Fui un general que contribuyó a formar el destino de América."

_____

4. "Di a conocer el Salto Ángel en 1935."

_____

4   **Lo que aprendiste** Write a complete definition of each item, based on what you have learned.

1. bolívar _____

_____

2. tribu yanomami _____

_____

3. Baruj Benacerraf _____

_____

4. lago de Maracaibo _____

_____

5. Petróleos de Venezuela _____

_____

6. Caracas _____

_____

7. Parque Central _____

_____

8. Simón Bolívar _____

_____

5   **El mapa de Venezuela** Label the map of Venezuela with the correct geographical names.

1. _____

2. _____

3. _____

4. _____

5. _____

6. _____

contextos

1 **Lo opuesto** Fill in the blanks with the terms that mean the opposite of the descriptions.

1. sedentario _____
2. con cafeína _____
3. fuerte _____
4. adelgazar _____

5. comer en exceso _____
6. con estrés _____
7. sufrir muchas presiones _____
8. fuera (*out*) de forma _____

2 **Vida sana** Complete the sentences with the correct terms.

1. Antes de correr, es importante hacer ejercicios de _____ para calentarse.

2. Para dormir bien por las noches, es importante tomar bebidas _____.

3. Para desarrollar músculos fuertes, es necesario _____.

4. Una persona que es muy sedentaria y ve mucha televisión es un _____.

5. _____ es bueno porque reduce la temperatura del cuerpo.

6. Para aliviar el estrés, es bueno hacer las cosas tranquilamente y sin _____.

7. Cuando tienes los músculos tensos, lo mejor es que te den un _____.

8. Las personas que dependen de las drogas son _____.

3 **Completar** Look at the drawings. Complete the sentences with the correct forms of the verbs from the word bank.

(no) apurarse
(no) consumir bebidas alcohólicas
(no) hacer ejercicios de estiramiento
(no) llevar una vida sana

1. Isabel debió _____.

2. Mi prima prefiere _____.

3. A Roberto no le gusta _____.

4. Adriana va a llegar tarde y tiene que _____.

4 **¿Negativo o positivo?** Categorize the terms in the word bank according to whether they are good or bad for one's health.

> buena nutrición
> colesterol alto
> comer comida
>   sin grasa
> comer en exceso
>
> consumir mucho
>   alcohol
> dieta equilibrada
> entrenarse
> exceso de cafeína
> fumar
>
> hacer ejercicios
>   de estiramiento
> hacer gimnasia
> levantar pesas
> llevar una
>   vida sana
>
> llevar una
>   vida sedentaria
> ser un drogadicto
> ser un teleadicto
> sufrir muchas
>   presiones
> tomar vitaminas

Bueno para la salud	Malo para la salud
_____	_____
_____	_____
_____	_____
_____	_____
_____	_____
_____	_____
_____	_____

5 **El/La entrenador(a)** You are a personal trainer, and your clients' goals are listed below. Give each one a different piece of advice, using familiar commands and expressions from **Contextos**.

1. "Quiero adelgazar." _____

2. "Quiero tener músculos bien definidos." _____

3. "Quiero quemar grasa." _____

4. "Quiero respirar sin problemas." _____

5. "Quiero correr un maratón." _____

6. "Quiero aumentar un poco de peso." _____

6 **Los alimentos** Write whether these food categories are rich in **vitaminas**, **minerales**, **proteínas**, or **grasas**.

1. carnes _____

2. agua mineral _____

3. mantequilla _____

4. frutas _____

5. huevos _____

6. aceite _____

7. verduras _____

8. cereales enriquecidos (*fortified*) _____

estructura

15.1 The present perfect

1 **¿Qué han hecho?** Complete each sentence with the present perfect of the verb in parentheses.

> **modelo**
>
> Marcos y Felipe _____ (hacer) sus tareas de economía.
> Marcos y Felipe **han hecho** sus tareas de economía.

1. Gloria y Samuel _____ (comer) comida francesa.

2. (yo) _____ (ver) la última película de ese director.

3. Pablo y tú _____ (leer) novelas de García Márquez.

4. Liliana _____ (tomar) la clase de economía.

5. (nosotros) _____ (ir) a esa heladería antes.

6. Tú le _____ (escribir) un mensaje eléctronico al profesor.

2 **¿Qué han hecho esta tarde?** Write sentences that say what these people have done this afternoon. Use the present perfect.

1. Luis y Marta

_____

2. Víctor

_____

3. (tú)

_____

4. Ricardo

_____

5. (yo)

_____

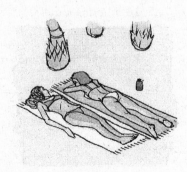

6. Claudia y yo

_____

Lección 15 Workbook Activities   **171**

Workbook

3 **Ha sido así** Rewrite the sentences, replacing the subject with the one in parentheses.

1. Hemos conocido a varios bolivianos este año. (tú)

_____

2. Gilberto ha viajado por todos los Estados Unidos. (yo)

_____

3. ¿Has ido al museo de arte de Boston? (ustedes)

_____

4. Paula y Sonia han hecho trabajos muy buenos. (Virginia)

_____

5. He asistido a tres conferencias de ese escritor. (los estudiantes)

_____

6. Mi hermano ha puesto la mesa todos los días. (mi madre y yo)

_____

4 **Todavía no** Rewrite the sentences to say that these things have not yet been done. Use the present perfect.

> **modelo**
>
> Su prima no va al gimnasio.
> Su prima todavía no ha ido al gimnasio.

1. Pedro y Natalia no nos dan las gracias.

_____

2. Los estudiantes no contestan la pregunta.

_____

3. Mi amigo Pablo no hace ejercicio.

_____

4. Esas chicas no levantan pesas.

_____

5. Tú no estás a dieta.

_____

6. Rosa y yo no sufrimos muchas presiones.

_____

15.2 The past perfect

1 Vida nueva Complete this paragraph with the past perfect forms of the verbs in parentheses.

Antes del accidente, mi vida (1) _____ (ser) tranquila y sedentaria. Hasta ese momento, (yo) siempre (2) _____ (mirar) mucho la televisión y (3) _____ (comer) en exceso. Nada malo me (4) _____ (pasar) nunca. El día en que pasó el accidente, mis amigos y yo nos (5) _____ (encontrar) para ir a nadar en un río. Nunca antes (6) _____ (ir) a ese río. Cuando llegamos, entré de cabeza al río. (Yo) No (7) _____ (ver) las rocas (*rocks*) que había debajo del agua. Me di con (*I hit*) las rocas en la cabeza. Mi hermana, que (8) _____ (ir) con nosotros al río, me sacó del agua. Todos mis amigos se (9) _____ (quedar) fuera del agua cuando vieron lo que me pasó. Me llevaron al hospital. En el hospital, los médicos me dijeron que yo (10) _____ (tener) mucha suerte. (Yo) No me (11) _____ (lastimar) demasiado la espalda, pero tuve que hacer terapia (*therapy*) física por muchos meses. (Yo) Nunca antes (12) _____ (preocuparse) por estar en buena forma, ni (13) _____ (querer) ir al gimnasio. Ahora hago gimnasia y soy una persona activa, flexible y fuerte.

2 Nunca antes Rewrite the sentences to say that these people had never done these things before.

modelo
Julián se compró un coche nuevo.
Julián nunca antes se había comprado un coche nuevo.

1. Tu novia fue al gimnasio por la mañana.

_____

2. Carmen corrió en el maratón de la ciudad.

_____

3. Visité los países de Suramérica.

_____

4. Los estudiantes escribieron trabajos de veinte páginas.

_____

5. Armando y Cecilia esquiaron en los Andes.

_____

6. Luis y yo tenemos un perro en casa.

_____

7. Condujiste el coche de tu papá.

_____

8. Ramón y tú nos prepararon la cena.

_____

3 **Ya había pasado** Combine the sentences, using the preterite and the past perfect tenses.

> **modelo**
>
> Elisa pone la televisión. Jorge ya se ha despertado.
> *Cuando Elisa puso la televisión, Jorge ya se había despertado.*

1. Lourdes llama a Carla. Carla ya ha salido.

_____

2. Tu hermano vuelve a casa. Ya has terminado de cenar.

_____

3. Llego a la escuela. La clase ya ha empezado.

_____

4. Ustedes nos buscan en casa. Ya hemos salido.

_____

5. Salimos a la calle. Ya ha empezado a nevar.

_____

6. Ellos van al centro comercial. Las tiendas ya han cerrado.

_____

7. Lilia y Juan encuentran las llaves. Raúl ya se ha ido.

_____

8. Preparas el almuerzo. Yo ya he comido.

_____

4 **Rafael Nadal** Write a paragraph about the things that Rafael Nadal had achieved by age 18. Use the phrases from the word bank with the past perfect. Start each sentence with **Ya**. The first one has been done for you.

empezar a jugar al tenis profesionalmente	jugar en torneos del Grand Slam
ganar un torneo Masters Series	recibir miles de dólares
ingresar a la lista de los 100 mejores jugadores de la ATP	ser el campeón (*champion*) de la Copa Davis

Cuando tenía 18 años, Rafael Nadal ya había empezado a jugar al tenis profesionalmente.

_____

_____

_____

_____

_____

_____

15.3 The present perfect subjunctive

1 **¡No estoy de acuerdo!** Your friend Lisa is contradicting everything you say. Using the present perfect subjunctive, complete her statements.

> **modelo**
>
> —He perdido las llaves muchas veces.
> —No es verdad *que hayas perdido las llaves muchas veces.*

1. —Éste ha sido tu mejor año. —No estoy segura _____.

2. —El ejercicio le ha aliviado el estrés. —Dudo _____.

3. —Rafael y tú han sufrido muchas presiones. —Niego _____.

4. —El gobierno ha estudiado el problema. —Es improbable _____.

5. —Ustedes han sido muy buenos amigos siempre. —No es cierto _____.

6. —Has hecho todo lo que pudiste. —No es seguro _____.

2 **De acuerdo** Lisa is in a better mood today and says everything you are thinking. Write her thoughts on these topics, using the expressions provided and the present perfect subjunctive.

> **modelo**
>
> Marina ha disfrutado de su dieta / improbable
> *Es improbable que Marina haya disfrutado de su dieta.*

1. Muchas niñas jóvenes han estado a dieta / terrible

_____

2. Ustedes no han llevado una vida sana hasta ahora / triste

_____

3. Los jugadores no han hecho ejercicios de estiramiento / una lástima

_____

4. Nosotros hemos aumentado de peso este verano / probable

_____

5. Algunos doctores del hospital han fumado en público / ridículo

_____

6. Mi esposo no ha engordado más / me alegro de

_____

7. Nunca he aliviado el estrés en mi trabajo / siento

_____

8. Tú y tu amiga se han mantenido en forma / qué bueno

_____

Lección 15 Workbook Activities   **175**

3 **La telenovela** Write a paragraph telling your best friend how glad you are that these things happened on the soap opera you both watch. Start each sentence with **Me alegro**. The first one has been done for you.

la vecina / poner la televisión	Alejandro y Leticia / ganar la lotería
Ligia Elena / separarse de Luis Javier	los padres de Juliana / encontrar la carta
la boda de Gema y Fernando / ser tan	de amor
elegante	(tú) / contarme lo que pasó ayer
Ricardo / conocer a Diana Carolina	(nosotros) / poder ver esta telenovela

Me alegro de que la vecina haya puesto la televisión. _____

_____

_____

_____

_____

_____

_____

_____

_____

_____

_____

Síntesis

On another sheet of paper, write an autobiographical essay about your time in school. Address:
- things that you have done that you are proud of and things you are embarrassed about. Use the present perfect.
- things that you had done by age eight and by age sixteen. Use the past perfect.

Use expressions such as **me alegro, me sorprende, siento, es una lástima, es triste, es extraño,** and **es ridículo** and the present perfect subjunctive. Cover such topics as academic and extracurricular achievements and failures, as well as achievements and failures in your social life.

panorama

Bolivia

1 **Información de Bolivia** Complete these sentences with information about Bolivia.

1. El área de Bolivia es igual al área total de _____.

2. Las personas de ascendencia indígena y europea representan _____.

3. Un 70% de la población boliviana vive en el _____.

4. La moneda de bolivia es el _____.

5. Los tres idiomas que se hablan en Bolivia son _____.

6. El lago navegable más alto del mundo es el _____.

7. El aeropuerto de La Paz se encuentra a _____ metros de altura.

8. Tiahuanaco es el nombre de unas ruinas y significa _____.

9. Se cree que Tiahuanaco fue fundado por los antepasados de _____.

10. _____ es un impresionante monumento que pesa unas 10 toneladas.

2 **¿Cierto o falso?** Indicate whether these statements are **cierto** or **falso**. Correct the false statements.

1. Bolivia tiene dos ciudades capitales diferentes.

_____

2. Jesús Lara fue un pintor y político boliviano.

_____

3. Bolivia tiene una costa en el océano Pacífico.

_____

4. El lago Titicaca es el lago más grande de Suramérica.

_____

5. Según la mitología aimará, los hijos del dios Sol fundaron su imperio.

_____

6. La música andina es el aspecto más conocido del folclore boliviano.

_____

7. Bolivia limita (*borders*) con Colombia, Perú y Brasil.

_____

8. Se piensa que los antepasados de los indígenas aimará fundaron Tiahuanaco hace 15.000 años.

_____

Workbook

3   **Términos bolivianos**   Fill in the blanks with the terms described.

1. _____ Son grupos indígenas que constituyen más de la mitad de la población de Bolivia.

2. _____ Es la sede del gobierno de Bolivia.

3. _____ Es la primera ciudad de Bolivia en número de habitantes.

4. _____ Fue político y presidente boliviano.

5. _____ Tipo de música compartida por Bolivia, Perú, Ecuador, Chile y Argentina. Es música popular de origen indígena.

6. _____ Es un grupo boliviano de música andina que lleva más de treinta años actuando en los escenarios internacionales.

4   **Letras desordenadas**   Unscramble the words according to the clues.

1. IICTATCA _____
(el segundo lago más grande de Suramérica)

2. BHABCMOCAA _____
(ciudad boliviana)

3. AUQHCUE _____
(uno de los idiomas oficiales de Bolivia)

4. OLAZCSAA _____
(apellido de una poeta boliviana)

5. SOL HSSCKIA _____
(grupo argentino de música andina)

6. URECS _____
(ciudad sede del Tribunal Supremo)

7. AEOMNLERCI _____
(tipo de centro que fue Tiahuanaco)

8. AALSKAASAY _____
(templo de las ruinas de Tiahuanaco)

repaso   **Lecciones 13–15**

1 **¿Subjuntivo o indicativo?** Write sentences, using the elements provided and either the subjunctive or the indicative, depending on the cues and context.

1. Jorge / esperar / su madre / conseguir un trabajo pronto

_____

2. (nosotros) / no negar / la clase de matemáticas / ser difícil

_____

3. ser imposible / una casa nueva / costar tanto dinero

_____

4. ustedes / alegrarse / la fiesta / celebrarse cerca de su casa

_____

5. ser una / lástima / Laura / no poder venir con nosotros

_____

_____

2 **En la oficina** Your boss is giving you and your co-workers some rules to follow in the office. Use affirmative or negative **nosotros** commands to write logical sentences.

1. poner todos los documentos en el archivo

_____

2. tomar dos horas para almorzar

_____

3. trabajar horas extra si es necesario

_____

4. llegar a tiempo por las mañanas

_____

5. ser amables con los clientes

_____

3 **Las conjunciones** Use the subjunctive or the indicative of the verbs in parentheses.

1. No quiero llegar a la fiesta después de que Marcelo _____ (irse).

2. Alicia siempre se levanta en cuanto _____ (sonar) el despertador.

3. No bebas ese vino a menos que _____ (ser) una ocasión especial.

4. Olga y Lisa tocan a la puerta hasta que su madre las _____ (oír).

5. Cuando (tú) _____ (llamar) a la oficina, pregunta por Gustavo.

6. Lilia llega a los lugares sin que nadie le _____ (decir) cómo llegar.

4 **Hemos dicho** Complete the sentences with the present perfect indicative, past perfect indicative, or present perfect subjunctive of the verbs in parentheses. Use the English cues to decide on the tense.

1. El entrenador (*has given*) _____ (dar) muchas clases de ejercicios aeróbicos antes.

2. Nosotros nunca antes (*had passed*) _____ (pasar) por esta parte de la ciudad.

3. Quiero conocer a alguien que (*has studied*) _____ (estudiar) psicología.

4. En la clase de literatura, ustedes (*have read*) _____ (leer) varias novelas interesantes.

5. Mi madre nos (*had heard*) _____ (oír) decir antes que queríamos una motocicleta.

6. Necesitas hablar con personas que (*have been*) _____ (estar) en Cuba.

5 **Los países** Use the past participles of the verbs from the word bank to complete the sentences about the countries in **Panorama**. Use each verb only once.

compartir	convertir	fundar	llamar	nacer
conectar	escribir	hacer	mantener	reflejar

1. En Colombia, los objetos de oro precolombino estaban _____ con un gran cuidado.

2. Las creencias (*beliefs*) de los indígenas colombianos sobre el oro están _____ en sus objetos.

3. *Cien años de soledad* está _____ en el estilo literario del "realismo mágico".

4. _____ en Caracas, el científico Baruj Benacerraf ganó el Premio Nobel en 1980.

5. Desde los años cincuenta, Caracas se ha _____ en una ciudad cosmopolita.

6. El interior de Venezuela está _____ con Caracas por carreteras y autopistas.

7. Simón Bolívar, _____ "El Libertador", fue el líder de la independencia suramericana.

8. Los grupos quechua y aimará de Bolivia han _____ sus culturas y lenguas.

9. La música andina es _____ por Bolivia, Perú, Ecuador, Chile y Argentina.

10. Se piensa que el centro ceremonial de Tiahuanaco, en Bolivia, fue _____ hace 15.000 años.

6 **Los derechos civiles** On another sheet of paper, write a brief paragraph in Spanish about a minority group in the U.S., using these questions as a guide:

- What injustices or unfair conditions has this group suffered in the past?
- What were the lives of the members of this group like in the past?
- What are your opinions about the injustices that occurred?
- What are some advances that this group has made? Under what conditions do the members of this group live today?
- What do you hope for the future of this group?
- What should we as a society do about the disadvantaged status of many minority groups?

contextos

Lección 16

1 **El anuncio** Answer the questions about this help-wanted ad, using complete sentences.

> **EMPRESA MULTINACIONAL BUSCA:**
> • Contador   • Gerente   • Secretario
> Salarios varían según la experiencia. Seguro[1] de salud, plan de jubilación (401k), dos semanas de vacaciones.
> Enviar currículum y carta de presentación por fax o por correo para concertar[2] una entrevista con el Sr. Martínez.
>
> [1]insurance   [2]schedule

1. ¿Cuántos puestos hay?

   _____

2. ¿Cuáles son los sueldos?

   _____

3. ¿Qué beneficios ofrece la empresa?

   _____

4. ¿Qué deben enviar los aspirantes?

   _____

5. ¿Quién es el señor Martínez?

   _____

6. ¿Dice el anuncio que hay que llenar una solicitud?

   _____

2 **Vida profesional** Complete the paragraph with items from the word bank.

anuncio	aspirante	currículum	entrevista	éxito	profesión	renunciar
ascenso	beneficios	empresa	entrevistadora	obtener	puesto	salario

Vi el (1) _____ en Internet. Se necesitaban personas para un

(2) _____ de editora en una pequeña (3) _____ que se

encontraba en el centro de la ciudad. Preparé mi (4) _____ con mucha atención

y lo envié por correo electrónico. Esa tarde me llamó la (5) _____, que se llamaba

la señora Piñeda. Me dijo que el (6) _____ que ofrecían no era demasiado alto,

pero que los (7) _____, como el seguro de salud, eran excelentes. Era una buena

oportunidad para (8) _____ experiencia. Me pidió que fuera a la oficina al día

siguiente para hacerme una (9) _____. Había otro (10) _____

en la sala de espera cuando llegué. Ese día decidí (11) _____ a mi trabajo

anterior (*previous*) y desde entonces ejerzo (*I practice*) la (12) _____ de editora.

¡He tenido mucho (13) _____!

3 **Una es diferente** Fill in the blanks with the words that don't belong in the groups.

1. ocupación, reunión, oficio, profesión, trabajo _____

2. pintor, psicólogo, maestro, consejero _____

3. arquitecta, diseñadora, pintora, bombera _____

4. invertir, currículum, corredor de bolsa, negocios _____

5. sueldo, beneficios, aumento, renunciar, ascenso _____

6. puesto, reunión, entrevista, videoconferencia _____

4 **Las ocupaciones** Fill in the blanks with the profession of the person who would make each statement.

1. "Decido dónde poner los elementos gráficos de las páginas de una revista."

_____

2. "Ayudo a las personas a resolver sus problemas. Hablan conmigo y buscamos soluciones."

_____

3. "Defiendo a mis clientes y les doy consejos legales."

_____

4. "Investigo las cosas que pasan y escribo artículos sobre los eventos."

_____

5. "Les doy clases a los niños en la escuela."

_____

6. "Hago experimentos y publico los resultados en una revista."

_____

5 **¿Quién lo usa?** Label each drawing with the profession associated with the objects.

1. _____

2. _____

3. _____

4. _____

estructura

16.1 The future

1 **Preguntas** Sabrina, your co-worker, needs some answers. Answer her questions with the future tense and the words in parentheses.

> **modelo**
> ¿Qué vas a hacer hoy? (el proyecto)
> Haré el proyecto hoy.

1. ¿Cuándo vamos a la reunión? (el jueves)

   _____

2. ¿Cuántas personas va a haber en la clase? (treinta)

   _____

3. ¿A qué hora vas a venir? (a las nueve)

   _____

4. ¿Quién va a ser el jefe de Delia? (Esteban)

   _____

5. ¿Dentro de cuánto va a salir Juan? (una hora)

   _____

6. ¿Quiénes van a estar en la fiesta del viernes? (muchos amigos)

   _____

2 **A los 30 años** Some friends in their late teens are talking about what they think they will be doing when they turn 30 years old. Complete the conversation with the correct form of the verbs in parentheses.

LETI Cuando tenga 30 años (1) _____ (ser) una arqueóloga famosa.

Yo (2) _____ (saber) mucho sobre las ruinas indígenas muy importantes.

SERGIO Yo (3) _____ (tener) un programa de viajes en la televisión. Mi cámara

de video y yo (4) _____ (visitar) lugares hermosos y muy interesantes.

SUSI Entonces (tú) (5) _____ (venir) a visitarme a mi restaurante de comida

caribeña que (6) _____ (abrir) en Santo Domingo, ¿verdad? *El Sabor*

Dominicano (7) _____ (tener) los mejores platos tradicionales y otros

creados (*created*) por mí.

SERGIO Claro que sí, (8) _____ (ir) a comer las especialidades y

(9) _____ (recomendarlo) a mis telespectadores (*viewers*). También (tú y

yo) (10) _____ (poder) visitar a Leti en sus expediciones.

LETI Sí, Susi (11) _____ (cocinar) platos exóticos en medio de la selva y todos

nosotros (12) _____ (disfrutar) de su deliciosa comida.

3 **Será así** Rewrite each sentence to express probability with the future tense. Each sentence should start with a verb in the future tense.

> modelo
>
> Creemos que se llega por esta calle.
> *Se llegará por esta calle.*

1. Es probable que sea la una de la tarde.

_____

2. Creo que ellas están en casa.

_____

3. Estamos casi seguros de que va a nevar hoy.

_____

4. Es probable que ellos vayan al cine luego.

_____

5. Creo que estamos enfermos.

_____

4 **Fin de semana entre amigos** Rosa, one of your friends, is telling you about some of the activities she has planned for this weekend. Write complete sentences to describe each image. Then keep using the future tense to write two activities that you will do this weekend.

Sábado por la mañana / nosotros   Después / ustedes   Mientras / yo

1. _____   2. _____   3. _____

_____   _____   _____

Por la noche / Julio, Lisa y Cata   Domingo por la mañana / yo   Domingo por la tarde / nosotros

4. _____   5. _____   6. _____

_____   _____   _____

7. _____

8. _____

16.2 The future perfect

1 **Optimista** Miguel is answering an e-mail from his friend Jorge. Answer Jorge's questions, saying that the people will have already done these things by the time indicated. Use the future perfect.

> **modelo**
> ¿Me enviarás un mensaje cuando llegues a Mérida?
> No, ya te habré enviado un mensaje cuando llegue a Mérida.

1. ¿Encontrarás un trabajo cuando te gradúes?

_____

2. ¿Le comprarás un regalo a Maru cuando te paguen?

_____

3. ¿Escribirá el Sr. Díaz una novela cuando se jubile?

_____

4. ¿Harás los preparativos para ir a España cuando termine el semestre?

_____

5. ¿Beberemos esta botella de vino cuando demos una fiesta?

_____

6. ¿Olvidaré a mi ex novia cuando me vaya de vacaciones?

_____

2 **¿Lo habrá hecho?** You expected these people to do something, and you're wondering if they have done it. Use the future perfect to ask yourself if they will have done it.

> **modelo**
> Le dije a Marcia que Pedro iba a llegar tarde. (esperar)
> ¿Lo habrá esperado?

1. Alma le dio el artículo a Javier. (leer)

_____

2. Le dejé comida a mi sobrino para el almuerzo. (comer)

_____

3. Mariela quería una falda nueva. (comprar)

_____

4. Rita iba a recoger a Julio al aeropuerto. (hacer)

_____

5. Ellas no querían viajar en tren. (decir)

_____

6. Mis amigos buscaban un pasaje barato. (encontrar)

_____

Lección 16 Workbook Activities

16.3 The past subjunctive

1 **Si pudiera** Complete the sentences with the past subjunctive forms of the verbs in parentheses.

1. El arqueólogo se alegró de que todos _____ (hacer) tantas preguntas.

2. Mi madre siempre quiso que yo _____ (estudiar) arquitectura.

3. Te dije que cuando (tú) _____ (ir) a la entrevista, llevaras tu currículum.

4. Tal vez no fue una buena idea que nosotros le _____ (escribir) esa carta.

5. Era una lástima que su esposo _____ (tener) que trabajar tanto.

6. Luisa dudaba que ese empleo _____ (ser) su mejor alternativa.

7. Era probable que Francisco _____ (llevarse) mal con sus jefes.

8. Laura buscaba intérpretes que _____ (saber) hablar inglés.

9. Ustedes no estaban seguros de que el gerente _____ (conocer) al contador.

10. Fue extraño que Daniela y tú _____ (solicitar) el mismo puesto.

2 **Si...** Daniel is talking to himself about the things that would make him happier. Complete his statements with the past subjunctive form of the verbs in parentheses. Then draw a portrait of yourself and write five sentences describing things that would make you happier. Try to use as many singular and plural forms as you can.

Sería (*I would be*) más feliz si...

1. (yo) _____ (ver) a mi novia todos los días.

2. mis papás _____ (venir) a mi ciudad a visitarme.

3. mi novia _____ (querer) hacer un viaje conmigo.

4. (yo) _____ (tener) una computadora más moderna.

5. mis nuevos amigos y yo _____ (viajar) juntos otra vez.

Sería más feliz si...

6. _____

7. _____

8. _____

9. _____

10. _____

3 **Chisme (*gossip*)** You overhear some coworkers gossiping about what's going on in the office, and they don't always agree. Complete their conversation so that the second sentence says the opposite of the first one.

> **modelo**
>
> Nadie dudaba que el candidato era muy bueno.
> **Nadie *estaba seguro de que el candidato fuera muy bueno.***

1. Nadie dudaba de que el ascenso de Andrés fue justo (*fair*).

   No estabas seguro de que _____.

2. Era obvio que todos los participantes sabían usar las computadoras.

   No fue cierto que _____.

3. Raquel estaba segura de que las reuniones no servían para nada.

   Pablo dudaba que _____.

4. Fue cierto que Rosa tuvo que ahorrar mucho dinero para invertirlo.

   No fue verdad que _____.

5. No hubo duda de que la videoconferencia fue un desastre (*disaster*).

   Tito negó que _____.

6. No negamos que los maestros recibieron salarios bajos.

   La directora negó que _____.

4 **El trabajo** Complete the conversation with the past subjunctive, the preterite, or the imperfect of the verbs in parentheses as appropriate.

MARISOL ¡Hola, Pepe! Me alegré mucho de que (tú) (1) _____ (conseguir) el trabajo de arquitecto.

PEPE Sí, aunque fue una lástima que (yo) (2) _____ (tener) que renunciar a mi puesto anterior.

MARISOL No dudé que (3) _____ (ser) una buena decisión.

PEPE No estaba seguro de que este puesto (4) _____ (ser) lo que quería, pero está muy bien.

MARISOL Estoy segura de que (tú) (5) _____ (hacer) muy bien la entrevista.

PEPE Me puse un poco nervioso, sin que eso (6) _____ (afectar) mis respuestas.

MARISOL Sé que ellos necesitaban a alguien que (7) _____ (tener) tu experiencia.

PEPE Es verdad que ellos (8) _____ (necesitar) a muchas personas para la oficina nueva.

Lección 16 Workbook Activities **187**

Síntesis

Write a two-part plan for your future.

- For the first part, write all of the things that you plan or wish to do with your life, using the future tense. Decide which things you will have accomplished by what age, using the future perfect. For example, "**A los veinticinco años, ya habré terminado la maestría** (*Master's degree*) **en negocios**".

- For the second part, imagine that you are elderly and reflecting on your life. What do you think of your accomplishments? At the time, what were you glad about, sorry about, scared about, annoyed about, and unsure about? What did you hope for and what did you deny yourself at the time? Use the preterite and the imperfect with the past subjunctive to write the story of your life.

_____

_____

_____

_____

_____

_____

_____

_____

_____

_____

_____

_____

_____

_____

_____

_____

_____

_____

_____

_____

_____

_____

Workbook

panorama

Nicaragua

1 **Datos nicaragüenses** Complete the sentences with information about Nicaragua.

1. Nicaragua, del tamaño (*size*) de Nueva York, es el país más grande de _____.

2. Managua es inestable geográficamente, con muchos _____ y _____.

3. Las _____ de Acahualinca son uno de los restos prehistóricos más famosos
   y antiguos de Nicaragua.

4. Desde joven, Ernesto Cardenal trabajó por establecer la _____ y la
   _____ en su país.

5. En los años 60, Cardenal estableció la comunidad artística del archipiélago de _____.

6. Ernesto Cardenal participó en la fundación de la organización _____.

7. Se cree que la isla _____ era un centro ceremonial indígena.

8. El nombre de la isla _____ significa "dos montañas" en náhuatl.

2 **El mapa** Label the map of Nicaragua.

1. _____

2. _____

3. _____

4. _____

5. _____

6. _____

3 **Datos rápidos** Identify the items and people described.

1. capital de Nicaragua _____

2. moneda nicaragüense _____

3. idiomas oficiales de Nicaragua _____

4. poeta nicaragüense nacido en el siglo XIX _____

5. política y ex presidenta nicaragüense _____

6. político y presidente nicaragüense _____

7. mujer poeta nicaragüense del siglo veinte _____

8. poeta y sacerdote que fue ministro de cultura _____

panorama

La República Dominicana

4 **¿Cierto o falso?** Indicate if each statement is **cierto** or **falso**. Then correct the false statements.

1. La República Dominicana y Haití comparten la isla La Española.

_____

2. La Fortaleza Ozama fue la tercera fortaleza construida en las Américas.

_____

3. La República Dominicana fue el primer país hispano en tener una liga de béisbol.

_____

4. Hoy día el béisbol es una afición nacional dominicana.

_____

5. El merengue es un tipo de música de origen dominicano que tiene sus raíces en el campo.

_____

6. El merengue siempre ha sido popular en las ciudades y ha tenido un tono urbano.

_____
_____

5 **Datos dominicanos** Complete the sentences with information about the Dominican Republic.

1. Los idiomas que se hablan en la República Dominicana son el _____ y el

_____.

2. _____ fue un político dominicano y padre de la patria en el siglo XIX.

3. Las señoras de la corte del Virrey de España paseaban por la _____.

4. El béisbol es un deporte muy practicado en todos los países del mar _____.

5. _____ y David Ortiz son dos beisbolistas dominicanos exitosos.

6. La _____ es un tambor característico de la República Dominicana.

7. Entre los años 1930 y 1960 se formaron las grandes _____ del merengue.

8. Uno de los cantantes más famosos de merengue dominicano es _____.

6 **En imágenes** Label these photos appropriately.

1. _____

2. _____

contextos

1 **¿Qué es?** Match each title to a genre.

canción	dibujos animados	obra de teatro	orquesta	poema
danza	festival	ópera	película	programa de entrevistas

1. *Carmen* _____

2. *Romeo y Julieta* _____

3. *Jimmy Kimmel Live!* _____

4. *Los Simpson* _____

5. *El cuervo* (raven) _____

6. *Gravedad* _____

7. *El cascanueces* (nutcracker) _____

8. *Feliz Navidad* _____

2 **¿Qué tipo de película es?** Label the type of movie shown on each screen.

1. _____

2. _____

3. _____

4. _____

Lección 17 Workbook Activities **191**

3 **Los artistas** Fill in each blank with the type of artist who would make the statement.

1. "Escribo obras de teatro para que las presenten al público." _____

2. "Dirijo a las estrellas y las cámaras para hacer películas." _____

3. "Trabajo con la computadora o con papel y pluma." _____

4. "Paso todo el día practicando las notas con mi instrumento." _____

5. "Soy muy famosa y estoy en las mejores películas." _____

6. "Me gusta escribir en versos, con palabras que riman (*rhyme*)." _____

7. "Hago grandes figuras de piedra de tres dimensiones." _____

8. "Sigo la música artísticamente con mi cuerpo." _____

9. "Pienso en la música y luego la escribo." _____

10. "Mi voz (*voice*) es mi instrumento." _____

4 **Las artes** Complete the newspaper article with the correct forms of the terms in the word bank.

artesanía	comedia	cultura	festival	moderno
clásico	cuento	escultura	folclórico	poema

Celebración de las artes

El (1) _____ artístico de la ciudad
comenzó ayer y en él van a participar diferentes cantantes,
grupos y orquestas. El viernes por la noche hay un
concierto de música (2) _____ de la
orquesta sinfónica de la ciudad. Tocarán la *Quinta*
sinfonía de Beethoven. El sábado tocarán durante el día varios grupos de música

(3) _____ de diferentes países. Será una oportunidad excelente para conocer más

sobre diversas (4) _____. El sábado por la tarde habrá un espectáculo de baile

expresivo, con música (5) _____. Además se exhibirá en los parques de la ciudad

una serie de grandes (6) _____ al aire libre. Por la noche, en el Teatro Central,

varios poetas le leerán sus (7) _____ al público. Finalmente, el domingo habrá

una feria (*fair*) de (8) _____, donde se venderá

cerámica y tejidos hechos a mano.

estructura

17.1 The conditional

1 **Si fuera famoso** Felipe is daydreaming about how his life would be if he were a famous artist. Complete the paragraph with the conditional form of the verbs.

Si yo fuera un artista famoso, creo que (1) _____ (ser) pintor;

(2) _____ (pintar) cuadros llenos de vida. Pero... no sé, también

(3) _____ (poder) ser cantante, (4) _____ (tener) una banda

de rock y juntos (5) _____ (viajar) por el mundo dando conciertos...

Ahhh, mejor (6) _____ (querer) ser poeta, mi musa Lola y yo

(7) _____ (vivir) en una villa y las personas (8) _____

(escuchar) mis poemas en el Teatro de la Ópera en Milán. Creo que Lola (9) _____

(ser) una bailarina extraordinaria; (10) _____ (bailar) en los teatros más

importantes, y por supuesto, yo (11) _____ (ir) con ella... Sin embargo, Lola y

yo (12) _____ (poder) ser muy buenos actores; nuestro público

(13) _____ (aplaudir) con entusiasmo en cada obra de teatro...

2 **La entrevista** Isabel is going to interview a famous author for an article in her college literary magazine. She e-mailed her journalism professor for advice. Rewrite the professor's advice in a paragraph, using the conditional of the verbs. The first sentence has been done for you.

buscar información en la biblioteca	grabar la entrevista
leer artículos de revista sobre la escritora	darle las gracias a la escritora
estudiar los cuentos de la escritora	al llegar a casa, transcribir la entrevista
preparar las preguntas antes de la entrevista	entonces escribir el artículo
vestirse de forma profesional	mostrárselo a la escritora antes de publicarlo
llegar temprano a casa de la escritora	sentirse muy orgullosa de su trabajo

Buscaría información en la biblioteca. _____

_____

_____

_____

_____

_____

_____

3 **Los buenos modales (manners)** Rewrite these commands with the conditional tense.

> **modelo**
> Termina el trabajo hoy antes de irte.
> ¿Terminarías el trabajo hoy antes de irte, por favor?

1. Tráigame una copa de vino. _____

2. Llama a Marcos esta tarde. _____

3. Encuéntreme un pasaje barato. _____

4. Pide una toalla más grande. _____

5. Venga a trabajar el sábado y el domingo. _____

6. Búscame en mi casa a las ocho. _____

4 **En el teatro** You and your friends are out for a night at the theater. React to each description of what happened by asking a question, using the conditional tense and the cues provided.

> **modelo**
> Adriana se durmió durante la película. (dormir bien anoche)
> ¿Dormiría bien anoche?

1. Natalia se fue temprano. (salir para ver otra obra de teatro)

_____

2. No encontré los boletos. (poner los boletos en mi cartera)

_____

3. Luz no fue al teatro. (tener otras cosas que hacer)

_____

4. Jaime e Isabel conocieron a los actores y actrices en una fiesta. (invitarlos el director)

_____

5 **Eso pensamos** Write sentences with the elements provided and the conditional of the verbs in parentheses.

> **modelo**
> Nosotros pensamos (ustedes / tener tiempo para ver el espectáculo)
> Nosotros pensamos que ustedes tendrían tiempo para ver el espectáculo.

1. Yo pensaba (el museo y el teatro / estar cerrados los domingos)

_____

2. Lisa y David dijeron (ese canal / presentar el documental ahora)

_____

3. Marta creía (sus estrellas de cine favoritas / salir en una nueva película)

_____

4. Lola dijo (Ramón / nunca hacer el papel de Romeo)

_____

17.2 The conditional perfect

1 **Pero no fue así** Write sentences with the elements provided. Use the conditional perfect of the verb in the first part of the sentence and the preterite of the verb in the second part.

> **modelo**
>
> Lidia / despertarse a las seis, // no oír el despertador
> Lidia se habría despertado a las seis, pero no oyó el despertador.

1. Tomás / ir al cine, // tener que quedarse estudiando

_____

2. (yo) / llamar a Marcela, // no conseguir su número de teléfono

_____

3. Antonio y Alberto / tocar bien en el concierto, // practicar poco

_____

4. (tú) / venir a mi casa, // no encontrar la dirección

_____

5. ustedes / conocer a mi novia, // llegar demasiado tarde

_____

6. mis amigos y yo / comer en tu casa, // comer en el restaurante

_____

2 **Viaje cancelado** You and your friends made plans to spend a week in New York City. However, you weren't able to go. Rewrite the paragraph to say what would have happened, using the conditional perfect. The first sentence has been done for you.

Iremos a ver una ópera famosa. Participaremos en un programa de entrevistas. Será un programa divertido. Mi prima nos conseguirá boletos para un espectáculo de baile. Nos quedaremos en casa de mis tíos. Conoceré al novio de mi prima. Mis tíos nos mostrarán la ciudad. Visitaremos la Estatua de la Libertad. Veremos a muchos turistas estadounidenses y extranjeros. Llamaré a mis padres para contarles todo. Habrá un festival en la calle. Bailaremos salsa y merengue en una discoteca. El novio de mi prima nos mostrará el documental que hizo. Escucharemos a algunos artistas recitar poemas en un café.

Habríamos ido a ver una ópera famosa. _____

_____

_____

_____

_____

_____

_____

Lección 17 Workbook Activities **195**

Workbook

17.3 The past perfect subjunctive

1 **En el pasado** Rewrite the sentences, replacing the subject in italics with the subject in parentheses and adjusting the form of the verb as necessary.

1. Mis padres se alegraron de que *yo* me hubiera graduado. (mi hermano)

_____

2. Marisol dudó que *nosotras* hubiéramos ido a la fiesta solas. (ustedes)

_____

3. Yo no estaba segura de que *mis hermanos* se hubieran despertado. (tú)

_____

4. Todos esperaban que *la conferencia* ya se hubiera acabado. (las clases)

_____

5. La clase empezó sin que *ustedes* hubieran hablado con el profesor. (nosotros)

_____

6. Fue una lástima que *mis amigos* no hubieran invitado a Roberto. (yo)

_____

2 **La obra de teatro** Your friends Eva and Tomás are walking home from the theater. Complete the conversation with the past perfect subjunctive form of the verbs.

EVA Ya había visto este espectáculo antes de que me invitaras. De todas maneras, me alegré de que

me (1) _____ (invitar) esta noche.

TOMÁS Si me (2) _____ (decir), habría cambiado de planes.

EVA Pues no importa. Ya vinimos y estuvo fabuloso. Claro que esperaba que

(3) _____ (elegir) mejores asientos.

TOMÁS Hice lo que pude. La verdad me molestó que en el teatro no me (4) _____

(ofrecer) más opciones. Me quejé (*I complained*) con el administrador, pero él no creía que yo

(5) _____ (pagar) esos boletos tan caros.

EVA Bueno, te creo. Pero esta tarde no me gustó nada que no me (6) _____

(llamar) antes. Anita me dijo que estabas con tus amigos, que habían ido al estadio...

TOMÁS ¡No es cierto que (7) _____ (ir) al estadio! Sí estaba con ellos, pero

sólo hablamos un rato. Oye, y no me dijiste con quién habías visto el espectáculo...

EVA Lo vi sola. Nadie pudo venir conmigo... Oye, y ¿por qué no invitaste a Paco y a Lulú? Se

habrían divertido mucho si (8) _____ (venir) con nosotros.

TOMÁS No creo. Aunque (*Although*) a Paco le (9) _____ (gustar) la idea,

Lulú no habría venido, lo sé. Estuvo insoportable en la boda de mi hermana. ¡Yo no podía

creer que se (10) _____ (quedar) dormida en la mesa!

3 **Las vacaciones** Complete the letter with the past perfect subjunctive of the verbs in parentheses.

3 de mayo

Querida Irma:

Me alegré mucho de que (tú) me (1) _____ (poder) visitar este verano. Además,

yo esperaba que (tú) te (2) _____ (quedar) unos días solamente, pero me alegré

cuando supe que te quedarías dos semanas. Si tú (3) _____ (estar) aquí todo el

mes, habríamos podido ver más zonas del país. Es probable que la playa de La Libertad te

(4) _____ (gustar) mucho, y también que (tú) (5) _____

(querer) hacer surf. ¡Ojalá (tú) (6) _____ (conocer) a mi hermano! Es probable

que tú y yo nos (7) _____ (divertir) muchísimo con él. ¡Lo habríamos pasado mejor

si (tú) (8) _____ (decidir) quedarte en El Salvador todo el verano!

Hasta pronto. Tu amiga,

Rosa

4 **No, no era cierto** Your grandmother is getting a little absentminded. Answer her questions negatively, using the past perfect subjunctive.

modelo

¿Era obvio que ustedes habían escrito la carta?
No, no era obvio que hubiéramos escrito la carta.

1. ¿Era verdad que el examen había sido muy difícil?

   _____

2. ¿Estaba Raquel segura de que él había tomado vino?

   _____

3. ¿Era cierto que todas las clases se habían llenado?

   _____

4. ¿Era obvio que ustedes habían limpiado la casa?

   _____

5. ¿Estabas seguro de que nosotros habíamos comido?

   _____

6. ¿Era cierto que yo había sido la última en llegar?

   _____

Síntesis

Interview a friend to find out what he or she would do if he or she won a million dollars in a game show. Then do the following:

- Write a paragraph that describes the things your friend would do. Use the conditional tense.
- Write a paragraph about what you would have done if you were the million-dollar winner. Use both the conditional perfect and the past perfect subjunctive tenses.

_____

_____

_____

_____

_____

_____

_____

_____

_____

_____

_____

_____

_____

_____

_____

_____

_____

_____

_____

_____

_____

_____

_____

_____

_____

_____

_____

Workbook

panorama

El Salvador

1 **Datos salvadoreños** Complete the sentences with information about El Salvador.

1. _____ es una poeta, novelista y cuentista salvadoreña.

2. El Salvador tiene unos 300 kilómetros de costa en el océano _____.

3. _____ es la playa que está más cerca de San Salvador.

4. Las condiciones de La Libertad son perfectas para el _____.

5. El Parque Nacional Montecristo se conoce también como _____.

6. En el Parque Nacional Montecristo se unen _____,

_____ y _____.

7. Los _____ del bosque Montecristo forman una bóveda que el sol no traspasa.

8. Las _____ de Ilobasco son pequeñas piezas de cerámica muy populares.

2 **¿Cierto o falso?** Indicate if each statement is **cierto** or **falso**. Then correct the false statements.

1. El Salvador es el país centroamericano más grande y más densamente poblado.

_____

2. Casi el 90 por ciento de la población salvadoreña es mestiza.

_____

3. Óscar Romero fue un arzobispo y activista por los derechos humanos.

_____

4. El pueblo de Ilobasco se ha convertido en un gran centro de surfing.

_____

5. El bosque nuboso Montecristo es una zona seca (*dry*).

_____

6. Los productos tradicionales de Ilobasco son los juguetes, los adornos y los utensilios de cocina.

_____

3 **Vistas de El Salvador** Label the places in the photos.

1. _____   2. _____

Lección 17 Workbook Activities

panorama

Honduras

4 **En Honduras** Answer the questions with complete sentences.

1. ¿Quiénes son los jicaque, los misquito y los paya?

_____

2. ¿Qué idiomas se hablan en Honduras?

_____

3. ¿Quién fue Argentina Díaz Lozano?

_____

4. ¿Qué cultura construyó la ciudad de Copán?

_____

5. ¿Para qué eran las canchas de Copán?

_____

6. ¿Por qué pudo intervenir la Standard Fruit Company en la política hondureña?

_____

5 **Datos hondureños** Briefly describe each person or item.

1. El Progreso _____

2. Carlos Roberto Reina _____

3. Copán _____

4. Rosalila _____

5. José Antonio Velásquez _____

6. las bananas _____

6 **Palabras hondureñas** Identify these people, places, or things.

1. capital de Honduras _____

2. Tegucigalpa, San Pedro Sula, El Progreso, La Ceiba _____

3. moneda hondureña _____

4. esculturas, cetros, templos, canchas _____

5. escritor hondureño _____

6. lugar adonde se empezaron a exportar las bananas hondureñas _____

contextos

Lección 18

1 **Identificar** Label the numbered items in the drawing.

1. _____

2. _____

3. _____

4. _____

5. _____

6. _____

7. _____

2 **Una es diferente** Fill in the blanks with the words that don't belong in the groups.

1. anunciar, comunicarse, luchar, transmitir, informar _____

2. racismo, sexismo, discriminación, desigualdad, prensa _____

3. libertad, tornado, huracán, tormenta, inundación _____

4. locutor, impuesto, ciudadano, político, reportero _____

5. crimen, guerra, violencia, derechos, choque _____

6. diario, noticiero, acontecimiento, artículo, informe _____

Workbook

3 **Crucigrama** Use the clues to complete the crossword puzzle.

Horizontales

1. Un carro golpea (*hits*) a otro carro.
2. Sucede cuando un río se llena demasiado de agua.
4. Es lo opuesto (*opposite*) a la democracia.
5. Se hace para saber quién va a ganar las elecciones.
7. Todos los días puedes leer las noticias en él.

Verticales

1. Quiere ser elegido para un puesto público.
3. Es el dinero que todos pagan al gobierno por lo que ganan.
6. Es una enfermedad del sistema inmune del cuerpo.

4 **La locutora** Complete the newscast with items from the word bank.

| candidatos | elecciones | encuestas | | noticias | prensa |
| discursos | elegir | medios de comunicación | | noticiero | votar |

Buenas tardes, y bienvenidos al (1) _____ de las cinco. Mañana, un mes

antes de las (2) _____ para la presidencia de los Estados Unidos, será el

primer debate entre los (3) _____. Ya ellos han pronunciado muchos

(4) _____, y todos hemos escuchado sus opiniones, pero mañana será la primera

vez que los candidatos se enfrentan (*face each other*). La (5) _____ internacional

está preparada para llevar las últimas noticias a los diarios de todo el mundo. Los

(6) _____, como la radio y la televisión, estarán bien representados. Las

(7) _____ no indican que alguno de los dos candidatos tenga una ventaja (*lead*)

clara. Lo más importante es ver cuántos ciudadanos irán a (8) _____ el día de las

elecciones. Son ellos los que decidirán a quién van a (9) _____. Volveremos a las

diez de la noche para darles las (10) _____ de la tarde. ¡Los esperamos!

estructura

18.1 Si clauses

1 **Sería así** Complete the sentences with the verbs in parentheses. Use the subjunctive and the conditional as appropriate.

> **modelo**
> Si yo **fuera** (ir) al cine, (yo) **vería** (ver) esa película.

1. Adriana y Claudia _____ (adelgazar) si _____ (comer) menos todos los días.

2. Si Gustavo _____ (conseguir) un trabajo mejor, (él) _____ (ganar) más dinero.

3. Si el amigo de Gerardo la _____ (invitar), Olga _____ (salir) con él al cine.

4. Alma y yo _____ (lavar) los platos si Alejandra _____ (pasar) la aspiradora.

5. Si (tú) _____ (tener) hambre, (tú) _____ (poder) almorzar en casa de mi tía.

6. Brenda nos _____ (venir) a buscar si (nosotras) _____ (estar) listas a tiempo.

7. Yo _____ (ir) a la ópera el sábado si ustedes _____ (tener) más boletos.

8. Si Pilar y tú _____ (querer), (nosotros) _____ (viajar) juntos por Suramérica.

9. Ustedes _____ (buscar) el libro en la librería si (ustedes) no lo _____ (encontrar) en casa.

10. Si Marcos y María _____ (poder), (ellos) _____ (comprar) una casa en mi barrio.

2 **Si fuera así...** Rewrite the sentences to describe a contrary-to-fact situation. Use the subjunctive and the conditional tenses.

> **modelo**
> Si me visitas en Montevideo, te invito a cenar.
> Si me visitaras en Montevideo, te invitaría a cenar.

1. Si buscas las llaves en la habitación, las encuentras enseguida.

_____

2. La madre de Rodrigo llama al médico si él está enfermo.

_____

3. Si ustedes saludan a Rosa y a Ramón, ellos son muy simpáticos.

_____

4. Si Luis me espera, voy con él al festival de música folclórica.

_____

5. Ana y Elena limpian la cocina y el baño si están sucios.

_____

6. Viajo a Uruguay con ustedes si tengo el dinero.

_____

3   **Si hubiera...** Write complete sentences about the images. Use the conditional perfect and the past perfect subjunctive.

> **modelo**
>
> (él) levantar pesas / mantenerse en forma
> Si hubiera levantado pesas, se habría mantenido en forma.

1. (ellos) / levantarse temprano / no llegar tarde

_____

_____

2. (yo) hacer ejercicios de estiramiento / no haberse lastimado

_____

_____

3. (ustedes) leer el libro / sacar buenas notas en el examen

_____

_____

4. (tú) llegar temprano / recibir un regalo

_____

_____

4   **Escribir oraciones** Write sentences with the elements provided to express conditions and events that are possible or likely to occur. Use the tenses in brackets.

> **modelo**
>
> Si Paco llega temprano / (ustedes / ir al cine) *[future]*
> Si Paco llega temprano, ustedes irán al cine.

1. Si quieres comer en mi casa / (tú / llamarme) *[command]*

_____

2. Si Luisa se enferma / (su novio / llevarla al doctor) *[present]*

_____

3. Si todos los ciudadanos votan / (el gobierno / ser mejor) *[near future]*

_____

4. Si Ana y tú estudian / (ustedes / aprobar el examen) *[future]*

_____

5. Si nos levantamos tarde / (nosotras / no llegar al discurso) *[near future]*

_____

18.2 Summary of the uses of the subjunctive

1 **¿Subjuntivo o indicativo?** Choose the correct verbs from the parentheses.

1. Cuando _____ (vienes, vengas) a buscarme, tráeme la mochila.

2. Nuestros primos nos llamaron después de que su madre se _____ (casó, casara).

3. Ricardo y Elena quieren que ella los llame en cuanto _____ (llega, llegue).

4. Ustedes se quitaron los abrigos tan pronto como _____ (pudieron, pudieran).

5. Ricardo va a correr en el parque hasta que se _____ (cansa, canse).

6. Después de que _____ (vamos, vayamos) al cine, quiero comer algo.

2 **¿Infinitivo o subjuntivo?** Rewrite the sentences, using the infinitive or the subjunctive form of the verb in parentheses, as needed.

1. Laura y Germán esperan que la tormenta no (causar) daños (*damage*).

_____

2. Los trabajadores temen (perder) sus derechos.

_____

3. Nosotros tenemos miedo de (conducir) en la ciudad.

_____

4. Gisela y tú se alegran de que Ricardo no (ser) antipático.

_____

5. Tú esperas (terminar) el trabajo antes de irte de vacaciones.

_____

6. Daniel teme que sus padres (vender) la casa en donde nació.

_____

3 **¿Hace o haga?** Complete the sentences with the indicative or subjunctive of the verbs in parentheses.

1. Roberto es el chico que _____ (trabajar) en el periódico universitario.

2. Álex y yo buscamos aspirantes que _____ (saber) usar bases de datos.

3. ¿Conoces a alguien que _____ (hablar) más de cuatro idiomas?

4. El amigo de Ana es un abogado que _____ (tener) muchos casos.

5. La señora López dice que no hay nadie que _____ (cocinar) mejor que ella.

6. Javier y yo somos artistas que _____ (dibujar) muy bien.

7. Mauricio quiere un asistente que _____ (vivir) en Quito.

8. Andrea tiene amigos que _____ (estudiar) en la UNAM.

Lección 18 Workbook Activities

4   **Planes de verano** Berta is writing an e-mail to her friend Pati about her plans for this summer. Complete the paragraph with the correct forms of the subjunctive.

Para: Pati	De: Berta	Asunto: Viaje de verano

Querida Pati:

Deseo que el semestre (1) _____ (terminar) pronto. Dudo que

(2) _____ (sacar) malas notas, pero ya tengo planes para el

verano. Tan pronto como (3) _____ (empezar) las vacaciones,

tomaré un avión a Montevideo. Si (4) _____ (comprar) mi

boleto hace dos meses, habría pagado menos dinero, pero me alegro de

que (5) _____ (aceptar) mi tarjeta de crédito en la agencia

de viajes. En cuanto (6) _____ (recibir) mi sueldo, compraré

un diario. Cuando (7) _____ (comenzar) mi viaje, voy a

escribir todas mis experiencias. Después de que (8) _____

(llegar) a Montevideo, mi amigo Alberto irá por mí al aeropuerto.

No descansaremos hasta que (9) _____ (visitar) todos los

lugares interesantes de su país. ¡Uf! Me alegro de que el verano

(10) _____ (durar) dos meses. En caso de que Alberto y yo

(11) _____ (necesitar) más tiempo, regresaré el próximo año.

Si tú (12) _____ (venir) con nosotros, disfrutarías mucho.

Siento mucho que (tú) no (13) _____ (poder) viajar este

verano y espero que ya (14) _____ (sentirse) mejor. Tan

pronto como (yo) (15) _____ (encontrar) un cibercafé en

Montevideo, te escribiré.

Saludos,
Berta

5   **Que sea así** Combine the sentences, using the present or past subjunctive in the adjective clause.

> **modelo**
> Patricia fue a buscar un escritorio. El escritorio debía ser grande.
> Patricia fue a buscar un escritorio que fuera grande.

1. Quiero elegir un candidato. El candidato debe ser inteligente y sincero.

   _____

2. La empresa iba a contratar un empleado. El empleado debía tener experiencia.

   _____

3. Norma y tú van a comprar una casa. La casa debe estar en buen estado (*condition*).

   _____

4. Iván quería casarse con una chica. La chica lo debía querer mucho.

   _____

5. Vamos a darle empleo a una señora. La señora debe saber cocinar.

   _____

6. Ellos estaban buscando una persona. La persona debía conocer a Sergio.

   _____

6 **¿Indicativo o subjuntivo?** Complete this letter with the present indicative or the present subjunctive of the verbs in parentheses.

Estimado cliente:

Le escribimos para informarle que su servicio de larga distancia ya (1) _____ (funcionar) a través de (*through*) nuestra empresa. Ahora las llamadas internacionales le (2) _____ (costar) 10 centavos por minuto a menos que usted (3) _____ (hacer) las llamadas en fin de semana. Puede llamarnos a nuestra línea de servicio al cliente cuando usted (4) _____ (querer). Nuestros agentes (5) _____ (responder) a las llamadas las 24 horas del día. Además, le ofrecemos nuestro servicio de Internet inalámbrico. Ahora usted (6) _____ (poder) conectarse a Internet sin que la distancia y el lugar (7) _____ (ser) un problema. Le sugerimos que (usted) (8) _____ (elegir) nuestra empresa para conectarse a Internet. Es cierto que usted (9) _____ (tener) muchas opciones, pero le aconsejamos que (usted) (10) _____ (conectarse) a través de nuestra empresa para obtener los mejores precios y servicios. Tan pronto como usted (11) _____ (decidir) usar nuestros servicios, llámenos. Nosotros le daremos toda la información que (usted) (12) _____ (necesitar).

7 **¿Qué habría pasado?** Write questions and answers with the elements provided to state what would have happened in each case.

modelo
si yo / haber estado en un incendio // (tú) / haber tenido miedo
¿Qué habría pasado si yo hubiera estado en un incendio?
Si hubieras estado en un incendio, habrías tenido miedo.

1. si don Diego / haber llegado tarde // (él) / no haber votado

_____
_____

2. si Jimena / haberte dicho eso // yo / no haber aceptado el trabajo

_____
_____

3. si Maru y tú / haber sido discriminados/as // (nosotros/as) / haber luchado contra la desigualdad

_____
_____

4. si Felipe y Miguel / haber visto al criminal // (ellos) / haber declarado en su contra (*against him*)

_____
_____

Workbook

■ Síntesis

Write an essay about a famous politician. Include various types of **si** clauses and different uses of the subjunctive as you address the following:

• State what you think about the person's life choices.
• With which aspects of the person's life do you agree and disagree?
• What do you like and dislike about him or her?
• What do you hope he or she will do in the future?
• Which of the things said about this person do you think are true and untrue?
• What would you have done and what would you do if you were this person?

_____

_____

_____

_____

_____

_____

_____

_____

_____

_____

_____

_____

_____

_____

_____

_____

_____

_____

_____

_____

_____

_____

Workbook

panorama

Paraguay

1 Preguntas sobre Paraguay Answer these questions about Paraguay.

1. ¿Cómo usan la lengua guaraní los paraguayos? _____

_____

2. ¿A qué se dedica el Teatro Guaraní? _____

_____

3. ¿Por qué se llaman "ñandutí" los encajes paraguayos? _____

_____

4. ¿Por qué visitan la represa Itaipú muchos turistas? _____

_____

5. ¿Qué ríos sirven de frontera entre Paraguay y Argentina? _____

_____

6. ¿Cuál es la importancia del río Paraná? _____

_____

2 Sopa de letras Use the clues to find terms about Paraguay in the puzzle. Then, write down the answers.

1. capital de Paraguay
2. central hidroeléctrica
3. ciudad de Paraguay
4. encaje artesanal paraguayo
5. estuario al final del río Paraná
6. guitarrista paraguayo
7. un idioma de Paraguay
8. lugar originario del ñandutí
9. una mujer de Paraguay
10. país que hace frontera con Paraguay
11. río con 3.200 km navegables
12. zona poco poblada de Paraguay

U	R	Í	O	D	E	L	A	P	L	A	T	A
X	I	R	M	Z	L	U	L	G	A	D	M	R
A	T	I	T	A	I	P	Ú	L	M	Ñ	B	G
S	A	D	Á	Q	Ñ	F	M	V	B	F	Í	E
U	U	S	G	R	A	N	C	H	A	C	O	N
N	G	U	A	R	A	N	Í	R	R	M	H	T
C	U	B	A	R	R	I	O	S	É	Í	C	I
I	Á	F	P	A	R	A	N	Á	L	U	X	N
Ó	Ñ	A	N	D	U	T	Í	G	O	R	Ñ	A
N	O	H	P	A	R	A	G	U	A	Y	A	R

1. _____
2. _____
3. _____
4. _____
5. _____
6. _____
7. _____
8. _____
9. _____
10. _____
11. _____
12. _____

panorama

Uruguay

3   **Datos uruguayos** Complete the sentences with information about Uruguay.

1. Montevideo está situada en la desembocadura del _____.

2. Hay numerosas playas que se extienden desde Montevideo hasta la ciudad de _____.

3. La _____ es un elemento esencial en la dieta diaria de los uruguayos.

4. El _____ es una infusión similar al té y es muy típico de la región.

5. El _____ es el deporte nacional de Uruguay.

6. En los años _____ se inició el período profesional del fútbol uruguayo.

7. El _____ de Montevideo dura unos cuarenta días y es el más largo del mundo.

8. La celebración más conocida del Carnaval de Montevideo es el _____.

4   **¿Cierto o falso?** Indicate if each statement is **cierto** or **falso**. Correct the false statements.

1. Punta del Este es una ciudad cosmopolita e intelectual.

_____

2. Jorge Drexler en un compositor y cantante uruguayo.

_____

3. El mate es una bebida de origen africano que está muy presente en Uruguay.

_____

4. Uruguay y Argentina desean ser la sede de la Copa Mundial de fútbol en 2030.

_____

5. Uno de los mejores carnavales de Suramérica se celebra en Salto.

_____

6. En el Desfile de Llamadas participan actores y actrices.

_____

5   **El mapa** Identify the places on this map of Uruguay.

1. _____   4. _____

2. _____   5. _____

3. _____   6. _____

repaso

1 **¿Cuándo ocurrirá?** Create sentences with the elements provided. First, use the future and the present subjunctive tenses. Then rewrite each sentence, using the future perfect and the present subjunctive.

modelo

(yo) / limpiar la casa // (nosotros) / ir al cine
Limpiaré la casa antes de que vayamos al cine.
Habré limpiado la casa cuando vayamos al cine.

1. Manuel / conseguir un trabajo // (tú) / comprar el coche

_____

_____

2. el candidato / cumplir (*keeps*) sus promesas // Ana / votar por él

_____

_____

3. Lola y yo / pintar el apartamento // ellos / mudarse

_____

_____

4. ustedes / terminar el trabajo // todos / llegar a la oficina

_____

_____

2 **Oraciones incompletas** Complete each sentence using the correct phrase from the word bank. Use each phrase once.

la cocina no estaría tan sucia	no pasaría nada malo
los dibujos saldrían mejor	tenían ganas
ganáramos más dinero	tuvieran más experiencia
hubieras venido ayer	yo habría aprendido más

1. Si me hubieras ayudado a estudiar, _____.

2. Ellos conseguirían ese trabajo si _____.

3. Habrías visto a Lucía si _____.

4. Si siempre pagaran a tiempo, _____.

5. Si la limpiáramos un poco, _____.

6. Estaríamos más contentos si _____.

7. Lilia y Marta nadaban si _____.

8. Si Gloria tuviera un papel de mejor calidad, _____.

Lecciones 16–18 Workbook Activities **211**

3 **El subjuntivo en acción** Complete the text with the correct forms of the verbs in parentheses. Use the present subjunctive, the past subjunctive, the conditional, the conditional perfect, the present perfect subjunctive, and the past perfect subjunctive as appropriate.

Si yo (1) _____ (vivir) en Uruguay, me gustaría vivir en Montevideo. No he

conocido a nadie que (2) _____ (estar) allí antes. Mi amigo Daniel me

recomendó el año pasado que (yo) (3) _____ (viajar) por Suramérica. Otros

amigos me recomiendan que (yo) (4) _____ (visitar) las islas del Caribe primero.

Mi novia quiere que yo la (5) _____ (llevar) de vacaciones a Costa Rica. Es

posible que este año mi familia (6) _____ (ir) de nuevo al Caribe en un crucero

(*cruise*). ¡Es una lástima que (nosotros) no (7) _____ (ver) muchos países de habla

hispana todavía! Espero que este año (nosotros) (8) _____ (poder) viajar más. Si

yo (9) _____ (tener) mucho dinero, (yo) (10) _____ (viajar)

siempre. Si mis abuelos (11) _____ (tener) las oportunidades de viajar que tienen

mis padres, habrían visto el mundo entero. Mi abuelo siempre nos aconsejó a nosotros que

(12) _____ (disfrutar) de la vida y que nunca (13) _____

(trabajar) tanto que no pudiéramos viajar. Si mi abuelo hubiera vivido hasta ahora, él

(14) _____ (ir) con nosotros a nuestro primer viaje en crucero. Y yo, ¡no dejaré de

viajar hasta que me (15) _____ (morir)! Espero que (nosotros) siempre

(16) _____ (tener) dinero, tiempo y salud para hacerlo.

4 **El extranjero** On a separate sheet of paper, write an essay in Spanish about life in the U.S. or Canada, a Spanish-speaking country, and your future home, using the following guidelines and keeping in mind the indicative and subjunctive tenses that you learned throughout your textbook.

- First, describe life in the U.S. or Canada: what you like, what bothers you, what is good, and what is bad. Mention at least one stereotype that you consider to be true and another that you feel is untrue about life in the U.S. or Canada. What would you recommend to someone who has recently moved to the U.S. or Canada? What other advice would you give that person?
- Next, write about a Spanish-speaking country. What would your childhood have been like if you had been born and had grown up there? What would your city and home be like? What would your parents be like? What would your education have been like?
- Finally, describe where you want to live in the future and why. Be sure to include some of the same topics in your explanation that you described in the other two sections.

Bienvenida, Marissa

Lección 1

Antes de ver el video

1 **¡Mucho gusto!** In this episode, Marissa will be meeting the **familia Díaz** for the first time. Look at the image and write down what you think Marissa, Mrs. Díaz, and Mr. Díaz are saying.

_____
_____
_____
_____
_____
_____

Mientras ves el video

2 **Completar** Watch **Bienvenida, Marissa** and fill in the blanks in the following sentences.

SRA. DÍAZ ¿(1)_____ hora es?

MARISSA (2)_____ las cuatro menos diez.

DON DIEGO Buenas tardes, (3)_____. Señorita, bienvenida a la Ciudad de México.

MARISSA ¡Muchas gracias! Me (4)_____ Marissa.
¿(5)_____ se llama usted?

DON DIEGO Yo soy Diego, mucho (6)_____.

MARISSA El gusto es (7)_____, don Diego.

DON DIEGO ¿Cómo (8)_____ usted hoy, señora Carolina?

SRA. DÍAZ Muy bien, gracias, ¿y (9)_____?

DON DIEGO Bien, (10)_____.

SRA. DÍAZ Ahí hay (11)_____ maletas. Son de Marissa.

DON DIEGO Con (12)_____.

3 **¿Cierto o falso?** Indicate whether each statement is **cierto** or **falso**.

	Cierto	Falso
1. Marissa es de Wisconsin.	○	○
2. Jimena es profesora.	○	○
3. La señora Díaz es de Cuba.	○	○
4. Felipe es estudiante.	○	○
5. El señor Díaz es de la Ciudad de México.	○	○
6. Marissa no tiene (*doesn't have*) diccionario.	○	○

Lección 1 Fotonovela Video Activities   **1**

Después de ver el video

4 **¿Quién?** Write the name of the person who said each of the following sentences.

1. Ellos son estudiantes. _____

2. Son las cuatro y veinticinco. _____

3. Hasta luego, señor Díaz. _____

4. La chica de Wisconsin. _____

5. Bienvenida, Marissa. _____

6. Nosotros somos tu diccionario. _____

7. Hay... tres cuadernos... un mapa... un libro de español... _____

8. Marissa, te presento a Roberto, mi esposo. _____

9. De nada. _____

10. Lo siento, Marissa. _____

11. ¿Cómo se dice mediodía en inglés? _____

12. No hay de qué. _____

13. ¿Qué hay en esta cosa? _____

14. ¿Quiénes son los dos chicos de las fotos? ¿Jimena y Felipe? _____

15. Gracias, don Diego. _____

5 **Ho, ho, hola...** Imagine that you have just met the man or woman of your dreams, and that person speaks only Spanish! Don't be shy! Write what the two of you would say in your first conversation.

_____

_____

_____

_____

_____

_____

_____

6 **En la clase** Imagine that you are in Mexico studying Spanish. Write your conversation with your Spanish professor on the first day you attend the university.

_____

_____

_____

_____

_____

_____

_____

¿Qué estudias?

Lección 2

Antes de ver el video

1 **Impresiones** Based on your impressions of Marissa, Felipe, and Jimena in **Lección 1**, write the names of the classes you think each person is taking or is most interested in. Circle the name of the person you believe is the most studious, and underline the name of the character you believe is the most talkative.

MARISSA	FELIPE	JIMENA
_____	_____	_____
_____	_____	_____
_____	_____	_____

Mientras ves el video

2 **¿Quién y a quién?** Watch **¿Qué estudias?** and say who asks these questions and to whom.

Preguntas	¿Quién?	¿A quién?
1. ¿A quién buscas?	_____	_____
2. ¿Cuántas clases tomas?	_____	_____
3. ¿Qué estudias?	_____	_____
4. ¿Dónde está tu diccionario?	_____	_____
5. ¿Hablas con tu mamá?	_____	_____

3 **¿Qué cosas hay?** Make a check mark beside the actions, items and places shown in **¿Qué estudias?**

_____ 1. libros _____ 5. comprar _____ 9. pizarra

_____ 2. laboratorio _____ 6. tiza _____ 10. dibujar

_____ 3. caminar _____ 7. hablar _____ 11. reloj

_____ 4. castillo _____ 8. horario _____ 12. mochila

4 **Completar** Fill in the blanks.

1. Marissa está en México para _____.

2. Marissa toma cuatro _____.

3. La _____ de Marissa es arqueología.

4. La especialización de Miguel es _____.

5. A Miguel le gusta _____.

6. Marissa _____ muy bien el español.

7. Juan Carlos toma química con el _____ Morales.

8. El profesor Morales enseña en un laboratorio sin _____.

9. A Felipe le gusta estar _____ el reloj y la puerta.

10. Maru _____ con su mamá.

Lección 2 Fotonovela Video Activities | **3**

Video Manual: *Fotonovela*

Después de ver el video

5   **Corregir** The underlined words in the following statements are incorrect. Fill in the blanks with the correct ones.

1. <u>Maru</u> es de los Estados Unidos. _____

2. <u>Miguel</u> toma una clase de computación. _____

3. <u>Felipe</u> necesita comprar libros. _____

4. En clase, a Marissa le gusta estar cerca <u>del reloj</u>. _____

5. <u>Felipe</u> es de Argentina. _____

6. Marissa toma español, <u>periodismo</u>, literatura y geografía. _____

7. Felipe busca a Juan Carlos y a <u>Maru</u>. _____

8. Felipe necesita practicar <u>español</u>. _____

6   **Asociar** Write the words or phrases in the box next to the names.

¿A la biblioteca?	cuatro clases	¿Por qué tomo química
arqueología	Ésta es la Ciudad de México.	y computación?
Buenos Aires	Hola, mamá, ¿cómo estás?	Te gusta la tarea.
ciencias ambientales	Me gusta mucho la cultura mexicana.	Y sin diccionario.

1. Marissa   _____   _____

           _____

2. Felipe   _____   _____

           _____

3. Juan Carlos   _____   _____

4. Maru   _____   _____

           _____

7   **¿Y tú?** Write a paragraph saying who you are, where you are from, where you study (city and name of university), and what classes you are taking this semester.

_____

_____

_____

_____

_____

_____

_____

_____

_____

Video Manual: *Fotonovela*

Un domingo en familia

Lección 3

Antes de ver el video

1

Examinar el título Look at the title of the episode. Based on the title and the image below, imagine what you think you will see.

_____
_____
_____
_____
_____
_____
_____

Mientras ves el video

2

Completar Fill in the blanks for each sentence from column A with a word from column B, according to **Un domingo en familia**.

A	B
1. Marta _____ ocho años.	trabajadora
2. Las hijas de Nayeli son simpáticas y _____.	tiene
3. La _____ de Ramón y Roberto se llama Ana María.	vive
4. Jimena dice que Felipe es _____ y feo.	gordo
5. Jimena es muy _____.	bonitas
6. Ana María _____ en Mérida.	hermana

3

En Xochimilco Check off each person or thing that appears.

____ 1. a Biology book   ____ 5. Felipe's uncle   ____ 9. people eating

____ 2. Marissa's grandparents   ____ 6. a soccer ball   ____ 10. Felipe's girlfriend

____ 3. Jimena's cousins   ____ 7. trajineras   ____ 11. Jimena's dad

____ 4. a desk   ____ 8. mariachis   ____ 12. Ana María's son-in-law

4

¿Cierto o falso? Indicate whether each statement is **cierto** or **falso**.

	Cierto	Falso
1. Felipe tiene mucha hambre.	○	○
2. El ex novio de Marissa es alemán.	○	○
3. Ana María tiene tres hijos.	○	○
4. Marissa tiene una sobrina que se llama Olivia.	○	○
5. La señora Díaz dice que su cuñada es muy simpática.	○	○

Después de ver el video

5 **Seleccionar** Select the letter of the word or phrase that goes in each sentence.

1. Roberto es el _____ de Felipe y Jimena.

   a. tío   b. primo   c. padre   d. sobrino

2. Los abuelos de Marissa son _____.

   a. ecuatorianos   b. españoles   c. mexicanos   d. alemanes

3. Adam es el _____ de Marissa.

   a. hermano menor   b. tío   c. primo   d. cuñado

4. Carolina tiene una _____ que se llama Ana María.

   a. tía   b. cuñada   c. hermana   d. prima

5. Las _____ de Nayeli son _____.

   a. primas; altas   b. hermanas; trabajadoras   c. hijas; simpáticas   d. sobrinas; guapas

6. La _____ de Nayeli es muy _____.

   a. sobrina; trabajadora   b. abuela; vieja   c. mamá; simpática   d. tía; alta

7. La _____ de Carolina tiene _____.

   a. tía; hambre   b. hija; sed   c. sobrina; frío   d. familia; sueño

8. Marissa decide ir a _____.

   a. la librería   b. la cafetería   c. Mérida   d. el estadio

6 **Preguntas** Answer the questions, using complete sentences.

1. ¿Quién tiene tres hermanos?

   _____

2. ¿Cuántos años tiene Valentina, la hija de Nayeli?

   _____

3. ¿Quién es hija única?

   _____

4. ¿Cómo se llama el hermano de Jimena?

   _____

5. ¿Cómo se llama el padre de Felipe?

   _____

7 **Preguntas personales** Answer the questions about your family.

1. ¿Cuántas personas hay en tu familia? ¿Cuál es más grande (*bigger*), tu familia o la familia de Jimena? _____

   _____

2. ¿Tienes hermanos/as? ¿Cómo se llaman? _____

   _____

3. ¿Tienes un(a) primo/a favorito/a? ¿Cómo es? _____

   _____

4. ¿Cómo es tu tío/a favorito/a? ¿Dónde vive? _____

   _____

Fútbol, cenotes y mole   Lección 4

Antes de ver el video

1 **El cenote** In this episode, Miguel, Maru, Marissa, and Jimena are going to a cenote to swim. What do you think they will see? What will they talk about?

_____
_____
_____
_____
_____
_____

Mientras ves el video

2 **Verbos** These sentences are taken from **Fútbol, cenotes y mole**. As you watch this segment, fill in the blanks with the missing verbs.

1. ¿No vamos a _____? ¿Qué es un cenote?

2. Ella nada y _____ al tenis y al golf.

3. Bueno, chicos, ya es hora, ¡_____!

4. Si _____, compramos el almuerzo.

3 **¿Qué ves?** Check what you see.

_____ 1. una pelota de fútbol   _____ 5. una bicicleta

_____ 2. un mensaje de correo electrónico   _____ 6. un restaurante

_____ 3. una mochila   _____ 7. una plaza

_____ 4. un videojuego   _____ 8. un cine

4 **Completar** Fill in the blanks in Column A with words from Column B.

A	B
1. Miguel dice que un cenote es una _____ natural.	montañas
2. Marissa dice que donde ella vive no hay _____.	pasatiempos
3. La tía Ana María tiene muchos _____ y actividades.	almorzar
4. La tía Ana María va al cine y a los _____.	museos
5. Eduardo y Pablo dicen que hay un partido de fútbol en el _____.	nadan
6. Don Guillermo dice que hay muchos _____ buenos en Mérida.	piscina
7. Felipe desea _____ mole.	restaurantes
8. Marissa y sus amigos _____ en el cenote.	parque

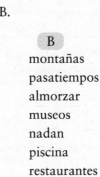

Lección 4 Fotonovela Video Activities   **7**

Video Manual: Fotonovela

Después de ver el video

5 **¿Qué hacen?** For numbers 1–11, fill in the missing letters in each word. For number 12, put the letters in the boxes in the right order.

1. Pablo dice que si no consigue más jugadores, su equipo va a ☐ __ __ d __ __.

2. Miguel dice que en México sólo hay __ __ n __ __ __ ☐ en la península de Yucatán.

3. Felipe dice que el restaurante del mole está en el __ __ __ ☐ __ o.

4. La tía Ana María sale mucho los __ __ n __ ☐ de semana.

5. Don Guillermo dice que hay un buen restaurante en la ☐ __ a __ __.

6. El mole de la tía Ana María es el __ __ v __ __ ☐ __ __ de Jimena.

7. Juan Carlos y Felipe van a __ __ __ __ ☐ r al fútbol con Eduardo y Pablo.

8. Felipe juega con la p ☐ __ __ __ __ después del partido.

9. Eduardo y Pablo van a pagar lo que Felipe y Juan Carlos van a ☐ __ m __ __ __ __ __.

10. Marissa no escala ☐ __ __ t __ __ __ __.

11. Los chicos hablan con don Guillermo después de jugar al __ __ __ b ☐ __.

12. La tía Ana María tiene muchos _____.

6 **Me gusta** Fill in the chart with the activities, hobbies, or sports that you enjoy. Also say when and where you do each activity.

Mis pasatiempos favoritos	¿Cuándo?	¿Dónde?

7 **Preguntas** Answer these questions in Spanish.

1. ¿Son aficionados/as a los deportes tus amigos/as? ¿Cuáles son sus deportes favoritos?

_____

_____

_____

2. ¿Qué hacen tú y tus amigos/as cuando tienen ratos libres?

_____

_____

_____

3. ¿Qué vas a hacer esta noche? ¿Vas a estudiar? ¿Descansar? ¿Mirar televisión? ¿Ver una película? ¿Por qué? _____

_____

_____

_____

¡Vamos a la playa!   Lección 5

Antes de ver el video

1 **¿Qué hacen?** The six friends have just arrived at the beach. Based on the image, what do you think Maru and Jimena are doing? What do you think they will do next?

_____

_____

_____

_____

_____

_____

_____

Mientras ves el video

2 **¿Quién?** Watch the episode and write the name of the person that goes with each expression.

Expresión	Nombre
1. En Yucatán hace mucho calor.	_____
2. ¿Están listos para su viaje a la playa?	_____
3. No podemos perder el autobús.	_____
4. Bienvenidas. ¿En qué puedo servirles?	_____
5. No está nada mal el hotel, ¿verdad? Limpio, cómodo.	_____

3 **¿Qué ves?** Check what is shown.

_____ 1. un inspector de aduanas   _____ 5. unas maletas   _____ 9. la planta baja del hotel

_____ 2. el mar   _____ 6. una pelota   _____ 10. unas llaves

_____ 3. un aeropuerto   _____ 7. una agencia de viajes   _____ 11. un libro

_____ 4. un botones   _____ 8. el campo   _____ 12. personas en la playa

4 **Completar** Fill in the blanks.

1. **TÍA ANA MARÍA**   Excelente, entonces… ¡A la _____!

2. **MARU**   Tenemos una _____ para seis personas para esta noche.

3. **EMPLEADO**   Dos _____ en el primer piso para seis huéspedes.

4. **MIGUEL**   Ellos son mis amigos. Ellos sí son _____ conmigo.

5. **MARISSA**   Yo estoy un poco _____. ¿Y tú? ¿Por qué no estás nadando?

Video Manual: *Fotonovela*

Después de ver el video

5 **¿Cierto o falso?** Say whether each statement is **cierto** or **falso**. Correct the false statements.

1. Miguel está enojado con Felipe.

_____

2. Felipe y Marissa hablan con un empleado del hotel.

_____

3. Los ascensores del hotel están a la izquierda.

_____

4. Maru y su novio quieren hacer windsurf, pero no tienen tablas.

_____

5. Felipe dice que el hotel es feo y desagradable.

_____

6. Jimena dice que estudiar en la playa es muy divertido.

_____

6 **Resumir** Write a summary of this episode in Spanish. Try not to leave out any important information.

_____

_____

_____

_____

_____

_____

_____

_____

7 **Preguntas** Answer these questions in Spanish.

1. ¿Te gusta ir de vacaciones? ¿Por qué? _____

_____

_____

2. ¿Adónde te gusta ir de vacaciones? ¿Por qué? _____

_____

_____

3. ¿Con quién(es) vas de vacaciones? _____

_____

_____

En el mercado

Lección 6

Antes de ver el video

1 **Describir** Look at the image and describe what you see, answering these questions: Where are Maru, Jimena, and Marissa? Who are they talking to? What is the purpose of their conversation?

_____

_____

_____

_____

_____

_____

Mientras ves el video

2 **Ordenar** Watch **En el mercado** and indicate the order in which you hear the following.

____ a. Acabamos de comprar tres bolsas por 480 pesos.

____ b. ¿Encontraron el restaurante?

____ c. Esta falda azul es muy elegante.

____ d. Le doy un muy buen precio.

____ e. Mira, son cuatro. Roja, amarilla, blanca, azul.

____ f. Acabo de ver una bolsa igual a ésta que cuesta 30 pesos menos.

3 **Mérida** Check each thing you see.

____ 1. una tarjeta de crédito

____ 2. una blusa

____ 3. un mercado

____ 4. un impermeable

____ 5. unos aretes

____ 6. un vendedor

4 **¿Quién lo dijo?** Indicate whether Marissa, Miguel, or don Guillermo said each sentence.

_____ 1. Quiero comprarle un regalo a Maru.

_____ 2. ¿Me das aquella blusa rosada? Me parece que hace juego con esta falda.

_____ 3. ¿Puedo ver ésos, por favor?

_____ 4. Hasta más tarde. Y ¡buena suerte!

_____ 5. Me contaron que los vendedores son muy simpáticos.

Lección 6 Fotonovela Video Activities **11**

Después de ver el video

5   **Completar** Complete the following sentences with words from the box.

azul	hermana	novia
camisetas	mercado	regatear
en efectivo	negro	vender

1. Juan Carlos, Felipe y Miguel creen que las chicas no saben _____.

2. Los seis amigos van de compras a un _____.

3. Marissa dice que el color _____ está de moda.

4. Miguel quiere comprarle un regalo a su _____ Maru.

5. Las _____ de Juan Carlos y Felipe costaron 200 pesos.

6. Las chicas pagan 480 pesos _____ por las bolsas.

6   **Corregir** All these statements are false. Rewrite them so they are true.

1. Jimena dice que la ropa del mercado es muy fea.

_____

2. Marissa usa la talla 6.

_____

3. Maru compró una blusa.

_____

4. Miguel compró un abrigo para Maru.

_____

7   **Preguntas** Answer these questions in Spanish.

1. ¿Te gusta ir de compras? ¿Por qué? _____

_____

2. ¿Adónde vas de compras? ¿Por qué? _____

_____

3. ¿Con quién(es) vas de compras? ¿Por qué? _____

_____

4. Imagina que estás en un centro comercial y que tienes mil dólares. ¿Qué vas a comprar? ¿Por qué?

_____

_____

5. Cuando compras un auto, ¿regateas con el/la vendedor(a)? _____

_____

¡Necesito arreglarme!   Lección 7

Antes de ver el video

1 **En el baño** In this episode, Marissa, Felipe, and Jimena want to get ready at the same time. What do you think they might say?

_____

_____

_____

_____

_____

_____

_____

Mientras ves el video

2 **¿Marissa o Felipe?** Watch **¡Necesito arreglarme!** and put a check mark in a column to show whether the plans are Marissa's or Felipe's.

Actividad	Marissa	Felipe
1. ir al cine	_____	_____
2. afeitarse	_____	_____
3. ir al café a molestar a su amigo	_____	_____
4. arreglarse el pelo	_____	_____
5. ir al café con Juan Carlos	_____	_____

3 **Ordenar** Number the following events from one to six, in the order they occurred.

____ a. Jimena termina de maquillarse.   ____ d. Las chicas comparten el espejo.

____ b. Todos quieren usar el espejo al mismo tiempo.   ____ e. Marissa busca una toalla.

____ c. Marissa quiere entrar al baño y la puerta está cerrada.   ____ f. Felipe entra al baño.

4 **Completar** Fill in the blanks.

1. **FELIPE** Cada vez que quiero usar el _____, una de ustedes está aquí.

2. **JIMENA** Me estoy _____ la cara.

3. **MARISSA** ¡_____ debe estudiar los viernes!

4. **JIMENA** ¿Por qué no te _____ por la mañana?

5. **FELIPE** Siempre hay _____ en vivo.

Lección 7 Fotonovela Video Activities   **13**

Después de ver el video

5 **Preguntas** Answer these questions in Spanish.

1. ¿Qué está haciendo Jimena cuando Marissa quiere entrar al baño?

_____

2. ¿Por qué Jimena quiere maquillarse primero?

_____

3. ¿Por qué se quiere afeitar Felipe?

_____

4. ¿Cómo es el café adonde van a ir Felipe y Juan Carlos?

_____

5. ¿Por qué Marissa quiere arreglarse?

_____

6. ¿Cuándo fue la última vez que Jimena vio a Juan Carlos?

_____

_____

6 **Preguntas personales** Answer these questions in Spanish.

1. ¿A qué hora te levantas durante la semana? ¿Y los fines de semana?

_____

_____

2. ¿Te gusta más bañarte o ducharte? ¿Por qué?

_____

_____

3. ¿Cuántas veces por día (*How many times a day*) te cepillas los dientes?

_____

_____

4. ¿Te lavas el pelo todos los días (*every day*)? ¿Por qué?

_____

_____

5. ¿Cómo cambia tu rutina los días que vas a la universidad y los días que sales con tus amigos?

_____

_____

7 **Escribir** Describe in Spanish what happened, from the point of view of Jimena, Marissa, or Felipe.

_____

_____

_____

_____

_____

_____

Video Manual: Fotonovela

Una cena... romántica **Lección 8**

Antes de ver el video

1 **En un restaurante** What do you do and say when you have dinner at a restaurant?

_____

_____

_____

_____

_____

_____

_____

_____

Mientras ves el video

2 **¿Quién?** Watch **Una cena... romántica** and write the name of the person who says each sentence.

Oración	Nombre
1. La ensalada viene con aceite y vinagre.	_____
2. Vino blanco para mí.	_____
3. Mejor pido la ensalada de pera con queso.	_____
4. Los espárragos están sabrosísimos esta noche.	_____
5. Señor, él es más responsable que yo.	_____

3 **Ordenar** Show the order in which the following took place.

_____ a. Felipe les pone pimienta a los platillos.

_____ b. Miguel pide una cerveza.

_____ c. El camarero recomienda la sopa de frijoles.

_____ d. El gerente llega a la mesa de Maru y Miguel.

4 **Completar** Fill in the missing words.

1. **MARU**   No sé qué pedir. ¿Qué me _____?

2. **CAMARERO**   ¿Ya decidieron qué quieren de _____?

3. **MARU**   Tienes razón, Felipe. Los espárragos están _____.

4. **FELIPE**   ¿Quién _____ jamón?

5. **JUAN CARLOS**   ¿Aquí vienen _____ mexicanos _____ extranjeros?

Después de ver el video

5 **Opiniones** Say who expressed the following opinions, either verbally or through body language.

_____ 1. Los mariscos parecen tan ricos como el jamón.

_____ 2. Este joven me está molestando con sus preguntas.

_____ 3. Los champiñones están deliciosos.

_____ 4. Felipe tiene la culpa (*is guilty*) de lo que pasó.

_____ 5. Vamos a la cocina para que paguen lo que hicieron.

6 **Corregir** Correct these statements.

1. Miguel le dice a Maru que la langosta se ve muy buena.

_____

2. De beber, Maru y Miguel piden té.

_____

3. El plato principal es ceviche de camarones con cilantro y limón.

_____

4. Maru pide el jamón con arvejas.

_____

5. Felipe dice que los champiñones saben a vinagre.

_____

6. Felipe dice que es el mejor camarero del mundo.

_____

7 **Preguntas personales** Answer these questions in Spanish.

1. ¿Almuerzas en la cafetería de tu universidad? ¿Por qué? _____

_____

2. ¿Cuál es tu plato favorito? ¿Por qué? _____

_____

3. ¿Cuál es el mejor restaurante de tu comunidad? Explica (*Explain*) tu opinión. _____

_____

4. ¿Cuál es tu restaurante favorito? ¿Cuál es la especialidad de ese restaurante? _____

_____

5. ¿Sales mucho a cenar con tus amigos/as? ¿Adónde van a cenar? _____

_____

El Día de Muertos   Lección 9

Antes de ver el video

1 **La celebración** In this episode, the Díaz family celebrates the Day of the Dead. What kinds of things do you expect to see?

_____

_____

_____

_____

_____

_____

Mientras ves el video

2 **Ordenar** Put the following events in order.

_____ a. La tía Ana María le dice a Marissa cómo se enamoraron sus papás.

_____ b. El señor Díaz brinda por los abuelos de la familia.

_____ c. Marissa prueba el mole que prepara la tía Ana María.

_____ d. Maite Fuentes habla del Día de Muertos en la televisión.

_____ e. Jimena pregunta dónde puso las galletas y el pastel.

3 **¿Qué ves?** Place a check mark beside each thing you see.

_____ 1. una botella de vino   _____ 5. calaveras de azúcar   _____ 9. un regalo de Navidad

_____ 2. una foto de boda   _____ 6. una quinceañera   _____ 10. helados

_____ 3. una graduación   _____ 7. galletas   _____ 11. un altar

_____ 4. flores   _____ 8. bolsas   _____ 12. un flan

4 **¿Quién lo dijo?** Write a name next to each sentence to indicate who says it.

_____ 1. Su familia es muy interesante.

_____ 2. El Día de Muertos se celebra en México el primero y el dos de noviembre.

_____ 3. ¡Estoy seguro que se lo van a pasar bien!

_____ 4. Al principio, mi abuela no quiso aceptar el matrimonio.

Después de ver el video

Video Manual: *Fotonovela*

5   **Corregir**   Rewrite these sentences to reflect what took place.

1. El Día de Muertos se celebra con flores, calaveras de azúcar, música y champán.

   _____

2. El mole siempre fue el plato favorito de la mamá de la tía Ana María.

   _____

3. Jimena intentó preparar mole para la fiesta de aniversario de sus tíos.

   _____

4. La tía Ana María se casó con un ingeniero que trabaja muchísimo.

   _____

5. Felipe y su papá prepararon pastel de chocolate para la familia.

   _____

6. A Valentina le gusta el helado.

   _____

6   **Eventos importantes**   Describe in Spanish the three most important events in this episode, and explain your choices.

   _____

   _____

   _____

   _____

   _____

   _____

   _____

7   **Preguntas personales**   Answer these questions in Spanish.

1. ¿Qué días de fiesta celebras con tu familia? _____

   _____

2. De los días de fiesta, ¿cuál es tu favorito? ¿Por qué? _____

   _____

3. ¿Qué haces el Día de Acción de Gracias? _____

   _____

4. ¿Cómo celebras tu cumpleaños? ¿Te gusta recibir regalos? _____

   _____

¡Qué dolor!   Lección 10

Antes de ver el video

1 **Una cita** Look at the image. Where do you think Jimena is? What is happening?

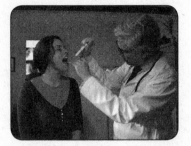

_____

_____

_____

_____

_____

_____

_____

_____

Mientras ves el video

2 **¿Quién?** Watch **¡Qué dolor!** and use check marks to show who said what.

Expresión	Jimena	Elena	Dr. Meléndez
1. ¿Cuáles son tus síntomas?	_____	_____	_____
2. Tengo un dolor de cabeza terrible.	_____	_____	_____
3. Empecé a toser esta mañana.	_____	_____	_____
4. Te voy a mandar algo para la garganta.	_____	_____	_____
5. ¡Es tan sólo un resfriado!	_____	_____	_____

3 **¿Qué ves?** Place a check mark beside the things you see in the video.

____ 1. un letrero (*sign*) que dice: "Se prohíbe fumar" ____ 6. una sala de emergencias

____ 2. un termómetro ____ 7. una receta

____ 3. pastillas para el resfriado ____ 8. un antibiótico

____ 4. una radiografía ____ 9. un doctor

____ 5. un consultorio ____ 10. una bolsa de la farmacia

4 **Completar** Write the name of the person who said each sentence and fill in the missing words.

_____ 1. A mi hermanito le dolía la _____ con frecuencia.

_____ 2. ¿Cuánto tiempo hace que tienes estos _____?

_____ 3. Tengo _____ y estoy congestionada.

_____ 4. Nunca tenía resfriados, pero me _____ el brazo dos veces.

_____ 5. No tienes _____. ¿Te pusiste un suéter anoche?

Lección 10 Fotonovela Video Activities   **19**

Video Manual: Fotonovela

Después de ver el video

5 **Seleccionar** Write the letter of the word or words that match each sentence.

1. ____ hizo cita con el Dr. Meléndez para llevar a Jimena.

   a. Don Diego   b. La señora Díaz   c. Elena   d. Miguel

2. Jimena puede ir inmediatamente a la ____ por los medicamentos.

   a. sala de emergencias   b. clínica   c. dentista   d. farmacia

3. Elena toma ____ para ____.

   a. aspirina; el dolor de cabeza   b. antibióticos; la gripe   c. pastillas; el resfriado

   d. medicamentos; el dolor de estómago

4. Elena dice que el té de jengibre es bueno para el dolor de ____.

   a. estómago   b. garganta   c. cabeza   d. brazos

5. La señora Díaz dice que a Jimena le dio ____ porque olvidó ponerse un suéter.

   a. fiebre   b. un resfriado   c. dolor de estómago   d. gripe

6. Cuando era niña, Jimena casi no ____.

   a. tomaba antibióticos   b. tomaba aspirinas   c. se rompía huesos   d. se enfermaba

6 **Preguntas** Answer the following questions in Spanish.

1. ¿Tiene fiebre Jimena? ¿Está mareada?

   _____

2. ¿Cuánto tiempo hace que a Jimena le duele la garganta? ¿Cuándo empezó a toser?

   _____

3. Según (*According to*) don Diego, ¿qué es lo mejor para los dolores de cabeza?

   _____

4. ¿Cuantas veces se rompió el brazo Elena?

   _____

5. ¿Qué le daban al hermanito de don Diego cuando le dolía la garganta?

   _____

7 **Preguntas personales** Answer these questions in Spanish.

1. ¿Te gusta ir al/a la médico/a? ¿Por qué? _____

   _____

2. ¿Tienes muchas alergias? ¿Eres alérgico/a a algún medicamento? _____

   _____

3. ¿Cuándo es importante ir a la sala de emergencias? _____

   _____

4. ¿Qué haces cuando tienes fiebre y te duele la garganta? _____

   _____

Video Manual: Fotonovela

En el taller

Antes de ver el video

1 **¿Qué pasa?** In this image, where do you think Miguel is? What do you think he is doing, and why?

_____

_____

_____

_____

_____

_____

Mientras ves el video

2 **¿Qué oíste?** Watch **En el taller** and place a check mark beside what you hear.

____ 1. ¿Cuál es tu dirección electrónica?

____ 2. ¿Está descompuesta tu computadora?

____ 3. ¿Y revisaste el aceite?

____ 4. El navegador GPS también está descompuesto.

____ 5. Mal día para la tecnología, ¿no?

____ 6. ¡Te están llamando!

____ 7. Se me acabó la pila.

____ 8. Me gusta mucho la televisión por cable.

____ 9. ¿Me pasas la llave?

____ 10. No manejes con el cofre abierto.

3 **¿Qué viste?** Place a check mark beside what you see.

____ 1. un teléfono celular

____ 2. una llave

____ 3. el cofre de un coche

____ 4. un reproductor de CD

____ 5. un mecánico

____ 6. la pantalla de un televisor

____ 7. una arroba

____ 8. una cámara de video

____ 9. un taller mecánico

____ 10. un archivo

4 **¿Quién dice?** Write the name of the person who said each sentence.

_____ 1. ¿Quién es el mecánico?

_____ 2. Está descargando el programa antivirus ahora.

_____ 3. Acaba de enviarme un mensaje de texto.

_____ 4. Este coche tiene más de 150.000 kilómetros.

_____ 5. Por favor, ¡arréglalo!

Después de ver el video

5 **Corregir** Rewrite these statements so they are true.

1. Miguel le llevó su coche a Felipe, el mecánico.

_____

2. La computadora de Maru funciona muy bien.

_____

3. Jorge no tiene problemas para arreglar el coche de Miguel.

_____

4. Se le acabó la pila al teléfono celular de Miguel.

_____

5. Maru necesita una cámara digital nueva y Miguel necesita un reproductor de MP3 nuevo.

_____

6. Jorge le dice a Miguel que revise el aceite cada mil kilómetros.

_____

6 **Un mensaje** Imagine that Maru is writing a short message to a friend about today's events. Write in Spanish what you think she would say.

_____

_____

_____

_____

_____

_____

7 **Preguntas personales** Answer these questions in Spanish.

1. Cuando tu carro está descompuesto, ¿lo llevas a un(a) mecánico/a o lo arreglas tú mismo/a?
¿Por qué? _____

_____

2. ¿Conoces a un(a) buen(a) mecánico/a? ¿Cómo se llama? _____

_____

3. ¿Tienes un teléfono celular? ¿Para qué lo usas? _____

_____

Video Manual: *Fotonovela*

Los quehaceres

Lección 12

Antes de ver el video

1 **En la casa** In this episode, Jimena and Felipe need to clean the house if they want to travel with Marissa to the Yucatan Peninsula. Look at the image and describe what you think is going on.

_____

_____

_____

_____

_____

_____

Mientras ves el video

2 **¿Cierto o falso?** Watch **Los quehaceres** and indicate whether each statement is **cierto** or **falso**.

	Cierto	Falso
1. A Jimena le gusta sacar la basura.	O	O
2. Felipe y Jimena deben limpiar la casa porque sus papás les pagaron el viaje.	O	O
3. Marissa sabe cómo cambiar la bolsa de la aspiradora.	O	O
4. Las servilletas estaban sobre la lavadora.	O	O
5. Hay quesadillas para cenar.	O	O

3 **¿Qué cosas ves?** Place a check mark beside what you see.

____ 1. un lavaplatos   ____ 4. vasos   ____ 7. platos

____ 2. un garaje   ____ 5. un sofá   ____ 8. un sótano

____ 3. un jardín   ____ 6. un autobús   ____ 9. tenedores

4 **Ordenar** Number the events from one to five, in the order they occur.

____ a. Don Diego les sugiere a las chicas que se organicen en equipos para limpiar.

____ b. Juan Carlos pone la mesa.

____ c. Marissa quiere quitar la bolsa de la aspiradora.

____ d. La señora Díaz entra a la cocina y saluda a sus hijos.

____ e. Jimena le dice a Felipe que limpie el baño.

Lección 12 Fotonovela Video Activities **23**

Video Manual: *Fotonovela*

Después de ver el video

5 **Seleccionar** Write the letter of the words that go in each sentence.

1. La señora Díaz les pide a sus hijos que quiten _____ de la mesa.

   a. los vasos   b. las tazas   c. los platos

2. La señora Díaz les _____ a sus hijos que limpien _____ si quieren viajar.

   a. ruega; el patio   b. sugiere; el apartamento   c. recomienda; el altillo

3. Jimena va a limpiar _____ y _____.

   a. el refrigerador; la estufa   b. el armario; la pared   c. el sillón; la lámpara

4. Don Diego le aconseja a Felipe que quite el polvo del _____.

   a. sótano   b. garaje   c. estante

5. Juan Carlos no sabe dónde están _____.

   a. las copas   b. los vasos   c. los tenedores

6 **Preguntas** Answer the following questions in Spanish.

1. Según el señor Díaz, ¿para qué hora deben preparar la cena Jimena y Felipe?

   _____

   _____

2. ¿Qué les piden sus padres a Marissa y a sus hermanos?

   _____

   _____

3. ¿Quiénes se sientan en el sofá para ver el partido de fútbol?

   _____

   _____

4. ¿Quién cambia la bolsa de la aspiradora?

   _____

   _____

5. ¿Qué dice la señora Díaz cuando ve el apartamento limpio?

   _____

   _____

7 **Escribir** Imagine that you are one of the characters. Write a paragraph from that person's point of view, summarizing what happened in the episode.

_____

_____

_____

_____

_____

_____

_____

Video Manual: *Fotonovela*

Aventuras en la naturaleza **Lección 13**

Antes de ver el video

1 **En Tulum** Marissa and Jimena visit a turtle sanctuary while Felipe and Juan Carlos take a tour through the jungle. What do you think the four friends will talk about when they are back together?

_____
_____
_____
_____
_____
_____
_____

Mientras ves el video

2 **Opiniones** Watch **Aventuras en la naturaleza** and place a check mark beside each opinion that is expressed.

____ 1. Necesitamos aprobar leyes para proteger a las tortugas.

____ 2. A menos que protejamos a los animales, muchos van a estar en peligro de extinción.

____ 3. No es posible hacer mucho para proteger el medio ambiente.

____ 4. Hoy estamos en Tulum, ¡y el paisaje es espectacular!

____ 5. El mar está muy contaminado.

3 **La aventura en la selva** As you watch Felipe and Juan Carlos' flashback about their adventure in the jungle, place a check mark beside what you see.

____ 1. un volcán   ____ 4. un desierto

____ 2. unos árboles   ____ 5. un teléfono celular

____ 3. unas plantas   ____ 6. una cámara

4 **¿Quién lo dijo?** Say who makes each statement, and fill in the blanks.

_____ 1. Espero que Felipe y Juan Carlos no estén perdidos en la _____...

_____ 2. No lo van a _____.

_____ 3. Estábamos muy emocionados porque íbamos a aprender sobre los

_____.

_____ 4. Por favor, síganme y eviten pisar las _____.

_____ 5. Decidí seguir un _____ que estaba cerca.

Lección 13 Fotonovela Video Activities   **25**

Después de ver el video

5 **¿Cierto o falso?** Indicate whether each sentence is **cierto** or **falso**. If an item is false, rewrite it so it is correct.

1. Marissa dice que el paisaje de Tulum es espectacular.

_____

2. A Jimena le gustaría viajar a Wisconsin para visitar a Marissa.

_____

3. Según la guía, hay compañías que cuidaron la selva.

_____

4. Felipe y Juan Carlos estaban muy aburridos porque iban a conocer la selva.

_____

5. Marissa y Jimena aprendieron las normas que existen para cazar tortugas.

_____

6 **Preguntas** Answer the following questions in Spanish.

1. ¿Por qué cree Jimena que ése es el último viaje del año que todos hacen juntos?

_____

2. ¿Por qué estaban emocionados Juan Carlos y Felipe antes de visitar la selva?

_____

_____

3. ¿Por qué se separaron del grupo Juan Carlos y Felipe?

_____

_____

4. ¿Marissa cree la historia de Felipe?

_____

_____

5. Según Jimena, ¿qué pasa ahora con la población de tortugas?

_____

_____

7 **Describir** List a few things that people can do to protect your community's environment.

_____

_____

_____

_____

_____

_____

Video Manual: *Fotonovela*

Nombre _____

Nombre _____   Fecha _____

Corriendo por la ciudad   **Lección 14**

Antes de ver el video

 En la calle In this episode, Maru needs to deliver a package but she experiences some problems. What do you think they might be?

_____
_____
_____
_____
_____
_____
_____

Mientras ves el video

 Ordenar Watch **Corriendo por la ciudad** and number the following events from one to five, in the order they occurred.

____ a. Maru le dice a Mónica que hay una joyería en el centro.

____ b. Mónica dice que el correo está cerca.

____ c. Maru busca el coche de Miguel.

____ d. Maru habla por teléfono con su mamá.

____ e. Maru cree que perdió el paquete.

3 **Completar** Fill in the blanks in the following sentences.

1. Voy a pasar al _____ porque necesito dinero.

2. ¿Puedes _____ por correo?

3. Estoy haciendo _____ y me gasté casi todo el efectivo.

4. Mi coche está en el _____ de la calle Constitución.

5. En esta esquina _____ a la derecha.

4 **¿Quién lo dijo?** Write the names of the people who said the following sentences.

_____ 1. Dobla a la avenida Hidalgo. Luego cruza la calle Independencia y dobla a la derecha.

_____ 2. Lo siento, tengo que ir a entregar un paquete.

_____ 3. Necesito ir a una joyería, pero la que está aquí al lado está cerrada.

_____ 4. Tengo que llegar al Museo de Antropología antes de que lo cierren.

_____ 5. Hay demasiado tráfico.

Después de ver el video

5 **Seleccionar** Write the letter of the word or words that complete each sentence.

1. Maru le dice a Miguel que está enfrente ____.

    a. del salón de belleza   b. de la panadería   c. de la joyería

2. Maru decide irse en taxi al ____.

    a. banco   b. correo   c. museo

3. Maru le ____ a Mónica porque no tiene efectivo.

    a. paga a plazos   b. pide dinero prestado   c. paga al contado

4. Mónica gastó el efectivo en la carnicería, la frutería y ____.

    a. al supermercado   b. el salón de belleza   c. la panadería

5. ____ de Maru estaba en el coche de Miguel.

    a. El paquete   b. El efectivo   c. La bolsa

6. Mónica ____ a la izquierda en el semáforo.

    a. hizo cola   b. dobló   c. cruzó

6 **Escribir** Write a summary of today's events from Maru's point of view.

_____

_____

_____

_____

_____

_____

_____

7 **Las diligencias** Write a paragraph describing some of the errands you ran last week. What did they involve, and what places in your community did you visit?

_____

_____

_____

_____

_____

_____

_____

_____

Chichén Itzá   Lección 15

Antes de ver el video

1 **Una excursión** List what you would probably do and say during a trip to an archeological site.

_____

_____

_____

_____

_____

_____

_____

Mientras ves el video

2 **¿Quién?** As you watch this episode of the **Fotonovela**, indicate who said each sentence.

_____ 1. Chichén Itzá es impresionante.

_____ 2. Nuestros papás nos trajeron cuando éramos niños.

_____ 3. Hay que estar en buena forma para recorrer las ruinas.

_____ 4. Pues, a mí me gustan las gorditas.

_____ 5. Qué lástima que no dejen subir hasta la cima.

3 **Completar** Fill in the blanks in these sentences.

1. _____ bajo mucha presión.

2. La universidad hace que seamos _____.

3. ¿Y Juan Carlos todavía no te _____ a salir?

4. Ofrecemos varios servicios para _____.

5. Su _____ es muy importante para nosotros.

4 **Ordenar** Number the events from one to four, putting them in order.

_____ a. Felipe y Juan Carlos corren.

_____ b. Marissa y Felipe toman fotos del lugar.

_____ c. Jimena y Juan Carlos se toman de las manos.

_____ d. Una empleada explica a los chicos qué ofrecen en el spa.

Video Manual: *Fotonovela*

Después de ver el video

5 **¿Cierto o falso?** Indicate whether each sentence is **cierto** or **falso**. If an item is false, rewrite it so that it is true.

1. Felipe quería regresar al D.F. desde que leyó el *Chilam Balam*.

   _____

2. Marissa lee en la guía que El Castillo fue construido entre el año 1000 y el 1200 d. C. y es una de las nuevas siete maravillas del mundo.

   _____

3. Según Felipe, algunos dicen que los mayas inventaron la gimnasia.

   _____

4. Jimena dice que se ha relajado mucho en la universidad últimamente.

   _____

5. Jimena ya había estudiado mucho antes de salir del D.F.

   _____

6 **Preguntas personales** Answer the following questions in Spanish.

1. ¿Haces ejercicio todos los días? ¿Por qué? _____

   _____

2. ¿Sacas muchas fotos cuando estás de vacaciones? ¿Por qué? _____

   _____

3. ¿Te gusta ir a un spa para aliviar la tensión? Explica por qué. _____

   _____

4. ¿Has visitado una zona arqueológica tan impresionante como la que visitaron Marissa, Felipe, Jimena y Juan Carlos? ¿Dónde? _____

   _____

5. ¿Quieres hacer una excursión como la que hicieron los cuatro estudiantes? Explica tu respuesta.

   _____

   _____

7 **Describir** Write a description of what you do or would like to do to reduce stress in your life.

_____

_____

_____

_____

_____

_____

Video Manual: Fotonovela

La entrevista de trabajo   **Lección 16**

Antes de ver el video

1   **Planes para el futuro**   Marissa, Jimena, Felipe, and Juan Carlos discuss their future plans in this episode. What do you think they will say?

_____

_____

_____

_____

_____

_____

_____

Mientras ves el video

2   **Planes y profesiones**   Watch **La entrevista de trabajo**. Then indicate who makes each statement, and fill in the blanks with the missing words.

_____ 1. Cuando yo termine la carrera, a ti ya te habrán despedido de tu

segundo _____.

_____ 2. Con el título de administrador de empresas seré _____.

_____ 3. Estoy muy feliz de poder ayudarte con _____.

_____ 4. Quiero trabajar en un museo y ser un _____ famoso.

_____ 5. Él será un excelente _____.

3   **Las profesiones**   Place a check mark beside the professions mentioned.

____ 1. arqueóloga   ____ 4. hombre de negocios

____ 2. política   ____ 5. reportero

____ 3. doctora   ____ 6. pintor

4   **Ordenar**   Number the following events from one to five, in the order they occur.

____ a. Marissa dice que no sabe cómo será su vida cuando tenga 30 años.

____ b. Miguel le da su currículum a la señora Díaz.

____ c. La señora Díaz dice que Miguel es un pintor talentoso y un excelente profesor.

____ d. Juan Carlos dice que estudia ciencias ambientales.

____ e. Marissa dice que Felipe será un excelente hombre de negocios.

Video Manual: *Fotonovela*

Después de ver el video

5 **Preguntas** Answer the following questions in Spanish.

1. ¿Quiénes van a crear una compañía de asesores de negocios?

_____

2. ¿Qué será Jimena en el futuro?

_____

3. ¿Quién trabaja en el Palacio de Bellas Artes desde hace cinco años?

_____

4. ¿Quién quiere seguir estudiando historia del arte?

_____

5. ¿Quién fue aceptada en el Museo de Antropología?

_____

_____

6 **En tu opinión** Answer the following questions in Spanish.

1. En tu opinión, ¿cuál de los personajes (*characters*) va a tener la profesión más interesante?
Explica tu respuesta. _____

_____

2. ¿Cuál de los personajes será el/la más rico/a? Explica tu opinión. _____

_____

3. ¿Cuál de los personajes será el/la más famoso/a? Explica tu opinión. _____

_____

4. ¿Cuál de los personajes será el/la más feliz? _____

_____

5. ¿Cuáles de los personajes van a lograr sus metas (*achieve their goals*)? Explica tu opinión.

_____

_____

7 **Tus planes** Write a description of what your life will be like in five years. Don't forget to mention your family, friends, residence, hobbies, and occupation.

_____

_____

_____

_____

_____

_____

_____

32 **Lección 16 Fotonovela** Video Activities

Una sorpresa para Maru

Lección 17

Antes de ver el video

1 **En el museo** In this episode, Maru y Miguel go to the museum. Based on the title and the image, what do you think will happen?

_____
_____
_____
_____
_____
_____
_____
_____

Mientras ves el video

2 **Ordenar** Watch **Una sorpresa para Maru** and number the following events from one to six, in the order they occurred.

_____ a. Juan Carlos dice que sus películas favoritas son las de ciencia ficción y de terror.

_____ b. Miguel le pide a Maru que se pare en una sala del museo.

_____ c. La gente aplaude a Maru y a Miguel.

_____ d. Jimena dice que su mamá va a la ópera con amigos del trabajo.

_____ e. Jimena dice que disfrutó mucho del espectáculo.

_____ f. Felipe dice que está de acuerdo con la relación de Jimena y Juan Carlos.

3 **La cultura en México** Place a check mark beside what you see.

_____ 1. escultoras _____ 5. un concierto

_____ 2. un cuento _____ 6. un instrumento musical

_____ 3. fotos _____ 7. artesanías en cerámica

_____ 4. un edificio blanco _____ 8. poetas

4 **Quién lo dijo** Indicate who made each statement, and fill in the blanks.

_____ 1. No he visto muchas representaciones de _____ contemporánea.

_____ 2. ¿Te gustan las películas _____?

_____ 3. El arte _____ nos cuenta la historia de su gente y su país.

_____ 4. Felipe intentó _____. ¡Qué horror!

_____ 5. Mi mamá hubiera querido que tocara algún _____.

Lección 17 Fotonovela Video Activities

Después de ver el video

5 **Seleccionar** Write the letter of the word or phrase that completes each sentence.

1. Jimena piensa ir con su mamá a la _____.

   a. obra   b. ópera   c. danza

2. A Maru le encanta ver las artesanías en cerámica y los _____.

   a. premios   b. cuentos   c. tejidos

3. A Jimena le gusta escuchar música en vivo e ir al _____.

   a. teatro   b. museo   c. programa de entrevistas

4. Juan Carlos puede ver las películas de _____ con Felipe.

   a. acción   b. aventuras   c. terror

5. A Jimena y a Juan Carlos les gustan los _____.

   a. dramas   b. documentales   c. escultores

6 **En tu opinión** Answer the following questions in Spanish.

1. ¿Crees que Maru y Miguel serán felices? Explica tu respuesta.

   _____

   _____

2. Juan Carlos y Jimena tienen intereses similares, pero ¿son compatibles? Explica tu opinión.

   _____

   _____

3. ¿Crees que Felipe y Marissa podrían ser novios algún día? ¿Por qué?

   _____

   _____

7 **En tu comunidad** Describe in Spanish a few cultural events in your community or area. You may invent them.

   _____

   _____

   _____

   _____

   _____

   _____

   _____

   _____

   _____

   _____

Video Manual: Fotonovela

Hasta pronto, Marissa

Lección 18

Antes de ver el video

1 **¿Qué pasa?** In this image, where do you think the friends are? What are they doing?

_____

_____

_____

_____

_____

_____

_____

Mientras ves el video

2 **Completar** As you watch **Hasta pronto, Marissa**, fill in the blanks.

1. Si _____ sabido que ellos no iban a estar aquí, me _____ despedido anoche.

2. Igualmente. Ella es Marissa. _____ el año con nosotros y hoy _____ a su casa, que es en los Estados Unidos.

3. Si te _____ la oportunidad de regresar a estudiar aquí, ¿_____?

4. Marissa, ¿cuál _____ tu experiencia _____ en México?

5. Marissa, espero que lo _____ pasado _____ en México.

6. Chichén Itzá fue muy _____ también. No puedo decidirme. ¡La he pasado de _____!

3 **¿Qué viste?** Place a check mark beside what you see.

____ 1. Marissa está triste por no poder despedirse de sus amigos.

____ 2. Don Diego conduce el carro de los Díaz.

____ 3. Marissa y el señor Díaz llegan a la fiesta sorpresa.

____ 4. Miguel dice que viajará a Bolivia.

____ 5. Marissa le da el diccionario a Felipe.

4 **Cosas y personas** Place a check mark beside what you see.

____ 1. una carta   ____ 3. una reportera   ____ 5. un soldado

____ 2. un choque   ____ 4. un periódico   ____ 6. una tormenta

Después de ver el video

5 **Preguntas** Answer these questions in Spanish.

1. Según la reportera, Maite Fuentes, ¿dónde tuvo lugar el terremoto? _____

_____

2. ¿Adónde quiere tomar unos cursos Marissa? _____

_____

3. Si Marissa tuviera que elegir una sola experiencia de las que vivió en México, ¿cuál elegiría?

_____

_____

4. Si le dieran la oportunidad, ¿Marissa volvería a estudiar en México?

_____

_____

5. ¿Qué le manda la tía Ana María a Marissa como regalo de despedida?

_____

_____

6 **Un artículo** Imagine that you are a reporter and you are going to interview Marissa about her experiences in Mexico. Write a brief article using what you saw in **Fotonovela**.

_____

_____

_____

_____

_____

_____

_____

_____

_____

7 **¿Qué va a pasar?** Marissa said goodbye to her friends and is returning to Wisconsin. What do you think the future holds for Marissa and her friends? Will Juan Carlos and Jimena continue dating? Will they get married? What will Miguel and Maru's wedding be like? Will the friends achieve their career goals?

_____

_____

_____

_____

_____

Panorama: Los Estados Unidos   Lección 1

Antes de ver el video

1 **Más vocabulario** Look over these useful words and expressions before you watch the video.

Vocabulario útil		
algunos *some, a few*	espectáculos *shows*	millón *million*
beisbolistas *baseball players*	estaciones *stations*	mucha *large*
comparsa *parade*	este *this*	muchos *many*
concursos *contests*	ligas mayores *major leagues*	por ciento *percent*
diseñador *designer*	más *more*	su *their*
disfraces *costumes*	mayoría *majority*	tiene *has*
escritora *writer*		

2 **Deportes** In this video, you are going to learn about some famous Dominican baseball players. In preparation, answer these questions about sports.

1. What sports are popular in the United States? _____

2. What is your favorite sport? _____

3. Do you play any sports? Which ones? _____

Mientras ves el video

3 **Cognados** Check off all the cognates you hear during the video.

___ 1. agosto   ___ 3. celebrar   ___ 5. democracia   ___ 7. festival   ___ 9. intuición

___ 2. carnaval   ___ 4. discotecas   ___ 6. famosos   ___ 8. independencia   ___ 10. populares

Después de ver el video

4 **Responder** Answer the questions in Spanish. Use complete sentences.

1. ¿Cuántos hispanos hay en Estados Unidos?

_____

2. ¿De dónde son la mayoría de los hispanos en Estados Unidos?

_____

3. ¿Quiénes son Pedro Martínez y Manny Ramírez?

_____

4. ¿Dónde hay muchas discotecas y estaciones de radio hispanas?

_____

5. ¿Qué son WADO y Latino Mix?

_____

6. ¿Es Julia Álvarez una escritora dominicana?

_____

Video Manual: Panorama cultural

Nombre _____ Fecha _____

Panorama: Canadá   Lección 1

Antes de ver el video

1 **Más vocabulario** Look over these useful words and expressions before you watch the video.

Vocabulario útil

|---|---|---|
bancos *banks*	hijas *daughters*	periódico *newspaper*
campo *field*	investigadora científica *research scientist*	que *that*
canal de televisión *TV station*	mantienen *maintain*	revista *magazine*
ciudad *city*	mayoría *majority*	seguridad *safety*
comunidad *community*	ofrecen *offer*	sus *her*
escuelas *schools*	otras *others*	trabajadores *workers*
estudia *studies*	pasa *spends*	vive *live*

2 **Responder** This video talks about the Hispanic community in Montreal. In preparation for watching the video, answer the following questions about your family's background.

1. Where were your parents born? And your grandparents? _____

2. If any of them came to the U.S. or Canada from another country, when and why did they come here? _____

3. Are you familiar with the culture of the country of your ancestors? What do you know about their culture? Do you follow any of their traditions? Which ones? _____

Mientras ves el video

3 **Marcar** Check off the nouns you hear while watching the video.

___ 1. apartamento   ___ 3. diario   ___ 5. horas   ___ 7. instituciones   ___ 9. lápiz

___ 2. comunidad   ___ 4. escuela   ___ 6. hoteles   ___ 8. laboratorio   ___ 10. el programa

Después de ver el video

4 **¿Cierto o falso?** Indicate whether these statements are **cierto** or **falso**. Correct the false statements.

1. La mayoría de los hispanos en Montreal son de Argentina. _____

2. En Montreal no hay canales de televisión en español. _____

3. En Montreal hay hispanos importantes. _____

4. Una hispana importante en el campo de la biología es Ana María Seifert. _____

5. Ella vive con sus dos hijas en una mansión en Montreal. _____

6. Ella pasa muchas horas en el museo. _____

7. En su casa mantienen muchas tradiciones argentinas. _____

8. Ella participa en convenciones nacionales e internacionales. _____

Video Manual: *Panorama cultural*

Lección 1 Panorama cultural Video Activities © 2016 by Vista Higher Learning, Inc. All rights reserved.

Panorama: España
Lección 2

Antes de ver el video

1 **Más vocabulario** Look over these useful words before you watch the video.

Vocabulario útil

antiguo *ancient*	**empezar** *to start*	**niños** *children*
blanco *white*	**encierro** *running of bulls*	**pañuelo** *neckerchief, bandana*
cabeza *head*	**esta** *this*	**peligroso** *dangerous*
calle *street*	**feria** *fair, festival*	**periódico** *newspaper*
cohete *rocket (firework)*	**fiesta** *party, festival*	**rojo** *red*
comparsa *parade*	**gente** *people*	**ropa** *clothing*
correr *to run*	**gigante** *giant*	**toro** *bull*
defenderse *to defend oneself*	**mitad** *half*	**ver** *to see*

2 **Festivales** In this video, you are going to learn about a Spanish festival. List the things you would probably do and see at a festival.

_____

_____

_____

_____

Mientras ves el video

3 **Ordenar** Number the items in the order in which they appear in the video.

_____ a. cohete   _____ c. gigante   _____ e. mitad hombre,

_____ b. cuatro mujeres en   _____ d. toros   mitad animal
       un balcón

Después de ver el video

4 **Fotos** Describe the video stills.

_____

_____

_____

_____

_____

Lección 2 Panorama cultural Video Activities **39**

Video Manual: *Panorama cultural*

_____
_____
_____
_____
_____

5   **Crucigrama** Complete these sentences and use the words to complete the crossword.

1. El Festival de San Fermín es la combinación de tres fiestas, una de ellas es las

     _____ comerciales.

2. Las _____ son los eventos favoritos de los niños.

3. La fiesta religiosa en honor a San Fermín, las ferias comerciales y los eventos taurinos son

     celebraciones _____.

4. Los Sanfermines es una de las _____ tradicionales españolas.

5. Las personas usan ropa blanca y _____ rojos.

6. En los encierros las personas corren delante de diecisiete _____.

7. En las comparsas hay figuras _____ hombre, mitad animal.

8. En los días del festival, hay ocho _____.

9. En las comparsas hay ocho _____.

10. Las comparsas pasan por las _____ de Pamplona.

11. Otras de las figuras tienen (*have*) enormes _____.

Panorama: Ecuador

Lección 3

Antes de ver el video

1   **Más vocabulario** Look over these useful words and expressions before you watch the video.

Vocabulario útil		
algunas *some*	otro *other*	todo *every*
científico *scientist*	pingüino *penguin*	tomar fotografías *to take pictures*
guía *guide*	recurso *resource*	tortuga *tortoise*

2   **Foto** Describe the video still. Write at least three sentences in Spanish.

_____
_____
_____
_____
_____
_____
_____

3   **Predecir** Look at the video still from the previous activity and write at least two sentences in Spanish about what you think you will see in this video.

_____
_____
_____

4   **Emparejar** Find the items in the second column that correspond to the ones in the first.

_____ 1. grande   a. near

_____ 2. pequeña   b. about

_____ 3. vieja   c. here

_____ 4. también   d. big

_____ 5. aquí   e. very

_____ 6. sobre   f. old

_____ 7. muy   g. also

_____ 8. cerca de   h. small

_____ 9. para   i. for

Video Manual: *Panorama cultural*

Lección 3 Panorama cultural Video Activities

Mientras ves el video

5 **Marcar** Check off the verbs you hear while watching the video.

_____ 1. aprender   _____ 5. escribir   _____ 9. tener

_____ 2. bailar   _____ 6. estudiar   _____ 10. tomar

_____ 3. beber   _____ 7. leer   _____ 11. vivir

_____ 4. comprar   _____ 8. recibir

Después de ver el video

6 **Responder** Answer the questions in Spanish. Use complete sentences.

1. ¿En qué océano están las islas Galápagos?

_____

_____

2. ¿Qué hacen los científicos que viven en las islas?

_____

_____

3. ¿Qué hacen los turistas que visitan las islas?

_____

_____

4. ¿Qué proyectos tiene la Fundación Charles Darwin?

_____

_____

5. ¿Cuáles son los animales más grandes que viven en las islas?

_____

_____

6. ¿Por qué son importantes estas islas?

_____

_____

7 **Preferencias** Of all the animals you saw in this video, which was your favorite? Write three sentences in Spanish describing your favorite animal.

_____

_____

_____

_____

Panorama: México
Lección 4

Antes de ver el video

1 **Más vocabulario** Look over these useful words before you watch the video.

Vocabulario útil			
día *day*	**estos** *these*	**gente** *people*	**sentir** *to feel*
energía *energy*	**fiesta** *party, celebration*	**para** *to*	**valle** *valley*

2 **Describir** In this video, you will learn about the archeological ruins of Teotihuacán where the celebration of the equinox takes place every year. Do you know what the equinox is? In English, try to write a description.

equinoccio: _____

_____

3 **Categorías** Categorize the words listed in the word bank.

arqueológicos	gente	increíble	mexicanos	Teotihuacán
capital mexicana	hacen	interesante	moderno	tienen
celebrar	hombres	jóvenes	mujeres	Valle de México
ciudad	importante	Latinoamérica	niños	van
escalar				

Lugares	Personas	Verbos	Adjetivos

Mientras ves el video

4 **Marcar** Check off the pastimes you see while watching the video.

_____ 1. pasear _____ 4. escalar (pirámides) _____ 7. visitar monumentos

_____ 2. nadar _____ 5. tomar el sol _____ 8. bucear

_____ 3. patinar _____ 6. ver películas

Lección 4 Panorama cultural Video Activities   **43**

Video Manual: *Panorama cultural*

Después de ver el video

5   **Completar** Fill in the blanks with the appropriate word(s).

la capital mexicana	muy interesante
la celebración del equinoccio	pasean
celebrar	sentir
comienzan	sol
manos	el Valle de México

1. Teotihuacán está a cincuenta kilómetros de _____.

2. A _____ van muchos grupos de música tradicional.

3. Todos quieren _____ la energía del sol en sus _____.

4. Ir a las pirámides de Teotihuacán es una experiencia _____.

5. Las personas _____ por las ruinas.

---

6   **¿Cierto o falso?** Indicate whether each statement is **cierto** or **falso**. Correct the false statements.

1. Las pirámides de Teotihuacán están lejos del Valle de México.

   _____

2. Muchas personas van a Teotihuacán todos los años para celebrar el equinoccio.

   _____

3. Turistas de muchas nacionalidades van a la celebración.

   _____

4. La gente prefiere ir a Teotihuacán los martes.

   _____

5. La celebración del equinoccio termina a las cinco de la mañana.

   _____

6. Las personas celebran la energía que reciben de Teotihuacán todos los años.

   _____

7   **Foto** Describe the video still. Write at least three sentences in Spanish.

_____

_____

_____

_____

_____

Panorama: Puerto Rico

Lección 5

Antes de ver el video

1 **Más vocabulario** Look over these useful words before you watch the video.

Vocabulario útil		
angosto *narrow*	calle *street*	plaza *square*
antiguo *old*	escultura *sculpture*	promocionar *to promote*
artesanías *handicrafts*	exposición *exhibition*	sitio *site*
bahía *bay*	fuente *fountain*	vender *to sell*
barrio *neighborhood*		

2 **Preferencias** This video describes the attractions that San Juan, the capital of Puerto Rico, has to offer. In Spanish, list at least three things that you like to do when you visit a new city.

_____

_____

_____

_____

_____

_____

_____

Mientras ves el video

3 **Cognados** Check off all the cognates you hear during the video.

_____ 1. aeropuerto

_____ 2. área

_____ 3. arte

_____ 4. artístico

_____ 5. cafés

_____ 6. calma

_____ 7. capital

_____ 8. construcciones

_____ 9. estrés

_____ 10. histórico

_____ 11. información

_____ 12. nacional

_____ 13. permanente

_____ 14. presidente

_____ 15. restaurantes

Video Manual: *Panorama cultural*

Después de ver el video

4 **Corregir** All of these statements are false. Rewrite them to correct the false information.

1. El Viejo San Juan es el barrio más moderno de la capital.

_____

2. El Morro es el centro artístico y cultural de Puerto Rico.

_____

3. Muchos artistas locales compran sus creaciones en las calles.

_____

4. En diciembre se celebra la Fiesta de la Calle San Sebastián con conciertos, exposiciones especiales de arte y un carnaval.

_____

5. En el Museo de las Américas presentan exposiciones relacionadas con la historia de Norteamérica.

_____

6. Todos los días, más de un millón de visitantes llegan al Centro de Información de Turismo del Viejo San Juan.

_____

5 **Completar** Complete the sentences with words from the word bank.

> camina   coloniales   excelente   galerías   promociona
> capital   esculturas   exposición   hermoso

1. En la bahía de la _____ de Puerto Rico está el Castillo de San Felipe del Morro.

2. Muchas de las construcciones del Viejo San Juan son _____.

3. En la mayoría de los parques hay _____ inspiradas en la historia del país.

4. El Instituto de Cultura Puertorriqueña _____ eventos culturales en la isla.

5. Hay muchas _____ de arte y museos.

6. En el Museo de San Juan hay una _____ permanente de la historia de Puerto Rico.

6 **Preferencias** Of all the places in San Juan that were described, which one did you find most interesting? In Spanish, describe this place and indicate why you found it so interesting.

_____

_____

_____

_____

_____

Video Manual: *Panorama cultural*

Panorama: Cuba   Lección 6

Antes de ver el video

1 **Más vocabulario** Look over these useful words before you watch the video.

Vocabulario útil	
conversar *to talk*	relacionadas *related to*
imágenes *images (in this case, of a religious nature)*	relaciones *relationships*
miembro *member*	sacerdote *priest*

2 **Responder** In this video you are going to see people visiting **santeros** to talk about their problems and their futures. In preparation for watching the video, answer the following questions about your behavior and beliefs.

1. ¿Hablas con alguien (*someone*) cuando tienes problemas? ¿Con quién?

_____

_____

_____

2. En tu opinión, ¿algunas personas pueden "ver" el futuro?

_____

_____

_____

Mientras ves el video

3 **Marcar** Check off the activities you see while watching the video.

_____ 1. hombre escribiendo

_____ 2. hombre leyendo

_____ 3. mujer corriendo

_____ 4. mujer llorando (*crying*)

_____ 5. niño jugando

_____ 6. personas bailando

_____ 7. personas caminando

_____ 8. personas cantando

_____ 9. personas conversando

Video Manual: *Panorama cultural*

Después de ver el video

4 **Responder** Answer the questions in Spanish using complete sentences.

1. ¿Qué es la santería?

_____

2. ¿Quiénes son los santeros?

_____

3. ¿Qué venden en las tiendas de santería?

_____

4. ¿Para qué visitan las personas a los santeros?

_____

5. ¿Quiénes son los sacerdotes?

_____

6. ¿Qué hacen los sacerdotes cuando van a las casas de las personas?

_____

5 **¿Cierto o falso?** Indicate whether each statement is **cierto** or **falso**. Correct the false statements.

1. Cada tres horas sale un barco de La Habana con destino a Regla.

_____

2. Regla es una ciudad donde se practica la santería.

_____

3. La santería es una práctica religiosa muy común en algunos países latinoamericanos.

_____

4. Los santeros no son personas importantes en su comunidad.

_____

5. La santería es una de las tradiciones cubanas más viejas.

_____

6 **Conversación** In this video, you see a **santero** talking with a woman. In Spanish, write a short conversation. Include what the woman would ask the **santero** and how he would respond to her problems.

_____

_____

_____

_____

Video Manual: *Panorama cultural*

Panorama: Perú   **Lección 7**

Antes de ver el video

1 **Más vocabulario** Look over these useful words and expressions before you watch the video.

Vocabulario útil		
canoa *canoe*	**exuberante naturaleza**	**ruta** *route, path*
dunas *sand dunes*	*lush countryside*	**tabla** *board*

2 **Preferencias** In this video you are going to learn about unusual sports. In preparation for watching the video, answer these questions about your interest in sports.

1. ¿Qué deportes practicas?

_____

2. ¿Dónde los practicas?

_____

3. ¿Qué deportes te gusta ver en televisión?

_____

Mientras ves el video

3 **Fotos** Describe the video stills. Write at least three sentences in Spanish for each still.

_____

_____

_____

_____

_____

_____

_____

_____

_____

_____

Lección 7 Panorama cultural Video Activities   **49**

Después de ver el video

4 **¿Cierto o falso?** Indicate whether each statement is **cierto** or **falso**. Correct the false statements.

1. Pachacamac es el destino favorito para los que pasean en bicicletas de montaña.

_____

2. El *sandboard* es un deporte antiguo en Perú.

_____

3. El *sandboard* se practica en Ocucaje porque en este lugar hay muchos parques.

_____

4. El Camino Inca termina en Machu Picchu.

_____

5. El Camino Inca se puede completar en dos horas.

_____

6. La pesca en pequeñas canoas es un deporte tradicional.

_____

5 **Completar** Complete the sentences with words from the word bank.

aventura	kilómetros	pesca
excursión	llamas	restaurante
exuberante	parque	tradicional

1. En Perú se practican muchos deportes de _____.

2. Pachacamac está a 31 _____ de Lima.

3. La naturaleza en Santa Cruz es muy _____.

4. En Perú, uno de los deportes más antiguos es la _____ en pequeñas canoas.

5. Caminar con _____ es uno de los deportes tradicionales en Perú.

6. Santa Cruz es un sitio ideal para ir de _____.

6 **Escribir** Imagine that you just completed the **Camino Inca**. In Spanish, write a short letter to a friend telling him or her about the things you did and saw.

_____

_____

_____

_____

_____

_____

_____

_____

Panorama: Guatemala   Lección 8

Antes de ver el video

1 **Más vocabulario** Look over these useful words and expressions before you watch the video.

Vocabulario útil		
alfombra *carpet*	destruir *to destroy*	ruinas *ruins*
artículos *items*	época colonial *colonial times*	sobrevivir *to survive*
calle *street*	indígenas *indigenous people*	terremoto *earthquake*

2 **Describir** In this video you are going to learn about an open-air market that takes place in Guatemala. In Spanish, describe one open-air market that you have been to or that you know about.

mercado: _____

_____

_____

_____

_____

3 **Categorías** Categorize the words listed in the word bank.

bonitas	espectaculares	indígenas	quieres
calles	grandes	mercado	región
colonial	habitantes	monasterios	sentir
conocer	iglesias	mujeres	vieja

Lugares	Personas	Verbos	Adjetivos

Lección 8 Panorama cultural Video Activities | **51**

Video Manual: Panorama cultural

Mientras ves el video

4   **Marcar**   Check off what you see while watching the video.

_____ 1. fuente (*fountain*)   _____ 6. niñas sonriendo

_____ 2. hombres con vestidos morados   _____ 7. niño dibujando

_____ 3. mujer bailando   _____ 8. personas hablando

_____ 4. mujer llevando bebé en el mercado   _____ 9. ruinas

_____ 5. mujeres haciendo alfombras de flores   _____ 10. turista mirando el paisaje

Después de ver el video

5   **Completar**   Complete the sentences with words from the word bank.

aire libre	alfombras	atmósfera	fijo	indígenas	regatear

1. En Semana Santa las mujeres hacen _____ con miles de flores.

2. En Chichicastenango hay un mercado al _____ los jueves y domingos.

3. En el mercado los artículos no tienen un precio _____.

4. Los clientes tienen que _____ cuando hacen sus compras.

5. En las calles de Antigua, los turistas pueden sentir la _____ del pasado.

6. Muchos _____ de toda la región van al mercado a vender sus productos.

6   **¿Cierto o falso?**   Indicate whether each statement is **cierto** or **falso**. Correct the false statements.

1. Antigua fue la capital de Guatemala hasta 1773.

_____

2. Una de las celebraciones más importantes de Antigua es la de la Semana Santa.

_____

3. En esta celebración, muchas personas se visten con ropa de color verde.

_____

4. Antigua es una ciudad completamente moderna.

_____

5. Chichicastenango es una ciudad mucho más grande que Antigua.

_____

6. El terremoto de 1773 destruyó todas las iglesias y monasterios en Antigua.

_____

7   **Comparar**   Write four sentences comparing the cities Antigua and Chichicastenango.

_____

_____

_____

_____

Panorama: Chile   Lección 9

Antes de ver el video

1 **Más vocabulario** Look over these useful words and expressions before you watch the video.

Vocabulario útil	
disfrutar (de) *to take advantage (of)*	isla *island*
grados *degrees*	recursos naturales *natural resources*
hace miles de años *thousands of years ago*	repartidas *spread throughout, distributed*
indígena *indigenous*	vista *view*

2 **Escribir** This video talks about Chile's Easter Island. In preparation for watching the video, answer the following questions.

1. ¿Has estado (*Have you been*) en una isla o conoces alguna? ¿Cómo se llama?

_____

2. ¿Dónde está? ¿Cómo es?

_____

Mientras ves el video

3 **Fotos** Describe the video stills. Write at least three sentences in Spanish for each still.

_____

_____

_____

_____

_____

_____

_____

_____

Video Manual: *Panorama cultural*

Lección 9 Panorama cultural Video Activities

Después de ver el video

4 **Completar** Complete the sentences with words from the word bank.

atracción	indígena
característico	llega
diferente	recursos
difícil	remoto
escalan	repartidas

1. *Rapa Nui* es el nombre de la isla de Pascua en la lengua _____ de la región.

2. Esta isla está en un lugar _____.

3. Los habitantes de esta isla no tenían muchos _____ naturales.

4. En un día de verano la temperatura _____ a los noventa grados.

5. Las esculturas *moái* son el elemento más _____ de esta isla.

6. Hay más de novecientas esculturas _____ por toda la isla.

7. Otra gran _____ de la isla es el gran cráter Rano Kau.

8. Los visitantes _____ el cráter para disfrutar de la espectacular vista.

5 **Preferencias** In Spanish, list at least two things you like about this video and explain your choices.

_____

_____

_____

_____

_____

_____

_____

_____

_____

_____

_____

_____

Video Manual: Panorama cultural

Panorama: Costa Rica

Lección 10

Antes de ver el video

 Más vocabulario Look over these useful words and expressions before you watch the video.

Vocabulario útil		
bosque *forest*	guía certificado *certified guide*	riqueza *wealth*
conservar *to preserve*	nuboso *cloudy*	tiendas de campaña *camping tents*
cubierto *covered*	permitir *to allow*	tocar *to touch*
entrar *to enter*	regla *rule*	tortugas marinas *sea turtles*

 Foto Describe the video still. Write at least three sentences in Spanish.

_____
_____
_____
_____
_____
_____
_____
_____

3 **Categorías** Categorize the words listed in the word bank.

bosque	guía	pedir	sacar
diferentes	hermosos	permite	Tortuguero
entrar	Monteverde	playa	turistas
exóticas	nuboso	pueblos	visitantes
frágil			

Lugares	Personas	Verbos	Adjetivos

Lección 10 Panorama cultural Video Activities

Mientras ves el video

4

Marcar While watching the video, check off the rules that have been put in place to protect nature.

_____ 1. En el parque Monteverde no pueden entrar más de 150 personas al mismo tiempo.

_____ 2. Los turistas tienen que dormir en tiendas de campaña.

_____ 3. Los turistas no pueden visitar Tortuguero en febrero.

_____ 4. Después de las 6 p.m. no se permite ir a la playa sin un guía certificado.

_____ 5. Los turistas no pueden tocar las tortugas.

_____ 6. En Tortuguero está prohibido tomar fotografías.

Después de ver el video

5

Completar Complete the sentences with words from the word bank.

acampan	entrar	pasan	prohíbe
conservan	estudiar	prefieren	transportan

1. En Monteverde se _____ más de dos mil especies diferentes de animales.

2. En este parque no pueden _____ más de 150 personas al mismo tiempo.

3. Algunos turistas _____ en Monteverde.

4. Otros _____ ir a los hoteles de los pueblos que están cerca de Monteverde.

5. Se _____ sacar fotografías.

6

Preferencias Write a brief paragraph in Spanish where you describe which place(s) you would like to visit in Costa Rica and why.

_____

_____

_____

_____

_____

_____

_____

_____

_____

_____

_____

Video Manual: *Panorama cultural*

Panorama: Argentina

Lección 11

Antes de ver el video

1 **Más vocabulario** Look over these useful words and expressions before you watch the video.

Vocabulario útil		
actualmente *nowadays*	gaucho *cowboy*	pintura *paint*
barrio *neighborhood*	género *genre*	salón de baile *ballroom*
cantante *singer*	homenaje *tribute*	suelo *floor*
exponer *to exhibit*	pareja *partner*	surgir *to emerge*
extrañar *to miss*	paso *step*	tocar *to play*

2 **Completar** The previous vocabulary will be used in this video. In preparation for watching the video, complete the sentences using words from the vocabulary list. Conjugate the verbs as necessary. Some words will not be used.

1. Los artistas _____ sus pinturas en las calles.

2. Beyoncé es una _____ famosa.

3. El tango tiene _____ muy complicados.

4. El jazz es un _____ musical que se originó en los Estados Unidos.

5. El tango _____ en Buenos Aires, Argentina.

6. La gente va a los _____ a bailar y divertirse.

7. Las personas _____ mucho su país cuando tienen que vivir en el extranjero.

Mientras ves el video

3 **Marcar** Check off the cognates you hear while watching the video.

_____ 1. adultos   _____ 7. dramático

_____ 2. aniversario   _____ 8. exclusivamente

_____ 3. arquitectura   _____ 9. famosos

_____ 4. artistas   _____ 10. gráfica

_____ 5. demostración   _____ 11. impacto

_____ 6. conferencia   _____ 12. musical

Lección 11 Panorama cultural Video Activities   **57**

Video Manual: *Panorama cultural*

Nombre _____   Fecha _____

Después de ver el video

4 **¿Cierto o falso?** Indicate whether each statement is **cierto** or **falso**. Correct the false statements.

1. Guillermo Alio dibuja en el suelo una gráfica para enseñar a cantar.

_____

2. El tango es música, danza, poesía y pintura.

_____

3. Alio es un artista que baila y canta al mismo tiempo.

_____

4. Alio y su pareja se ponen pintura verde en los zapatos.

_____

5. Ahora los tangos son historias de hombres que sufren por amor.

_____

6. El tango tiene un tono dramático y nostálgico.

_____

5 **Completar** Complete the sentences with words from the word bank.

| actualmente | compositor | fiesta | género | homenaje | pintor | surgió | toca |

1. El tango es un _____ musical que se originó en Argentina en 1880.
2. El tango _____ en el barrio La Boca.
3. _____ este barrio se considera un museo al aire libre.
4. En la calle Caminito se _____ y se baila el tango.
5. Carlos Gardel fue el _____ de varios de los tangos más famosos.
6. En el aniversario de su muerte, sus aficionados le hacen un _____.

6 **Responder** Answer the questions in Spanish. Use complete sentences.

1. ¿Por qué crees que el tango es tan famoso en todo el mundo? _____

_____

2. ¿Te gustaría (*Would you like*) aprender a bailar tango? ¿Por qué? _____

_____

3. ¿Qué tipo de música te gusta? Explica tu respuesta. _____

_____

Video Manual: Panorama cultural

58   **Lección 11 Panorama cultural** Video Activities   © 2016 by Vista Higher Learning, Inc. All rights reserved.

Panorama: Panamá

Lección 12

Antes de ver el video

1 **Más vocabulario** Look over these useful words before you watch the video.

Vocabulario útil

anualmente *annually*	impresionante *incredible*	según *according to*
arrecife *reef*	lado *side*	sitio *site*
disfrutar *to enjoy*	peces *fish*	torneo *tournament*
especies *species*	precioso *beautiful*	

2 **Responder** This video talks about the best places to dive and surf in Panama. In preparation for watching this video, answer these questions about surfing.

1. ¿Te gusta el *surf*? ¿Por qué?

_____

_____

_____

2. ¿Practicas este deporte? ¿Conoces a alguien que lo practique? ¿Dónde lo practica(s)?

_____

_____

_____

Mientras ves el video

3 **Ordenar** Number the items in the order in which they appear in the video.

a. _____

b. _____

c. _____

Lección 12 Panorama cultural Video Activities

Después de ver el video

4 **Emparejar** Find the items in the second column that correspond to the ones in the first.

1. La isla Contadora es la más grande _____
2. Allí siempre hace calor, _____
3. En Panamá, los visitantes pueden bucear en el océano Pacífico por la mañana _____
4. Las islas de San Blas son 365, _____
5. En Santa Catarina los deportistas disfrutan de _____

a. por la noche.
b. del archipiélago.
c. la playa blanca y el agua color turquesa.
d. por eso se puede bucear en todas las estaciones.
e. una para cada día del año.
f. y en el mar Caribe por la tarde.

5 **Responder** Answer the questions in Spanish. Use complete sentences.

1. ¿Qué país centroamericano tiene archipiélagos en el océano Pacífico y en el mar Caribe?

_____
_____

2. ¿Por qué Las Perlas es un buen lugar para bucear?

_____
_____

3. ¿Cómo llegan los turistas a la isla Contadora?

_____
_____

4. ¿Cómo se llaman los indígenas que viven en las islas San Blas?

_____
_____

5. ¿Adónde van los mejores deportistas de *surfing* del mundo?

_____
_____

6 **Pasatiempos** Complete this chart in Spanish.

Mis deportes/ pasatiempos favoritos	Por qué me gustan	Dónde/cuándo los practico

Nombre _____ Fecha _____

Antes de ver el video

1 **Más vocabulario** Look over these useful words and expressions before you watch the video.

Vocabulario útil	
alrededores *surrounding area*	delfín *dolphin*
belleza natural *natural beauty*	desfile *parade*
campesinos *country/rural people*	disfrutar (de) *to enjoy*
carroza *float*	feria *fair; festival*
cordillera *mountain range*	fiesta *festival*
costas *coasts*	orquídea *orchid*

Mientras ves el video

2 **Preguntas** Answer the questions about these video stills. Use complete sentences.

¿Cómo se llama esta celebración?

1. _____

   _____

   _____

¿Dónde vive este animal?

2. _____

   _____

   _____

Lección 13 Panorama cultural Video Activities

61

Video Manual: *Panorama cultural*

Después de ver el video

3 **Emparejar** Find the items in the second column that correspond to the ones in the first.

_____ 1. El grano colombiano que se exporta mucho.   a. el café

_____ 2. el Carnaval de Barranquilla   b. Río Amazonas

_____ 3. En Colombia crecen muchas.   c. un desfile de carrozas decoradas

_____ 4. Aquí vive el delfín rosado.   d. orquídeas

_____ 5. desfile de los silleteros   e. Feria de las Flores

_____ 6. Aquí vive el cóndor.   f. Nevado del Huila

4 **Completar** Complete the sentences with words from the list.

Amazonas	carrozas	el cóndor	flor
campesinos	celebra	encuentra	reserva

1. En el Parque de Orquídeas hay más de tres mil especies de esta _____.

2. En los alrededores del Parque Nevado del Huila vive _____.

3. El río _____ está al sur de Colombia.

4. El Parque Amaracayu es una _____ natural.

5. Los _____ participan en el desfile de los silleteros.

6. El domingo de carnaval se hace un desfile con _____ decoradas.

5 **Responder** Answer these questions in Spanish. Use complete sentences.

1. ¿Qué es lo primero que piensas cuando oyes la palabra "carnaval"?

_____

_____

_____

2. ¿Cuál crees que es el carnaval más famoso del mundo? ¿Por qué?

_____

_____

_____

3. ¿Cuál es el carnaval más famoso de tu país? ¿Cómo se celebra?

_____

_____

_____

Video Manual: *Panorama cultural*

Panorama: Venezuela   Lección 14

Antes de ver el video

1 **Más vocabulario** Look over these useful words before you watch the video.

Vocabulario útil		
castillo *castle*	fuerte *fort*	plana *flat*
catarata *waterfall*	maravilla *wonder*	según *according to*
cima *top*	medir *to measure*	teleférico *cable railway*

2 **Preferencias** In this video you are going to learn about two of the most famous tourist attractions in Venezuela: its mountains and beaches. In preparation for watching the video, complete these sentences.

1. Me gusta/No me gusta ir a la playa porque _____

_____

_____

2. Me gusta/No me gusta ir de excursión a las montañas porque _____

_____

_____

Mientras ves el video

3 **Marcar** Check off the cognates you hear while watching the video.

_____ 1. animales

_____ 2. arquitectura

_____ 3. construcción

_____ 4. diversa

_____ 5. famoso

_____ 6. geológicas

_____ 7. horizontales

_____ 8. marina

_____ 9. mitología

_____ 10. naturales

_____ 11. plantas

_____ 12. verticales

Lección 14 Panorama cultural Video Activities   **63**

Video Manual: *Panorama cultural*

Después de ver el video

4 **¿Cierto o falso?** Indicate whether each statement is **cierto** or **falso**. Correct the false statements.

1. El Fortín Solano es la capital comercial de la isla Margarita.

_____

2. "Tepuyes" es el nombre que los indígenas piaroas le dan a las montañas.

_____

3. Se cree que en el Parque Nacional Canaima hay muchas especies de plantas y animales que nunca han sido clasificadas.

_____

4. El Salto Ángel es la catarata más alta del mundo.

_____

5. Según la mitología de los piaroas, el tepuy Autana representa la muerte.

_____

6. La isla Margarita es conocida como la Perla del Amazonas.

_____

5 **Completar** Complete the sentences with words from the word bank. Some words will not be used.

clase	islas	metros	río	verticales
fuertes	marina	planas	teleférico	

1. En Venezuela hay castillos y _____ que sirvieron para proteger al país hace muchos años.

2. En Venezuela hay más de 311 _____.

3. La isla Margarita tiene una fauna _____ muy diversa.

4. Los hoteles de isla Margarita son de primera _____.

5. El Parque Nacional Canaima tiene 38 grandes montañas de paredes _____ y cimas _____.

6. Venezuela también tiene el _____ más largo del mundo.

6 **Escribir** In Spanish, list the three things you found most interesting in this video and explain your choices. Use complete sentences.

_____

_____

_____

_____

_____

_____

Panorama: Bolivia   **Lección 15**

Antes de ver el video

 Más vocabulario Look over these useful words before you watch the video.

Vocabulario útil	
alimento *food*	**salar** *salt flat*
enorme *enormous*	**tratamiento** *treatment*
particular *unique*	

2 **Foto** Describe the video still. Write at least three sentences in Spanish.

_____
_____
_____
_____
_____
_____
_____
_____

3 **Predecir** Based on the still in the previous activity, what do you think this video episode is going to be about?

_____
_____
_____

Mientras ves el video

4 **Marcar** Check off the cognates you hear while watching the video.

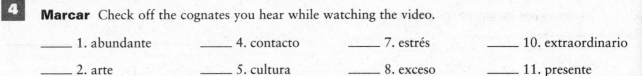

_____ 1. abundante	_____ 4. contacto	_____ 7. estrés	_____ 10. extraordinario
_____ 2. arte	_____ 5. cultura	_____ 8. exceso	_____ 11. presente
_____ 3. color	_____ 6. diversa	_____ 9. exótico	_____ 12. región

Lección 15 Panorama cultural Video Activities   **65**

Video Manual: *Panorama cultural*

Después de ver el video

5   **Palabra correcta** The underlined elements in these statements are incorrect. Write the correct word in the space provided.

1. El salar de Uyuni está al <u>norte</u> de Bolivia.

   La palabra correcta es: _____

2. La sal, sin exceso, es <u>mala</u> para las personas que sufren de enfermedades de los huesos.

   La palabra correcta es: _____

3. Los hoteles de esta región se hicieron con cuidado porque el contacto en exceso con la sal es <u>excelente</u> para la salud.

   La palabra correcta es: _____

4. Estos hoteles ofrecen a los huéspedes masajes y otros tratamientos para aliviar el <u>acné</u>.

   La palabra correcta es: _____

5. La sal se usa en Uyuni para <u>dañar</u> los alimentos.

   La palabra correcta es: _____

6. El salar de Uyuni parece un gran <u>parque</u> de color blanco.

   La palabra correcta es: _____

6   **Preferencias** Would you like to stay in a hotel where everything is made out of salt? In Spanish, give two reasons why you think you would like to stay in such a place and two more why you would not. Explain your reasons.

Razones por las que me gustaría:

_____

_____

_____

_____

_____

Razones por las que no me gustaría:

_____

_____

_____

_____

_____

_____

Video Manual: *Panorama cultural*

Panorama: Nicaragua   Lección 16

Antes de ver el video

1 **Más vocabulario** Look over these useful words and expressions before you watch the video.

Vocabulario útil		
artesanías *handicrafts, craft work*	dioses *gods*	ofrendas *offerings*
atractivos *attractions*	laguna *lagoon*	venado *deer*
burlarse de *to make fun of*	obras artesanales *handicrafts*	venerar *to worship*

2 **Categorías** Categorize the words listed in the word bank.

artesanales	creían	famosa	pueblo	significan
autoridades	deriva	habitantes	reciente	tradicionales
bailan	enojados	laguna	región	venden
capital	extensas	políticos		

Lugares	Personas	Verbos	Adjetivos

Mientras ves el video

3 **Marcar** Check off the verbs you hear while watching the video.

_____ 1. bailan   _____ 5. correr   _____ 9. jugar

_____ 2. burlan   _____ 6. creían   _____ 10. venden

_____ 3. calmar   _____ 7. deriva   _____ 11. veneraban

_____ 4. comer   _____ 8. estudiar   _____ 12. ver

Después de ver el video

4   **Emparejar** Find the items in the second column that correspond to the ones in the first.

_____ 1. erupciones del Volcán Masaya en los últimos 500 años   a. una celebración

_____ 2. Los indígenas les daban esto a los dioses para calmar   b. ofrendas

      al volcán.   c. El volcán hacía erupción.

_____ 3. *mazalt* y *yan*   d. nombre *Masaya* en lengua indígena

_____ 4. Pasaba cuando los dioses estaban enojados.   e. diecinueve

_____ 5. el Torovenado

---

5   **Respuestas** Answer the questions in Spanish. Use complete sentences.

1. ¿Cómo se llama el pueblo donde está situada la laguna de Masaya? _____

_____

2. ¿De dónde se deriva el nombre *Masaya*? _____

_____

3. ¿Cuál es la fiesta más importante que se celebra en Masaya? _____

_____

4. ¿De quiénes se burlan los habitantes en estas fiestas? _____

_____

5. ¿Por qué se le conoce a Masaya como la capital del folclor nicaragüense? _____

_____

6. ¿Qué venden en el mercado, además de frutas y verduras? _____

_____

6   **Escribir** Write a short summary of this video in Spanish.

_____

_____

_____

_____

_____

_____

_____

_____

_____

_____

Video Manual: *Panorama cultural*

Panorama: República Dominicana Lección 16

Antes de ver el video

1 **Más vocabulario** Look over these useful words and expressions before you watch the video.

Vocabulario útil	
crear *to create, to form*	papel *role*
emigrantes *emigrants*	ritmos *rhythms*
fiestas nacionales *national festivals*	tocar (música) *to play (music)*

2 **Preguntas** This video talks about two musical genres famous in the Dominican Republic. In preparation for watching the video, answer these questions.

1. ¿Cuál es el género (*genre*) musical estadounidense con más fama internacional? _____

_____

2. ¿Te gusta esta música? ¿Por qué? _____

_____

Mientras ves el video

3 **Marcar** Check off the activities and places you see in the video.

_____ 1. niños sonriendo   _____ 6. espectáculo de baile en teatro

_____ 2. mujer vendiendo ropa   _____ 7. bandera (*flag*) de la República Dominicana

_____ 3. parejas bailando   _____ 8. mujer peinándose

_____ 4. hombre tocando acordeón   _____ 9. bulevar (*boulevard*)

_____ 5. niño jugando al fútbol   _____ 10. playa

Después de ver el video

4 **Corregir** The underlined elements in the sentences are incorrect. Write the correct words in the spaces provided.

1. Uno de los mejores ejemplos de la mezcla (*mix*) de culturas en la República Dominicana es la <u>arquitectura</u>.

La palabra correcta es: _____

2. El Festival del Merengue se celebra en las <u>plazas</u> de Santo Domingo todos los veranos.

La palabra correcta es: _____

3. La música de la República Dominicana está influenciada por la música tradicional de <u>Asia</u>.

La palabra correcta es: _____

Lección 16 Panorama cultural Video Activities | **69**

Video Manual: Panorama cultural

4. En todo el país hay discotecas donde se toca y se baila la bachata y el <u>jazz</u>.

La palabra correcta es: _____

5. El veintisiete de febrero de cada año los dominicanos celebran el día de la <u>madre</u>.

La palabra correcta es: _____

6. La bachata y el merengue son ritmos <u>poco</u> populares en la República Dominicana.

La palabra correcta es: _____

---

5   **Emparejar** Find the items in the second column that correspond to the ones in the first.

_____ 1. Aquí la gente baila la bachata y el merengue.

_____ 2. Este músico recibió en 1966 la Medalla Presidencial.

_____ 3. *El Bachatón*

_____ 4. Juan Luis Guerra, Johnny Ventura y Wilfredo Vargas

_____ 5. La música dominicana recibió la influencia de estas personas.

a. Johnny Pacheco

b. varios de los muchos músicos de bachata y merengue con fama internacional

c. los indígenas que vivían en la región

d. las discotecas de la ciudad

e. En este programa de televisión sólo se toca la bachata.

---

6   **Seleccionar** Select the sentence that best summarizes what you saw in this video.

_____ 1. Por muchos años, muchos emigrantes llegaron a la República Dominicana y crearon la actual cultura dominicana.

_____ 2. Todas las estaciones de radio tocan bachata y hay un programa de televisión muy popular dedicado exclusivamente a esta música, llamado *El Bachatón*.

_____ 3. Los ritmos más populares de la República Dominicana, la bachata y el merengue, son producto de varias culturas y forman parte integral de la vida de los dominicanos.

_____ 4. Una fiesta tradicional dominicana es el Festival del Merengue, que se celebra todos los veranos desde 1966 por las calles de Santo Domingo.

---

7   **Responder** Answer the questions in Spanish. Use complete sentences.

1. ¿Cuál es tu música favorita? ¿Por qué? _____

_____

2. ¿Dónde escuchas esta música? ¿Cuándo? _____

_____

3. ¿Quiénes son los intérpretes más famosos de esta música? ¿Cuál de ellos te gusta más? _____

_____

4. ¿Te gusta bailar? ¿Qué tipo de música bailas? _____

_____

5. ¿Es la música algo importante en tu vida? ¿Por qué? _____

_____

Video Manual: Panorama cultural

Panorama: El Salvador   Lección 17

Antes de ver el video

1 **Más vocabulario** Look over these useful words before you watch the video.

Vocabulario útil	
alimento *food*	**grano** *grain*
fuente *source*	**salsa** *sauce*

2 **Categorías** Categorize the words listed in the word bank.

arepas	comerciales	restaurantes
buena	importante	tamales
catedrales	maíz	tradicionales
cebolla	mercados	usa
centrales	plazas	Valle de México
ciudades	postre	venden
comenzaron	queso	vivían

Lugares	Comida	Verbos	Adjetivos

Mientras ves el video

3 **Marcar** Check off the verbs you hear while watching the video.

_____ 1. bailar   _____ 5. describir   _____ 8. saber   _____ 11. vender

_____ 2. cocinar   _____ 6. hacer   _____ 9. servir   _____ 12. usar

_____ 3. comer   _____ 7. limpiar   _____ 10. tocar   _____ 13. vivir

_____ 4. decir

Video Manual: *Panorama cultural*

Lección 17 Panorama cultural Video Activities   **71**

Después de ver el video

4 **Completar** Complete the sentences with words from the word bank.

aceite	fuente	pupusas
arroz	maíz	sal
camarón	postre	símbolo

1. En El Salvador el _____ es el alimento principal de la dieta diaria.

2. Las pupusas se comen a veces como _____ acompañadas de frutas y chocolate.

3. En todos los lugares importantes de las ciudades y pueblos de El Salvador se venden

   _____ .

4. Para hacer las pupusas se usa maíz, agua, _____ y sal.

5. El maíz es una buena _____ de carbohidratos.

6. El maíz se ha usado como _____ religioso.

5 **Foto** Describe the video still. Write at least three sentences in Spanish.

_____

_____

_____

_____

6 **Escribir** Write about your favorite food and explain how to prepare it. Don't forget to include all the necessary ingredients.

_____

_____

_____

_____

_____

_____

_____

Video Manual: Panorama cultural

Panorama: Honduras   Lección 17

Antes de ver el video

1 **Más vocabulario** Look over these useful words and expressions before you watch the video.

Vocabulario útil	
astrónomo *astronomer*	obras de arte *works of art*
claro/a *clear*	quetzal *quetzal (a type of bird)*
dentro de *inside*	ruinas *ruins*
escala *scale*	serpiente *snake*
impresionante *amazing*	

2 **Predecir** Do you remember the video from **Lección 4**? It was about the pyramids of Teotihuacán. In this lesson you are going to hear about other pyramids, those in the city of Copán, Honduras. Write a paragraph about the things you think you will see in this video.

_____

_____

_____

_____

_____

_____

_____

Mientras ves el video

3 **Marcar** Check off the words you hear while watching the video.

_____ 1. azteca

_____ 2. bailes

_____ 3. cultura precolombina

_____ 4. grupos

_____ 5. maya

_____ 6. ochocientos

_____ 7. quetzal

_____ 8. Rosalila

_____ 9. Sol

_____ 10. Tegucigalpa

Video Manual: *Panorama cultural*

Después de ver el video

4   **Seleccionar**   Choose the option that best completes each sentence.

1. Una ciudad muy importante de la cultura _____ es Copán.
     a. olmeca   b. salvadoreña   c. azteca   d. maya

2. Desde mil novecientos _____ y cinco, científicos han trabajado en estas ruinas.
     a. cincuenta   b. setenta   c. sesenta   d. noventa

3. Los mayas fueron grandes artistas, _____, matemáticos, astrónomos y médicos.
     a. maestros   b. estudiantes   c. arquitectos   d. cantantes

4. Ricardo Agurcia descubrió un templo _____ una pirámide.
     a. afuera de   b. cerca de   c. dentro de   d. a un lado de

5. En Copán encontraron el texto más _____ que dejó la gran civilización maya.
     a. extenso   b. corto   c. interesante   d. divertido

6. En Copán está el Museo de _____ Maya.
     a. Arte   b. Pintura   c. Escultura   d. Texto

7. La puerta del museo tiene la forma de la boca de _____.
     a. una serpiente   b. un gato   c. un puma   d. un quetzal

8. En la sala principal se encuentra la réplica _____ Rosalila.
     a. de la pirámide   b. de la ciudad   c. del Templo   d. de la ruina

5   **Fotos**   Describe the video stills. Write at least three sentences in Spanish for each still.

_____
_____
_____
_____
_____

_____
_____
_____
_____
_____

6   **Escribir**   Imagine that you went to Copán; write a postcard to a friend about everything you saw there.

_____
_____
_____
_____
_____

Panorama: Paraguay   **Lección 18**

Antes de ver el video

1 **Más vocabulario** Look over these useful words and expressions before you watch the video.

Vocabulario útil		
alimento *food*	cultivar *to cultivate*	quemar *to burn*
amargo *bitter*	empresas *companies*	sagrada *sacred*
asegurar *to maintain*	fuente *source*	suplemento alimenticio
calabaza *pumpkin*	hervir *to boil*	*dietary supplement*
cortar *to cut*	hojas *leaves*	

2 **Preferencias** In this video you are going to learn about the importance of a coffee-like beverage in the Paraguayan diet. Do you like coffee? Is it popular in your country? Why? Is it good for your health? Write a paragraph in Spanish to answer these questions.

_____

_____

_____

_____

_____

_____

_____

_____

Mientras ves el video

3 **Ordenar** Number the sentences in the order in which they appear in the video.

_____ a. El mate es un alimento.

_____ b. Hay muchas técnicas para preparar el mate.

_____ c. Tomar mate era ilegal.

_____ d. El mate se toma a toda hora.

_____ e. La yerba mate crece en América del Sur.

_____ f. El mate tiene vitaminas, minerales y antioxidantes.

_____ g. El mate tiene un sabor amargo.

_____ h. Los indígenas guaraní creían que esta planta era un regalo de sus antepasados.

_____ i. El mate es típico de Paraguay, Argentina y Uruguay.

_____ j. El mate es usado por personas que quieren adelgazar.

Después de ver el video

4 **Fotos** Describe the video stills. Write at least three sentences in Spanish for each one.

_____
_____
_____
_____
_____
_____
_____
_____
_____
_____
_____
_____

5 **Responder** Answer the questions in Spanish.

1. ¿Qué es el mate? _____
_____

2. ¿Dónde es típico el mate? _____
_____

3. ¿Cómo usaban el mate los indígenas guaraní? _____
_____

4. ¿Cómo se usa el mate hoy en día? _____
_____

5. ¿Por qué durante la colonia era ilegal tomar mate? _____
_____

6. ¿Qué características tiene el mate? _____
_____

6 **Escribir** Write a short summary of this video in Spanish.

_____
_____
_____
_____
_____
_____

Video Manual: *Panorama cultural*

Panorama: Uruguay

Lección 18

Antes de ver el video

1 **Más vocabulario** Look over these useful words and expressions before you watch the video.

Vocabulario útil		
asado *barbecue*	campos *rural areas*	jineteadas *rodeo*
cabalgatas colectivas *caravans*	ganadería *ranching*	ranchos ganaderos *cattle ranches*
caballos *horses*	gauchos *cowboys*	siglos *centuries*

2 **Predecir** Based on the video stills, write what you think the video will be about.

_____

_____

_____

_____

Mientras ves el video

3 **Describir** Write a short description of the items.

1. Las estancias son _____

_____

2. Los gauchos son _____

_____

3. Las cabalgatas colectivas son _____

_____

4. Las jineteadas son _____

_____

Lección 18 Panorama cultural Video Activities

Video Manual: *Panorama cultural*

Después de ver el video

4 **Responder** Answer the questions in Spanish.

1. ¿Te gustaría quedarte por unos días en una estancia? ¿Por qué?

_____

2. ¿Por qué crees que a los turistas les gustan estos lugares? ¿Por qué son tan especiales?

_____

3. ¿Hay en tu país hoteles parecidos a las estancias? ¿Cómo son?

_____

5 **Imaginar** Imagine that you are a travel agent and that you need to create an itinerary for a client going to an **estancia**. Write the itinerary in the space below.

lunes	
martes	
miércoles	
jueves	
viernes	
sábado	
domingo	

6 **Escribir** Now imagine that you are a **gaucho**. What is your daily routine? Describe the activities you do every day.

En la mañana yo _____

_____

_____.

En la tarde yo _____

_____

_____.

En la noche yo _____

_____

_____.

Encuentros en la plaza

Lección 1

Antes de ver el video

1 **Vos** Most Argentinians use the pronoun **vos** instead of **tú** when talking to friends. In some cases, the verb in the **vos** form is different from the **tú** form; in others, it is the same. Look at these questions with **vos**. Can you guess what the **tú** equivalent is?

> **modelo**
> Vos: ¿Cómo te llamás?
> Tú: ¿Cómo te llamas?

1. Y vos, ¿cómo estás?

_____

2. ¿De dónde sos?

_____

2 **¡En español!** Look at the video still. Imagine a conversation between two of these people.

¡Hola! ¿Cómo te va? _____

_____

_____

_____

_____

_____

Mientras ves el video

3 **Completar** What does Silvina say when she meets her friends? Complete these conversations.

   A. (3:42–3:51)

     CHICO Hola.

     CHICA ¿(1)_____?

     CHICA Y CHICO ¡Cuánto tiempo! (*It's been so long!*)

     SILVINA Sí, hace mucho, ¿no?

     CHICA ¡Qué (2)_____ verte (*to see you*)!

     SILVINA ¿(3)_____ están ustedes? ¿Bien?

     CHICA Y CHICO (4)_____.

   B. (4:12–4:19)

     SILVINA Quiero (*I want*) presentarles a mi (5)_____ Gonzalo.

     CHICA Hola, ¿qué (6)_____?

     GONZALO Hola. Gonzalo. ¿Tú cómo te (7)_____?

     CHICA Mariana.

     GONZALO (8)_____, Mariana.

   Lección 1 Flash cultura Video Activities

Después de ver el video

4 **Ordenar** Pay attention to Silvina's actions and put them in the correct order.

_____ a. presenta una amiga a Mark

_____ b. dice (*she says*): ¿Como están ustedes? ¿Bien?

_____ c. da (*she gives*) un beso y un abrazo

_____ d. camina (*she walks*) por la Plaza de Mayo

_____ e. dice: ¡Hasta pronto!

5 **¿Quién?** Indicate who would make each of these statements.

Statements	Long-time friends at a plaza	People meeting for the first time
1. ¡Qué bueno verte!		
2. Sí, hace mucho, ¿no?		
3. Les presento a mi amigo.		
4. ¿Cómo estás?		
5. Mucho gusto.		

6 **¡Cuánto tiempo!** Write a conversation you would have with a friend whom you have not seen in a long time. Include the expressions provided.

¡Cuánto tiempo!	¡Qué bueno verte!
Hace mucho.	¿Qué tal?

_____

_____

_____

_____

_____

7 **Encuentros en la plaza** Describe two aspects of this episode that caught your attention: people, their physical proximity, activities they do, etc. Then, explain how those are similar or different in your own culture. You may use English.

_____

_____

_____

_____

_____

_____

Video Manual: *Flash cultura*

Los estudios

Lección 2

Antes de ver el video

1 **Más vocabulario** Look over these useful words before you watch the video.

Vocabulario útil	
las ciencias biológicas y de la salud *biological and health sciences*	el cuarto año de la carrera *the fourth year of college*
las ciencias físico-matemáticas *physical and mathematical sciences*	dé clases *teaches*
¿Conoces a algún ex alumno reconocido? *¿Do you know any renowned alumni?*	los estudios superiores *higher education* la psicoterapia *psychotherapy*

2 **¡En español!** Look at the video still and answer these questions in Spanish. Carlos is in Mexico City; can you guess what place? Who is Carlos talking to? What do you think this person does?

Carlos López, México, D.F.

_____

_____

_____

_____

_____

_____

Mientras ves el video

3 **Conversaciones** Complete these conversations between Carlos López and two students.

CARLOS LÓPEZ ¿(1)_____ te llamas?

ESTUDIANTE Héctor.

CARLOS LÓPEZ Héctor. ¿Y qué estudias?

ESTUDIANTE (2)_____.

CARLOS LÓPEZ ¿Y cuál es tu materia favorita?

ESTUDIANTE Este... ahorita, (3)_____ de Roma.

CARLOS LÓPEZ ¿De dónde (4)_____?

ESTUDIANTE De Corea.

CARLOS LÓPEZ De Corea. ¿Te gusta estudiar en la (5)_____?

ESTUDIANTE Sí, me gusta mucho.

CARLOS LÓPEZ ¿Qué estudias?

ESTUDIANTE Estoy estudiando (6)_____.

4 **Identificar** Indicate which area of study each of these students and alumni is likely to study or have studied.

| Ciencias Biológicas y de la Salud | Ciencias Sociales |
| Ciencias Físico-Matemáticas | Humanidades |

Octavio Paz
Escritor

1. _____ 2. _____ 3. _____

Después de ver el video

5 **Oraciones** Complete each statement with the correct option.

autobuses	estudio	profesor
derecho	ex alumno	residencia estudiantil
estudiantes	México, D.F.	universidad

1. _____ es un importante centro económico y cultural.

2. La UNAM es una _____ en la Ciudad de México.

3. La UNAM es como (*like*) una ciudad con _____, policía y gobierno (*government*) propios (*own*).

4. Los _____ de la UNAM son de diferentes países.

5. Hay cuatro áreas principales de _____.

6. Manuel Álvarez Bravo es un _____ famoso de la UNAM.

6 **¡Carlos López de visita (*on a visit*)!** Imagine that Carlos López visits your school and wants to find out about the institution, campus or facilities, classes, and students. Write a brief paragraph about what you would say.

> **modelo**
>
> ¡Hola, Carlos! Me llamo Rosa Estévez y estudio en la Universidad de Toronto.
> Hay muchos estudiantes de diferentes países. Este (*This*) semestre tomo clases...

_____

_____

_____

_____

_____

La familia   Lección 3

Antes de ver el video

1 **Más vocabulario** Look over these useful words before you watch the video.

<table>
<tr><td colspan="2" align="center">**Vocabulario útil**</td></tr>
<tr>
<td>el canelazo *typical drink from Ecuador*
la casa *house*
Día de la Madre *Mother's Day*
Ésta es la cocina. *This is the kitchen.*
Éste es un patio interior.
  This is an interior patio.</td>
<td>¡Qué familia tan grande tiene! *Your family is so big!*
¡Qué grande es tu casa…! *Your house is so big!*
¿Quién pelea con quién? *Who fights with whom?*
te muestro *I'll show you*
Vamos. *Let's go.*</td>
</tr>
</table>

2 **¡En español!** Look at the video still. Imagine what Mónica will say about families in Ecuador, and write a two- or three-sentence introduction to this episode.

Mónica, Quito

¡Hola, amigos! Bienvenidos a otra aventura de *Flash cultura*. Hoy

vamos (*we are going*) a hablar de… _____

_____

_____

_____

_____

_____

_____

Mientras ves el video

3 **Identificar** Identify which family these people belong to: **los Valdivieso**, **los Bolaños**, or both.

Personas	Los Valdivieso	Los Bolaños
1. abuelos	_____	_____
2. novia	_____	_____
3. esposo	_____	_____
4. esposa	_____	_____
5. sobrinos	_____	_____
6. dos hijos y una hija	_____	_____

4 **Emparejar** Watch as Mrs. Valdivieso gives Mónica a tour of the house. Match the captions to the appropriate images.

1. _____   2. _____   3. _____

a. Y éste es el comedor…
   Todos comemos aquí.

b. Vamos, te enseño el
   resto de la casa.

c. Éste es un patio interior.
   Aquí hacemos reuniones
   familiares.

d. Finalmente, ésta es
   la cocina.

e. ¿Qué están haciendo hoy
   en el parque?

Después de ver el video

5 **¿Cierto o falso?** Indicate whether each statement is **cierto** (*true*) or **falso** (*false*).

1. En el parque, una familia celebra el Día de la Madre. _____

2. La familia Valdivieso representa la familia moderna y la familia Bolaños representa la
   familia tradicional. _____

3. Los Bolaños no viven en Quito. _____

4. Bernardo tiene animales en su casa. _____

5. Los Valdivieso toman canelazo. _____

6 **¿Qué te gusta?** Imagine that you are one of the Valdivieso children and that Mónica asks you about your likes and dislikes. Select one of the children and write a paragraph using the cues provided.

| bailar | dibujar | hermanos | padres |

_____

_____

_____

_____

7 **Andy, un chico con novia** Andy's parents just found out that he has a girlfriend. Imagine that they are being introduced to her for the first time. Write five questions they would ask her.

_____

_____

_____

_____

¡Fútbol en España!   **Lección 4**

Antes de ver el video

1   **Más vocabulario**   Look over these useful words before you watch the video.

Vocabulario útil		
la afición *fans*	nunca *never*	seguro/a *sure*
más allá *beyond*	se junta (con) *is intertwined (with)*	la válvula de escape *outlet*

2   **¡En español!**   Look at the video still. Imagine what Mari Carmen will say about soccer in Spain, and write a two- or three-sentence introduction to this episode.

Mari Carmen Ortiz, Barcelona

¡Hola, amigos! ¡Bienvenidos a *Flash cultura*! Hoy vamos a

hablar de… _____

_____

_____

_____

_____

_____

Mientras ves el video

3   **Identificar**   You might see any of these actions in a video about soccer in Spain. Check off the items you see in this episode.

___ a. celebrar un gol (*goal*)   ___ d. hablar con un jugador famoso   ___ f. pasear en bicicleta

___ b. comer churros   ___ e. jugar al fútbol   ___ g. celebrar en las calles (*streets*)

___ c. ganar un premio (*award*)   ___ h. jugar al fútbol americano

4   **Emparejar**   Indicate which teams these people are affiliated with.

1.   2.   3.

○ Barça	○ Barça	○ Barça
○ Real Madrid	○ Real Madrid	○ Real Madrid
○ no corresponde	○ no corresponde	○ no corresponde

Después de ver el video

5 **Completar** Complete each statement with the correct option.

aficionados al fútbol	churros	estadio	gol	Red Sox

1. En España hay muchos _____.

2. Camp Nou es un _____ en Barcelona.

3. La rivalidad entre el Barça y el Real Madrid es comparable con la rivalidad entre los Yankees y los _____ en béisbol.

4. Mari Carmen compra _____.

6 **Aficionados** Who are these fans? Imagine what they would say if they introduced themselves. Write information like their name, age, origin, team affiliation, and any other details that come to mind.

> **modelo**
>
> **Aficionado:** ¡Hola! Soy José Artigas y soy de Madrid. Mi equipo favorito es el Real Madrid. Miro todos los partidos en el estadio. ¡VIVA EL REAL MADRID! ¡Nunca pierde!

_____

_____

_____

_____

_____

_____

_____

_____

_____

7 **Un futbolista** Imagine that you are Mari Carmen and you decide to interview a famous soccer player in Spain. Write five questions you would ask him.

> **modelo**
>
> ¿Dónde prefieres vivir?

_____

_____

_____

_____

¡Vacaciones en Perú!

Antes de ver el video

1 **Más vocabulario** Look over these useful words before you watch the video.

Vocabulario útil		
aislado/a *isolated*	**disfrutar** *to enjoy*	**se salvó** *was saved*
andino/a *Andean*	**el esfuerzo** *effort*	**la selva** *jungle*
ayudó *helped*	**hemos contratado** *we have hired*	**subir** *to climb, to go up*
el cultivo *farming*	**la obra** *work (of art)*	**la vuelta al mundo** *around the world*

2 **Completar** Complete these sentences. Make the necessary changes.

1. Machu Picchu es una _____ muy importante de la civilización inca.

   Esta (*This*) ciudad inca está rodeada (*surrounded*) de una gran _____.

2. Los incas fueron (*were*) grandes artistas y expertos en técnicas de _____

   como el sistema de terrazas (*terraces*).

3. Hoy muchos turistas van a _____ de las ruinas incas y del maravilloso

   paisaje andino.

4. Cada año miles de personas deciden _____ hasta Machu Picchu por el Camino Inca.

3 **¡En español!** Look at the video still. Imagine what Omar will say about Machu Picchu, and write a two- or three-sentence introduction to this episode.

Omar Fuentes, Perú

¡Bienvenidos a otra aventura de *Flash cultura*! Hoy estamos en…

_____

_____

_____

_____

Mientras ves el video

4 **Descripción** What does Noemí say about the lost city of Machu Picchu? Complete this quote.

"Omar, te cuento (*let me tell you*) que Machu Picchu se salvó de la invasión (1)_____

gracias a que se encuentra (*it's located*) (2)_____ sobre esta (3)_____,

como tú puedes ver. Y también la (4)_____ ayudó mucho… lo cubrió (*covered*)

rápidamente, y eso también contribuye."

Lección 5 Flash cultura Video Activities

5 **Emparejar** Watch the tourists describe their impressions of Machu Picchu. Match the captions to the appropriate people.

1. _____   2. _____

3. _____   4. _____

a. enigma y misterio   b. magnífico y misterioso   c. algo esplendoroso, algo único…

d. ¡Fantástico!   e. Nos encanta muchísimo.

Después de ver el video

6 **¿Cierto o falso?** Indicate whether each statement is **cierto** or **falso**.

1. Las ruinas de Machu Picchu están al lado del mar. _____

2. Hay menos de (*less than*) cien turistas por día en el santuario (*sanctuary*) inca. _____

3. Cuando visitas Machu Picchu, puedes contratar a un guía experto. _____

4. Todos los turistas llegan a Machu Picchu en autobús. _____

5. Omar pregunta a los turistas por qué visitan Machu Picchu. _____

7 **¡La vuelta al mundo!** Imagine that you are a travel agent and that the French globetrotting family you saw in the video is planning their next destination. Write a conversation between you and the mother. Suggest an exciting destination, describe the activities the family can do together, and then work out how to get there, where to stay, and for how long.

_____

_____

_____

_____

_____

Comprar en los mercados   Lección 6

Antes de ver el video

1 **Más vocabulario** Look over these useful words before you watch the video.

Vocabulario útil		
las artesanías *handicrafts*	la heladería *ice-cream shop*	la soda (C.R.) *food stall*
el camarón *shrimp*	el helado *ice cream*	la sopa de mondongo *tripe soup*
la carne *meat*	el pescado *fish*	suave *soft*
la flor *flower*	¡Pura vida! *Cool!, Alright!*	el/la tico/a *person from Costa Rica*
la fruta *fruit*	el regateo *haggling, bargaining*	vale *it costs*

2 **¡En español!** Look at the video still. Imagine what Randy will say about markets in Costa Rica, and write a two- or three-sentence introduction to this episode.

Randy Cruz, Costa Rica

¡Hola a todos! Hoy estamos en… _____

_____

_____

_____

_____

Mientras ves el video

3 **¿Qué compran?** Identify which item(s) these people buy at the market.

1. _____   2. _____   3. _____

    a. frutas   b. artesanías   c. carne y pescado

    d. camarones y flores e. zapatos

Lección 6 Flash cultura Video Activities |

4 **Completar** Watch Randy bargain, and complete this conversation.

RANDY ¿(1)_____ vale?

VENDEDOR Trescientos (*300*) (2)_____.

RANDY Trescientos colones el kilo. Me puede hacer un (3)_____, ¿sí?

VENDEDOR Perfecto.

VENDEDOR OK... (4)_____ cuatro ochenta... cuatro y medio.

RANDY Cuatrocientos (*400*).

VENDEDOR Cuatro (5)_____.

RANDY Cuatrocientos cuarenta.

VENDEDOR Sí, señor.

Después de ver el video

5 **Ordenar** Put Randy's actions in the correct order.

_____ a. Busca la heladería en el Mercado Central.

_____ b. Regatea el precio de unas papayas.

_____ c. Va al mercado al aire libre.

_____ d. Entrevista a personas en el Mercado Central.

_____ e. Toma sopa de mondongo, un plato (*dish*) típico de Costa Rica.

6 **¡Aquí no hay descuentos!** Imagine that Randy wants to buy an item of clothing that he really likes, but he doesn't have enough money to pay the full price. Write a conversation between Randy and a salesperson in which Randy negotiates the price. Be creative!

_____

_____

_____

_____

_____

7 **Preguntas** Answer these questions.

1. ¿En qué lugares o tipos de tiendas haces las compras generalmente? ¿Pequeñas tiendas, grandes almacenes o centros comerciales? _____

_____

2. ¿Con quién(es) sales generalmente a comprar ropa: solo/a (*alone*), con amigos o con alguien (*someone*) de tu familia? ¿Por qué? _____

_____

3. ¿Cómo prefieres pagar tus compras: en efectivo o con tarjeta de crédito? ¿Por qué? _____

_____

4. ¿Esperas las rebajas para comprar cosas que quieres o no te importa (*you don't mind*) pagar el precio normal? _____

Tapas para todos los días   **Lección 7**

Antes de ver el video

1 **Más vocabulario** Look over these useful words before you watch the video.

Vocabulario útil		
los caracoles *snails*	informal *casual, informal*	preparaban unos platillos
Cataluña *Catalonia (an*	País Vasco *Basque Country*	*used to prepare little dishes*
autonomous community	*(autonomous community*	las tortillas de patata *Spanish*
in Spain)	*in Spain)*	*potato omelets*
contar los palillos *counting*	el pan *bread*	el trabajo *job; work*
the toothpicks	las porciones de comida	único/a *unique*
la escalivada *grilled vegetables*	*food portions*	

2 **Completar** Complete this paragraph about **tapas**.

Las tapas son pequeñas (1)_____ que se sirven en bares y restaurantes de España.
Hay diferentes tipos de tapas: los (2)_____ y las (3)_____ son
algunos ejemplos. En algunos bares, los camareros (*waiters*) traen la comida, pero en lugares más
(*more*) (4)_____ el cliente toma las tapas en la barra (*bar*). Es muy común salir
solo o con amigos a tomar tapas después del trabajo. Sin duda, ¡salir de tapas en España es una
experiencia fantástica y (5)_____!

3 **¡En español!** Look at the video still. Imagine what Mari Carmen will say about **tapas** in Barcelona,
and write a two- or three-sentence introduction to this episode.

Mari Carmen, España

¡Hola! Hoy estamos en Barcelona. Esta bonita ciudad... _____

_____

_____

_____

_____

Mientras ves el video

4 **Montaditos** Indicate whether these statements about **montaditos** are **cierto** or **falso**.

1. Los cajeros cuentan los palillos para saber cuánto deben pagar los clientes. _____

2. Los montaditos son informales. _____

3. Los montaditos son caros. _____

4. Los montaditos se preparan siempre con pan. _____

5. Hay montaditos en bares al aire libre solamente. _____

5 **Completar** (03:13–03:29) Watch these people talk about **tapas,** and complete this conversation.

MARI CARMEN ¿Cuándo sueles venir a (1)_____ tapas?

HOMBRE Generalmente (2)_____ del trabajo. Cuando al salir de trabajar

(3)_____ hambre, vengo (4)_____.

MARI CARMEN ¿Y vienes solo, vienes con amigos o da igual (*doesn't it matter*)?

HOMBRE Da igual. Si alguien (5)_____ conmigo, mejor; y si no, vengo solo.

Después de ver el video

6 **¿Cierto o falso?** Indicate whether these statements are **cierto** or **falso.**

1. Mari Carmen pasea en motocicleta por el centro de Barcelona. _____

2. Mari Carmen entrevista a personas sobre sus hábitos después de salir del trabajo. _____

3. Una versión sobre el origen de las tapas dice que un rey (*king*) necesitaba (*needed*) comer pocas veces al día. _____

4. Los restaurantes elegantes y caros sirven montaditos. _____

5. La tradición del montadito proviene (*comes from*) del País Vasco. _____

6. Los pinchos son sólo platos fríos. _____

7 **Un día en la vida de...** Select one of these people and imagine a typical workday. Consider his or her daily routine as well as the time he or she gets up, goes to work, spends with friends, goes back home, and goes to sleep. Use the words provided.

| más tarde | se acuesta | se levanta |
| por la noche | se cepilla los dientes | va al trabajo |

_____

_____

_____

_____

_____

_____

_____

Video Manual: *Flash cultura*

La comida latina   Lección 8

Antes de ver el video

1 **Más vocabulario** Look over these useful words before you watch the video.

Vocabulario útil		
el arroz congrí *mixed rice and beans from Cuba*	el frijol *bean*	la rebanada *slice*
el azafrán *saffron*	el perejil *parsley*	el taco al pastor *Shepherd-style taco*
la carne molida *ground beef*	el picadillo a la habanera *Cuban-style ground beef*	la torta al pastor *traditional sandwich from Tijuana*
la carne picada *diced beef*	el plátano *banana*	
el cerdo *pork*	el pollo *chicken*	la ropa vieja *Cuban shredded beef*

2 **¡En español!** Look at the video still. Imagine what Leticia will say about **la comida latina** in Los Angeles, and write a two- or three-sentence introduction to this episode.

Leticia, Estados Unidos

¡Hola! Soy Leticia Arroyo desde Los Ángeles. Hoy vamos a

hablar sobre… _____

_____

_____

_____

_____

_____

_____

Mientras ves el video

3 **Completar** (04:15–04:48) Watch Leticia ask other customers in the restaurant for recommendations, and complete this conversation.

LETICIA Señoritas, ¿qué estamos (1)_____ de rico?

CLIENTE 1 Mojito.

LETICIA ¿Y de qué se trata el (2)_____?

CLIENTE 1 Es pollo con cebolla, arroz blanco, (3)_____ negros y plátanos fritos. Es delicioso.

LETICIA Rico. ¿Y el tuyo?

CLIENTE 2 Yo estoy comiendo (4)_____ con pollo, que es arroz amarillo, pollo y plátanos fritos.

LETICIA ¿Y otras cosas en el (5)_____ que están ricas también?

CLIENTE 2 A mí me (6)_____ la ropa vieja.

Video Manual: *Flash cultura*

4 **Ordenar** Put these events in the correct order.

_____ a. Toma un café en el restaurante cubano.

_____ b. Leticia habla con el gerente (*manager*) de un supermercado.

_____ c. Leticia come picadillo, un plato típico cubano.

_____ d. La dueña de una taquería mexicana le muestra a Leticia diferentes platos mexicanos.

_____ e. Leticia compra frutas y verduras en un supermercado hispano.

Después de ver el video

5 **Emparejar** Match these expressions to the appropriate situations.

_____ 1. ¿Qué me recomienda?   _____ 4. ¿Está listo/a para ordenar?

_____ 2. ¡Se me hace agua la boca!   _____ 5. A la orden.

_____ 3. ¡Que se repita!

    a. Eres un(a) empleado/a de una tienda. Ayudaste a un(a) cliente/a a hacer una compra. Él/Ella te dice gracias. ¿Qué le respondes?

    b. Estás en un restaurante. Miraste el menú, pero todavía no sabes qué quieres comer. ¿Qué le dices al/a la camarero/a?

    c. El/La camarero/a te dio el menú hace cinco minutos y ahora se acerca para preguntarte si sabes lo que quieres pedir. ¿Qué pregunta te hace?

    d. Terminas de comer y pagas, estás muy contento/a por la comida y el servicio que recibiste. ¿Qué le dices al/a la camarero/a?

    e. Acabas de entrar en un supermercado. Tienes mucha hambre y ves unos postres que te parecen (*seem*) deliciosos. ¿Qué dices?

6 **Un plato típico** Research one of these typical dishes or drinks from the Hispanic world. Find out about its ingredients, where it is typical, and any other information that you find interesting.

ropa vieja	picadillo a la habanera	horchata
Inca Kola	malta Hatuey	mate

_____

_____

_____

_____

_____

_____

_____

Las fiestas

Lección 9

Antes de ver el video

1 **Más vocabulario** Look over these useful words before you watch the video.

Vocabulario útil		
alegrar *to make happy*	el cartel *poster*	la parranda *party*
las artesanías *crafts*	la clausura *closing ceremony*	la pintura *painting*
el/la artesano/a *craftsperson;* *artisan*	destacarse *to stand out*	el santo de palo *wooden saint*
los cabezudos *carnival figures with large heads*	el Día de Reyes *Three Kings' Day*	tocar el tambor *playing drums*
la canción de Navidad *Christmas carol*	las frituras *fried foods; fritters*	los Tres Santos Reyes/Reyes Magos *Three Kings*
	la madera *wood*	
	la misa *mass*	

2 **Completar** Complete this paragraph about **la Navidad** in Puerto Rico.

En Puerto Rico, las Navidades no terminan después del (1)_____, como en el resto de los países hispanos, sino después de las Fiestas de la Calle San Sebastián. Hay muchas expresiones artísticas de (2)_____ locales; entre ellas se destacan los (3)_____, que son pequeñas estatuas (*statues*) de madera de vírgenes y santos. La (4)_____ empieza por la noche cuando las personas salen a disfrutar del baile y la música con amigos y familiares.

3 **¡En español!** Look at the video still. What do you think this episode will be about? Imagine what Diego will say, and write a two- or three-sentence introduction to this episode.

Diego Palacios, Puerto Rico

¡Bienvenidos! Soy Diego Palacios, de Puerto Rico. Hoy les quiero

mostrar… _____

_____

_____

_____

Mientras ves el video

4 **Ordenar** Ordena cronológicamente lo que Diego hizo (*did*).

_____ a. Les preguntó a personas qué disfrutaban más de las fiestas.

_____ b. Bailó con los cabezudos en la calle.

_____ c. Habló con artesanos sobre los santos de palo.

_____ d. Tomó un helado de coco.

_____ e. Comió unas frituras.

Lección 9 Flash cultura Video Activities

5 **Emparejar** Match the captions to the appropriate elements.

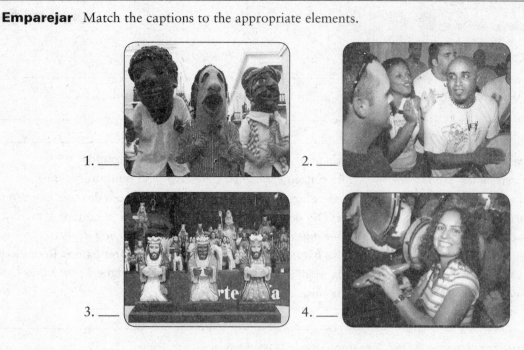

1. ____   2. ____

3. ____   4. ____

a. el güiro   b. los cabezudos   c. los santos de palo   d. el pandero   e. los carteles

Después de ver el video

6 **¿Cierto o falso?** Indicate whether each statement is **cierto** or **falso**.

1. Las Navidades en Puerto Rico terminan con el Día de Reyes. _____

2. Los artistas hacen cuadros y carteles sobre la Navidad. _____

3. En Puerto Rico, todas las celebraciones navideñas son religiosas. _____

4. Los santos de palo representan a personajes puertorriqueños. _____

5. Según un artesano, la pieza de artesanía más popular es la de los Tres Santos Reyes.

_____

6. El güiro y el pandero son algunos de los instrumentos típicos de la música de estas fiestas.

_____

7 **¡De parranda!** Imagine that you are an exchange student in Puerto Rico and that you are attending this celebration. You are dancing on the street when suddenly Diego spots you and decides to interview you. Tell him how you feel and what cultural aspects catch your attention. Make sure to include these words.

| artistas | bailar | cabezudos | de parranda | en la calle | tocar el tambor |

_____

_____

_____

_____

La salud

Lección 10

Antes de ver el video

1 **Más vocabulario** Look over these useful words before you watch the video.

Vocabulario útil		
atender *to treat; to see (in a hospital)*	**cumplir (una función)** *to fulfill (a function/role)*	**gratuito** *free (of charge)*
atendido/a *treated*	**esperar** *to wait*	**herido/a** *injured*
brindar *to offer*	**estar de guardia** *to be on call*	**el reportaje** *story*
chocar *to crash*	**golpeado/a** *bruised*	**se atienden pacientes** *patients are treated*

2 **¡En español!** Look at the video still. Imagine what Silvina will say about hospitals in Argentina, and write a two- or three-sentence introduction to this episode.

Silvina Márquez, Argentina

¡Hola a todos! Hoy estamos en… _____

_____

_____

_____

_____

_____

Mientras ves el video

3 **Problemas de salud** Match these statements to their corresponding video stills.

1. ___

2. ___

3. ___

a. Tengo dolor de cabeza y me golpeé la cabeza.

d. Me chocó una bici.

b. Mi abuela estaba con un poco de tos.

e. Me salió una alergia.

c. Estoy congestionada.

4 **Completar** Watch Silvina interview a patient, and complete this conversation.

SILVINA ¿Y a vos qué te pasa? ¿Por qué estás aquí en la (1)_____?

PACIENTE Porque me salió una (2)_____ en la (3)_____ hace dos días y quería saber qué tenía. ¿Y a vos qué te pasó?

SILVINA Yo tuve un accidente. Me (4)_____ una bici en el centro y mirá cómo quedé…

PACIENTE … toda lastimada (*hurt*)…

SILVINA Sí, y aquí también, aquí también… Estoy toda (5)_____.

Después de ver el video

5 **Ordenar** Put Silvina's actions in the correct order.

_____ a. Le dio sus datos personales a la enfermera.

_____ b. Llegó a la guardia del hospital.

_____ c. Fue atendida por el doctor.

_____ d. Tuvo un accidente con una bicicleta.

_____ e. Entrevistó a pacientes.

6 **El sistema de salud en Argentina** Identify the main characteristics of the health system in Argentina. Use these guiding questions.

1. ¿Cómo es el sistema de salud: público, privado o mixto?

2. ¿Hay que pagar en los hospitales públicos?

3. ¿Qué son las guardias?

4. ¿Hay que esperar mucho para ser atendido/a?

5. ¿Cómo es la carrera de medicina?

6. ¿Qué similitudes y diferencias existen entre el sistema de salud en Argentina y el de tu país?

7 **¿Un pequeño accidente?** You were exploring the city of Buenos Aires when an aggressive pedestrian knocked you to the ground. You arrived in great pain at the **guardia** only to find the wait very long. Write your conversation with a nurse in which you explain your symptoms to convince him/her that this is *not* a minor accident and you should receive immediate care.

_____

_____

_____

_____

_____

_____

_____

_____

_____

Maravillas de la tecnología
Lección 11

Antes de ver el video

1   **Más vocabulario**   Look over these useful words before you watch the video.

Vocabulario útil		
la afirmación cultural *cultural affirmation*	chatear *to chat*	la masificación *spread*
alejado/a *remote*	el desarrollo *development*	mejorar *to improve*
beneficiarse *to benefit*	el esfuerzo *effort*	el/la proveedor(a) *supplier*
el/la cuzqueño/a *person from Cuzco*	al extranjero *abroad*	servirse de *to make use of*
	mandar *to send*	el/la usuario/a *user*

2   **La tecnología**   Complete this paragraph about technology in Peru.

En Perú, la (1)_____ de Internet benefició el (2)_____ de la agricultura

en las comunidades indígenas. Para estas comunidades es una herramienta (*tool*) importante para obtener

e intercambiar información. También, en ciudades como Cuzco, los artistas y comerciantes que son

(3)_____ de Internet pueden (4)_____ el nivel (*level*) de ventas porque se

conectan (5)_____ y así pueden vender sus productos en otros países.

3   **¡En español!**   Look at the video still. Imagine what Omar will say about technology in Peru, and write a two- or three-sentence introduction to this episode.

Omar Fuentes, Perú

¡Hola a todos! ¿Saben de qué vamos a hablar hoy? _____

_____

_____

_____

_____

Mientras ves el video

4   **Completar**   Watch Omar interview a young man, and complete their conversation.

OMAR ¿Qué haces en medio de la Plaza de Armas usando una (1)_____?

JOVEN Estoy mandándole un (2)_____ a mi novia en Quito.

OMAR ... en Quito... ¿Así que tú eres (3)_____?

JOVEN Sí, soy ecuatoriano.

OMAR Y... ¿qué tal? ¿Qué te (4)_____ el Cuzco? ¿Qué te parece el Perú?

JOVEN Me encanta Cuzco porque se parece mucho a mi ciudad, pero me gusta un poco más

porque puedo usar (5)_____ en medio de la plaza y (6)_____

me molesta.

5 **Emparejar** Identify what these people use cell phones and Internet for.

1. ___    2. ___    3. ___

a. para escribir mensajes
   a su novia

b. para comunicarse con su
   proveedor

c. para vender sus productos
   en el extranjero

d. para hacer una videoconferencia
   y hablar con su familia

e. para chatear con amigos

Después de ver el video

6 **¿Cierto o falso?** Indicate whether each statement is **cierto** or **falso**.

1. En Perú, los cibercafés son lugares exclusivos para los turistas. _____

2. Los cibercafés son conocidos como "cabinas de Internet" en Perú y están por todo el país. _____

3. A diferencia de los cibercafés, los teléfonos celulares ayudan a la comunicación rápida
   y económica. _____

4. La comunidad indígena de Perú se beneficia de las ventajas que ofrecen los cibercafés. _____

5. En la Plaza de Armas de Cuzco es posible navegar en la red de manera inalámbrica. _____

6. Las tecnologías de la comunicación no permiten a las comunidades indígenas reafirmarse
   culturalmente. _____

7 **Preguntas** Answer these questions.

1. ¿Para qué usas Internet?
   _____

2. ¿Cómo te comunicas con tu familia y tus amigos cuando viajas?
   _____

3. ¿Piensas que la masificación de la tecnología es buena? ¿Por qué?
   _____

4. ¿Piensas que el servicio de Internet debe ser gratuito para todas las personas? ¿Por qué?
   _____

8 **Un mensaje** Remember the young man who was writing an e-mail to his girlfriend at the Plaza de Armas in Cuzco? Imagine you are the young man and write an e-mail to his girlfriend telling her about living in Cuzco and how technology is used there.

¡Hola, mi amor! En este momento estoy en la Plaza de Armas de Cuzco. _____

_____

_____

_____

_____

La casa de Frida   Lección 12

Antes de ver el video

1 **Más vocabulario** Look over these useful words before you watch the video.

Vocabulario útil		
el alma *soul*	contar con *to have; to feature*	el relicario *locket*
la artesanía *crafts*	convertirse en *to become*	el retrato *portrait*
el barro *clay*	la muleta *crutch*	la urna *urn*
la ceniza *ash*	el recorrido *tour*	el vidrio soplado *blown glass*

2 **Emparejar** Match each definition to the appropriate word.

1. Es un aparato que ayuda a caminar a las personas que no pueden hacerlo por sí solas (*by themselves*). _____

2. Es el recipiente (*container*) donde se ponen las cenizas de la persona muerta. _____

3. Es una pintura de una persona. _____

4. tener, poseer _____

5. camino o itinerario en un museo, en parques, etc. _____

6. Transformarse en algo distinto de lo que era antes. _____

3 **¡En español!** Look at the video still. Imagine what Carlos will say about **La casa de Frida,** and write a two- or three-sentence introduction to this episode.

Carlos López, México

¡Bienvenidos a otro episodio de *Flash cultura*! Soy Carlos López

desde… _____

_____

_____

_____

Mientras ves el video

4 **¿Dónde están?** Identify where these items are located in Frida's museum.

¿Dónde están?	La cocina	La habitación
1. barro verde de Oaxaca		
2. la urna con sus cenizas		
3. los aparatos ortopédicos		
4. vidrio soplado		
5. la cama original		
6. artesanía de Metepec		

5 **Impresiones** Listen to what these people say, and match the captions to the appropriate person.

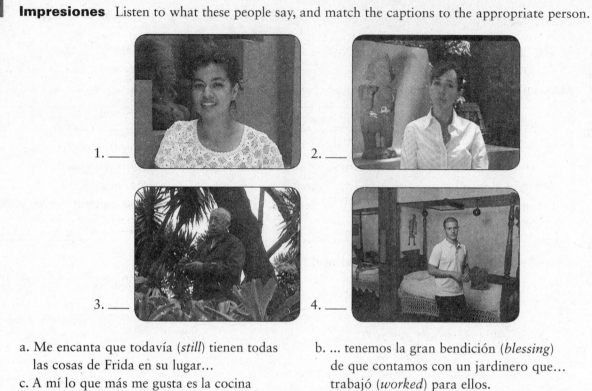

1. ___

2. ___

3. ___

4. ___

a. Me encanta que todavía (*still*) tienen todas las cosas de Frida en su lugar…

c. A mí lo que más me gusta es la cocina y los jardines.

e. … para mí fueron unas buenas personas…

b. … tenemos la gran bendición (*blessing*) de que contamos con un jardinero que… trabajó (*worked*) para ellos.

d. El espacio más impresionante de esta casa es la habitación de Frida.

Después de ver el video

6 **Ordenar** Put Carlos' actions in the correct order.

_____ a. Habló con distintas personas sobre el museo y sus impresiones.

_____ b. Caminó por las calles de Coyoacán.

_____ c. Pasó por el estudio y terminó el recorrido en la habitación de Frida.

_____ d. Mostró el cuadro *Viva la vida* y otras pinturas de Frida.

_____ e. Recorrió la cocina.

_____ f. Llegó al Museo Casa de Frida Kahlo.

7 **¿Qué te gustó más?** Choose an aspect of Frida's house and describe it. Is it similar to or different from your own house? What do you find interesting about it?

_____

_____

_____

_____

_____

_____

_____

_____

Naturaleza en Costa Rica — Lección 13

Antes de ver el video

1 **Más vocabulario** Look over these useful words before you watch the video.

Vocabulario útil		
el balneario *spa*	las faldas *foot (of a mountain or volcano)*	el piso *ground*
el Cinturón de Fuego *Ring of Fire*		la profundidad *depth*
	lanzar *to throw*	refrescarse *to refresh oneself*
cuidadoso/a *careful*	mantenerse fuera *to keep outside*	el rugido *roar*
derramado/a *spilled*	el milagro *miracle*	el ruido *noise*

2 **Los volcanes** Complete this paragraph about volcanoes in Central America.

Los países centroamericanos crearon "La Ruta Colonial y de los volcanes" para atraer turismo cultural y ecológico a esta región. El recorrido (*tour*) de los volcanes es el itinerario favorito de los visitantes, ya que éstos pueden escuchar los (1)_____ volcánicos y sentir el (2)_____ vibrando cuando caminan cerca. Es posible caminar por las (3)_____ de los volcanes que no están activos y observar la lava (4)_____ en antiguas erupciones. ¡Centroamérica es un (5)_____ de la naturaleza!

3 **¡En español!** Look at the video still. Imagine what Alberto will say about volcanoes and hot springs in Costa Rica, and write a two- or three-sentence introduction to this episode.

Alberto Cuadra, Costa Rica

¡Bienvenidos a Costa Rica! Hoy vamos a visitar... _____

_____

_____

_____

_____

Mientras ves el video

4 **¿Qué ves?** Identify the items you see in the video.

____ 1. cuatro monos juntos

____ 2. las montañas

____ 3. un volcán

____ 4. una tortuga marina

____ 5. el mar

____ 6. dos ballenas

____ 7. las aguas termales

____ 8. muchos pumas

5 **Completar** Complete this conversation between Alberto and the guide.

ALBERTO ¿Qué tan activo es el (1)_____ Arenal?

GUÍA El volcán Arenal se encuentra dentro de los volcanes más (2)_____ en el mundo. Se pueden observar las (3)_____ incandescentes, sobre todo en la noche… y en este momento, el sonido que (4)_____ es efecto de la actividad activa del volcán.

ALBERTO ¿Por qué es que el volcán produce ese sonido?

GUÍA Bueno, es el efecto de las erupciones; la combinación también del aire, del (5)_____; cuando la (6)_____ sale y tiene el contacto con la parte externa.

Después de ver el video

6 **Ordenar** Put Alberto's actions in the correct order.

_____ a. Se cubrió con una toalla porque tenía frío.

_____ b. Caminó hasta el Parque Nacional Volcán Arenal.

_____ c. Vio caer las rocas incandescentes desde la ventana de su hotel.

_____ d. Cuando sintió que se movía el piso, tuvo miedo y salió corriendo.

_____ e. Se bañó en las aguas termales de origen volcánico.

_____ f. Conversó sobre el volcán con el guía.

7 **¡Defendamos el volcán!** Imagine that you are a forest ranger at the **volcán Arenal** park and you just learned that a highly polluting company plans to move its plant near the park. Write a conversation between you and your colleagues at work in which you try to convince them to take action to prevent it.

_____

_____

_____

_____

8 **Ecoturismo** Alberto says that ecotourism represents the fastest growing subsector of the tourist industry. Identify the positive and negative aspects of ecotourism and then write a brief paragraph about it. You may use examples from the video.

Aspectos positivos	Aspectos negativos

_____

_____

_____

_____

_____

_____

El Metro del D.F.

Lección 14

Antes de ver el video

Video Manual: *Flash cultura*

1 **Más vocabulario** Look over these useful words before you watch the video.

Vocabulario útil		
ancho/a *wide*	contar con *to have, to offer*	repartido/a *spread*
el boleto *ticket*	debajo *underneath*	el siglo *century*
el camión *bus (Mexico)*	gratuito/a *free*	superado/a *surpassed*
el castillo *castle*	imponente *imposing, impressive*	la superficie *surface*
construido/a *built*	recorrer *to cover (traveling)*	ubicado/a *located*

2 **Completar** Complete these sentences.

1. En México se le dice _____ a un autobús.
2. Los autobuses _____ distintos puntos de México, D.F.
3. El Metro tiene estaciones _____ por toda la ciudad.
4. El Bosque de Chapultepec está _____ en el centro de México, D.F.
5. El Metro es un servicio _____ para personas de más de 60 años.

3 **¡En español!** Look at the video still. Imagine what Carlos will say about **el Metro** in Mexico City, and write a two- or three-sentence introduction to this episode.

Carlos López, México

¡Hola! Hoy vamos a hablar de… _____

_____

_____

_____

_____

Mientras ves el video

4 **¿Qué les gusta?** Identify what each of these passengers likes about **el Metro**.

1. ___

2. ___

3. ___

a. Es útil para ir a la escuela y visitar a mis compañeros. b. Hay una parada (*stop*) cerca de mi casa.
c. Es un transporte seguro, rápido y cómodo. d. Es barato y siempre me dan un descuento.
e. Hay mucha variedad de gente.

Lección 14 Flash cultura Video Activities

5 **¿Qué dice?** Identify the places Carlos mentions in the video.

_____ 1. una joyería del siglo pasado

_____ 2. las estaciones de metro superficiales

_____ 3. la Catedral Metropolitana

_____ 4. una panadería

_____ 5. un castillo construido en un cerro (*hill*)

_____ 6. el correo

_____ 7. un zoológico

_____ 8. un bosque en el centro de la ciudad

Después de ver el video

6 **¿Cierto o falso?** Indicate whether these statements are **cierto** or **falso**.

1. Carlos dice que el Metrobús es el sistema favorito de los ciudadanos. _____

2. Los tranvías circulan bajo la superficie de la ciudad. _____

3. En el Metro puedes recorrer los principales atractivos de México, D.F. _____

4. El Zócalo es la plaza principal de la capital mexicana. _____

7 **¿Cómo llego?** Imagine that you are in Mexico City. You want to go to **Ciudad Azteca** and decided to take the subway, but got confused and end up in **Barranca del Muerto**, the other end of the city! On a separate piece of paper, write a conversation in which you ask a person for directions to help you get to your destination. Use some of these expressions. You can also find a map of the **Metro** online.

cambiar de tren
las estaciones
    de transbordo
estar perdido
hasta
al norte
seguir derecho

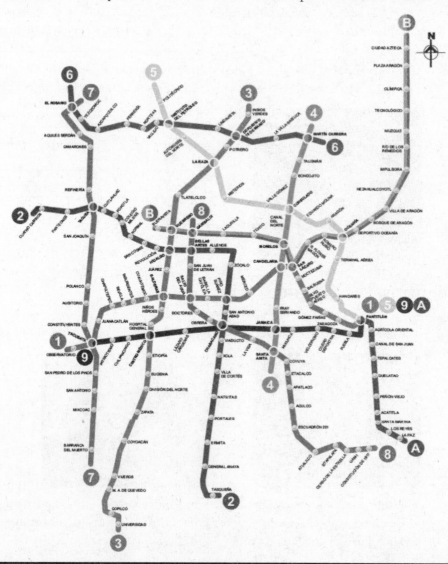

¿Estrés? ¿Qué estrés?   Lección 15

Antes de ver el video

1 **Más vocabulario** Look over these useful words before you watch the video.

Vocabulario útil		
el ambiente *atmosphere*	el/la madrileño/a	remontarse *to go back (in time)*
el descanso *rest*	*person from Madrid*	retirarse *to retreat*
el espectáculo *show*	mantenerse sano/a	*(to a peaceful place)*
el estanque *pond*	*to stay healthy*	el retiro *retreat*
judío/a *Jewish*	el paseo *walk*	trotar *to jog*
llevadero/a *bearable*	remar *to row*	el vapor *steam*

2 **Completar** Complete this paragraph about **baños árabes**.

Madrid fue lugar de encuentro de tres culturas: musulmana, cristiana y (1)_____.
Los musulmanes, por ejemplo, introdujeron los famosos baños árabes, que eran lugares de
(2)_____ donde las personas iban a (3)_____ a lugares tranquilos y a
socializar. Aunque en la actualidad los (4)_____ continúan disfrutando de estos baños,
existen muchas otras alternativas para mantenerse sanos y sin estrés.

3 **¡En español!** Look at the video still. Imagine what Miguel Ángel will say about **el estrés** in Madrid,
and write a two- or three-sentence introduction to this episode.

Miguel Ángel Lagasca, España

¡Bienvenidos a Madrid! Hoy les quiero mostrar… _____

_____

_____

_____

_____

_____

_____

_____

Mientras ves el video

4 **Completar** Listen to a man talking about his dog, and complete his comments.

HOMBRE Bueno, a mí me espera además un (1)_____. Yo tengo un perro que se
llama Curro, que es un fenómeno... Gracias a él, pues, aparte del (2)_____ de
Madrid, sirve para (3)_____ y dar un paseíto, ¿eh?, y resulta muy agradable.
Más (4)_____ [...] Yo insisto que lo mejor en Madrid es tener un perro, si es
(5)_____ que se llame Curro, y dar un (6)_____ con él, y es
muy divertido.

5 **¿Estrés en Madrid?** Being the capital of Spain, Madrid has the hustle and bustle of any big city. Identify why these **madrileños** are stressed out.

1. ____

2. ____

3. ____

a. Porque durmieron en el parque para conseguir boletos.

b. Porque hay mucho tráfico en la ciudad.

c. Porque hay personas que les quieren quitar el lugar en la cola.

d. Porque tiene un perro muy agresivo.

e. Porque tienen que hacer largas colas para todo, sobre todo para espectáculos culturales.

Después de ver el video

6 **Preguntas** Answer each of these questions.

1. ¿Qué problema tiene Madrid que es típico de una gran ciudad?

_____

2. Menciona dos lugares adonde los madrileños van para desestresarse.

_____

3. ¿Quién es Curro? ¿Qué opina su dueño de él?

_____

4. ¿Cuáles son tres actividades saludables que se pueden hacer en el Parque del Retiro?

_____

5. ¿Cuántas salas de baños árabes tiene el Medina Mayrit?

_____

7 **No hablo español** Remember the American who cut the line for the show? The couple behind him did not succeed in making him go at the end. What would you say to him? Write a conversation in which you tell him to go to the back of the line!

_____

_____

_____

_____

_____

_____

_____

_____

_____

_____

El mundo del trabajo

Lección 16

Antes de ver el video

1 **Más vocabulario** Look over these useful words before you watch the video.

Vocabulario útil		
el desarrollo *development*	(ser) exitoso/a *(to be)*	la madera *wood*
el destino *destination*	*successful*	el nivel *level*
la elevación *height*	la fidelidad *loyalty*	la oportunidad *opportunity*

2 **Emparejar** Match each definition to the appropriate word.

_____ 1. Alguien o algo que tiene muy buena aceptación.   a. elevación

_____ 2. Meta, punto de llegada.   b. madera

_____ 3. Conveniencia de tiempo y de lugar.   c. desarrollo

_____ 4. Parte sólida de los árboles cubierta por la corteza (*bark*).   d. exitoso

_____ 5. Altura que algo alcanza, o a la que está colocado.   e. nivel

_____ 6. Distancia vertical de un punto de la tierra respecto al nivel del mar.   f. destino

_____ 7. Progresar, crecer económica, social, cultural o políticamente.   g. fidelidad

_____ 8. Lealtad que alguien debe a otra persona.   h. oportunidad

3 **¡En español!** Look at the video still. Imagine what Mónica will say about jobs in Ecuador, and write a two- or three-sentence introduction to this episode.

Mónica, Ecuador

Hola, los saluda Mónica... _____

_____

_____

_____

_____

_____

_____

Mientras ves el video

4 **Marcar** Check off what you see while watching the video.

_____ 1. vendedor de periódicos   _____ 6. hombre policía

_____ 2. payaso   _____ 7. médico

_____ 3. dentista   _____ 8. pintora

_____ 4. heladero   _____ 9. artesano

_____ 5. barrendera   _____ 10. mesero

Lección 16 Flash cultura Video Activities

5 **Impresiones** Listen to what these people say, and match the captions to the appropriate person.

1. ____   2. ____   3. ____

a. Claro que sí. Soy la jefa.

b. Odio mi trabajo. Me pagan poquísimo (*very little*) y aparte, mi jefa es súper fastidiosa...

c. Lo que más me gusta de trabajar en Klein Tours es que ayudamos al desarrollo de nuestro país.

d. Bueno, la persona que quiera estar conmigo deberá recibirme con mi profesión, ya que yo no tengo un horario de oficina normal.

Después de ver el video

6 **¿Cierto o falso?** Indicate whether each statement is **cierto** or **falso**. Correct the false statements.

1. Quito es una de las capitales de mayor elevación del mundo. _____

2. La mujer policía trabaja desde muy temprano en la mañana. _____

3. La peluquería de don Alfredo está ubicada en la calle García Moreno, debajo del Mercado Central en el centro de Quito. _____

4. La profesión de don Alfredo es una tradición familiar. _____

5. Klein Tours es una agencia de viajes especializada solamente en excursiones a las islas Galápagos.

_____

6. Las principales áreas de trabajo de Klein Tours son ventas, operaciones, *marketing* y el área administrativa. _____

7 **Escribir** Choose a profession that you would like to work in from the following list. Then, write three **ventajas** and three **desventajas** for that profession.

artista	enfermero/a	peluquero/a
barrendero/a	mesero/a	policía
dentista	payaso/a	vendedor/a

Ventajas	Desventajas
1. _____	1. _____
2. _____	2. _____
3. _____	3. _____

Palacios del arte   Lección 17

Antes de ver el video

1 **Más vocabulario** Look over these words before you watch the video.

Vocabulario útil

alucinante *amazing*	la infanta *princess*	la pieza *piece*
brillar *to shine*	infantil *childlike*	la planta *floor*
la corte (real) *(royal) court*	ladrar *to bark*	recto/a *straight*
dorado/a *golden*	el lienzo *canvas*	el Renacimiento *Renaissance*
la época *time, period*	magistral *masterly*	el siglo *century*
el estilo *style*	majo/a *good-looking; nice*	

2 **Completar** Complete this paragraph about the painting *Las meninas* by Diego Velázquez.

Las meninas es una de las (1) _____ más famosas del pintor español Diego Velázquez. Fue hecha a mediados del (2) _____ XVI y es un buen ejemplo del (3) _____ magistral de este artista. Originalmente, esta pintura se llamó *La familia de Felipe IV*, pero se le cambió el nombre porque en el centro del cuadro aparece la (4) _____ Margarita de Austria con dos damas de honor o meninas. Entre los personajes del cuadro, hay un perro, y es tan real que parece a punto de (5) _____.

3 **¡En español!** Look at the image. Imagine what Mari Carmen will say about **el arte** in Madrid, and write a two- or three-sentence introduction to this episode.

Mari Carmen, España

¡Hola a todos! Hoy estamos en Madrid _____

_____

_____

_____

_____

_____

_____

Mientras ves el video

4 **Marcar** Identify the painters Mari Carmen mentions in the video.

_____ 1. Salvador Dalí   _____ 6. Diego Rivera

_____ 2. Frida Kahlo   _____ 7. Francisco de Goya

_____ 3. Diego Velázquez   _____ 8. Joan Miró

_____ 4. Pablo Picasso   _____ 9. Vincent van Gogh

_____ 5. El Greco   _____ 10. Fernando Botero

5 **Emparejar** Match each name with a painting.

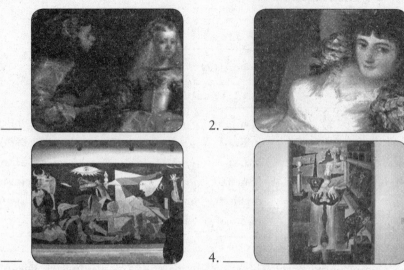

1. ___   2. ___

3. ___   4. ___

a. *La Inmaculada Concepción*   b. *El hombre invisible*   c. *Las meninas*
d. *Guernica*   e. *La maja vestida*

Después de ver el video

6 **Ordenar** Put Mari Carmen's actions in order.

_____ a. Recorrió el Museo Nacional Centro de Arte Reina Sofía.

_____ b. Entró al Museo del Prado.

_____ c. Habló con distintas personas sobre el *Guernica*, de Pablo Picasso.

_____ d. Mostró el cuadro *Campesino catalán con guitarra*, de Joan Miró.

_____ e. Caminó por el Paseo del Prado.

_____ f. Mostró el cuadro *La Inmaculada Concepción*, de El Greco.

7 **Guía de turistas** Imagine that you work as a tour guide in Madrid and you've been asked to show your tour group the city's museums. Which of the museums that you saw in the video would you take them to first? Write a description of what you would tell the tour group about the paintings there.

_____

_____

_____

_____

_____

_____

_____

_____

_____

_____

_____

_____

Puerto Rico: ¿nación o estado?   Lección 18

Video Manual: *Flash cultura*

Antes de ver el video

1 **Más vocabulario** Look over these words before you watch the video.

Vocabulario útil		
el agua de coco *coconut water*	la isla *island*	las relaciones exteriores
el/la boricua *Puerto Rican*	los lazos *ties*	*foreign policy*
convertirse *to become*	la nación independiente	la soberanía *sovereignty*
la estadidad *statehood*	*independent nation*	la vacuna *vaccine*
el estado libre asociado	permanecer *to stay; to remain*	valorar *to value*
associated free state	el productor *producer*	

2 **Completar** Fill in the blanks in these sentences.

1. En Puerto Rico, el _____ es una bebida muy popular.

2. Otro nombre para los puertorriqueños es _____.

3. Para viajar a Puerto Rico desde los EE.UU. no hacen falta las _____.

4. Hay puertorriqueños que quieren que su país siga siendo un estado _____ asociado.

5. Algunos puertorriqueños desean que su país se convierta en una nación _____.

3 **¡En español!** Look at the image. Imagine what Diego will say about politics in Puerto Rico, and write a two- or three-sentence introduction to this episode.

Diego Palacios, Puerto Rico

Saludos y bienvenidos... _____

_____

_____

_____

_____

_____

_____

Mientras ves el video

4 **¿Qué ves?** Identify what you see in the video.

_____ 1. un caballo   _____ 5. un mapa

_____ 2. un avión   _____ 6. un cajero automático

_____ 3. una ballena   _____ 7. un gimnasio

_____ 4. el mar   _____ 8. un buzón

5 **Opiniones** Listen to what these people say, and match the caption with a person.

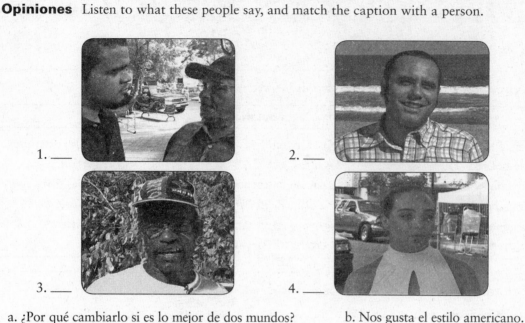

1. ___

2. ___

3. ___

4. ___

a. ¿Por qué cambiarlo si es lo mejor de dos mundos?   b. Nos gusta el estilo americano.

c. Yo prefiero que Puerto Rico se quede como está.   d. Yo quiero la estadidad, no hay nada más.

e. Yo creo que Puerto Rico debe ser independiente ahora.

Después de ver el video

6 **¿Cierto o falso?** Indicate whether each statement is **cierto** or **falso**.

1. En Puerto Rico, hay casi dos millones de habitantes. _____

2. Los puertorriqueños pueden votar para elegir al presidente de los Estados Unidos. _____

3. Puerto Rico es un territorio de los Estados Unidos. _____

4. La moneda de Puerto Rico es el dólar estadounidense. _____

5. La aduana de la isla está a cargo del gobierno de Puerto Rico. _____

6. Todos los puertorriqueños están de acuerdo en que su país sea un estado libre asociado. _____

7 **Eres de Puerto Rico** Imagine that you are Puerto Rican and you are preparing to address Congress. Write a speech explaining your position on the status of Puerto Rico and defend your argument.

_____

_____

_____

_____

_____

_____

_____

_____

_____

_____

_____

contextos   Lección 1

1 **Identificar** You will hear six short exchanges. For each one, decide whether it is a greeting, an introduction, or a leave-taking. Mark the appropriate column with an **X**.

> **modelo**
>
> *You hear:* RAQUEL David, te presento a Paulina.
>   DAVID Encantado.
> *You mark:* an **X** under *Introduction*.

	Greeting	Introduction	Leave-taking
Modelo	_____	**X**	_____
1.	_____	_____	_____
2.	_____	_____	_____
3.	_____	_____	_____
4.	_____	_____	_____
5.	_____	_____	_____
6.	_____	_____	_____

2 **Asociar** You will hear three conversations. Look at the drawing and write the number of the conversation under the appropriate group of people.

3 **Preguntas** Listen to each question or statement and respond with an answer from the list in your lab manual. Repeat the correct response after the speaker.

a. Bien, gracias.   c. Lo siento.   e. Nada.
b. Chau.   d. Mucho gusto.   f. Soy de los Estados Unidos.

Lección 1 Lab Activities   **1**

pronunciación

The Spanish alphabet

The Spanish and English alphabets are almost identical, with a few exceptions. For example, the Spanish letter **ñ (eñe)** doesn't occur in the English alphabet. Furthermore, the letters **k (ka)** and **w (doble ve)** are used only in words of foreign origin. Examine the chart below to find other differences.

Letra	Nombre(s)	Ejemplo(s)	Letra	Nombre(s)	Ejemplo(s)
a	a	adiós	n	ene	nacionalidad
b	be	bien, problema	ñ	eñe	mañana
c	ce	cosa, cero	o	o	once
ch*	che	chico	p	pe	profesor
d	de	diario, nada	q	cu	qué
e	e	estudiante	r	ere	regular, señora
f	efe	foto	s	ese	señor
g	ge	gracias, Gerardo, regular	t	te	tú
h	hache	hola	u	u	usted
i	i	igualmente	v	ve	vista, nuevo
j	jota	Javier	w	doble ve	*walkman*
k	ka, ca	kilómetro	x	equis	existir, México
l	ele	lápiz	y	i griega, ye	yo
ll*	elle	llave	z	zeta, ceta	zona
m	eme	mapa			

* Ch and ll are no longer considered separate letters.

1 **El alfabeto** Repeat the Spanish alphabet and example words after the speaker.

2 **Práctica** When you hear the number, say the corresponding word aloud and then spell it. Then listen to the speaker and repeat the correct response.

1. nada
2. maleta
3. quince
4. muy
5. hombre
6. por favor
7. San Fernando
8. Estados Unidos
9. Puerto Rico
10. España
11. Javier
12. Ecuador
13. Maite
14. gracias
15. Nueva York

3 **Dictado** You will hear six people introduce themselves. Listen carefully and write the people's names as they spell them.

1. _____

2. _____

3. _____

4. _____

5. _____

6. _____

estructura

1.1 Nouns and articles

1 **Identificar** You will hear a series of words. Decide whether the word is masculine or feminine, and mark an **X** in the appropriate column.

> **modelo**
>
> *You hear:* lección
> *You mark:* an **X** under *feminine*.

	Masculine	**Feminine**
Modelo	_____	X _____
1.	_____	_____
2.	_____	_____
3.	_____	_____
4.	_____	_____
5.	_____	_____
6.	_____	_____
7.	_____	_____
8.	_____	_____

2 **Transformar** Change each word from the masculine to the feminine. Repeat the correct answer after the speaker. (6 *items*)

> **modelo**
>
> el chico
> la chica

3 **Cambiar** Change each word from the singular to the plural. Repeat the correct answer after the speaker. (8 *items*)

> **modelo**
>
> una palabra
> unas palabras

4 **Completar** Listen as Silvia reads her shopping list. Write the missing words in your lab manual.

_____ diccionario

un _____

_____ cuadernos

_____ mapa de _____

_____ lápices

Lección 1 Lab Activities   **3**

1.2 Numbers 0–30

1 **¡Bingo!** You are going to play two games (**juegos**) of bingo. As you hear each number, mark it with an **X** on your bingo card.

Juego 1		
1	3	5
29	25	6
14	18	17
9	12	21

Juego 2		
0	30	27
10	3	2
16	19	4
28	22	20

2 **Números** Use the cue in your lab manual to tell how many there are of each item. Repeat the correct response after the speaker.

> **modelo**
> *You see:* 18 chicos
> *You say:* dieciocho chicos

1. 15 lápices
2. 4 computadoras
3. 8 cuadernos

4. 22 días
5. 9 lecciones
6. 30 fotos

7. 1 palabra
8. 26 diccionarios
9. 12 países

10. 3 problemas
11. 17 escuelas
12. 25 turistas

3 **Completar** You will hear a series of math problems. Write the missing numbers and solve the problems.

1. _____ + ____11____ = _____

2. _____ − ____5____ = _____

3. ____8____ + _____ = _____

4. _____ − ____12____ = _____

5. ____3____ + _____ = _____

6. _____ + ____0____ = _____

4 **Preguntas** Look at the drawing and answer each question you hear. Repeat the correct response after the speaker. (*6 items*)

1.3 Present tense of **ser**

1 Identificar Listen to each sentence and mark an **X** in the column for the subject of the verb.

You hear: Son pasajeros.
You mark: an **X** under **ellos**.

	yo	tú	él	nosotros	ellos
Modelo	___	___	___	___	X
1.	___	___	___	___	___
2.	___	___	___	___	___
3.	___	___	___	___	___
4.	___	___	___	___	___
5.	___	___	___	___	___
6.	___	___	___	___	___

2 Cambiar Form a new sentence using the cue you hear as the subject. Repeat the correct answer after the speaker. (*8 items*)

modelo

Isabel es de los Estados Unidos. (yo)
Yo soy de los Estados Unidos.

3 Escoger Listen to each question and choose the most logical response.

1. a. Soy Patricia.   b. Es la señora Gómez.
2. a. Es de California.   b. Él es conductor.
3. a. Es de Canadá.   b. Es un diccionario.
4. a. Es de Patricia.   b. Soy estudiante.
5. a. Él es conductor.   b. Es de España.
6. a. Es un cuaderno.   b. Soy de los Estados Unidos.

4 Preguntas Answer each question you hear using the cue in your lab manual. Repeat the correct response after the speaker.

modelo

You hear: ¿De dónde es Pablo?
You see: Estados Unidos
You say: Él es de los Estados Unidos.

1. España   2. California   3. México   4. Ecuador   5. Puerto Rico   6. Colorado

5 ¿Quiénes son? Listen to this conversation and write the answers to the questions in your lab manual.

1. ¿Cómo se llama el hombre? _____   4. ¿De dónde es ella? _____
2. ¿Cómo se llama la mujer? _____   5. ¿Quién es estudiante? _____
3. ¿De dónde es él? _____   6. ¿Quién es profesor? _____

1.4 Telling time

1 **La hora** Look at the clock and listen to the statement. Indicate whether the statement is **cierto** or **falso**.

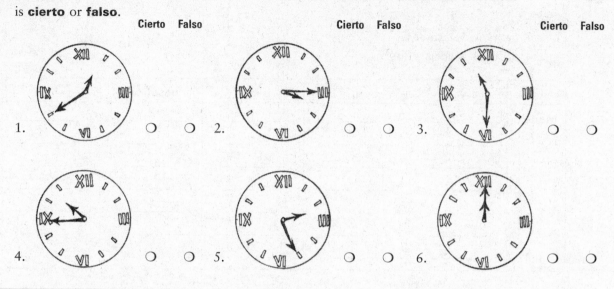

	Cierto	Falso		Cierto	Falso		Cierto	Falso
1.	○	○	2.	○	○	3.	○	○
4.	○	○	5.	○	○	6.	○	○

2 **Preguntas** Some people want to know what time it is. Answer their questions, using the cues in your lab manual. Repeat the correct response after the speaker.

> **modelo**
> *You hear:* ¿Qué hora es, por favor?
> *You see:* 3:10 p.m.
> *You say:* Son las tres y diez de la tarde.

1. 1:30 p.m. 3. 2:05 p.m. 5. 4:54 p.m.
2. 9:06 a.m. 4. 7:15 a.m. 6. 10:23 p.m.

3 **¿A qué hora?** You are trying to plan your class schedule. Ask your counselor what time these classes meet and write the answer.

> **modelo**
> *You see:* la clase de economía
> *You say:* ¿A qué hora es la clase de economía?
> *You hear:* Es a las once y veinte de la mañana.
> *You write:* 11:20 a.m.

1. la clase de biología: _____   4. la clase de literatura: _____

2. la clase de arte: _____   5. la clase de historia: _____

3. la clase de matemáticas: _____   6. la clase de sociología: _____

vocabulario

You will now hear the vocabulary found in your textbook on the last page of this lesson. Listen and repeat each Spanish word or phrase after the speaker.

contextos

Lección 2

1 **Identificar** Look at each drawing and listen to the statement. Indicate whether the statement is **cierto** or **falso**.

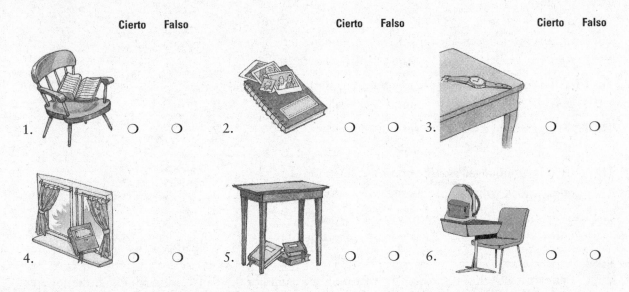

	Cierto	Falso		Cierto	Falso		Cierto	Falso
1.	○	○	2.	○	○	3.	○	○
4.	○	○	5.	○	○	6.	○	○

2 **¿Qué día es?** Your friend Diego is never sure what day of the week it is. Respond to his questions saying that it is the day before the one he mentions. Then repeat the correct answer after the speaker. (6 items)

> **modelo**
> Hoy es domingo, ¿no?
> No, hoy es sábado.

3 **Preguntas** You will hear a series of questions. Look at Susana's schedule for today and answer each question. Then repeat the correct response after the speaker.

martes 18	
○	
9:00 economía — Sr. Rivera	1:30 prueba de contabilidad — Sr. Ramos
11:00 química — Sra. Hernández	3:00 matemáticas — Srta. Torres
12:15 cafetería — Carmen	4:30 laboratorio de computación — Héctor
○	

Lección 2 Lab Activities

pronunciación

Spanish vowels

Spanish vowels are never silent; they are always pronounced in a short, crisp way without the glide sounds used in English.

a	e	i	o	u

The letter **a** is pronounced like the *a* in *father*, but shorter.

Álex   cl**a**se   n**a**d**a**   enc**a**nt**a**d**a**

The letter **e** is pronounced like the *e* in *they*, but shorter.

el   **e**n**e**   m**e**sa   **e**l**e**fant**e**

The letter **i** sounds like the *ee* in *beet*, but shorter.

Inés   ch**i**ca   t**i**za   señor**i**ta

The letter **o** is pronounced like the *o* in *tone*, but shorter.

h**o**la   c**o**n   libr**o**   d**o**n Francisc**o**

The letter **u** sounds like the *oo* in *room*, but shorter.

uno   reg**u**lar   sal**u**dos   g**u**sto

---

1   **Práctica**   Practice the vowels by repeating the names of these places in Spain after the speaker.

1. Madrid
2. Alicante
3. Tenerife
4. Toledo
5. Barcelona
6. Granada
7. Burgos
8. La Coruña

---

2   **Oraciones**   Repeat each sentence after the speaker, focusing on the vowels.

1. Hola. Me llamo Ramiro Morgado.
2. Estudio arte en la Universidad de Salamanca.
3. Tomo también literatura y contabilidad.
4. Ay, tengo clase en cinco minutos. ¡Nos vemos!

---

3   **Refranes**   Repeat each saying after the speaker to practice vowels.

1. Del dicho al hecho hay un gran trecho.
2. Cada loco con su tema.

---

4   **Dictado**   You will hear a conversation. Listen carefully and write what you hear during the pauses. The entire conversation will then be repeated so you can check your work.

JUAN _____

_____

_____

ROSA _____

JUAN _____

ROSA _____

---

8   **Lección 2** Lab Activities

estructura

2.1 Present tense of -ar verbs

1 **Identificar** Listen to each sentence and mark an **X** in the column for the subject of the verb.

> **modelo**
> *You hear:* Trabajo en la cafetería.
> *You mark:* an **X** under **yo**.

	yo	tú	él/ella	nosotros/as	ellos/ellas
Modelo	X	___	___	___	___
1.	___	___	___	___	___
2.	___	___	___	___	___
3.	___	___	___	___	___
4.	___	___	___	___	___
5.	___	___	___	___	___
6.	___	___	___	___	___
7.	___	___	___	___	___
8.	___	___	___	___	___

2 **Cambiar** Form a new sentence using the cue you hear as the subject. Repeat the correct answer after the speaker. (*6 items*)

> **modelo**
> María practica los verbos ahora. (José y María)
> *José y María practican los verbos ahora.*

3 **Preguntas** Answer each question you hear in the negative. Repeat the correct response after the speaker. (*8 items*)

> **modelo**
> ¿Estudias geografía?
> *No, yo no estudio geografía.*

4 **Completar** Listen to the following description and write the missing words in your lab manual.

Teresa y yo (1) _____ en la Universidad Autónoma de Madrid. Teresa

(2) _____ lenguas extranjeras. Ella (3) _____ trabajar

en las Naciones Unidas (*United Nations*). Yo (4) _____ clases de periodismo.

También me gusta (5) _____ y (6) _____. Los sábados

(7) _____ con una tuna. Una tuna es una orquesta (*orchestra*) estudiantil.

Los jóvenes de la tuna (8) _____ por las calles (*streets*) y

(9) _____ canciones (*songs*) tradicionales de España.

2.2 Forming questions in Spanish

1 **Escoger** Listen to each question and choose the most logical response.

1. a. Porque mañana es la prueba.   b. Porque no hay clase mañana.
2. a. Viaja en autobús.   b. Viaja a Toledo.
3. a. Llegamos el 3 de abril.   b. Llegamos al estadio.
4. a. Isabel y Diego dibujan.   b. Dibujan en la clase de arte.
5. a. No, enseña física.   b. No, enseña en la Universidad Politécnica.
6. a. Escuchan un video.   b. Escuchan música clásica.
7. a. Sí, me gusta mucho.   b. Miro la televisión en la residencia.
8. a. Hay diccionarios en la biblioteca.   b. Hay tres.

2 **Cambiar** Change each sentence into a question using the cue in your lab manual. Repeat the correct response after the speaker.

> **modelo**
>
> *You hear:* Los turistas toman el autobús.
> *You see:* ¿Quiénes?
> *You say:* ¿Quiénes toman el autobús?

1. ¿Dónde?   3. ¿Qué?, (tú)   5. ¿Cuándo?   7. ¿Quiénes?
2. ¿Cuántos?   4. ¿Quién?   6. ¿Dónde?   8. ¿Qué?, (tú)

3 **¿Lógico o ilógico?** You will hear some questions and the responses. Decide if they are **lógico** (*logical*) or **ilógico** (*illogical*).

1. Lógico   Ilógico   3. Lógico   Ilógico   5. Lógico   Ilógico
2. Lógico   Ilógico   4. Lógico   Ilógico   6. Lógico   Ilógico

4 **Un anuncio** Listen to this radio advertisement and answer the questions in your lab manual.

1. ¿Dónde está (*is*) la Escuela Cervantes? _____

_____

2. ¿Qué cursos ofrecen (*do they offer*) en la Escuela Cervantes? _____

_____

3. ¿Cuándo practican los estudiantes el español? _____

_____

4. ¿Adónde viajan los estudiantes de la Escuela Cervantes? _____

_____

2.3 Present tense of **estar**

1   **Describir** Look at the drawing and listen to each statement. Indicate whether the statement is **cierto** or **falso**.

	Cierto	Falso			Cierto	Falso			Cierto	Falso
1.	○	○		3.	○	○		5.	○	○
2.	○	○		4.	○	○		6.	○	○

2   **Cambiar** Form a new sentence using the cue you hear. Repeat the correct answer after the speaker. (*8 items*)

> **modelo**
> Irma está en la biblioteca. (Irma y Hugo)
> Irma y Hugo *están en la biblioteca.*

3   **Escoger** You will hear some sentences with a beep in place of the verb. Decide which form of **ser** or **estar** should complete each sentence and circle it.

> **modelo**
> *You hear:* Javier (*beep*) estudiante.
> *You circle:* **es** because the sentence is **Javier es estudiante**.

1. es	está	5. es	está
2. es	está	6. eres	estás
3. es	está	7. son	están
4. Somos	Estamos	8. Son	Están

    Lección 2 Lab Activities   **11**

2.4 Numbers 31 and higher

1 **Números de teléfono** You want to invite some classmates to a party, but you don't have their telephone numbers. Ask the person who sits beside you what their telephone numbers are, and write the answer.

> **modelo**
>
> *You see:* Elián
> *You say:* ¿Cuál es el número de teléfono de Elián?
> *You hear:* Es el ocho, cuarenta y tres, cero, ocho, treinta y cinco.
> *You write:* 843-0835

1. Arturo: _____

2. Alicia: _____

3. Roberto: _____

4. Graciela: _____

5. Simón: _____

6. Eva: _____

7. José Antonio: _____

8. Mariana: _____

2 **Dictado** Listen carefully and write each number as numerals rather than words.

1. _____   4. _____   7. _____

2. _____   5. _____   8. _____

3. _____   6. _____   9. _____

3 **Mensaje telefónico** Listen to this telephone conversation and complete the phone message in your lab manual with the correct information.

Mensaje telefónico

Para (*For*) _____

De parte de (*From*) _____

Teléfono _____

Mensaje _____

_____

_____

_____

---

vocabulario

You will now hear the vocabulary found in your textbook on the last page of this lesson. Listen and repeat each Spanish word or phrase after the speaker.

contextos

Lección 3

1 **Escoger** You will hear some questions. Look at the family tree and choose the correct answer to each question.

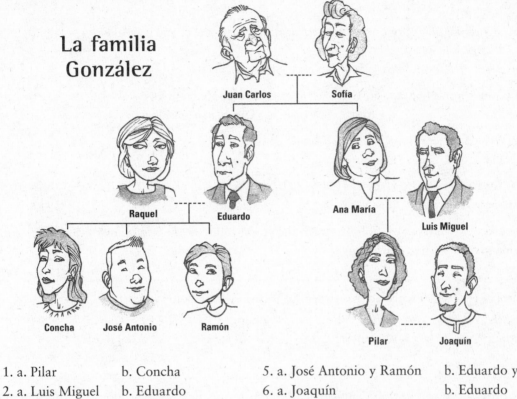

La familia González

1. a. Pilar   b. Concha   5. a. José Antonio y Ramón   b. Eduardo y Ana María
2. a. Luis Miguel b. Eduardo   6. a. Joaquín   b. Eduardo
3. a. Sofía   b. Ana María   7. a. Ana María   b. Sofía
4. a. Raquel   b. Sofía   8. a. Luis Miguel   b. Juan Carlos

2 **La familia González** Héctor wants to verify the relationship between various members of the González family. Look at the drawing and answer his questions with the correct information. Repeat the correct response after the speaker. (*6 items*)

> **modelo**
> Juan Carlos es el abuelo de Eduardo, ¿verdad?
> No, Juan Carlos es el padre de Eduardo.

3 **Profesiones** Listen to each statement and write the number of the statement below the drawing it describes.

a. _____   b. _____   c. _____   d. _____

Diphthongs and linking

In Spanish, **a**, **e**, and **o** are considered strong vowels. The weak vowels are **i** and **u**.

herm**a**n**o**   ni**ña**   cu**ña**d**o**

A diphthong is a combination of two weak vowels or of a strong vowel and a weak vowel. Diphthongs are pronounced as a single syllable.

r**ui**do   par**ie**ntes   per**io**dista

Two identical vowel sounds that appear together are pronounced like one long vowel.

l**a** **a**buela   m**i** **hi**jo   una clas**e** **e**xcelente

Two identical consonants together sound like a single consonant.

co**n** **N**atalia   su**s** **s**obrinos   la**s** **s**illas

A consonant at the end of a word is always linked with the vowel sound at the beginning of the next word.

E**s** **i**ngeniera.   mi**s** **a**buelos   su**s** **hi**jos

A vowel at the end of a word is always linked with the vowel sound at the beginning of the next word.

m**i** **h**ermano   s**u** **e**sposa   nuestr**o** **a**migo

1 Práctica Repeat each word after the speaker, focusing on the diphthongs.

1. historia
2. nieto
3. parientes
4. novia
5. residencia
6. prueba
7. puerta
8. ciencias
9. lenguas
10. estudiar
11. izquierda
12. ecuatoriano

2 Oraciones When you hear the number, read the corresponding sentence aloud. Then listen to the speaker and repeat the sentence.

1. Hola. Me llamo Anita Amaral. Soy del Ecuador.
2. Somos seis en mi familia.
3. Tengo dos hermanos y una hermana.
4. Mi papá es del Ecuador y mi mamá es de España.

3 Refranes Repeat each saying after the speaker to practice diphthongs and linking sounds.

1. Cuando una puerta se cierra, otra se abre.
2. Hablando del rey de Roma, por la puerta se asoma.

4 Dictado You will hear eight sentences. Each will be said twice. Listen carefully and write what you hear.

1. _____
2. _____
3. _____
4. _____
5. _____
6. _____
7. _____
8. _____

estructura

3.1 Descriptive adjectives

1 Transformar Change each sentence from the masculine to the feminine. Repeat the correct answer after the speaker. (*6 items*)

> **modelo**
> El chico es mexicano.
> La chica es mexicana.

2 Cambiar Change each sentence from the singular to the plural. Repeat the correct answer after the speaker. (*6 items*)

> **modelo**
> El profesor es ecuatoriano.
> Los profesores son ecuatorianos.

3 Mis compañeros de clase Describe your classmates, using the cues in your lab manual. Repeat the correct response after the speaker.

> **modelo**
> *You hear:* María
> *You see:* alto
> *You say:* María es alta.

1. simpático
2. rubio
3. inteligente
4. pelirrojo y muy bonito
5. alto y moreno
6. delgado y trabajador
7. bajo y gordo
8. tonto

4 Completar Listen to the following description and write the missing words in your lab manual.

Mañana mis parientes llegan de Guayaquil. Son cinco personas: mi abuela Isabel, tío Carlos y tía Josefina, y mis primos Susana y Tomás. Mi prima es (1)_____ y (2)_____. Baila muy bien. Tomás es un niño (3)_____, pero es (4)_____. Tío Carlos es (5)_____ y (6)_____. Tía Josefina es (7)_____ y (8)_____. Mi abuela es (9)_____ y muy (10)_____.

5 La familia Rivas Look at the photo of the Rivas family and listen to each statement. Indicate whether the statement is **cierto** or **falso**.

	Cierto	Falso
1.	○	○
2.	○	○
3.	○	○
4.	○	○
5.	○	○
6.	○	○
7.	○	○

3.2 Possessive adjectives

1   **Identificar** Listen to each statement and mark an **X** in the column for the possessive adjective you hear.

> **modelo**
>
> *You hear*: Es mi diccionario de español.
> *You mark*: an **X** under **my**.

	my	*your* (familiar)	*your* (formal)	*his/her*	*our*	*their*
Modelo	X					
1.						
2.						
3.						
4.						
5.						
6.						
7.						
8.						

2   **Escoger** Listen to each question and choose the most logical response.

1. a. No, su hijastro no está aquí.
   b. Sí, tu hijastro está aquí.
2. a. No, nuestros abuelos son argentinos.
   b. Sí, sus abuelos son norteamericanos.
3. a. Sí, tu hijo trabaja ahora.
   b. Sí, mi hijo trabaja en la librería Goya.
4. a. Sus padres regresan hoy a las nueve.
   b. Mis padres regresan hoy a las nueve.
5. a. Nuestra hermana se llama Margarita.
   b. Su hermana se llama Margarita.
6. a. Tus plumas están en el escritorio.
   b. Sus plumas están en el escritorio.
7. a. No, mi sobrino es ingeniero.
   b. Sí, nuestro sobrino es programador.
8. a. Su horario es muy bueno.
   b. Nuestro horario es muy bueno.

3   **Preguntas** Answer each question you hear in the affirmative using the appropriate possessive adjective. Repeat the correct response after the speaker. (*7 items*)

> **modelo**
>
> ¿Es tu lápiz?
> Sí, *es mi lápiz.*

3.3 Present tense of -er and -ir verbs

1 **Identificar** Listen to each statement and mark an **X** in the column for the subject of the verb.

> **modelo**
> *You hear:* Corro con Dora mañana.
> *You mark:* an **X** under **yo**.

	yo	tú	él/ella	nosotros/as	ellos/ellas
Modelo	X	_____	_____	_____	_____
1.	_____	_____	_____	_____	_____
2.	_____	_____	_____	_____	_____
3.	_____	_____	_____	_____	_____
4.	_____	_____	_____	_____	_____
5.	_____	_____	_____	_____	_____
6.	_____	_____	_____	_____	_____

2 **Cambiar** Listen to the following statements. Using the cues you hear, say that these people do the same activities. Repeat the correct answer after the speaker. (*8 items*)

> **modelo**
> Julia aprende francés. (mi amigo)
> **Mi amigo también aprende francés.**

3 **Preguntas** Answer each question you hear in the negative. Repeat the correct response after the speaker. (*8 items*)

> **modelo**
> ¿Viven ellos en una residencia estudiantil?
> **No, ellos no viven en una residencia estudiantil.**

4 **Describir** Listen to each statement and write the number of the statement below the drawing it describes.

a. _____   b. _____   c. _____   d. _____

Lección 3 Lab Activities   **17**

3.4 Present tense of **tener** and **venir**

1 Cambiar Form a new sentence using the cue you hear as the subject. Repeat the correct answer after the speaker. (*6 items*)

> modelo
> Alicia viene a las seis. (David y Rita)
> David y Rita vienen a las seis.

2 Consejos (Advice) Some people are not doing what they should. Say what they have to do. Repeat the correct response after the speaker. (*6 items*)

> modelo
> Elena no trabaja.
> Elena tiene que trabajar.

3 Preguntas Answer each question you hear using the cue in your lab manual. Repeat the correct answer after the speaker.

> modelo
> ¿Tienen sueño los niños? (no)
> No, los niños no tienen sueño.

1. sí, (yo)   3. no, (nosotros)   5. sí, (mi abuela)   7. el domingo
2. Roberto   4. sí, dos, (yo)   6. mis tíos

4 Situaciones Listen to each situation and choose the appropriate **tener** expression. Each situation will be repeated.

1. a. Tienes sueño.   b. Tienes prisa.
2. a. Tienen mucho cuidado.   b. Tienen hambre.
3. a. Tenemos mucho calor.   b. Tenemos mucho frío.
4. a. Tengo sed.   b. Tengo hambre.
5. a. Ella tiene razón.   b. Ella no tiene razón.
6. a. Tengo miedo.   b. Tengo sueño.

5 Mi familia Listen to the following description. Then read the statements in your lab manual and decide whether they are **cierto** or **falso**.

	Cierto	Falso		Cierto	Falso
1. Francisco desea ser periodista.	○	○	4. Él tiene una familia pequeña.	○	○
2. Francisco tiene 20 años.	○	○	5. Su madre es ingeniera.	○	○
3. Francisco vive con su familia.	○	○	6. Francisco tiene una hermana mayor.	○	○

vocabulario

You will now hear the vocabulary found in your textbook on the last page of this lesson. Listen and repeat each Spanish word or phrase after the speaker.

contextos

Lección 4

1 **Lugares** You will hear six people describe what they are doing. Choose the place that corresponds to the activity.

1. _____
2. _____
3. _____
4. _____
5. _____
6. _____

a. el museo

b. el café

c. la piscina

d. el cine

e. el estadio

f. las montañas

g. el parque

h. la biblioteca

2 **Describir** For each drawing, you will hear two statements. Choose the one that corresponds to the drawing.

1. a.   b.

2. a.   b.

3. a.   b.

4. a.   b.

3 **Completar** Listen to this description and write the missing words in your lab manual.

Chapultepec es un (1) _____ muy grande en el (2) _____ de

la (3) _____ de México. Los (4) _____ muchas

(5) _____ llegan a Chapultepec a pasear, descansar y practicar

(6) _____ como (like) el (7) _____, el fútbol, el vóleibol y

el (8) _____. Muchos turistas también (9) _____ por

Chapultepec. Visitan los (10) _____ y el (11) _____ a los

Niños Héroes.

pronunciación

Word stress and accent marks

Every Spanish syllable contains at least one vowel. When two vowels are joined in the same syllable, they form a diphthong. A monosyllable is a word formed by a single syllable.

pe - **lí** - cu - la   e - **di** - fi - **cio**   ver   **yo**

The syllable of a Spanish word that is pronounced most emphatically is the "stressed" syllable.

bi - blio - **te** - ca   vi - si - **tar**   **par** - que   **fút** - bol

Words that end in **n**, **s**, or a **vowel** are usually stressed on the next-to-last syllable.

pe - **lo** - ta   pis - **ci** - na   **ra** - tos   **ha** - blan

If words that end in **n**, **s**, or a **vowel** are stressed on the last syllable, they must carry an accent mark on the stressed syllable.

na - ta - **ción**   pa - **pá**   in - **glés**   Jo - **sé**

Words that do not end in **n**, **s**, or a **vowel** are usually stressed on the last syllable.

bai - **lar**   es - pa - **ñol**   u - ni - ver - si - **dad**   tra - ba - ja - **dor**

If words that do not end in **n**, **s**, or a **vowel** are stressed on the next-to-last syllable, they must carry an accent mark on the stressed syllable.

béis - bol   **lá** - piz   **ár** - bol   **Gó** - mez

---

1   **Práctica**   Repeat each word after the speaker, stressing the correct syllable.

1. profesor	4. Mazatlán	7. niños	10. México
2. Puebla	5. examen	8. Guadalajara	11. están
3. ¿Cuántos?	6. ¿Cómo?	9. programador	12. geografía

---

2   **Conversación**   Repeat the conversation after the speaker to practice word stress.

MARINA   Hola, Carlos. ¿Qué tal?

CARLOS   Bien. Oye, ¿a qué hora es el partido de fútbol?

MARINA   Creo que es a las siete.

CARLOS   ¿Quieres ir?

MARINA   Lo siento, pero no puedo. Tengo que estudiar biología.

---

3   **Refranes**   Repeat each saying after the speaker to practice word stress.

1. Quien ríe de último, ríe mejor.   2. En la unión está la fuerza.

---

4   **Dictado**   You will hear six sentences. Each will be said twice. Listen carefully and write what you hear.

1. _____

2. _____

3. _____

4. _____

5. _____

6. _____

---

estructura

4.1 Present tense of ir

1 **Identificar** Listen to each sentence and mark an **X** in the column for the subject of the verb you hear.

> **modelo**
>
> *You hear:* Van a ver una película.
> *You mark:* an **X** under **ellos/ellas**.

	yo	tú	él/ella	nosotros/as	ellos/ellas
Modelo	_____	_____	_____	_____	X _____
1.	_____	_____	_____	_____	_____
2.	_____	_____	_____	_____	_____
3.	_____	_____	_____	_____	_____
4.	_____	_____	_____	_____	_____
5.	_____	_____	_____	_____	_____
6.	_____	_____	_____	_____	_____

2 **Cambiar** Form a new sentence using the cue you hear as the subject. Repeat the correct answer after the speaker. (*8 items*)

> **modelo**
>
> Ustedes van al Museo Frida Kahlo. (yo)
> *Yo voy al Museo Frida Kahlo.*

3 **Preguntas** Answer each question you hear using the cue in your lab manual. Repeat the correct response after the speaker.

> **modelo**
>
> *You hear:* ¿Quiénes van a la piscina?
> *You see:* Gustavo y Elisa
> *You say:* Gustavo y Elisa van a la piscina.

1. mis amigos   3. al partido de baloncesto   5. sí
2. en el Café Tacuba   4. no   6. pasear en bicicleta

4 **¡Vamos!** Listen to this conversation. Then read the statements in your lab manual and decide whether they are **cierto** or **falso**.

	Cierto	Falso
1. Claudia va a ir al gimnasio.	○	○
2. Claudia necesita comprar una mochila.	○	○
3. Sergio va a visitar a su tía.	○	○
4. Sergio va al gimnasio a las ocho de la noche.	○	○
5. Sergio va a ir al cine a las seis.	○	○
6. Claudia y Sergio van a ver una película.	○	○

4.2 Stem-changing verbs: e→ie, o→ue

1 **Identificar** Listen to each sentence and write the infinitive form of the verb you hear.

> **modelo**
> You hear: No entiendo el problema.
> You write: *entender*

1. _____   4. _____   7. _____

2. _____   5. _____   8. _____

3. _____   6. _____

2 **Preguntas** Answer each question you hear using the cue in your lab manual. Repeat the correct response after the speaker.

> **modelo**
> You hear: ¿A qué hora comienza el partido?
> You see: 2:15 p.m.
> You say: *El partido comienza a las dos y cuarto de la tarde.*

1. el jueves, (nosotros)   3. sí   5. leer una revista, (yo)   7. a las tres, (nosotros)

2. no, (yo)   4. sí, (ustedes)   6. mirar la televisión   8. Samuel

3 **Diversiones** Look at these listings from the entertainment section in a newspaper. Then listen to the questions and write the answers in your lab manual.

23D

MÚSICA	Pinturas de José Clemente	**Campeonato de baloncesto**
Palacio de Bellas Artes	Orozco	Los Universitarios vs. Los Toros
Ballet folclórico	De martes a domingo,	Gimnasio Municipal
Viernes 9, 8:30 p.m.	de 10:00 a.m. a 6:00 p.m.	Sábado 10, 7:30 p.m.
	Entrada libre	
Bosque de Chapultepec		**Torneo de Golf**
Concierto de música mexicana	**DEPORTES**	con Lee Treviño
Domingo, 1:00 p.m.	**Copa Internacional de Fútbol**	Club de Golf Atlas
	México vs. Guatemala	Domingo 8, 9:00 a.m.
MUSEOS	Estadio Martín	
Museo de Arte Moderno	Viernes 9, 8:30 p.m.	

1. _____

2. _____

3. _____

4. _____

5. _____

4.3 Stem-changing verbs: e→i

1 Completar Listen to this radio broadcast and fill in the missing words.

Este fin de semana los excursionistas (*hikers*) (1) _____ más senderos (*trails*).

Dicen que ir de (2) _____ a las montañas es una (3) _____

muy popular y (4) _____ que (5) _____ más senderos. Si lo

(6) _____, la gente va a (7) _____ muy feliz. Si no, ustedes

pueden (8) _____ la historia aquí, en Radio Montaña.

2 Escoger Listen to each question and choose the most logical response.

1. a. Normalmente pido tacos.   b. Voy al restaurante los lunes.

2. a. Consigo novelas en la biblioteca.   b. Consigo revistas en el centro.

3. a. Repiten la película el sábado.   b. No deseo ver la película.

4. a. Sigue un programa de baloncesto.   b. No, prefiere bucear.

5. a. Nunca pido pizza.   b. Nunca pido perdón.

6. a. Prefiere visitar un monumento.   b. Prefiere buscar en la biblioteca.

7. a. ¿Quién fue el primer presidente?   b. A las cuatro de la tarde.

8. a. Sí, es muy interesante.   b. Sí, mi hermano juega.

3 Conversación Listen to the conversation and answer the questions.

1. ¿Qué quiere Paola?

_____

2. ¿Por qué repite Paola las palabras?

_____

3. ¿Hace Miguel el favor que pide Paola?

_____

4. ¿Dónde puede conseguir la revista?

_____

4.4 Verbs with irregular **yo** forms

1 **Describir** For each drawing, you will hear two statements. Choose the one that corresponds to the drawing.

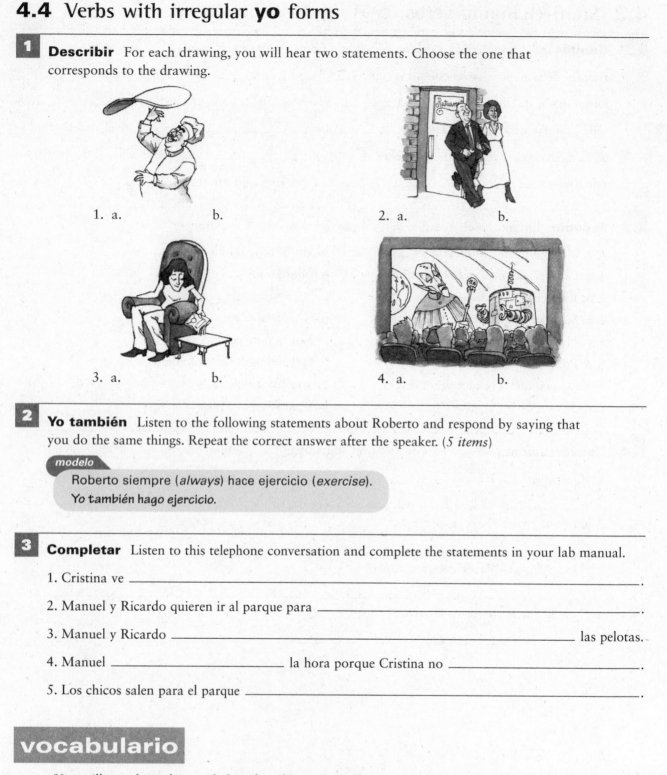

1. a. _____ b. _____

2. a. _____ b. _____

3. a. _____ b. _____

4. a. _____ b. _____

2 **Yo también** Listen to the following statements about Roberto and respond by saying that you do the same things. Repeat the correct answer after the speaker. (*5 items*)

> **modelo**
> Roberto siempre (*always*) hace ejercicio (*exercise*).
> Yo también hago ejercicio.

3 **Completar** Listen to this telephone conversation and complete the statements in your lab manual.

1. Cristina ve _____.

2. Manuel y Ricardo quieren ir al parque para _____.

3. Manuel y Ricardo _____ las pelotas.

4. Manuel _____ la hora porque Cristina no _____.

5. Los chicos salen para el parque _____.

vocabulario

You will now hear the vocabulary found in your textbook on the last page of this lesson. Listen and repeat each Spanish word or phrase after the speaker.

contextos   **Lección 5**

1 **Identificar** You will hear a series of words. Write the word that does not belong in each series.

1. _____   5. _____

2. _____   6. _____

3. _____   7. _____

4. _____   8. _____

2 **Describir** For each drawing, you will hear two statements. Choose the one that corresponds to the drawing.

1. a.   b.   2. a.   b.   3. a.   b.

3 **En la agencia de viajes** Listen to this conversation between Mr. Vega and a travel agent. Then read the statements in your lab manual and decide whether they are **cierto** or **falso**.

	Cierto	Falso
1. El señor Vega quiere esquiar, pescar y bucear.	○	○
2. El señor Vega va a Puerto Rico.	○	○
3. El señor Vega quiere ir de vacaciones la primera semana de mayo.	○	○
4. Una habitación en Las Tres Palmas cuesta (*costs*) $85,00.	○	○
5. El hotel tiene restaurante, piscina y *jacuzzi*.	○	○

4 **Escoger** Listen to each statement and choose the most appropriate activity for that weather condition.

1. a. Vamos a ir a la piscina.   b. Vamos a poner la televisión.

2. a. Voy a escribir una carta.   b. Voy a bucear.

3. a. Vamos al museo.   b. Vamos a tomar el sol.

4. a. Mañana voy a pasear en bicicleta.   b. Mañana voy a esquiar.

5. a. Queremos ir al cine.   b. Queremos nadar.

6. a. Voy a correr en el parque.   b. Voy a leer un libro.

7. a. Quiero escuchar música.   b. Quiero jugar al golf.

Lección 5 Lab Activities   **25**

pronunciación

Spanish b and v

There is no difference in pronunciation between the Spanish letters **b** and **v**. However, each letter can be pronounced two different ways, depending on which letters appear next to them.

bueno **v**ólei**b**ol **bib**lioteca **vi**vir

B and **v** are pronounced like the English hard **b** when they appear either as the first letter of a word, at the beginning of a phrase, or after **m** or **n**.

bonito **v**iajar tam**b**ién in**v**estigar

In all other positions, **b** and **v** have a softer pronunciation, which has no equivalent in English. Unlike the hard **b**, which is produced by tightly closing the lips and stopping the flow of air, the soft **b** is produced by keeping the lips slightly open.

de**b**er no**v**io a**b**ril cer**v**eza

In both pronunciations, there is no difference in sound between **b** and **v**. The English v sound, produced by friction between the upper teeth and lower lip, does not exist in Spanish. Instead, the soft **b** comes from friction between the two lips.

bola **v**ela Cari**b**e decli**v**e

When **b** or **v** begins a word, its pronunciation depends on the previous word. At the beginning of a phrase or after a word that ends in **m** or **n**, it is pronounced as a hard **b**.

Verónica y su esposo cantan ‿**b**oleros.

Words that begin with **b** or **v** are pronounced with a soft **b** if they appear immediately after a word that ends in a vowel or any consonant other than **m** or **n**.

Benito es de ‿**B**oquerón pero ‿**v**ive en ‿**V**ictoria.

---

1 **Práctica** Repeat these words after the speaker to practice the **b** and the **v**.

1. hablamos
2. trabajar
3. botones
4. van
5. contabilidad
6. bien
7. doble
8. novia
9. béisbol
10. nublado
11. llave
12. invierno

2 **Oraciones** When you hear the number, read the corresponding sentence aloud, focusing on the **b** and **v** sounds. Then listen to the speaker and repeat the sentence.

1. Vamos a Guaynabo en autobús.
2. Voy de vacaciones a la Isla Culebra.
3. Tengo una habitación individual en el octavo piso.
4. Víctor y Eva van por avión al Caribe.
5. La planta baja es bonita también.
6. ¿Qué vamos a ver en Bayamón?
7. Beatriz, la novia de Víctor, es de Arecibo, Puerto Rico.

3 **Refranes** Repeat each saying after the speaker to practice the **b** and the **v**.

1. No hay mal que por bien no venga.
2. Hombre prevenido vale por dos.

4 **Dictado** You will hear four sentences. Each will be said twice. Listen carefully and write what you hear.

1. _____
2. _____
3. _____
4. _____

estructura

5.1 Estar with conditions and emotions

1 **Describir** For each drawing, you will hear two statements. Choose the one that corresponds to the drawing.

1. a. _____ b. _____   2. a. _____ b. _____

3. a. _____ b. _____   4. a. _____ b. _____

2 **Cambiar** Form a new sentence using the cue you hear as the subject. Repeat the correct answer after the speaker. (*8 items*)

> **modelo**
> Rubén está enojado con Patricia. (mamá)
> Mamá *está enojada con* Patricia.

3 **Preguntas** Answer each question you hear using the cues in your lab manual. Repeat the correct response after the speaker.

> **modelo**
> *You hear:* ¿Está triste Tomás?
> *You see:* no / contento/a
> *You say:* No, Tomás *está contento.*

1. no / abierto/a   3. su hermano   5. no / sucio/a

2. sí, (nosotros)   4. no / ordenado/a   6. estar de vacaciones, (yo)

4 **Situaciones** You will hear four brief conversations. Choose the statement that expresses how the people feel in each situation.

1. a. Ricardo está nervioso.   b. Ricardo está cansado.

2. a. La señora Fuentes está contenta.   b. La señora Fuentes está preocupada.

3. a. Eugenio está aburrido.   b. Eugenio está avergonzado.

4. a. Rosario y Alonso están equivocados. b. Rosario y Alonso están enojados.

5.2 The present progressive

1 **Escoger** Listen to what these people are doing. Then read the statements in your lab manual and choose the appropriate description.

1. a. Es profesor.   b. Es estudiante.

2. a. Es botones.   b. Es inspector de aduanas.

3. a. Eres artista.   b. Eres huésped.

4. a. Son jugadoras de fútbol.   b. Son programadoras.

5. a. Es ingeniero.   b. Es botones.

6. a. Son turistas.   b. Son empleados.

2 **Transformar** Change each sentence from the present tense to the present progressive. Repeat the correct answer after the speaker. (6 *items*)

> *modelo*
>
> Adriana confirma su reservación.
> Adriana *está confirmando su reservación.*

3 **Preguntas** Answer each question you hear using the cue in your lab manual and the present progressive. Repeat the correct response after the speaker.

> *modelo*
>
> *You hear:* ¿Qué hacen ellos?
> *You see:* jugar a las cartas
> *You say:* Ellos *están jugando a las cartas.*

1. hacer las maletas   3. dormir   5. hablar con el botones
2. pescar en el mar   4. correr en el parque   6. comer en el café

4 **Describir** You will hear some questions. Look at the drawing and respond to each question. Repeat the correct answer after the speaker. (6 *items*)

5.3 Ser and estar

1 **Escoger** You will hear some questions with a beep in place of the verb. Decide which form of **ser** or **estar** should complete each question and circle it.

> **modelo**
>
> *You hear:* ¿Cómo (*beep*)?
> *You circle:* **estás** because the question is **¿Cómo estás?**

1. es	está	4. Es	Está
2. Son	Están	5. Es	Está
3. Es	Está	6. Es	Está

2 **¿Cómo es?** You just met Rosa Beltrán at a party. Describe her to a friend by using **ser** or **estar** with the cues you hear. Repeat the correct response after the speaker. (*6 items*)

> **modelo**
>
> muy amable
> *Rosa es muy amable.*

3 **¿Ser o estar?** You will hear the subject of a sentence. Complete the sentence using a form of **ser** or **estar** and the cue in your lab manual. Repeat the correct response after the speaker.

> **modelo**
>
> *You hear:* Papá
> *You see:* en San Juan
> *You say:* Papá está en San Juan.

1. inspector de aduanas	3. a las diez	5. el 14 de febrero
2. la estación de tren	4. ocupados	6. corriendo a clase

4 **¿Lógico o no?** You will hear some statements. Decide if they are **lógico** or **ilógico**.

1. Lógico	Ilógico	4. Lógico	Ilógico
2. Lógico	Ilógico	5. Lógico	Ilógico
3. Lógico	Ilógico	6. Lógico	Ilógico

5 **Ponce** Listen to Carolina's description of her vacation and answer the questions in your lab manual.

1. ¿Dónde está Ponce?

_____

2. ¿Qué tiempo está haciendo?

_____

3. ¿Qué es el Parque de Bombas?

_____

4. ¿Que día es hoy?

_____

5. ¿Por qué no va Carolina al Parque de Bombas hoy?

_____

5.4 Direct object nouns and pronouns

1 **Escoger** Listen to each question and choose the most logical response.

1. a. Sí, voy a comprarlo.
   b. No, no voy a comprarla.

2. a. Joaquín lo tiene.
   b. Joaquín la tiene.

3. a. Sí, los puedo llevar.
   b. No, no te puedo llevar.

4. a. Irene los tiene.
   b. Irene las tiene.

5. a. Sí, te llevamos al partido.
   b. Sí, nos llevas al partido.

6. a. No, vamos a hacerlo mañana.
   b. No, vamos a hacerla mañana.

7. a. Va a conseguirlos mañana.
   b. Va a conseguirlas mañana.

8. a. Pienso visitarla el fin de semana.
   b. Pienso visitarte el fin de semana.

2 **Cambiar** Restate each sentence you hear using a direct object pronoun. Repeat the correct answer after the speaker. (*6 items*)

> *modelo*
> Isabel está mirando la televisión.
> Isabel está mirándola.

Isabel está mirando la televisión con Diego.

3 **No veo nada** You just broke your glasses and now you can't see anything. Respond to each statement using a direct object pronoun. Repeat the correct answer after the speaker. (*6 items*)

> *modelo*
> Allí está el Museo de Arte e Historia.
> ¿Dónde? No lo veo.

4 **Preguntas** Answer each question you hear in the negative. Repeat the correct response after the speaker. (*6 items*)

> *modelo*
> ¿Haces tu maleta?
> No, no la hago.

vocabulario

You will now hear the vocabulary found in your textbook on the last page of this lesson. Listen and repeat each Spanish word or phrase after the speaker.

contextos

Lección 6

1 **¿Lógico o ilógico?** Listen to each statement and indicate if it is **lógico** or **ilógico**.

1. Lógico   Ilógico
2. Lógico   Ilógico
3. Lógico   Ilógico
4. Lógico   Ilógico

5. Lógico   Ilógico
6. Lógico   Ilógico
7. Lógico   Ilógico
8. Lógico   Ilógico

2 **Escoger** Listen as each person talks about the clothing he or she needs to buy. Then choose the activity for which the clothing would be appropriate.

1. a. ir a la playa
2. a. jugar al golf
3. a. salir a bailar
4. a. montar a caballo
5. a. jugar al vóleibol
6. a. hacer un viaje

b. ir al cine
b. buscar trabajo (*work*)
b. ir a las montañas
b. jugar a las cartas
b. comer en un restaurante elegante
b. patinar en línea

3 **Preguntas** Respond to each question saying that the opposite is true. Repeat the correct answer after the speaker. (*6 items*)

> **modelo**
> Las sandalias cuestan mucho, ¿no?
> No, las sandalias cuestan poco.

4 **Describir** You will hear some questions. Look at the drawing and write the answer to each question.

Diana   Carmen

1. _____
2. _____
3. _____
4. _____

pronunciación

The consonants **d** and **t**

Like **b** and **v**, the Spanish **d** can have a hard sound or a soft sound, depending on which letters appear next to it.

     ¿**D**ónde?   ven**d**er   na**d**ar   ver**d**a**d**

At the beginning of a phrase and after **n** or **l**, the letter **d** is pronounced with a hard sound. This sound is similar to the English d in *dog*, but a little softer and duller. The tongue should touch the back of the upper teeth, not the roof of the mouth.

     Don   **d**inero   tien**d**a   fal**d**a

In all other positions, **d** has a soft sound. It is similar to the English *th* in *there*, but a little softer.

     me**d**ias   ver**d**e   vesti**d**o   huéspe**d**

When **d** begins a word, its pronunciation depends on the previous word. At the beginning of a phrase or after a word that ends in **n** or **l**, it is pronounced as a hard **d**.

     Don **D**iego no tiene el **d**iccionario.

Words that begin with **d** are pronounced with a soft **d** if they appear immediately after a word that ends in a vowel or any consonant other than **n** or **l**.

     Doña **D**olores es **d**e la capital.

When pronouncing the Spanish **t**, the tongue should touch the back of the upper teeth, not the roof of the mouth. In contrast to the English *t*, no air is expelled from the mouth.

     traje   pan**t**alones   **t**arje**t**a   **t**ien**d**a

1 **Práctica** Repeat each phrase after the speaker to practice the **d** and the **t**.

1. Hasta pronto.	5. No hay de qué.	9. Es estupendo.
2. De nada.	6. ¿De dónde es usted?	10. No tengo computadora.
3. Mucho gusto.	7. ¡Todos a bordo!	11. ¿Cuándo vienen?
4. Lo siento.	8. No puedo.	12. Son las tres y media.

2 **Oraciones** When you hear the number, read the corresponding sentence aloud, focusing on the **d** and **t** sounds. Then listen to the speaker and repeat the sentence.

1. Don Teodoro tiene una tienda en un almacén en La Habana.
2. Don Teodoro vende muchos trajes, vestidos y zapatos todos los días.
3. Un día un turista, Federico Machado, entra en la tienda para comprar un par de botas.
4. Federico regatea con don Teodoro y compra las botas y también un par de sandalias.

3 **Refranes** Repeat each saying after the speaker to practice the **d** and the **t**.

1. En la variedad está el gusto.   2. Aunque la mona se vista de seda, mona se queda.

4 **Dictado** You will hear four sentences. Each will be said twice. Listen carefully and write what you hear.

1. _____

2. _____

3. _____

4. _____

estructura

6.1 Saber and conocer

1 **¿Saber o conocer?** You will hear some sentences with a beep in place of the verb. Decide which form of **saber** or **conocer** should complete each sentence and circle it.

> **modelo**
> You hear: (*Beep*) cantar.
> You circle: **Sé** because the sentence is **Sé cantar**.

1. Sé   Conozco   3. Sabemos   Conocemos   5. Sabes   Conoces
2. Saben   Conocen   4. Sé   Conozco   6. Sabes   Conoces

2 **Cambiar** Listen to the following statements and say that you do the same activities. Repeat the correct answer after the speaker. (*5 items*)

> **modelo**
> Julia sabe nadar.
> Yo también sé nadar.

3 **Preguntas** Answer each question using the cue you hear. Repeat the correct response after the speaker. (*6 items*)

> **modelo**
> ¿Conocen tus padres Antigua? (Sí)
> Sí, mis padres conocen Antigua.

4 **Mi compañera de cuarto** Listen as Jennifer describes her roommate. Then read the statements in your lab manual and decide whether they are **cierto** or **falso**.

	Cierto	Falso
1. Jennifer conoció (*met*) a Laura en la escuela primaria.	O	O
2. Laura sabe hacer muchas cosas.	O	O
3. Laura sabe hablar alemán.	O	O
4. Laura sabe buscar gangas.	O	O
5. Laura sabe patinar en línea.	O	O
6. Laura conoce a algunos muchachos simpáticos.	O	O

5 **De compras** Listen to this conversation between Carmen and Rosalía. Then choose the correct answers to the questions in your lab manual.

1. ¿Cuál es el problema de Carmen cuando va de compras?
   a. Siempre encuentra gangas.   b. Nunca encuentra ofertas.
2. ¿Conoce Carmen el nuevo centro comercial?
   a. No lo conoce, pero sabe dónde está.   b. Ni lo conoce, ni sabe dónde está.
3. ¿Qué quiere comprar Rosalía en el centro comercial?
   a. Quiere comprar zapatos.   b. No quiere comprar nada.
4. ¿Cuándo van Carmen y Rosalía de compras?
   a. Mañana antes del trabajo.   b. Mañana después del trabajo.

Lección 6 Lab Activities   **33**

6.2 Indirect object pronouns

1 **Escoger** Listen to each question and choose the most logical response.

1. a. Sí, le muestro el abrigo.

   b. Sí, me muestra el abrigo.

2. a. No, no le presto el suéter azul.

   b. No, no te presto el suéter azul.

3. a. Voy a comprarles ropa interior.

   b. Vamos a comprarle ropa interior.

4. a. Sí, nos dan las nuevas sandalias.

   b. Sí, me dan las nuevas sandalias.

5. a. Nos cuestan veinte dólares.

   b. Les cuestan veinte dólares.

6. a. Sí, nos trae un sombrero.

   b. Sí, te traigo un sombrero.

2 **Transformar** Cecilia is shopping. Say for whom she buys these items using indirect object pronouns. Repeat the correct answer after the speaker. (6 *items*)

> **modelo**
>
> Cecilia compra una bolsa para Dora.
> *Cecilia le compra una bolsa.*

3 **Preguntas** Answer each question you hear using the cue in your lab manual. Repeat the correct response after the speaker.

> **modelo**
>
> *You hear:* ¿Quién está esperándote?
> *You see:* Mauricio
> *You say:* Mauricio está esperándome.

1. sí	3. no	5. Antonio
2. $50,00	4. su traje nuevo	6. bluejeans

4 **En el centro comercial** Listen to this conversation and answer the questions in your lab manual.

1. ¿Quién es Gustavo?

_____

2. ¿Qué está haciendo Gustavo?

_____

3. ¿Qué le pregunta Gustavo a José?

_____

4. ¿Por qué le presta dinero José?

_____

5. ¿Cuándo va a regalarle (to give) la falda a Norma?

_____

6.3 Preterite tense of regular verbs

1 **Identificar** Listen to each sentence and decide whether the verb is in the present or the preterite tense. Mark an **X** in the appropriate column.

> **modelo**
> You hear: Alejandro llevó un suéter marrón.
> You mark: an **X** under **Preterite**.

	Present	*Preterite*
Modelo	_____	**X**
1.	_____	_____
2.	_____	_____
3.	_____	_____
4.	_____	_____
5.	_____	_____
6.	_____	_____
7.	_____	_____
8.	_____	_____

2 **Cambiar** Change each sentence from the present to the preterite. Repeat the correct answer after the speaker. (*8 items*)

> **modelo**
> Compro unas sandalias baratas.
> *Compré unas sandalias baratas.*

3 **Preguntas** Answer each question you hear using the cue in your lab manual. Repeat the correct response after the speaker.

> **modelo**
> You hear: ¿Dónde conseguiste tus botas?
> You see: en la tienda Lacayo
> You say: *Conseguí mis botas en la tienda Lacayo.*

1. $26,00   2. ayer   3. Marta   4. no   5. no   6. no

4 **¿Estás listo?** Listen to this conversation between Matilde and Hernán. Make a list of the tasks Hernán has already done in preparation for his trip and a list of the tasks he still needs to do.

Tareas completadas

_____

_____

_____

_____

Tareas que necesita hacer

_____

_____

_____

_____

6.4 Demonstrative adjectives and pronouns

1 **En el mercado** A group of tourists is shopping at an open-air market. Listen to what they say, and mark an **X** in the column for the demonstrative adjective you hear.

> *modelo*
>
> *You hear:* Me gusta mucho esa bolsa.
> *You mark:* an **X** under *that*.

	this	*that*	*these*	*those*
Modelo	_____	**X**	_____	_____
1.	_____	_____	_____	_____
2.	_____	_____	_____	_____
3.	_____	_____	_____	_____
4.	_____	_____	_____	_____

2 **Cambiar** Form a new sentence using the cue you hear. Repeat the correct answer after the speaker. (*6 items*)

> *modelo*
>
> Quiero este suéter. (chaqueta)
> *Quiero esta chaqueta.*

3 **Transformar** Form a new sentence using the cue you hear. Repeat the correct answer after the speaker. (*6 items*)

> *modelo*
>
> Aquel abrigo es muy hermoso. (corbatas)
> *Aquellas corbatas son muy hermosas.*

4 **Preguntas** Answer each question you hear in the negative using a form of the demonstrative pronoun **ése**. Repeat the correct response after the speaker. (*8 items*)

> *modelo*
>
> ¿Quieres esta blusa?
> *No, no quiero ésa.*

5 **De compras** Listen to this conversation. Then read the statements in your lab manual and decide whether they are **cierto** or **falso**.

	Cierto	Falso
1. Flor quiere ir al almacén Don Guapo.	O	O
2. Enrique trabaja en el almacén Don Guapo.	O	O
3. El centro comercial está lejos de los chicos.	O	O
4. Van al almacén que está al lado del Hotel Plaza.	O	O

vocabulario

You will now hear the vocabulary found in your textbook on the last page of this lesson. Listen and repeat each Spanish word or phrase after the speaker.

contextos

Lección 7

1 **Describir** For each drawing, you will hear two statements. Choose the one that corresponds to the drawing.

1. a. _____ b. _____

2. a. _____ b. _____

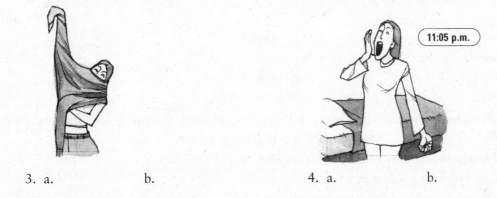

3. a. _____ b. _____   4. a. _____ b. _____

2 **Preguntas** Clara is going to baby-sit your nephew. Answer her questions about your nephew's daily routine using the cues in your lab manual. Repeat the correct response after the speaker.

> **modelo**
> *You hear:* ¿A qué hora va a la escuela?
> *You see:* 8:30 a.m.
> *You say:* Va a la escuela a las ocho y media de la mañana.

1. 7:00 a.m.   4. champú para niños
2. se lava la cara   5. 9:00 p.m.
3. por la noche   6. después de comer

3 **Entrevista** Listen to this interview. Then read the statements in your lab manual and decide whether they are **cierto** or **falso**.

	Cierto	Falso
1. Sergio Santos es jugador de fútbol.	○	○
2. Sergio se levanta a las 5:00 a.m.	○	○
3. Sergio se ducha por la mañana y por la noche.	○	○
4. Sergio se acuesta a las 11:00 p.m.	○	○

Lección 7 Lab Activities   **37**

pronunciación

The consonant r

In Spanish, **r** has a strong trilled sound at the beginning of a word. No English words have a trill, but English speakers often produce a trill when they imitate the sound of a motor.

    ropa   rutina   rico   **R**amón

In any other position, **r** has a weak sound similar to the English *tt* in *better* or the English *dd* in *ladder*. In contrast to English, the tongue touches the roof of the mouth behind the teeth.

    gustar   durante   prime**r**o   crema

The letter combination **rr**, which only appears between vowels, always has a strong trilled sound.

    piza**rr**a   co**rr**o   ma**rr**ón   abu**rr**ido

Between vowels, the difference between the strong trilled **rr** and the weak **r** is very important, as a mispronunciation could lead to confusion between two different words.

    ca**r**o   ca**rr**o   pe**r**o   pe**rr**o

1   **Práctica** Repeat each word after the speaker, to practice the **r** and the **rr**.

1. Perú	5. comprar	9. Arequipa
2. Rosa	6. favor	10. tarde
3. borrador	7. rubio	11. cerrar
4. madre	8. reloj	12. despertador

2   **Oraciones** When you hear the number, read the corresponding sentence aloud, focusing on the **r** and **rr** sounds. Then listen to the speaker and repeat the sentence.

1. Ramón Robles Ruiz es programador. Su esposa Rosaura es artista.
2. A Rosaura Robles le encanta regatear en el mercado.
3. Ramón nunca regatea… le aburre regatear.
4. Rosaura siempre compra cosas baratas.
5. Ramón no es rico, pero prefiere comprar cosas muy caras.
6. ¡El martes Ramón compró un carro nuevo!

3   **Refranes** Repeat each saying after the speaker to practice the **r** and the **rr**.

1. Perro que ladra no muerde.
2. No se ganó Zamora en una hora.

4   **Dictado** You will hear seven sentences. Each will be said twice. Listen carefully and write what you hear.

1. _____
2. _____
3. _____
4. _____
5. _____
6. _____
7. _____

estructura

7.1 Reflexive verbs

1 **Describir** For each drawing, you will hear two statements. Choose the one that corresponds to the drawing.

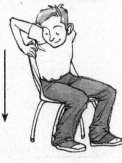

1. a.   b.   2. a.   b.

3. a.   b.   4. a.   b.

2 **Preguntas** Answer each question you hear in the affirmative. Repeat the correct response after the speaker. (*7 items*)

> **modelo**
>
> ¿Se levantó temprano Rosa?
> Sí, Rosa se levantó temprano.

3 **¡Esto fue el colmo! (*The last straw!*)** Listen as Julia describes what happened in her dorm yesterday. Then choose the correct ending for each statement in your lab manual.

1. Julia se ducha en cinco minutos porque...
   a. siempre se levanta tarde.   b. las chicas de su piso comparten un cuarto de baño.
2. Ayer la chica nueva...
   a. se quedó dos horas en el baño.   b. se preocupó por Julia.
3. Cuando salió, la chica nueva...
   a. se enojó mucho.   b. se sintió (*felt*) avergonzada.

7.2 Indefinite and negative words

1 **¿Lógico o ilógico?** You will hear some questions and the responses. Decide if they are **lógico** or **ilógico**.

	Lógico	Ilógico		Lógico	Ilógico
1.	○	○	5.	○	○
2.	○	○	6.	○	○
3.	○	○	7.	○	○
4.	○	○	8.	○	○

2 **¿Pero o sino?** You will hear some sentences with a beep in place of a word. Decide if **pero** or **sino** should complete each sentence and circle it.

modelo
You hear: Ellos no viven en Lima (*beep*) en Arequipa.
You circle: **sino** *because the sentence is* **Ellos no viven en Lima sino en Arequipa.**

1.	pero	sino	5.	pero	sino
2.	pero	sino	6.	pero	sino
3.	pero	sino	7.	pero	sino
4.	pero	sino	8.	pero	sino

3 **Transformar** Change each sentence you hear to say the opposite is true. Repeat the correct answer after the speaker. (*5 items*)

modelo
Nadie se ducha ahora.
Alguien se ducha ahora.

4 **Preguntas** Answer each question you hear in the negative. Repeat the correct response after the speaker. (*6 items*)

modelo
¿Qué estás haciendo?
No estoy haciendo nada.

5 **Entre amigos** Listen to this conversation between Felipe and Mercedes. Then decide whether the statements in your lab manual are **cierto** or **falso**.

	Cierto	Falso
1. No hay nadie en la residencia.	○	○
2. Mercedes quiere ir al Centro Estudiantil.	○	○
3. Felipe tiene un amigo peruano.	○	○
4. Mercedes no visitó ni Machu Picchu ni Cuzco.	○	○
5. Felipe nunca visitó Perú.	○	○

7.3 Preterite of **ser** and **ir**

1   **Escoger**   Listen to each sentence and indicate whether the verb is a form of **ser** or **ir**.

1. ser   ir   5. ser   ir
2. ser   ir   6. ser   ir
3. ser   ir   7. ser   ir
4. ser   ir   8. ser   ir

2   **Cambiar**   Change each sentence from the present to the preterite. Repeat the correct answer after the speaker. (*8 items*)

> **modelo**
> Ustedes van en avión.
> Ustedes fueron en avión.

3   **Preguntas**   Answer each question you hear using the cue in your lab manual. Repeat the correct response after the speaker.

> **modelo**
> *You hear:* ¿Quién fue tu profesor de química?
> *You see:* el señor Ortega
> *You say:* El señor Ortega fue mi profesor de química.

1. al mercado al aire libre   4. fabulosa
2. muy buenas   5. al parque
3. no   6. difícil

4   **¿Qué hicieron (*did they do*) anoche?**   Listen to this telephone conversation and answer the questions in your lab manual.

1. ¿Adónde fue Carlos anoche?

_____

2. ¿Cómo fue el partido? ¿Por qué?

_____

3. ¿Adónde fueron Katarina y Esteban anoche?

_____

4. Y Esteban, ¿qué hizo (*did he do*) allí?

_____

7.4 Verbs like **gustar**

1 Escoger Listen to each question and choose the most logical response.

1. a. Sí, me gusta.   b. Sí, te gusta.
2. a. No, no le interesa.   b. No, no le interesan.
3. a. Sí, les molestan mucho. b. No, no les molesta mucho.
4. a. No, no nos importa.   b. No, no les importa.
5. a. Sí, le falta.   b. Sí, me falta.
6. a. Sí, les fascina.   b. No, no les fascinan.

2 Cambiar Form a new sentence using the cue you hear. Repeat the correct answer after the speaker. (*6 items*)

> **modelo**
> A ellos les interesan las ciencias. (a Ricardo)
> A Ricardo le interesan las ciencias.

3 Preguntas Answer each question you hear using the cue in your lab manual. Repeat the correct response after the speaker.

> **modelo**
> *You hear:* ¿Qué te encanta hacer?
> *You see:* patinar en línea
> *You say:* Me encanta patinar en línea.

1. la familia y los amigos   4. $2,00   7. no / nada
2. sí   5. el baloncesto y el béisbol 8. sí
3. las computadoras   6. no

4 Preferencias Listen to this conversation. Then fill in the chart with Eduardo's preferences and answer the question in your lab manual.

Le gusta	No le gusta

¿Qué van a hacer los chicos esta tarde? _____

_____

vocabulario

You will now hear the vocabulary found in your textbook on the last page of this lesson. Listen and repeat each Spanish word or phrase after the speaker.

contextos

1 **Identificar** Listen to each question and mark an **X** in the appropriate category.

> modelo
>
> *You hear:* ¿Qué es la piña?
> *You mark:* an **X** under **fruta.**

	carne	pescado	verdura	fruta	bebida
Modelo	_____	_____	_____	**X**	_____
1.	_____	_____	_____	_____	_____
2.	_____	_____	_____	_____	_____
3.	_____	_____	_____	_____	_____
4.	_____	_____	_____	_____	_____
5.	_____	_____	_____	_____	_____
6.	_____	_____	_____	_____	_____
7.	_____	_____	_____	_____	_____
8.	_____	_____	_____	_____	_____

2 **Describir** Listen to each sentence and write the number of the sentence below the drawing of the food or drink mentioned.

a. _____ b. _____ c. _____ d. _____

e. _____ f. _____ g. _____ h. _____

i. _____ j. _____

3 **En el restaurante** You will hear a couple ordering a meal in a restaurant. Write the items they order in the appropriate categories.

	SEÑORA	SEÑOR
Primer plato		
Plato principal		
Bebida		

pronunciación

ll, ñ, c, and z

Most Spanish speakers pronounce **ll** like the *y* in *yes*.

pollo   llave   ella   cebolla

The letter **ñ** is pronounced much like the *ny* in *canyon*.

mañana   señor   baño   niña

Before **a**, **o**, or **u**, the Spanish **c** is pronounced like the *c* in *car*.

café   colombiano   cuando   rico

Before **e** or **i**, the Spanish **c** is pronounced like the *s* in *sit*. In parts of Spain, **c** before **e** or **i** is pronounced like the *th* in *think*.

cereales   delicioso   conducir   conocer

The Spanish **z** is pronounced like the *s* in *sit*. In parts of Spain, **z** is pronounced like the *th* in *think*.

zeta   zanahoria   almuerzo   cerveza

1   **Práctica** Repeat each word after the speaker to practice pronouncing **ll**, **ñ**, **c**, and **z**.

1. mantequilla	5. español	9. quince
2. cuñado	6. cepillo	10. compañera
3. aceite	7. zapato	11. almorzar
4. manzana	8. azúcar	12. calle

2   **Oraciones** When the speaker pauses, repeat the corresponding sentence or phrase, focusing on **ll**, **ñ**, **c**, and **z**.

1. Mi compañero de cuarto se llama Toño Núñez. Su familia es de la Ciudad de Guatemala y de Quetzaltenango.
2. Dice que la comida de su mamá es deliciosa, especialmente su pollo al champiñón y sus tortillas de maíz.
3. Creo que Toño tiene razón porque hoy cené en su casa y quiero volver mañana para cenar allí otra vez.

3   **Refranes** Repeat each saying after the speaker to practice pronouncing **ll**, **ñ**, **c**, and **z**.

1. Las aparencias engañan.
2. Panza llena, corazón contento.

4   **Dictado** You will hear five sentences. Each will be said twice. Listen carefully and write what you hear.

1. _____
2. _____
3. _____
4. _____
5. _____

estructura

8.1 Preterite of stem-changing verbs

1   **Identificar** Listen to each sentence and decide whether the verb is in the present or the preterite tense. Mark an **X** in the appropriate column.

> **modelo**
>
> You hear: Pido bistec con papas fritas.
> You mark: an **X** under **Present**.

	Present	Preterite
Modelo	X	
1.		
2.		
3.		
4.		
5.		
6.		
7.		
8.		

2   **Cambiar** Change each sentence you hear substituting the new subject given. Repeat the correct response after the speaker. (5 items)

> **modelo**
>
> Tú no dormiste bien anoche. (Los niños)
> Los niños no durmieron bien anoche.

3   **Preguntas** Answer each question you hear using the cue in your lab manual. Repeat the correct response after the speaker.

> **modelo**
>
> You hear: ¿Qué pediste?
> You see: pavo asado con papas y arvejas
> You say: Pedí pavo asado con papas y arvejas.

1. Sí   3. leche   5. No
2. No   4. Sí   6. la semana pasada

4   **Un día largo** Listen as Ernesto describes what he did yesterday. Then read the statements in your lab manual and decide whether they are **cierto** or **falso**.

	Cierto	Falso
1. Ernesto se levantó a las seis y media de la mañana.	○	○
2. Se bañó y se vistió en poco tiempo.	○	○
3. Los clientes empezaron a llegar a la una.	○	○
4. Almorzó temprano.	○	○
5. Pidió pollo asado con papas.	○	○
6. Después de almorzar, Ernesto y su primo siguieron trabajando.	○	○

     Lección 8 Lab Activities   **45**

8.2 Double object pronouns

1 Escoger The manager of El Gran Pavo Restaurant wants to know what items the chef is going to serve to the customers today. Listen to each question and choose the correct response.

> **modelo**
> *You hear:* ¿Les vas a servir sopa a los clientes?
> *You read:* a. Sí, se la voy a servir.   b. No, no se lo voy a servir.
> *You mark:* **a** because it refers to **la sopa.**

1. a. Sí, se las voy a servir.   b. No, no se los voy a servir.

2. a. Sí, se la voy a servir.   b. No, no se lo voy a servir.

3. a. Sí, se los voy a servir.   b. No, no se las voy a servir.

4. a. Sí, se los voy a servir.   b. No, no se las voy a servir.

5. a. Sí, se la voy a servir.   b. No, no se lo voy a servir.

6. a. Sí, se lo voy a servir.   b. No, no se la voy a servir.

2 Cambiar Repeat each statement, replacing the direct object noun with a pronoun. (*6 items*)

> **modelo**
> María te hace ensalada.
> María te la hace.

3 Preguntas Answer each question using the cue you hear and object pronouns. Repeat the correct response after the speaker. (*5 items*)

> **modelo**
> ¿Me recomienda usted los mariscos? (sí)
> Sí, se los recomiendo.

4 Una fiesta Listen to this conversation between Eva and Marcela. Then read the statements in your lab manual and decide whether they are **cierto** or **falso**.

	Cierto	Falso
1. Le van a hacer una fiesta a Sebastián.	O	O
2. Le van a preparar langosta.	O	O
3. Le van a preparar una ensalada de mariscos.	O	O
4. Van a tener vino tinto, cerveza, agua mineral y té helado.	O	O
5. Clara va a comprar cerveza.	O	O
6. Le compraron un cinturón.	O	O

8.3 Comparisons

1 **Escoger** You will hear a series of descriptions. Choose the statement in your lab manual that expresses the correct comparison.

1. a. Yo tengo más dinero que Rafael.
   b. Yo tengo menos dinero que Rafael.
2. a. Elena es mayor que Juan.
   b. Elena es menor que Juan.
3. a. Enrique come más hamburguesas que José.
   b. Enrique come tantas hamburguesas como José.
4. a. La comida de la Fonda es mejor que la comida del Café Condesa.
   b. La comida de la Fonda es peor que la comida del Café Condesa.
5. a. Las langostas cuestan tanto como los camarones.
   b. Los camarones cuestan menos que las langostas.

2 **Comparar** Look at each drawing and answer the question you hear with a comparative statement. Repeat the correct response after the speaker.

1.   **Ricardo**   **Sara**   2.   **Héctor**   **Alejandro**

3.   **Leonor**   **Melissa**

3 **Al contrario** You are babysitting Anita, a small child, who starts boasting about herself and her family. Respond to each statement using a comparative of equality. Then repeat the correct answer after the speaker. (6 items)

> **modelo**
> Mi mamá es más bonita que tu mamá.
> Al contrario, mi mamá es tan bonita como tu mamá.

8.4 Superlatives

1 **Superlativos** You will hear a series of descriptions. Choose the statement in your lab manual that expresses the correct superlative.

1. a. Tus pantalones no son los más grandes de la tienda.

   b. Tus pantalones son los más grandes de la tienda.

2. a. La camisa blanca es la más bonita del centro comercial.

   b. La camisa blanca no es tan bonita como otras camisas de la tienda.

3. a. Las rebajas del centro comercial son peores que las rebajas de la tienda.

   b. En el centro comercial puedes encontrar las mejores rebajas.

4. a. El vestido azul es el más caro de la tienda.

   b. El vestido azul es el más barato de la tienda.

5. a. Sebastián es el mejor vendedor de la tienda.

   b. Sebastián es el peor vendedor de la tienda.

2 **Preguntas** Answer each question you hear using the absolute superlative. Repeat the correct response after the speaker. (*6 items*)

> **modelo**
> La comida de la cafetería es mala, ¿no?
> Sí, *es malísima.*

3 **Anuncio** Listen to this advertisement. Then read the statements and decide whether they are **cierto** or **falso**.

	Cierto	Falso
1. Ningún almacén de la ciudad es tan grande como El Corte Inglés.	○	○
2. La mejor ropa es siempre carísima.	○	○
3. Los zapatos de El Corte Inglés son muy elegantes.	○	○
4. En El Corte Inglés gastas menos dinero y siempre tienes muy buena calidad.	○	○
5. El horario de El Corte Inglés es tan flexible como el horario de otras tiendas del centro.	○	○

vocabulario

You will now hear the vocabulary found in your textbook on the last page of this lesson. Listen and repeat each Spanish word or phrase after the speaker.

contextos

Lección 9

1 **¿Lógico o ilógico?** You will hear some statements. Decide if they are **lógico** or **ilógico**.

1. Lógico   Ilógico   5. Lógico   Ilógico
2. Lógico   Ilógico   6. Lógico   Ilógico
3. Lógico   Ilógico   7. Lógico   Ilógico
4. Lógico   Ilógico   8. Lógico   Ilógico

2 **Escoger** For each drawing, you will hear three statements. Choose the one that corresponds to the drawing.

1. a.   b.   c.   2. a.   b.   c.

3. a.   b.   c.   4. a.   b.   c.

3 **Una celebración** Listen as señora Jiménez talks about a party she has planned. Then answer the questions in your lab manual.

1. ¿Para quién es la fiesta?

_____

2. ¿Cuándo es la fiesta?

_____

3. ¿Por qué hacen la fiesta?

_____

4. ¿Quiénes van a la fiesta?

_____

5. ¿Qué van a hacer los invitados en la fiesta?

_____

pronunciación

The letters **h**, **j**, and **g**

The Spanish **h** is always silent.

    helado   **h**ombre   **h**ola   **h**ermosa

The letter **j** is pronounced much like the English *h* in *his*.

    José   **j**ubilarse   de**j**ar   pare**j**a

The letter **g** can be pronounced three different ways. Before **e** or **i**, the letter **g** is pronounced much like the English *h*.

    a**g**encia   **g**eneral   **G**il   **G**isela

At the beginning of a phrase or after the letter **n**, the Spanish **g** is pronounced like the English *g* in *girl*.

    Gustavo, **g**racias por llamar el domin**g**o.

In any other position, the Spanish **g** has a somewhat softer sound.

    Me **g**radué en a**g**osto.

In the combinations **gue** and **gui**, the **g** has a hard sound and the **u** is silent. In the combination **gua**, the **g** has a hard sound and the **u** is pronounced like the English *w*.

    Guerra   conse**gui**r   **gua**ntes   a**gua**

1   **Práctica** Repeat each word after the speaker to practice pronouncing **h**, **j**, and **g**.

1. hamburguesa	4. guapa	7. espejo	10. gracias	13. Jorge
2. jugar	5. geografía	8. hago	11. hijo	14. tengo
3. oreja	6. magnífico	9. seguir	12. galleta	15. ahora

2   **Oraciones** When you hear the number, read the corresponding sentence aloud. Then listen to the speaker and repeat the sentence.

1. Hola. Me llamo Gustavo Hinojosa Lugones y vivo en Santiago de Chile.
2. Tengo una familia grande; somos tres hermanos y tres hermanas.
3. Voy a graduarme en mayo.
4. Para celebrar mi graduación, mis padres van a regalarme un viaje a Egipto.
5. ¡Qué generosos son!

3   **Refranes** Repeat each saying after the speaker to practice pronouncing **h**, **j**, and **g**.

1. A la larga, lo más dulce amarga.   2. El hábito no hace al monje.

4   **Dictado** Victoria is talking to her friend Mirta on the phone. Listen carefully and during the pauses write what she says. The entire passage will then be repeated so that you can check your work.

_____

_____

_____

_____

estructura

9.1 Irregular preterites

1 **Escoger** Listen to each question and choose the most logical response.

1. a. No, no conduje hoy. b. No, no condujo hoy.
2. a. Te dije que tengo una cita con b. Me dijo que tiene una cita con
   Gabriela esta noche. Gabriela esta noche.
3. a. Estuvimos en la casa de Marta. b. Estuvieron en la casa de Marta.
4. a. Porque tuvo que estudiar. b. Porque tiene que estudiar.
5. a. Lo supiste la semana pasada. b. Lo supimos la semana pasada.
6. a. Los pusimos en la mesa. b. Los pusiste en la mesa.
7. a. No, sólo tradujimos un poco. b. No, sólo traduje un poco.
8. a. Sí, le di $20. b. Sí, le dio $20.

2 **Cambiar** Change each sentence from the present to the preterite. Repeat the correct answer after the speaker. (*8 items*)

> **modelo**
> Él pone el flan sobre la mesa.
> Él *puso el flan sobre la mesa.*

3 **Preguntas** Answer each question you hear using the cue in your lab manual. Substitute object pronouns for the direct object when possible. Repeat the correct answer after the speaker.

> **modelo**
> *You hear:* ¿Quién condujo el auto?
> *You see:* yo
> *You say:* Yo lo conduje.

1. Gerardo 3. nosotros 5. ¡Felicitaciones!
2. Mateo y Yolanda 4. muy buena 6. mi papá

4 **Completar** Listen to the dialogue and write the missing words in your lab manual.

(1) _____ por un amigo que los Márquez (2) _____ a visitar

a su hija. Me (3) _____ que (4) _____ desde

Antofagasta y que se (5) _____ en el Hotel Carrera. Les

(6) _____ una llamada (*call*) anoche, pero no (7) _____

el teléfono. Sólo (8) _____ dejarles un mensaje. Hoy ellos me

(9) _____ y me (10) _____ si mi esposa y yo teníamos

tiempo para almorzar con ellos. Claro que les (11) _____ que sí.

9.2 Verbs that change meaning in the preterite

1 **Identificar** Listen to each sentence and mark an **X** in the column for the subject of the verb.

> **modelo**
>
> *You hear:* ¿Cuándo lo supiste?
> *You mark:* an **X** under **tú.**

	yo	tú	él/ella	nosotros/as	ellos/ellas
Modelo	___	X	___	___	___
1.	___	___	___	___	___
2.	___	___	___	___	___
3.	___	___	___	___	___
4.	___	___	___	___	___
5.	___	___	___	___	___
6.	___	___	___	___	___
7.	___	___	___	___	___
8.	___	___	___	___	___

2 **Preguntas** Answer each question you hear using the cue in your lab manual. Substitute object pronouns for the direct object when possible. Repeat the correct response after the speaker.

> **modelo**
>
> *You hear:* ¿Conocieron ellos a Sandra?
> *You see:* sí
> *You say:* Sí, la conocieron.

1. sí   2. en la casa de Ángela   3. el viernes   4. no   5. no   6. anoche

3 **¡Qué lástima! (*What a shame!*)** Listen as José talks about some news he recently received. Then read the statements and decide whether they are **cierto** or **falso.**

	Cierto	Falso
1. Supieron de la muerte ayer.	○	○
2. Se sonrieron cuando oyeron las noticias (*news*).	○	○
3. Carolina no se pudo comunicar con la familia.	○	○
4. Francisco era (*was*) joven.	○	○
5. Mañana piensan llamar a la familia de Francisco.	○	○

4 **Relaciones amorosas** Listen as Susana describes what happened between her and Pedro. Then answer the questions in your lab manual.

1. ¿Por qué no pudo salir Susana con Pedro? _____

2. ¿Qué supo por su amiga? _____

3. ¿Cómo se puso Susana cuando Pedro llamó? _____

4. ¿Qué le dijo Susana a Pedro? _____

9.3 ¿Qué? and ¿cuál?

1 **¿Lógico o ilógico?** You will hear some questions and the responses. Decide if they are **lógico** or **ilógico**.

1. Lógico	Ilógico	5. Lógico	Ilógico
2. Lógico	Ilógico	6. Lógico	Ilógico
3. Lógico	Ilógico	7. Lógico	Ilógico
4. Lógico	Ilógico	8. Lógico	Ilógico

2 **Preguntas** You will hear a series of responses to questions. Using **¿qué?** or **¿cuál?**, form the question that prompted each response. Repeat the correct answer after the speaker. (*8 items*)

> modelo
> Santiago de Chile es la capital de Chile.
> ¿Cuál es la capital de Chile?

3 **De compras** Look at Marcela's shopping list for Christmas and answer each question you hear. Repeat the correct response after the speaker. (*6 items*)

Raúl	2 camisas, talla 17
Cristina	blusa, color azul
Pepe	bluejeans y tres pares de calcetines blancos
Abuelo	cinturón
Abuela	suéter blanco

4 **Escoger** Listen to this radio commercial and choose the most logical response to each question.

1. ¿Qué hace Fiestas Mar?

   a. Organiza fiestas.   b. Es una tienda que vende cosas para fiestas.   c. Es un club en el mar.

2. ¿Para qué tipo de fiesta no usaría Fiestas Mar?

   a. Para una boda.   b. Para una fiesta de sorpresa.   c. Para una cena con los suegros.

3. ¿Cuál de estos servicios no ofrece Fiestas Mar?

   a. Poner las decoraciones.   b. Proveer (*Provide*) el lugar.   c. Proveer los regalos.

4. ¿Qué tiene que hacer el cliente si usa los servicios de Fiestas Mar?

   a. Tiene que preocuparse por la lista de invitados.   b. Tiene que preocuparse por la música.

   c. Tiene que preparar la comida.

5. Si uno quiere contactar Fiestas Mar, ¿qué debe hacer?

   a. Debe escribirles un mensaje electrónico.   b. Debe llamarlos.   c. Debe ir a Casa Mar.

9.4 Pronouns after prepositions

1   **Cambiar**   Listen to each statement and say that the feeling is not mutual. Use a pronoun after the preposition in your response. Then repeat the correct answer after the speaker. (*6 items*)

> **modelo**
> Carlos quiere desayunar con nosotros.
> *Pero nosotros no queremos desayunar con él.*

2   **Preguntas**   Answer each question you hear using the appropriate pronoun after the preposition and the cue in your lab manual. Repeat the correct response after the speaker.

> **modelo**
> *You hear:* ¿Almuerzas con Alberto hoy?
> *You see:* No
> *You say:* No, no almuerzo con él hoy.

1. Sí
2. Luis
3. Sí
4. Sí
5. No
6. Francisco

3   **Preparativos (*Preparations*)**   Listen to this conversation between David and Andrés. Then answer the questions in your lab manual.

1. ¿Qué necesitan comprar para la fiesta?

2. ¿Con quién quiere Alfredo ir a la fiesta?

3. ¿Por qué ella no quiere ir con él?

4. ¿Con quién va Sara a la fiesta?

5. ¿Para quién quieren comprar algo especial?

vocabulario

You will now hear the vocabulary found in your textbook on the last page of this lesson. Listen and repeat each Spanish word or phrase after the speaker.

contextos

Lección 10

1 **Identificar** You will hear a series of words. Write each one in the appropriate category.

> *modelo*
> *You hear:* el hospital
> *You write:* **el hospital** under **Lugares**.

Lugares	Medicinas	Condiciones y síntomas médicos
el hospital		

2 **Describir** For each drawing, you will hear two statements. Choose the one that corresponds to the drawing.

1. a.   b.

2. a.   b.

3. a.   b.

4. a.   b.

Lección 10 Lab Activities

pronunciación

c (before a consonant) and q

In Lesson 8, you learned that, in Spanish, the letter **c** before the vowels **a**, **o**, and **u** is pronounced like the *c* in the English word *car*. When the letter **c** appears before any consonant except **h**, it is also pronounced like the *c* in *car*.

clínica	biciCleta	crema	doCtora	oCtubre

In Spanish, the letter **q** is always followed by an **u**, which is silent. The combination **qu** is pronounced like the *k* sound in the English word *kitten*. Remember that the sounds **kwa**, **kwe**, **kwi**, **kwo**, and **koo** are always spelled with the combination **cu** in Spanish, never with **qu**.

querer	parque	queso	química	mantequilla

1 **Práctica** Repeat each word after the speaker, focusing on the **c** and **q** sounds.

1. quince
2. querer
3. pequeño
4. equipo
5. conductor
6. escribir
7. contacto
8. increíble
9. aquí
10. ciclismo
11. electrónico
12. quitarse

2 **Oraciones** When you hear the number, read the corresponding sentence aloud. Then listen to the speaker and repeat the sentence.

1. El doctor Cruz quiso sacarle un diente.
2. Clara siempre se maquilla antes de salir de casa.
3. ¿Quién perdió su equipaje?
4. Pienso comprar aquella camisa porque me queda bien.
5. La chaqueta cuesta quinientos cuarenta dólares, ¿no?
6. Esa cliente quiere pagar con tarjeta de crédito.

3 **Refranes** Repeat each saying after the speaker to practice the **c** and the **q** sounds.

1. Ver es creer. [1]
2. Quien mal anda, mal acaba. [2]

4 **Dictado** You will hear five sentences. Each will be said twice. Listen carefully and write what you hear.

1. _____
2. _____
3. _____
4. _____
5. _____
   _____

[1] *Seeing is believing.*

[2] *He who lives badly, ends badly.*

estructura

10.1 The imperfect tense

1 **Identificar** Listen to each sentence and circle the verb tense you hear.

1. a. present   b. preterite   c. imperfect   6. a. present   b. preterite   c. imperfect
2. a. present   b. preterite   c. imperfect   7. a. present   b. preterite   c. imperfect
3. a. present   b. preterite   c. imperfect   8. a. present   b. preterite   c. imperfect
4. a. present   b. preterite   c. imperfect   9. a. present   b. preterite   c. imperfect
5. a. present   b. preterite   c. imperfect   10. a. present   b. preterite   c. imperfect

2 **Cambiar** Form a new sentence using the cue you hear. Repeat the correct answer after the speaker. (6 *items*)

> modelo
>
> Iban a casa. (Eva)
> Eva iba a casa.

3 **Preguntas** A reporter is writing an article about funny things people used to do when they were children. Answer her questions, using the cues in your lab manual. Then repeat the correct response after the speaker.

> modelo
>
> *You hear:* ¿Qué hacía Miguel de niño?
> *You see:* ponerse pajitas (*straws*) en la nariz
> *You say:* Miguel se ponía pajitas en la nariz.

1. quitarse los zapatos en el restaurante   4. jugar con un amigo invisible
2. vestirnos con la ropa de mamá   5. usar las botas de su papá
3. sólo querer comer dulces   6. comer con las manos

4 **Completar** Listen to this description of Ángela's medical problem and write the missing words in your lab manual.

(1) _____ Ángela porque (2) _____ día y noche.

(3) _____ que (4) _____ un resfriado, pero se

(5) _____ bastante saludable. Se (6) _____ de la biblioteca después

de poco tiempo porque les (7) _____ a los otros estudiantes. Sus amigas, Laura y

Petra, siempre le (8) _____ que (9) _____ alguna alergia. Por fin,

decidió hacerse un examen médico. La doctora le dijo que ella (10) _____

alérgica y que (11) _____ muchas medicinas para las alergias. Finalmente, le

recetó unas pastillas. Al día siguiente (*following*), Ángela se (12) _____ mejor

porque (13) _____ cuál era el problema y ella dejó de estornudar después de

tomar las pastillas.

Lección 10 Lab Activities

10.2 The preterite and the imperfect

1 Identificar Listen to each statement and identify the verbs in the preterite and the imperfect. Write them in the appropriate column.

> **modelo**
> *You hear:* Cuando llegó la ambulancia, el esposo estaba mareado.
> *You write:* **llegó** under *preterite*, and **estaba** under *imperfect*.

	preterite	*imperfect*
Modelo	llegó	estaba
1.		
2.		
3.		
4.		
5.		
6.		
7.		
8.		

2 Responder Answer the questions using the cues in your lab manual. Substitute direct object pronouns for the direct object nouns when appropriate. Repeat the correct response after the speaker.

> **modelo**
> *You hear:* ¿Por qué no llamaste al médico la semana pasada?
> *You see:* perder su número de teléfono
> *You say:* **Porque perdí su número de teléfono.**

1. en la mesa de la cocina
2. tener ocho años
3. lastimarse el tobillo
4. no, ponerla en la mochila
5. tomarse las pastillas
6. no, pero tener una grave infección de garganta
7. toda la mañana
8. necesitar una radiografía de la boca

3 ¡Qué nervios! Listen as Sandra tells a friend about her day. Then read the statements in your lab manual and decide whether they are **cierto** or **falso**.

	Cierto	Falso
1. Sandra tenía mucha experiencia poniendo inyecciones.	○	○
2. La enfermera tenía un terrible dolor de cabeza.	○	○
3. La enfermera le dio una pastilla a Sandra.	○	○
4. El paciente trabajaba en el hospital con Sandra.	○	○
5. El paciente estaba muy nervioso.	○	○
6. Sandra le puso la inyección mientras él hablaba.	○	○

10.3 Constructions with **se**

1 **Escoger** Listen to each question and choose the most logical response.

1. a. Ay, se te quedó en casa.
   b. Ay, se me quedó en casa.

2. a. No, se le olvidó llamarlo.
   b. No, se me olvidó llamarlo.

3. a. Se le rompieron jugando al fútbol.
   b. Se les rompieron jugando al fútbol.

4. a. Ay, se les olvidaron.
   b. Ay, se nos olvidó.

5. a. No, se me perdió.
   b. No, se le perdió.

6. a. Se nos rompió.
   b. Se le rompieron.

2 **Preguntas** Answer each question you hear using the cue in your lab manual and the impersonal **se**. Repeat the correct response after the speaker.

> **modelo**
> *You hear:* ¿Qué lengua se habla en Costa Rica?
> *You see:* español
> *You say:* Se habla español.

1. a las seis
2. gripe
3. en la farmacia

4. en la caja
5. en la Oficina de Turismo
6. tomar el autobús #3

3 **Letreros (*Signs*)** Some or all of the type is missing on the signs in your lab manual. Listen to the speaker and write the appropriate text below each sign. The text for each sign will be repeated.

_____
_____
_____

_____
_____
_____

_____
_____
_____

_____
_____
_____

Lección 10 Lab Activities

10.4 Adverbs

1 **Completar** Listen to each statement and circle the word or phrase that best completes it.

1. a. casi   b. mal   c. ayer
2. a. con frecuencia   b. además   c. ayer
3. a. poco   b. tarde   c. bien
4. a. a menudo   b. muy   c. menos
5. a. así   b. apenas   c. tranquilamente
6. a. bastante   b. a tiempo   c. normalmente

2 **Cambiar** Form a new sentence by changing the adjective in your lab manual to an adverb. Repeat the correct answer after the speaker.

> **modelo**
> You hear: Juan dibuja.
> You see: fabuloso
> You say: Juan dibuja fabulosamente.

1. regular   4. constante
2. rápido   5. general
3. feliz   6. fácil

3 **Preguntas** Answer each question you hear in the negative, using the cue in your lab manual. Repeat the correct response after the speaker.

> **modelo**
> You hear: ¿Salió bien la operación?
> You see: mal
> You say: No, la operación salió mal.

1. lentamente   4. nunca
2. tarde   5. tristemente
3. muy   6. poco

4 **Situaciones** You will hear four brief conversations. Choose the phrase that best completes each sentence in your lab manual.

1. Mónica…
   a. llegó tarde al aeropuerto.
   b. casi perdió el avión a San José.
   c. decidió no ir a San José.

2. Pilar…
   a. se preocupa por la salud de Tomás.
   b. habla con su médico.
   c. habla con Tomás sobre un problema médico.

3. La señora Blanco…
   a. se rompió la pierna hoy.
   b. quiere saber si puede correr mañana.
   c. se lastimó el tobillo hoy.

4. María está enojada porque Vicente…
   a. no va a recoger (*to pick up*) su medicina.
   b. no recogió su medicina ayer.
   c. no debe tomar antibióticos.

vocabulario

You will now hear the vocabulary found in your textbook on the last page of this lesson. Listen and repeat each Spanish word or phrase after the speaker.

contextos

Lección 11

1 **Asociaciones** Circle the word or words that are not logically associated with each word you hear.

1. la impresora	la velocidad	la pantalla
2. guardar	imprimir	funcionar
3. la carretera	el motor	el sitio web
4. el tanque	el ratón	el aceite
5. conducir	el cibercafé	el reproductor de MP3
6. el archivo	la televisión	la llanta

2 **¿Lógico o ilógico?** You will hear some statements. Decide if they are **lógico** or **ilógico**.

	Lógico	Ilógico		Lógico	Ilógico
1.	○	○	4.	○	○
2.	○	○	5.	○	○
3.	○	○	6.	○	○

3 **Identificar** For each drawing in your lab manual, you will hear two statements. Choose the statement that best corresponds to the drawing.

1. a.   b.

2. a.   b.

3. a.   b.

4. a.   b.

pronunciación

c (before e or i), s, and z

In Latin America, **c** before **e** or **i** sounds much like the *s* in *sit*.

medi**c**ina   **c**elular   cono**c**er   pa**c**iente

In parts of Spain, **c** before **e** or **i** is pronounced like the *th* in *think*.

condu**c**ir   poli**c**ía   **c**ederrón   velo**c**idad

The letter **s** is pronounced like the *s* in *sit*.

subir   be**s**ar   **s**onar   impre**s**ora

In Latin America, the Spanish **z** is pronounced like the s in *sit*.

cabe**z**a   nari**z**   abra**z**ar   embara**z**ada

The **z** is pronounced like the *th* in *think* in parts of Spain.

zapatos   **z**ona   pla**z**a   bra**z**o

1 **Práctica** Repeat each word after the speaker to practice pronouncing **s**, **z**, and **c** before **i** and **e**.

1. funcionar	4. sitio	7. zanahoria	10. perezoso
2. policía	5. disco	8. marzo	11. quizás
3. receta	6. zapatos	9. comenzar	12. operación

2 **Oraciones** When you hear each number, read the corresponding sentence aloud. Then listen to the speaker and repeat the sentence.

1. Vivió en Buenos Aires en su niñez, pero siempre quería pasar su vejez en Santiago.

2. Cecilia y Zulaima fueron al centro a cenar al restaurante Las Delicias.

3. Sonó el despertador a las seis y diez, pero estaba cansado y no quiso oírlo.

4. Zacarías jugaba al baloncesto todas las tardes después de cenar.

3 **Refranes** Repeat each saying after the speaker to practice pronouncing **s**, **z**, and **c** before **i** and **e**.

1. Zapatero, a tus zapatos. [1]

2. Primero es la obligación que la devoción. [2]

4 **Dictado** You will hear a friend describing Azucena's weekend experiences. Listen carefully and write what you hear during the pauses. The entire passage will be repeated so that you can check your work.

_____

_____

_____

_____

_____

_____

_____

[1] *Mind your P's and Q's. (lit. Shoemaker, to your shoes.)*

[2] *Business before pleasure.*

estructura

11.1 Familiar commands

1 Identificar You will hear some sentences. If the verb is a **tú** command, circle **Sí** in your lab manual. If the verb is not a **tú** command, circle **No**.

> *modelo*
>
> *You hear:* Ayúdanos a encontrar el control remoto.
> *You circle:* **Sí** *because* **Ayúdanos** *is a* **tú** *command.*

1.	Sí	No		
2.	Sí	No		
3.	Sí	No		
4.	Sí	No		
5.	Sí	No		

6. Sí   No
7. Sí   No
8. Sí   No
9. Sí   No
10. Sí   No

2 Cambiar Change each command you hear to the negative. Repeat the correct answer after the speaker. (*8 items*)

> *modelo*
>
> Cómprame un reproductor de DVD.
> *No me compres un reproductor de DVD.*

3 Preguntas Answer each question you hear using an affirmative **tú** command. Repeat the correct response after the speaker. (*7 items*)

> *modelo*
>
> ¿Estaciono aquí?
> *Sí, estaciona aquí.*

4 Consejos prácticos You will hear a conversation among three friends. Using **tú** commands and the ideas presented, write six pieces of advice that Mario can follow to save some money.

1. _____

2. _____

3. _____

4. _____

5. _____

6. _____

Lección 11 Lab Activities   **63**

11.2 Por and para

1   **Escoger** You will hear some sentences with a beep in place of a preposition. Decide if **por** or **para** should complete each sentence.

> **modelo**
>
> *You hear:* El teclado es (*beep*) la computadora de Nuria.
> *You mark:* an **X** under **para**.

	por	para
Modelo	___	**X**
1.	___	___
2.	___	___
3.	___	___
4.	___	___
5.	___	___
6.	___	___
7.	___	___
8.	___	___

2   **La aventura** Complete each phrase about Jaime with **por** or **para** and the cue in your lab manual. Repeat each correct response after the speaker.

> **modelo**
>
> *You hear:* Jaime estudió
> *You see:* médico
> *You say:* Jaime estudió para médico.

1. unos meses
2. hacer sus planes
3. mil dólares
4. ver a sus padres

5. la ciudad
6. su mamá
7. pesos
8. las montañas

3   **Los planes** Listen to the telephone conversation between Antonio and Sonia and then select the best response for the questions in your lab manual.

1. ¿Por dónde quiere ir Sonia para ir a Bariloche?
   a. Quiere ir por Santiago de Chile.
   b. Va a ir por avión.
2. ¿Para qué va Sonia a Bariloche?
   a. Va para esquiar.
   b. Va para comprar esquíes.

3. ¿Por qué tiene que ir de compras Sonia?
   a. Para comprar una bolsa.
   b. Necesita un abrigo para el frío.
4. ¿Por qué quiere ir Antonio con ella hoy?
   a. Quiere ir para estar con ella.
   b. Quiere ir para comprar un regalo.

11.3 Reciprocal reflexives

1 **Escoger** Listen to each question and, in your lab manual, choose the most logical response.

1. a. Hace cuatro años que nos conocimos.
   b. Se vieron todos los fines de semana.
2. a. Nos besamos antes de salir a trabajar.
   b. No, creo que se besaron en la segunda.
3. a. Nos llevamos mal sólo el último año.
   b. Se llevaron mal siempre.
4. a. Sí, se saludan con un abrazo y también con un beso.
   b. Nos saludamos desde lejos.
5. a. Casi nunca me miraban.
   b. Creo que se miraban con mucho amor.
6. a. Sólo nos ayudamos para el examen.
   b. Se ayudan a menudo.
7. a. Creo que se hablan todas las noches.
   b. Le hablan mucho porque tienen celulares.
8. a. Cuando se casaron se querían mucho.
   b. Cada día nos queremos más.

2 **Responder** Answer each question in the affirmative. Repeat the correct answer after the speaker. (6 *items*)

> **modelo**
>
> ¿Se abrazaron tú y Carolina en la primera cita?
> Sí, nos abrazamos en la primera cita.

3 **Los amigos** Listen to a description of a friendship and then, in your lab manual, choose the phrase that best completes each sentence.

1. Desde los once años, los chicos _____ con frecuencia.
   a. se veían   b. se ayudaban   c. se besaban
2. Samuel y Andrea _____ por la amistad (*friendship*) de sus madres.
   a. se escribían   b. se entendían   c. se conocieron
3. Las madres de Andrea y Samuel...
   a. se ayudaban.   b. se conocían bien.   c. se odiaban.
4. Andrea y Samuel no _____ por un tiempo debido a (*due to*) un problema.
   a. se conocieron   b. se hablaron   c. se ayudaron
5. Después de un tiempo...
   a. se besaron.   b. se pidieron perdón. c. se odiaron.
6. La separación sirvió para enseñarles que...
   a. se querían.   b. se hablaban mucho.   c. se conocían bien.
7. No es cierto. Andrea y Samuel no...
   a. se casaron.   b. se entendían bien.   c. se querían.
8. Los dos amigos _____ por un tiempo.
   a. se besaban   b. se comprometieron   c. se llevaron mal

Lección 11 Lab Activities   **65**

11.4 Stressed possessive adjectives and pronouns

1 Identificar Listen to each statement and mark an **X** in the column identifying the possessive pronoun you hear.

> **modelo**
>
> *You hear:* Ya arreglaron todos los coches, pero el tuyo no.
> *You write:* an **X** under **yours**.

	mine	*yours*	*his/hers*	*ours*	*theirs*
Modelo	_____	**X**	_____	_____	_____
1.	_____	_____	_____	_____	_____
2.	_____	_____	_____	_____	_____
3.	_____	_____	_____	_____	_____
4.	_____	_____	_____	_____	_____
5.	_____	_____	_____	_____	_____
6.	_____	_____	_____	_____	_____
7.	_____	_____	_____	_____	_____
8.	_____	_____	_____	_____	_____

2 Transformar Restate each sentence you hear, using the cues in your lab manual. Repeat the correct answer after the speaker.

> **modelo**
>
> *You hear:* ¿De qué año es el carro suyo?
> *You see:* mine
> *You say:* ¿De qué año es el carro mío?

1. *his*
2. *ours*
3. *yours (fam.)*
4. *theirs*
5. *mine*
6. *hers*

3 ¿Cierto o falso? You will hear two brief conversations. Listen carefully and then indicate whether the statements in your lab manual are **cierto** or **falso**.

Conversación 1

	Cierto	Falso
1. Pablo dice que el carro es de Ana.	○	○
2. Ana necesita la computadora para su trabajo.	○	○
3. Las películas de Ana son mejores que las de Pablo.	○	○

Conversación 2

	Cierto	Falso
4. La computadora de Adela es muy rápida.	○	○
5. El navegador GPS de la prima de Adela es muy bueno.	○	○
6. El navegador es más de Adela que de ellos dos.	○	○

vocabulario

You will now hear the vocabulary found in your textbook on the last page of this lesson. Listen and repeat each Spanish word or phrase after the speaker.

contextos   Lección 12

1   Describir   Listen to each sentence and write the number of the sentence below the drawing of the household item mentioned.

a. _____   b. _____   c. _____

d. _____   e. _____   f. _____

g. _____   h. _____

2   Identificar   You will hear a series of words. Write the word that does not belong in each series.

1. _____   4. _____   7. _____

2. _____   5. _____   8. _____

3. _____   6. _____

3   Quehaceres domésticos   Your children are complaining about the state of things in your house. Respond to their complaints by telling them what household chores they should do to correct the situation. Repeat the correct response after the speaker. (*6 items*)

modelo

La ropa está arrugada (*wrinkled*).
Debes planchar la ropa.

4   En la oficina de la agente inmobiliaria   Listen to this conversation between Mr. Fuentes and a real estate agent. Then read the statements in your lab manual and decide whether they are **cierto** or **falso**.

	Cierto	Falso
1. El señor Fuentes quiere alquilar una casa.	○	○
2. El señor Fuentes quiere vivir en las afueras.	○	○
3. Él no quiere pagar más de 900 balboas al mes.	○	○
4. Él vive solo (*alone*).	○	○
5. El edificio de apartamentos tiene ascensor.	○	○
6. El apartamento tiene lavadora.	○	○

Lección 12 Lab Activities   **67**

pronunciación

The letter x

In Spanish, the letter **x** has several sounds. When the letter **x** appears between two vowels, it is usually pronounced like the *ks* sound in *eccentric* or the *gs* sound in *egg salad*.

con**exi**ón   **exa**men   **saxo**fón

If the letter **x** is followed by a consonant, it is pronounced like *s* or *ks*.

ex**p**licar   sex**t**o   ex**c**ursión

In Old Spanish, the letter **x** had the same sound as the Spanish **j**. Some proper names and some words from native languages like Náhuatl and Maya have retained this pronunciation.

Don Qui**x**ote   Oa**x**aca   Te**x**as

1 **Práctica** Repeat each word after the speaker, focusing on the **x** sound.

1. éxito
2. reflexivo
3. exterior
4. excelente
5. expedición
6. mexicano
7. expresión
8. examinar
9. excepto
10. exagerar
11. contexto
12. Maximiliano

2 **Oraciones** When you hear the number, read the corresponding sentence aloud. Then listen to the speaker and repeat the sentence.

1. Xavier Ximénez va de excursión a Ixtapa.
2. Xavier es una persona excéntrica y se viste de trajes extravagantes.
3. Él es un experto en lenguas extranjeras.
4. Hoy va a una exposición de comidas exóticas.
5. Prueba algunos platos exquisitos y extraordinarios.

3 **Refranes** Repeat each saying after the speaker to practice the **x** sound.

1. Ir por extremos no es de discretos. [1]
2. El que de la ira se deja vencer, se expone a perder. [2]

4 **Dictado** You will hear five sentences. Each will be said twice. Listen carefully and write what you hear.

1. _____
2. _____
3. _____
4. _____
5. _____

[1] *Prudent people don't go to extremes.*

[2] *He who allows anger to overcome him, risks losing.*

estructura

12.1 Relative pronouns

1 **Escoger** You will hear some sentences with a beep in place of the relative pronoun. Decide whether **que**, **quien**, or **lo que** should complete each sentence and circle it.

> **modelo**
>
> *You hear:* (Beep) me gusta de la casa es el jardín.
> *You circle:* **Lo que** because the sentence is **Lo que me gusta de la casa es el jardín**.

1. que	quien	lo que		6. que	quien	lo que
2. que	quien	lo que		7. Que	Quien	Lo que
3. que	quien	lo que		8. que	quien	lo que
4. que	quien	lo que		9. que	quien	lo que
5. que	quien	lo que		10. que	quien	lo que

2 **Completar** You will hear some incomplete sentences. Choose the correct ending for each sentence.

1. a. con que trabaja tu amiga.
   b. que se mudó a Portobelo.
2. a. que vende muebles baratos.
   b. que trabajábamos.
3. a. a quienes escribí son mis primas.
   b. de quien te escribí.
4. a. con que barres el suelo.
   b. que queremos vender.
5. a. lo que deben.
   b. que deben.
6. a. que te hablo es ama de casa.
   b. en quien pienso es ama de casa.

3 **Preguntas** Answer each question you hear using a relative pronoun and the cues in your lab manual. Repeat the correct response after the speaker.

> **modelo**
>
> *You hear:* ¿Quiénes son los chicos rubios?
> *You see:* mis primos / viven en Colón
> *You say:* Son mis primos que viven en Colón.

1. chica / conocí en el café
2. el cliente / llamó ayer
3. chico / se casa Patricia
4. agente / nos ayudó
5. vecinos / viven en la casa azul
6. chica / trabajo

4 **Un robo (break-in)** There has been a theft at the Riveras' house. The detective they have hired has gathered all the family members in the living room to reveal the culprit. Listen to his conclusions. Then complete the list of clues (**pistas**) in your lab manual and answer the question.

Pistas

1. El reloj que _____.
2. La taza que _____.
3. La almohada que _____.

Pregunta

¿Quién se llevó las cucharas de la abuela y por qué se las llevó? _____
_____

12.2 Formal (usted/ustedes) commands

1 **Identificar** You will hear some sentences. If the verb is a formal command, circle **Sí**. If the verb is not a command, circle **No**.

> **modelo**
>
> *You hear:* Saque la basura.
> *You circle:* **Sí** because **Saque** is a formal command.

1. Sí No   6. Sí No
2. Sí No   7. Sí No
3. Sí No   8. Sí No
4. Sí No   9. Sí No
5. Sí No   10. Sí No

2 **Cambiar** A physician is giving a patient advice. Change each sentence you hear from an indirect command to a formal command. Repeat the correct answer after the speaker. (*6 items*)

> **modelo**
>
> Usted tiene que dormir ocho horas cada noche.
> *Duerma ocho horas cada noche.*

3 **Preguntas** Answer each question you hear in the affirmative using a formal command and a direct object pronoun. Repeat the correct response after the speaker. (*8 items*)

> **modelo**
>
> ¿Cerramos las ventanas?
> *Sí, ciérrenlas.*

4 **Más preguntas** Answer each question you hear using a formal command and the cue in your lab manual. Repeat the correct response after the speaker.

> **modelo**
>
> *You hear:* ¿Debo llamar al señor Rodríguez?
> *You see:* no / ahora
> *You say:* No, no lo llame ahora.

1. no   4. no
2. a las cinco   5. el primer día del mes
3. sí / aquí   6. que estamos ocupados

5 **¿Cómo llegar?** Julia is going to explain how to get to her home. Listen to her instructions, then number the instructions in your lab manual in the correct order. Two items will not be used.

_____ a. entrar al edificio que está al lado del Banco Popular

_____ b. tomar el ascensor al cuarto piso

_____ c. buscar las llaves debajo de la alfombra

_____ d. ir detrás del edificio

_____ e. bajarse del metro en la estación Santa Rosa

_____ f. subir las escaleras al tercer piso

_____ g. caminar hasta el final del pasillo

12.3 The present subjunctive

1   **Escoger**   You will hear some sentences with a beep in place of a verb. Decide which verb should complete each sentence and circle it.

> **modelo**
>
> *You hear:* Es urgente que (*beep*) al médico.
> *You see:* vas vayas
> *You circle:* **vayas** *because the sentence is* **Es urgente que vayas al médico**.

1. tomamos	tomemos		5. se acuestan	se acuesten
2. conduzcan	conducen		6. sabes	sepas
3. aprenda	aprende		7. almorcemos	almorzamos
4. arreglas	arregles		8. se mude	se muda

2   **Cambiar**   You are a Spanish instructor, and it's the first day of class. Tell your students what it is important for them to do using the cues you hear. (*8 items*)

> **modelo**
>
> hablar español en la clase
> **Es importante que ustedes hablen español en la clase.**

3   **Transformar**   Change each sentence you hear to the subjunctive mood using the expression in your lab manual. Repeat the correct answer after the speaker.

> **modelo**
>
> *You hear:* Pones tu ropa en el armario.
> *You see:* Es necesario
> *You say:* **Es necesario que pongas tu ropa en el armario.**

1. Es mejor   4. Es importante
2. Es urgente   5. Es bueno
3. Es malo   6. Es necesario

4   **¿Qué pasa aquí?**   Listen to this conversation. Then choose the phrase that best completes each sentence in your lab manual.

1. Esta conversación es entre…
   a. un empleado y una clienta.
   b. un hijo y su madre.
   c. un camarero y la dueña de un restaurante.
2. Es necesario que Mario…
   a. llegue temprano.
   b. se lave las manos.
   c. use la lavadora.
3. Es urgente que Mario…
   a. ponga las mesas.
   b. quite las mesas.
   c. sea listo.

12.4 Subjunctive with verbs of will and influence

1 **Identificar** Listen to each sentence. If you hear a verb in the subjunctive, mark **Sí**. If you don't hear the subjunctive, mark **No**.

1. Sí No
2. Sí No
3. Sí No

4. Sí No
5. Sí No
6. Sí No

2 **Transformar** Some people are discussing what they or their friends want to do. Say that you don't want them to do those things. Repeat the correct response after the speaker. (*6 items*)

> **modelo**
>
> Esteban quiere invitar a tu hermana a una fiesta.
> No quiero que Esteban invite a mi hermana a una fiesta.

3 **Situaciones** Listen to each situation and make a recommendation using the cues in your lab manual. Repeat the correct response after the speaker.

> **modelo**
>
> *You hear:* Sacamos una "F" en el examen de química.
> *You see:* estudiar más
> *You say:* Les recomiendo que estudien más.

1. ponerte un suéter
2. quedarse en la cama
3. regalarles una tostadora

4. no hacerlo
5. comprarlas en la Casa Bonita
6. ir a La Cascada

4 **¿Qué hacemos?** Listen to this conversation and answer the questions in your lab manual.

1. ¿Qué quiere el señor Barriga que hagan los chicos?

_____

2. ¿Qué le pide el chico?

_____

3. ¿Qué les sugiere el señor a los chicos?

_____

4. ¿Qué tienen que hacer los chicos si no consiguen el dinero?

_____

5. Al final, ¿en qué insiste el señor Barriga?

_____

vocabulario

You will now hear the vocabulary found in your textbook on the last page of this lesson. Listen and repeat each Spanish word or phrase after the speaker.

contextos

1 **¿Lógico o ilógico?** You will hear some questions and the responses. Decide if they are **lógico** or **ilógico**.

1. Lógico   Ilógico   4. Lógico   Ilógico
2. Lógico   Ilógico   5. Lógico   Ilógico
3. Lógico   Ilógico   6. Lógico   Ilógico

2 **Eslóganes** You will hear some slogans created by environmentalists. Write the number of each slogan next to the ecological problem it addresses.

_____ a. la contaminación del aire   _____ d. la contaminación del agua
_____ b. la deforestación urbana   _____ e. el ecoturismo
_____ c. la extinción de animales   _____ f. la basura en las calles

3 **Preguntas** Look at the drawings and answer each question you hear. Repeat the correct response after the speaker.

1.

2.

3.

4.

4 **Completar** Listen to this radio advertisement and write the missing words in your lab manual.

Para los que gustan del (1) _____, la agencia Eco-Guías los invita a viajar a la

(2) _____ amazónica. Estar en el Amazonas es convivir (*to coexist*) con la

(3) _____. Venga y (4) _____ los misterios del

(5) _____. Admire de cerca las diferentes (6) _____ y

(7) _____ mientras navega por un (8) _____ que parece

mar. Duerma bajo un (9) _____ lleno de (10) _____.

pronunciación

l, ll, and y

In Spanish, the letter **l** is pronounced much like the *l* sound in the English word *lemon*.

cielo   lago   lata   luna

In Lesson 8, you learned that most Spanish speakers pronounce **ll** like the *y* in the English word *yes*. The letter **y** is often pronounced in the same manner.

estrella   valle   mayo   playa

When the letter **y** occurs at the end of a syllable or by itself, it is pronounced like the Spanish letter **i**.

ley   muy   voy   y

1 **Práctica** Repeat each word after the speaker focusing on the **l**, **ll**, and **y** sounds.

1. lluvia   6. pasillo   11. yogur
2. desarrollar   7. limón   12. estoy
3. animal   8. raya   13. taller
4. reciclar   9. resolver   14. hay
5. llegar   10. pantalla   15. mayor

2 **Oraciones** When you hear the number, read the corresponding sentence aloud. Then listen to the speaker and repeat the sentence.

1. Ayer por la mañana Leonor se lavó el pelo y se maquilló.
2. Ella tomó café con leche y desayunó pan con mantequilla.
3. Después su yerno vino a su casa para ayudarla.
4. Pero él se cayó en las escaleras del altillo y se lastimó la rodilla.
5. Leonor lo llevó al hospital.
6. Allí le dieron unas pastillas para el dolor.

3 **Refranes** Repeat each saying after the speaker to practice the **l**, **ll**, and **y** sounds.

1. Quien no oye consejo no llega a viejo. [1]
2. A caballo regalado, no le mires el diente. [2]

4 **Dictado** You will hear five sentences. Each will be said twice. Listen carefully and write what you hear.

1. _____
2. _____
3. _____
4. _____
5. _____

[1] *He who doesn't listen to advice doesn't reach old age.*

[2] *Don't look a gift horse in the mouth.*

estructura

13.1 The subjunctive with verbs of emotion

1 **Escoger** Listen to each statement and, in your lab manual, choose the most logical response.

1. a. Ojalá que se mejore pronto.
   b. Me alegro de que esté bien.
2. a. Espero que podamos ir a nadar mañana.
   b. Es una lástima que ya no lo podamos usar.
3. a. Me sorprende que venga temprano.
   b. Siento que se pierda la película.
4. a. Temo que el río esté contaminado.
   b. Me alegro de que vea bien.

5. a. Es ridículo que el gobierno controle cuándo nos bañamos.
   b. Me gusta cepillarme los dientes.
6. a. Es triste que la gente cuide las playas.
   b. Me molesta que no hagamos nada para mejorar la situación.

2 **Transformar** Change each sentence you hear to the subjunctive mood using the expression in your lab manual. Repeat the correct answer after the speaker.

> **modelo**
> You hear: Cada año hay menos árboles en el mundo.
> You see: Es una lástima.
> You say: Es una lástima que cada año haya menos árboles en el mundo.

1. Es triste.
2. Es extraño.
3. Es terrible.
4. Es ridículo.
5. Es una lástima.
6. Me molesta.

3 **Preguntas** Answer each question you hear using the cues in your lab manual. Repeat the correct response after the speaker.

> **modelo**
> You hear: ¿De qué tienes miedo?
> You see: nosotros / no resolver la crisis de energía
> You say: Tengo miedo de que nosotros no resolvamos la crisis de energía.

1. Ricardo / estudiar ecología
2. muchas personas / no preocuparse por el medio ambiente
3. tú / hacer un viaje a la selva
4. el gobierno / controlar el uso de la energía nuclear
5. los turistas / recoger las flores
6. haber / tantas plantas en el desierto

4 **El Club de Ecología** Listen to this conversation. Then read the statements in your lab manual and decide whether they are **cierto** or **falso**.

	Cierto	Falso
1. Carmen se alegra de que la presidenta del club empiece un programa de reciclaje.	○	○
2. Héctor espera que Carmen se enoje con la presidenta.	○	○
3. Carmen teme que los otros miembros (*members*) quieran limpiar las playas.	○	○
4. A Carmen le gusta ir a la playa.	○	○
5. A Héctor le sorprende que Carmen abandone (*resigns from*) el club.	○	○
6. Carmen cree que la presidenta va a cambiar de idea.	○	○

13.2 The subjunctive with doubt, disbelief, and denial

1 **Identificar** Listen to each sentence and decide whether you hear a verb in the indicative or the subjunctive in the subordinate clause. Mark an **X** in the appropriate column.

> **modelo**
>
> *You hear:* Creo que Nicolás va de excursión.
> *You mark:* an **X** under **indicative** because you heard **va**.

	indicative	subjunctive
Modelo	X	
1.		
2.		
3.		
4.		
5.		
6.		
7.		

2 **Cambiar** Change each sentence you hear to the negative. Repeat the correct answer after the speaker. (*7 items*)

> **modelo**
>
> Dudo que haga frío en Bogotá.
> *No dudo que hace frío en Bogotá.*

3 **Te ruego** Listen to this conversation between a father and daughter. Then choose the word or phrase in your lab manual that best completes each sentence.

1. Juanita quiere ir a la selva amazónica para...
   a. vivir con los indios.   b. estudiar las aves tropicales.   c. estudiar las plantas tropicales.
2. Ella _____ que quiere ir.
   a. está segura de   b. no está segura de   c. niega
3. Su papá _____ que se enferme de malaria.
   a. está seguro   b. teme   c. niega
4. Juanita _____ que se enferme.
   a. duda   b. no duda   c. cree
5. _____ que el papá no quiera que ella vaya.
   a. Es cierto   b. No es cierto   c. No hay duda de
6. El papá dice que _____ que la selva amazónica es un lugar fantástico.
   a. es improbable   b. es imposible   c. no cabe duda de
7. _____ Juanita va a la selva amazónica.
   a. Es seguro que   b. Tal vez   c. No es probable que
8. Juanita _____ que su papá es el mejor papá del mundo.
   a. duda   b. no cree   c. cree

13.3 The subjunctive with conjunctions

1 **¿Lógico o ilógico?** You will hear some sentences. Decide if they are **lógico** or **ilógico**.

1. Lógico   Ilógico   4. Lógico   Ilógico
2. Lógico   Ilógico   5. Lógico   Ilógico
3. Lógico   Ilógico   6. Lógico   Ilógico

2 **A la entrada del parque** Listen to the park ranger's instructions. Then number the drawings in your lab manual in the correct order.

a. _____   b. _____

c. _____   d. _____

3 **Identificar** Listen to each sentence and mark an **X** in the appropriate column to indicate whether the subordinate clause expresses a future action, a habitual action, or a past action.

> **modelo**
>
> *You hear:* Voy a ir a caminar por el sendero tan pronto como llegues a casa.
> *You mark:* an **X** under **future action**.

	future action	habitual action	past action
Modelo	X		
1.			
2.			
3.			
4.			
5.			
6.			

vocabulario

You will now hear the vocabulary found in your textbook on the last page of this lesson. Listen and repeat each Spanish word or phrase after the speaker.

Nombre _____Fecha _____

1 **¿Lógico o ilógico?** You will hear some questions and the responses. Decide if they are **lógico** or **ilógico**.

1. Lógico   Ilógico   3. Lógico   Ilógico   5. Lógico   Ilógico   7. Lógico   Ilógico
2. Lógico   Ilógico   4. Lógico   Ilógico   6. Lógico   Ilógico   8. Lógico   Ilógico

2 **Hacer diligencias** Look at the drawing in your lab manual and listen to Sofía's description of her day. During each pause, write the name of the place she went. The first one has been done for you.

| Lavandería Rosa | Zapatería Valencia | Correo | Peluquería Violeta | Pastelería Simón |
| | | | | Joyería Andes |

Calle Flores

Plaza Ángel — **Calle Campos**

Colegio La Salle
Librería Gallegos
Banco Nacional

N
O←→E
S

1. _____Lavandería Rosa_____   5. _____
2. _____   6. _____
3. _____   7. _____
4. _____   8. _____

3 **Preguntas** Look once again at the drawing in activity 2 in your lab manual and answer each question you hear with the correct information. Repeat the correct response after the speaker. (*5 items*)

> modelo
> La joyería está al norte de la plaza, ¿verdad?
> No, la joyería está al este de la plaza.

4 **Perdidos en el centro** Listen to Carlos and Victoria's conversation and answer the questions in your lab manual.

1. ¿Qué buscan Carlos y Victoria? _____

2. ¿Quién les indica cómo llegar? _____

3. ¿Qué deben hacer en el semáforo? _____

4. ¿A cuántas cuadras está el lugar del semáforo? _____

pronunciación

m and n

The letter **m** is pronounced like the *m* in the English word *made*.

    mamá   **m**arzo   **m**andar   **m**esa

The letter **n** is pronounced like the *n* in the English word *none*.

    Norte   **n**adie   **n**unca   **n**ieto

When **n** is followed by the letter **v**, the **n** is pronounced like the Spanish **m**.

    e**n**viar   i**n**vierno   i**n**vitado   co**n** **V**íctor

1   **Práctica** Repeat each word or phrase after the speaker to practice pronouncing **m** and **n**.

1. imposible	5. número	9. enamorado	13. matrimonio
2. mañana	6. invitar	10. monumento	14. confirmar
3. mano	7. moreno	11. empleado	15. con Víctor
4. manejar	8. envase	12. encima	16. ningún

2   **Oraciones** When you hear each number, read the corresponding sentence aloud. Then listen to the speaker and repeat the sentence.

1. A mí no me gustan nada los mariscos.
2. En el mercado compro naranjas, melocotones y manzanas.
3. Mañana invito a Mario Martín a cenar conmigo.
4. Mario es el mejor mecánico de motocicletas del mundo.
5. También le importa mucho la conservación del medio ambiente.
6. Siempre envía los envases de aluminio al centro de reciclaje en Valencia.

3   **Refranes** Repeat each saying after the speaker to practice pronouncing **m** and **n**.

1. Más vale poco y bueno que mucho y malo. [1]
2. Mala hierba nunca muere. [2]

4   **Dictado** You will hear a paragraph. Listen carefully and write what you hear during the pauses. The entire paragraph will then be repeated so that you can check your work.

_____

_____

_____

_____

_____

[1] *Quality is more important than quantity.*

[2] *Like a bad penny, it just keeps turning up. (lit. Bad grass never dies.)*

estructura

14.1 The subjunctive in adjective clauses

1 **Identificar** Listen to each statement or question. If it refers to a person, place, or thing that clearly exists or is known, mark an **X** in the **Sí** row. If it refers to a person, place, or thing that either does not exist or whose existence is uncertain, mark an **X** in the **No** row.

> **modelo**
> *You hear:* Buscamos un hotel que tenga piscina.
> *You mark:* an **X** in the **No** row because the existence of the hotel is uncertain.

	Modelo	1.	2.	3.	4.	5.	6.
Sí	___	___	___	___	___	___	___
No	X	___	___	___	___	___	___

2 **Escoger** You will hear some sentences with a beep in place of the verb. Decide which verb best completes each sentence and circle it.

> **modelo**
> *You hear:* Tengo una cuenta corriente que (*beep*) gratis.
> *You circle:* **es** because the existence of the **cuenta corriente** is not in doubt.

1. tiene   tenga   2. vende   venda   3. vende   venda   4. hacen   hagan

3 **Cambiar** Change each sentence you hear into the negative. Repeat the correct answer after the speaker. (*6 items*)

> **modelo**
> Hay un restaurante aquí que sirve comida venezolana.
> No hay ningún restaurante aquí que sirva comida venezolana.

4 **Buscando amistad** Read the ads for pen pals found in your lab manual. Then listen to the four recorded personal ads. In your lab manual, write the name of the person whose written ad best suits each recorded personal ad.

Nombre: Gustavo Carrasquillo
Dirección: Casilla 204, La Paz, Bolivia
Edad: 20 años
Pasatiempos: Ver películas en inglés, leer revistas de política, escalar montañas, esquiar y hacer amistad con jóvenes de todo el mundo. Me pueden escribir en inglés o alemán.

Nombre: Claudia Morales
Dirección: Calle 4–14, Guatemala, Guatemala
Edad: 18 años
Pasatiempos: Ir a conciertos de rock, escuchar la radio, ver películas extranjeras, mandar y recibir correo electrónico.

Nombre: Alicia Duque
Dirección: Avenida Gran Capitán 26, Córdoba, España
Edad: 18 años
Pasatiempos: Ir al cine, a fiestas, bailar, hablar por teléfono y escribir canciones de amor. Pueden escribirme en francés.

Nombre: Antonio Ávila
Dirección: Apartado Postal 3007, Panamá, Panamá
Edad: 21 años
Pasatiempos: Entre mis pasatiempos están escribir cartas a amigos de todas partes del mundo, escuchar la radio, practicar deportes y leer revistas.

Nombre: Rosalinda Guerrero
Dirección: Calle 408 #3, Hatillo, Puerto Rico
Edad: 19 años
Pasatiempos: Navegar por Internet, leer sobre política, ir a conciertos y visitar museos de arte.

1. _____   3. _____
2. _____   4. _____

14.2 Nosotros/as commands

1 **Identificar** Listen to each statement. Mark an **X** in the **Sí** row if it is a command. Mark an **X** in the **No** row if it is not.

> **modelo**
> *You hear:* Abramos la tienda.
> *You mark:* an **X** next to **Sí**.

	Modelo	1.	2.	3.	4.	5.	6.
Sí	X	___	___	___	___	___	___
No	___	___	___	___	___	___	___

2 **Cambiar** Change each sentence you hear to a **nosotros/as** command. Repeat the correct answer after the speaker. (*8 items*)

> **modelo**
> Vamos a visitar la Plaza Bolívar.
> Visitemos la Plaza Bolívar.

3 **Preguntas** Answer each question you hear negatively. Then make another suggestion using the cue in your lab manual and a **nosotros/as** command.

> **modelo**
> *You hear:* ¿Cocinamos esta noche?
> *You see:* comer en el Restaurante Cambur
> *You say:* No, no cocinemos esta noche. Comamos en el Restaurante Cambur.

1. jugar a las cartas
2. esquiarla

3. ir a la biblioteca
4. limpiar el sótano

4 **¿Cierto o falso?** Listen to Manuel and Elisa's conversation. Then read the statements in your lab manual and decide whether they are **cierto** or **falso**.

	Cierto	Falso
1. Manuel está muy ocupado.	○	○
2. Manuel va a acompañar a Elisa a hacer diligencias.	○	○
3. Primero van a ir al correo para comprar sellos.	○	○
4. Elisa quiere depositar el cheque primero.	○	○
5. Manuel y Elisa van a comprar el postre antes de ir al banco.	○	○
6. Elisa sugiere cortarse el pelo después de hacer todo lo demás.	○	○

14.3 Past participles used as adjectives

1 **Identificar** Listen to each sentence and write the past participle that is being used as an adjective.

> **modelo**
>
> *You hear:* Los programas musicales son divertidos.
> *You write:* divertidos

1. _____   5. _____

2. _____   6. _____

3. _____   7. _____

4. _____   8. _____

2 **Preguntas** It has been a very bad day. Answer each question using the cue in your lab manual. Repeat the correct response after the speaker.

> **modelo**
>
> *You hear:* ¿Dónde está el libro?
> *You see:* perder
> *You say:* El libro está perdido.

1. romper   3. divorciar   5. caer   7. abrir   9. vender

2. morir   4. gastar   6. comer   8. dañar

3 **¿Cierto o falso?** Look at the drawing in your lab manual and listen to each statement. Indicate whether each statement is **cierto** or **falso**.

	Cierto	Falso
1.	○	○
2.	○	○
3.	○	○
4.	○	○
5.	○	○
6.	○	○

vocabulario

You will now hear the vocabulary found in your textbook on the last page of this lesson. Listen and repeat each Spanish word or phrase after the speaker.

contextos

1 **Identificar** You will hear a series of words or phrases. Write the word or phrase that does not belong in each group.

1. _____   3. _____   5. _____

2. _____   4. _____   6. _____

2 **Describir** For each drawing, you will hear a brief description. Indicate whether it is **cierto** or **falso** according to what you see.

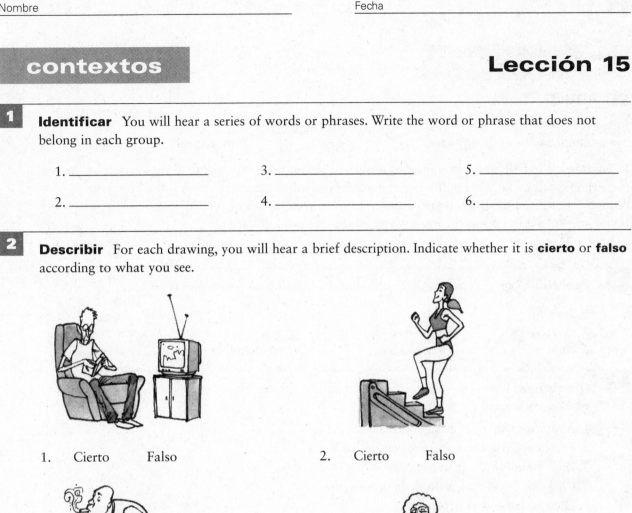

1.   Cierto   Falso

2.   Cierto   Falso

3.   Cierto   Falso

4.   Cierto   Falso

3 **A entrenarse** Listen as Marisela describes her new fitness program. Then list the activities she plans to do each day in your lab manual.

lunes: _____

martes: _____

miércoles: _____

jueves: _____

viernes: _____

sábado: _____

domingo: _____

pronunciación

ch and p

In Spanish, **ch** is pronounced like the *ch* sound in *church* and *chair*.

    Co**ch**abamba   no**che**   mo**ch**ila   mu**ch**a**ch**o   que**ch**ua

In English, the letter *p* at the beginning of a word is pronounced with a puff of air. In contrast, the Spanish **p** is pronounced without the puff of air. It is somewhat like the *p* sound in *spin*. To check your pronunciation, hold the palm of your hand in front of your mouth as you say the following words. If you are making the **p** sound correctly, you should not feel a puff of air.

    La **P**az   **p**eso   **p**iscina   a**p**urarse   **p**roteína

1   **Práctica** Repeat each word after the speaker, focusing on the **ch** and **p** sounds.

1. archivo	4. lechuga	7. pie	10. chuleta
2. derecha	5. preocupado	8. cuerpo	11. champiñón
3. chau	6. operación	9. computadora	12. leche

2   **Oraciones** When you hear the number, read the corresponding sentence aloud. Then listen to the speaker and repeat the sentence.

1. A muchos chicos les gusta el chocolate.
2. Te prohibieron comer chuletas por el colesterol.
3. ¿Has comprado el champán para la fiesta?
4. Chela perdió el cheque antes de depositarlo.
5. Levanto pesas para perder peso.
6. ¿Me prestas el champú?

3   **Refranes** Repeat each saying after the speaker to practice the **ch** and **p** sounds.

1. Del dicho al hecho, hay mucho trecho. [1]
2. A perro flaco todo son pulgas. [2]

4   **Dictado** You will hear eight sentences. Each will be said twice. Listen carefully and write what you hear.

1. _____
2. _____
3. _____
4. _____
5. _____
6. _____
7. _____
8. _____

[1] *It's easier said than done.*
[2] *It never rains, but it pours.*

estructura

15.1 The present perfect

1 Identificar Listen to each statement and mark an **X** in the column for the subject of the verb.

> **modelo**
> *You hear:* Nunca han hecho ejercicios aeróbicos.
> *You mark:* an **X** under **ellos**.

	yo	tú	él/ella	nosotros/as	ellos
Modelo	___	___	___	___	X
1.	___	___	___	___	___
2.	___	___	___	___	___
3.	___	___	___	___	___
4.	___	___	___	___	___
5.	___	___	___	___	___
6.	___	___	___	___	___

2 Transformar Change each sentence you hear from the present indicative to the present perfect indicative. Repeat the correct answer after the speaker. (*8 items*)

> **modelo**
> Pedro y Ernesto salen del gimnasio.
> *Pedro y Ernesto han salido del gimnasio.*

3 Preguntas Answer each question you hear using the cue in your lab manual. Repeat the correct response after the speaker.

> **modelo**
> *You hear:* ¿Ha adelgazado Miguel?
> *You see:* sí / un poco
> *You say:* Sí, Miguel ha adelgazado un poco.

1. sí   3. no   5. no
2. sí   4. sí   6. no / todavía

4 Consejos de una amiga Listen to this conversation between Eva and Manuel. Then choose the correct ending for each statement in your lab manual.

1. Ellos están hablando de…
   a. que fumar es malo.   b. la salud de Manuel.   c. los problemas con sus clases.
2. Manuel dice que sufre presiones cuando…
   a. tiene exámenes.   b. hace gimnasia.   c. no puede dormir y fuma mucho.
3. Eva dice que ella…
   a. estudia durante el día.   b. ha estudiado poco.   c. también está nerviosa.
4. Eva le dice a Manuel que…
   a. deje de fumar.   b. estudie más.   c. ellos pueden estudiar juntos.

15.2 The past perfect

1 **¿Lógico o ilógico?** You will hear some brief conversations. Indicate if they are **lógico** or **ilógico**.

1. Lógico   Ilógico
2. Lógico   Ilógico
3. Lógico   Ilógico
4. Lógico   Ilógico
5. Lógico   Ilógico
6. Lógico   Ilógico

2 **Transformar** Change each sentence you hear from the preterite to the past perfect indicative. Repeat the correct answer after the speaker. (*6 items*)

> **modelo**
> Marta nunca sufrió muchas presiones.
> Marta nunca había sufrido muchas presiones.

3 **Describir** Using the cues in your lab manual, describe what you and your friends had already done before your parents arrived for a visit. Repeat the correct answer after the speaker.

> **modelo**
> *You see:* preparar la cena
> *You hear:* mis amigas
> *You say:* Mis amigas ya habían preparado la cena.

1. limpiar el baño y la sala
2. sacar la basura
3. sacudir los muebles
4. poner la mesa
5. hacer las camas
6. darle de comer al gato

4 **Completar** Listen to this conversation and write the missing words in your lab manual. Then answer the questions.

JORGE ¡Hola, chico! Ayer vi a Carmen y no me lo podía creer, me dijo que te

(1) _____ (2) _____ en el gimnasio. ¡Tú, que siempre

(3) _____ (4) _____ tan sedentario! ¿Es cierto?

RUBÉN Pues, sí. (5) _____ (6) _____ mucho de peso y me dolían las rodillas. Hacía

dos años que el médico me (7) _____ (8) _____ que tenía que mantenerme

en forma. Y finalmente, hace cuatro meses, decidí hacer gimnasia casi todos los días.

JORGE Te felicito (*I congratulate you*), amigo. Yo también (9) _____ (10) _____

hace un año a hacer gimnasia. ¿Qué días vas? Quizás nos podemos encontrar allí.

RUBÉN (11) _____ (12) _____ todos los días al salir del trabajo. ¿Y tú? ¿Vas con Carmen?

JORGE Siempre (13) _____ (14) _____ juntos hasta que compré mi propio carro.

Ahora voy cuando quiero. Pero la semana que viene voy a tratar de ir después del trabajo para

verte por allí.

15. ¿Por qué es extraño que Rubén esté en el gimnasio?

_____

16. ¿Qué le había dicho el médico a Rubén?

_____

17. ¿Por qué no va Jorge con Carmen al gimnasio?

_____

15.3 The present perfect subjunctive

1 **Identificar** Listen to each sentence and decide whether you hear a verb in the present perfect indicative, the past perfect indicative, or the present perfect subjunctive.

1. a. present perfect   b. past perfect   c. present perfect subjunctive
2. a. present perfect   b. past perfect   c. present perfect subjunctive
3. a. present perfect   b. past perfect   c. present perfect subjunctive
4. a. present perfect   b. past perfect   c. present perfect subjunctive
5. a. present perfect   b. past perfect   c. present perfect subjunctive
6. a. present perfect   b. past perfect   c. present perfect subjunctive
7. a. present perfect   b. past perfect   c. present perfect subjunctive
8. a. present perfect   b. past perfect   c. present perfect subjunctive

2 **Completar** Complete each sentence you hear using the cue in your lab manual and the present perfect subjunctive. Repeat the correct response after the speaker.

> **modelo**
>
> *You see:* usted / llegar muy tarde
> *You hear:* Temo que...
> *You say:* Temo que usted haya llegado muy tarde.

1. ella / estar enferma
2. tú / dejar de fumar
3. ellos / salir de casa ya
4. nosotros / entrenarnos lo suficiente
5. él / ir al gimnasio
6. yo / casarme

3 **En el Gimnasio Cosmos** Listen to this conversation between Eduardo and a personal trainer, then complete the form in your lab manual.

```
GIMNASIO COSMOS
Tel. 52-9023
Datos del cliente
Nombre: _____

Edad: _____

¿Cuándo fue la última vez que hizo ejercicio?

_____

¿Qué tipo de vida ha llevado últimamente: activa o pasiva?

_____

¿Consume alcohol?

_____

¿Fuma o ha fumado alguna vez?

_____
```

vocabulario

You will now hear the vocabulary found in your textbook on the last page of this lesson. Listen and repeat each Spanish word or phrase after the speaker.

   Lección 15 Lab Activities

contextos

1 **Identificar** Listen to each description and then complete the sentence by identifying the person's occupation.

> **modelo**
> *You hear:* La señora Ortiz enseña a los estudiantes. Ella es...
> *You write:* maestra.

1. _____.   3. _____.   5. _____.

2. _____.   4. _____.   6. _____.

2 **Anuncios clasificados** Look at the ads and listen to each statement. Then decide if the statement is **cierto** or **falso**.

EMPRESA INTERNACIONAL
Busca
CONTADOR

Requisitos:
• Tenga estudios de administración de empresas
• Hable español e inglés

Se ofrece:
• Horario flexible
• Salario semanal de 700 córdobas
• Posibilidades de ascenso

Contacto: Sr. Flores
Tel.: 492 2043

SE BUSCA DISEÑADOR

• Se ofrece un salario anual de 250.000 córdobas.
• Excelentes beneficios
• Debe tener cinco años de experiencia.

Si está interesado, envíe currículum a
EMPRESA LÓPEZ
Fax: 342 2396

	Cierto	Falso			Cierto	Falso			Cierto	Falso
1.	○	○	3.		○	○	5.		○	○
2.	○	○	4.		○	○	6.		○	○

3 **Publicidad** Listen to this radio advertisement and answer the questions in your lab manual.

1. ¿Qué tipo de empresa es Mano a Obra?

_____

2. ¿Qué hace esta empresa?

_____

3. ¿Cuál es la ocupación del señor Mendoza?

_____

4. ¿Qué le va a dar la empresa al señor Mendoza en un año?

_____

5. ¿En qué profesiones se especializa (*specializes*) Mano a Obra?

_____

pronunciación

Intonation

Intonation refers to the rise and fall in the pitch of a person's voice when speaking. Intonation patterns in Spanish are not the same as those in English, and they vary according to the type of sentence.

In normal statements, the pitch usually rises on the first stressed syllable.

A **mí** me ofrecieron un ascenso.   **Ca**da aspirante debe entregar una solicitud.

In exclamations, the pitch goes up on the first stressed syllable.

¡Oja**lá** venga!   ¡**Cla**ro que sí!

In questions with *yes* or *no* answers, the pitch rises to the highest level on the last stressed syllable.

¿Trajiste el cu**rrí**culum?   ¿Es usted arqui**tec**to?

In questions that request information, the pitch is highest on the stressed syllable of the interrogative word.

¿**Cuán**do renunciaste al trabajo?   ¿**Cuál** es su número de teléfono?

1 **Práctica** Repeat each sentence after the speaker, imitating the intonation.

1. ¿Vas a venir a la reunión?
2. ¿Dónde trabajaba anteriormente?
3. ¡Qué difícil!
4. Estoy buscando un nuevo trabajo.
5. Quiero cambiar de profesión.
6. ¿Te interesa el puesto?

2 **Oraciones** When you hear the number, say the speaker's lines in this dialogue aloud. Then listen to the speaker and repeat the sentences.

1. **REPARTIDOR (DELIVERY MAN)** Trabajo para la Compañía de Transportes Alba. ¿Es usted el nuevo jefe?
2. **JEFE** Sí. ¿Qué desea?
3. **REPARTIDOR** Aquí le traigo los muebles de oficina. ¿Dónde quiere que ponga el escritorio?
4. **JEFE** Allí delante, debajo de la ventana. ¡Tenga cuidado! ¿Quiere romper la computadora?
5. **REPARTIDOR** ¡Perdón! Ya es tarde y estoy muy cansado.
6. **JEFE** Perdone usted, yo estoy muy nervioso. Hoy es mi primer día en el trabajo.

3 **Dictado** You will hear a phone conversation. Listen carefully and write what you hear during the pauses. The entire conversation will then be repeated so that you can check your work.

PACO _____

_____

ISABEL _____

_____

PACO _____

_____

ISABEL _____

_____

PACO _____

_____

92 **Lección 16** Lab Activities

Nombre _____ Fecha _____

estructura

16.1 The future

1 Identificar Listen to each sentence and mark an **X** in the column for the subject of the verb.

> **modelo**
> You hear: Iré a la reunión.
> You mark: an **X** under **yo**.

	yo	tú	ella	nosotros	ustedes
Modelo	X				
1.					
2.					
3.					
4.					
5.					
6.					
7.					
8.					

2 Cambiar Change each sentence you hear to the future tense. Repeat the correct answer after the speaker. (*8 items*)

> **modelo**
> Ellos van a salir pronto.
> Ellos saldrán pronto.

3 Preguntas Answer each question you hear using the cues in your lab manual. Repeat the correct response after the speaker.

> **modelo**
> You hear: ¿Con quién saldrás esta noche?
> You see: Javier
> You say: Yo saldré con Javier.

1. no / nada
2. el lunes por la mañana
3. Santo Domingo
4. esta noche
5. 2:00 p.m.
6. sí
7. de periodista
8. la próxima semana

4 Nos mudamos Listen to this conversation between Fernando and Marisol. Then read the statements in your lab manual and decide whether they are **cierto** or **falso**.

	Cierto	Falso
1. Marisol y Emilio se mudarán a Granada.	○	○
2. Ellos saben cuándo se mudan.	○	○
3. Marisol y Emilio harán una excursión a la selva y las playas antes de que él empiece su nuevo trabajo.	○	○
4. Fernando no podrá visitarlos en Nicaragua en un futuro próximo.	○	○

Lección 16 Lab Activities **93**

16.2 The future perfect

1 **¿Lógico o ilógico?** You will hear some brief conversations. Indicate if they are **lógico** or **ilógico**.

	Lógico	Ilógico		Lógico	Ilógico
1.	○	○	5.	○	○
2.	○	○	6.	○	○
3.	○	○	7.	○	○
4.	○	○	8.	○	○

2 **Cambiar** Change each sentence from the future to the future perfect. Repeat the correct response after the speaker. (*8 items*)

> *modelo*
>
> Yo ganaré un millón de dólares.
> *Yo habré ganado un millón de dólares.*

3 **Preguntas** Look at the time line, which shows future events in Sofía's life, and answer each question you hear. Then repeat the correct response after the speaker. (*5 items*)

> *modelo*
>
> *You hear:* ¿Qué habrá hecho Sofía en el año 2025?
> *You see:* 2025 / graduarse
> *You say:* En el año 2025 Sofía se habrá graduado.

4 **Planes futuros** Listen to this conversation between Germán and Vivian. Then choose the correct answer for each question in your lab manual.

1. ¿Qué va a pasar dentro de un mes?
   a. Se habrá acabado el semestre.
   b. Germán se habrá puesto nervioso.

2. ¿Qué habrá hecho el novio de Vivian?
   a. Se habrá ido de viaje.
   b. Habrá hecho las reservaciones.

3. Normalmente, ¿qué hace Germán durante las vacaciones?
   a. Él trabaja en la empresa de su familia.
   b. Él se va a Santo Domingo.

4. ¿Qué puesto habrá conseguido Germán dentro de dos años?
   a. Él será jefe de arquitectos.
   b. Él será gerente de un banco.

5. ¿Por qué dice Vivian que Germán no debe pensar tanto en el futuro?
   a. Porque ahora necesita preocuparse por los exámenes.
   b. Porque en el futuro no tendrá tiempo para ir de vacaciones.

16.3 The past subjunctive

1 **Identificar** Listen to the following verbs. Mark **Sí** if the verb is in the past subjunctive and **No** if it is in another tense.

1. Sí   No   7. Sí   No
2. Sí   No   8. Sí   No
3. Sí   No   9. Sí   No
4. Sí   No   10. Sí   No
5. Sí   No   11. Sí   No
6. Sí   No   12. Sí   No

2 **Cambiar** Form a new sentence using the cue you hear. Repeat the correct answer after the speaker. (*8 items*)

> **modelo**
> Marisa quería que yo dejara el trabajo. (mi hermana)
> **Marisa quería que mi hermana dejara el trabajo.**

3 **Completar** Complete each phrase you hear using the cue in your lab manual and the past subjunctive. Repeat the correct response after the speaker.

> **modelo**
> *You hear:* Esperábamos que tú...
> *You see:* seguir otra carrera
> *You say:* **Esperábamos que tú siguieras otra carrera.**

1. ir a renunciar al puesto   5. poner un anuncio en los periódicos
2. darte el aumento   6. llegar temprano al trabajo
3. invertir en su empresa   7. ofrecerles mejores beneficios
4. saber la verdad   8. gastar menos dinero

4 **El mundo de los negocios** Listen to this conversation between two coworkers and answer the questions in your lab manual.

1. ¿Qué le pidió el jefe a Elisa cuando la llamó por teléfono? _____

_____

2. ¿Qué le pidió el jefe a la empleada cuando entró (*entered*) a su oficina? _____

_____

3. ¿Qué le preguntó el jefe a Elisa? _____

_____

4. ¿Qué le contestó Elisa? _____

_____

vocabulario

You will now hear the vocabulary found in your textbook on the last page of this lesson. Listen and repeat each Spanish word or phrase after the speaker.

Lección 16 Lab Activities   **95**

contextos

1 **Describir** For each drawing, you will hear a description. Decide whether it is **cierto** or **falso**.

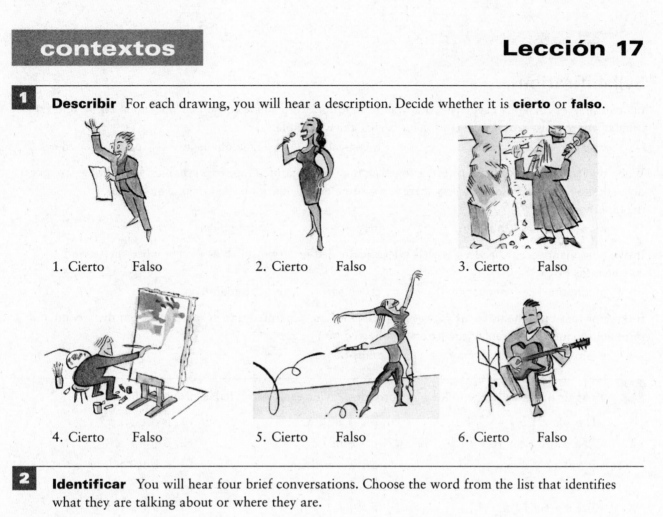

1. Cierto   Falso

2. Cierto   Falso

3. Cierto   Falso

4. Cierto   Falso

5. Cierto   Falso

6. Cierto   Falso

2 **Identificar** You will hear four brief conversations. Choose the word from the list that identifies what they are talking about or where they are.

1. _____

2. _____

3. _____

4. _____

a. la orquesta
b. el poema
c. el tejido
d. la cerámica
e. los dibujos animados
f. el concurso

3 **La programación** Listen to this announcement about this afternoon's TV programs. Then answer the questions in your lab manual.

1. ¿Qué canal ofrece estos programas?

_____

2. ¿Qué programa empieza a las cuatro de la tarde?

_____

3. ¿Qué tipo de programa es *De tú a tú*?

_____

4. ¿Quién es Juan Muñoz?

_____

5. ¿Qué tipo de película es *Corazón roto*?

_____

Lección 17 Lab Activities

pronunciación

Syllabification

In Spanish, every syllable has only one vowel or diphthong. If a single consonant (including **ch**, **ll**, and **rr**) occurs between two vowels, the consonant begins a new syllable.

    co-che   dra-ma   mu-si-cal   ma-qui-lla-je   pe-rro   to-car

When two strong vowels (**a**, **e**, **o**) occur together, they are separated into two syllables. Diphthongs are never divided into separate syllables unless there is a written accent mark on the **i** or **u**, which breaks the diphthong.

    ar-te-sa-ní-a   ma-es-tro   his-to-ria   tra-ge-dia

If two consonants occur between vowels, they are divided into two syllables, except when the second consonant is **l** or **r**.

    al-fom-bra   or-ques-ta   pu-bli-car   ro-mán-ti-co

If three or four consonants occur between vowels, they are separated into syllables between the second and third consonants unless one of the letters is followed by **l** or **r**.

    e-jem-plo   ins-pec-tor   trans-por-te

---

1 **Práctica** Listen to the following words and divide each into syllables using slashes.

1. e s c u l p i r
2. c o n c i e r t o
3. i n s t r u m e n t o
4. c o n c u r s o
5. e s t r e l l a
6. a c a m p a r
7. p r e m i o
8. a p l a u d i r
9. b a i l a r í n
10. e x t r a n j e r a
11. p o e s í a
12. ó p e r a
13. a b u r r i r s e
14. c a n t a n t e
15. e n t r a d a

---

2 **Refranes** Repeat each saying after the speaker.

1. De músico, poeta y loco, todos tenemos un poco. [1]
2. Tener más hambre que un maestro. [2]

---

3 **Dictado** You will hear a conversation. Listen carefully and write what you hear during the pauses. The entire conversation will then be repeated so that you can check your work.

RAMÓN _____

_____

CELIA _____

RAMÓN _____

_____

CELIA _____

_____

RAMÓN _____

[1] *We are all part musician, part poet, and part fool.*
[2] *To be as poor as a churchmouse.*

---

estructura

17.1 The conditional

1 **Identificar** Listen to each sentence and decide whether you hear a verb in the future, the conditional, or the imperfect tense.

1. a. future   b. conditional   c. imperfect
2. a. future   b. conditional   c. imperfect
3. a. future   b. conditional   c. imperfect
4. a. future   b. conditional   c. imperfect
5. a. future   b. conditional   c. imperfect
6. a. future   b. conditional   c. imperfect
7. a. future   b. conditional   c. imperfect
8. a. future   b. conditional   c. imperfect
9. a. future   b. conditional   c. imperfect
10. a. future   b. conditional   c. imperfect

2 **Cambiar** Form a new sentence replacing the **iba a** + [*infinitive*] construction with the corresponding verb in the conditional. Repeat the correct answer after the speaker. (*6 items*)

> *modelo*
>
> Andrea dijo que iba a tocar el piano.
> Andrea dijo que tocaría el piano.

3 **Entrevista** You are considering taking a job as the director of a new soap opera, and a reporter wants to know what the new show would be like. Answer his questions using the cues in your lab manual. Then repeat the correct response after the speaker.

> *modelo*
>
> *You hear:* ¿Cómo se llamaría la telenovela?
> *You see:* Amor eterno
> *You say:* Se llamaría *Amor eterno.*

1. 23
2. San Salvador
3. romántica
4. Hispania y Univisión
5. Sí / muchísimo
6. $500.000

4 **Una exposición (*A show*)** Cristina is planning an exhibition for her artwork. Listen to her ideas and then indicate whether the statements in your lab manual are **cierto** or **falso**.

	Cierto	Falso
1. La fiesta sería al aire libre.	O	O
2. Invitaría al director de una revista.	O	O
3. Sus amigos podrían llevar algo de comer y beber.	O	O
4. Sus compañeros de trabajo irían a la fiesta.	O	O
5. Presentaría las pinturas de su primo.	O	O
6. A Cristina le gustaría publicar un libro sobre su escultura.	O	O

17.2 The conditional perfect

1   **Identificar**   Listen to each statement and mark an **X** in the column for the subject of the verb.

> **modelo**
>
> *You hear:* Habrían preferido ir al concierto.
> *You mark:* an **X** under **ellos**.

	yo	tú	él	nosotros	ellos
Modelo	___	___	___	___	X
1.	___	___	___	___	___
2.	___	___	___	___	___
3.	___	___	___	___	___
4.	___	___	___	___	___
5.	___	___	___	___	___
6.	___	___	___	___	___

2   **¿Lógico o ilógico?**   You will hear six brief conversations. Indicate if they are **lógico** or **ilógico**.

1. Lógico   Ilógico   4. Lógico   Ilógico
2. Lógico   Ilógico   5. Lógico   Ilógico
3. Lógico   Ilógico   6. Lógico   Ilógico

3   **¿Qué habría pasado?**   Look at the program for an art conference that was canceled at the last minute and answer the questions you hear. Repeat the correct response after the speaker.

15F

VI CONFERENCIA ANUAL SOBRE EL ARTE

PROGRAMA DEL DÍA (Martes, 24)

10:00   Café y pasteles para todos.

10:15   Presentación de todos los artistas que participan en la conferencia.

Conferencias

10:30   El mundo de la televisión: el futuro de los canales públicos. Presentada por Marisa Monleón.

11:00   La artesanía: expresión cultural de los pueblos. Presentada por Roberto González.

11:30   El cuento hispanoamericano. Presentada por Mercedes Román.

12:00   Las canciones populares como formas poéticas. Presentada por Federico Martínez.

12:30   Las bellas artes en El Salvador. Presentada por Francisco Ruiz.

Espectáculos

4:00   Concierto de la Orquesta Tegucigalpa.

5:00   Lectura de poesía hondureña, por Renato Lafuente.

17.3 The past perfect subjunctive

1   **Identificar** Listen to each sentence and decide whether you hear a verb in the conditional, the conditional perfect, or the past perfect subjunctive tense in the subordinate clause.

1. a. conditional   b. conditional perfect   c. past perfect subjunctive
2. a. conditional   b. conditional perfect   c. past perfect subjunctive
3. a. conditional   b. conditional perfect   c. past perfect subjunctive
4. a. conditional   b. conditional perfect   c. past perfect subjunctive
5. a. conditional   b. conditional perfect   c. past perfect subjunctive
6. a. conditional   b. conditional perfect   c. past perfect subjunctive

2   **Escoger** You will hear some sentences with a beep in place of the verb. Decide which verb should complete each sentence and circle it.

> **modelo**
> You hear: Yo dudaba que él (*beep*) un buen actor.
> You circle: **hubiera sido** because the sentence is
>   **Yo dudaba que él hubiera sido un buen actor**.

1. había vivido   hubiera vivido   5. había empezado   hubiera empezado
2. habíamos bailado   hubiéramos bailado   6. habías estado   hubieras estado
3. había trabajado   hubiera trabajado   7. había conocido   hubiera conocido
4. habías dicho   hubieras dicho   8. había bebido   hubiera bebido

3   **Cambiar** Say that you didn't believe what these people had done using the past perfect subjunctive and the cues you hear. Repeat the correct answer after the speaker. (*7 items*)

> **modelo**
> Martín / ver el documental
> *No creía que Martín hubiera visto el documental.*

4   **Hoy en el cine** Listen to this talk show and answer the questions in your lab manual.

1. ¿Creyó Olivia que Óscar había ido a la fiesta?

_____

2. ¿Era cierto que Óscar había sido invitado a la fiesta?

_____

3. ¿Creyó Óscar que José Santiago había hecho bien el papel de malo en *Acción final*?

_____

4. ¿Cómo habría tenido más éxito la película *El profesor*?

_____

vocabulario

You will now hear the vocabulary found in your textbook on the last page of this lesson. Listen and repeat each Spanish word or phrase after the speaker.

   Lección 17 Lab Activities   **101**

contextos

Lección 18

1 **Definiciones** You will hear some definitions. Write the letter of the word being defined.

1. _____   a. el terremoto

2. _____   b. el impuesto

3. _____   c. la tormenta

4. _____   d. la paz

5. _____   e. la guerra

6. _____   f. el tornado

7. _____   g. la encuesta

8. _____   h. las noticias

2 **¿Lógico o ilógico?** Listen to each news item and indicate if it is **lógico** or **ilógico**.

1. Lógico   Ilógico   5. Lógico   Ilógico

2. Lógico   Ilógico   6. Lógico   Ilógico

3. Lógico   Ilógico   7. Lógico   Ilógico

4. Lógico   Ilógico

3 **Describir** Look at the drawing and write the answer to each question you hear.

1. _____

2. _____

3. _____

4. _____

pronunciación

Review of word stress and accentuation

In Lesson 4, you learned that an accent mark is required when a word ends in a vowel, **n**, or **s**, and the stress does *not* fall on the next-to-last syllable.

pren-sa   ar-**tí**-cu-lo   ca-**fé**   hu-ra-**cán**   **pú**-bli-co

If a word ends in any consonant other than **n** or **s**, and the stress does *not* fall on the last syllable, it requires an accent mark.

de-**ber**   a-**zú**-car   **cés**-ped   **fá**-cil   **mó**-dem

Accent marks are also used in Spanish to distinguish the meaning of one word from another. This is especially important for verbs where the stress often determines the tense and person.

el *(the)*   él *(he)*   mi *(my)*   mí *(me)*   tu *(your)*   tú *(you)*

compro *(I buy)*   compró *(he bought)*   pague *(Ud. command)*   pagué *(I paid)*

1 **Práctica** Repeat each word after the speaker and add an accent mark where necessary.

1. contaminacion
2. policia
3. voto
4. ejercito
5. declaro
6. dificil
7. rapido
8. sofa
9. todavia
10. opera
11. arbol
12. luche

2 **Oraciones** When you hear the number, read the corresponding sentence aloud, focusing on the word stress. Then listen to the speaker and repeat the sentence.

1. Ramón Gómez informó ayer desde Radio Bolívar que había peligro de inundación cerca del río Paraná.
2. Él explicó que toda la población necesitaba prepararse para cualquier cosa *(anything)* que pudiera ocurrir.
3. El ejército, ayudado de la policía, recorrió la región e informó a todos del peligro.

3 **Refranes** Repeat each saying after the speaker to practice word stress.

1. Quien perseveró, alcanzó. [1]
2. A fácil perdón, frecuente ladrón. [2]

4 **Dictado** You will hear a conversation. Listen carefully and write what you hear during the pauses. The entire conversation will be repeated so that you can check your work.

MERCEDES _____

ENRIQUE _____

MERCEDES _____

ENRIQUE _____

_____

MERCEDES _____

_____

[1] *He who perseveres, succeeds.*

[2] *Pardon one offense and you encourage many.*

estructura

18.1 **Si** clauses

1 **Escoger** You will hear some incomplete sentences. Choose the correct ending for each sentence.

1. a. llovía mucho.   b. lloviera mucho.
2. a. te gustó algún candidato.   b. te hubiera gustado algún candidato.
3. a. podemos ir de vacaciones juntos.   b. pudiéramos ir de vacaciones juntos.
4. a. el conductor hubiera tenido cuidado.   b. el conductor habría tenido cuidado.
5. a. yo trabajaré con los pobres.   b. yo trabajaría con los pobres.
6. a. todos fuéramos ciudadanos responsables.   b. todos éramos ciudadanos responsables.
7. a. el presidente va a hablar esta tarde.   b. el presidente vaya a hablar esta tarde.
8. a. me lo pedirás.   b. me lo pidieras.
9. a. Eva sale con él.   b. Eva salga con él.
10. a. te habías comunicado con el dueño.   b. te hubieras comunicado con el dueño.

2 **Cambiar** Change each sentence from the future to the conditional. Repeat the correct answer after the speaker. (6 *items*)

> **modelo**
> Carlos se informará si escucha la radio.
> *Carlos se informaría si escuchara la radio.*

3 **Preguntas** Answer each question you hear using the cue in your lab manual. Repeat the correct response after the speaker.

> **modelo**
> *You hear:* ¿Qué harías si vieras un crimen?
> *You see:* llamar a la policia
> *You say:* Si yo viera un crimen, llamaría a la policía.

1. pedir un préstamo   3. buscar un trabajo nuevo   5. ir a Montevideo
2. ayudar a los pobres   4. quedarse en casa   6. hacer un viaje

4 **Un robo (A break-in)** Alicia and Fermín's house was burglarized. Listen to their conversation and answer the questions in your lab manual.

1. Según (*According to*) Fermín, ¿qué habría pasado si hubieran cerrado la puerta con llave?

   _____

2. Según Alicia, ¿qué habría pasado si hubieran cerrado la puerta con llave? _____

   _____

3. ¿Qué haría Alicia si Fermín y ella tuvieran suficiente dinero? _____

   _____

4. ¿Por qué se está poniendo nerviosa Alicia? _____

   _____

Lección 18 Lab Activities   **105**

18.2 Summary of the uses of the subjunctive

1 **Escoger** You will hear some incomplete sentences. Choose the correct ending for each sentence.

1. a. el terremoto había durado más de dos minutos.
   b. el terremoto durara más de dos minutos.

2. a. escribió sobre el incendio?
   b. escriba sobre el incendio?

3. a. no podían comunicarse con nosotros.
   b. no pudieran comunicarse con nosotros.

4. a. tenemos unos días de vacaciones.
   b. tengamos unos días de vacaciones.

5. a. los resultados de la encuesta están equivocados.
   b. los resultados de la encuesta estén equivocados.

6. a. ver el reportaje sobre el sexismo en los Estados Unidos.
   b. que ven el reportaje sobre el sexismo en los Estados Unidos.

7. a. te habrás enojado.
   b. te habrías enojado.

8. a. donde hay terremotos.
   b. donde haya habido terremotos.

2 **Transformar** Change each sentence you hear to the negative. Repeat the correct answer after the speaker. (*6 items*)

> **modelo**
> Creía que era muy peligroso.
> No creía que fuera muy peligroso.

3 **Preguntas** Answer each question you hear using the cue in your lab manual. Repeat the correct response after the speaker.

> **modelo**
> *You hear:* ¿Qué te pidió el jefe?
> *You see:* escribir los informes
> *You say:* El jefe me pidió que escribiera los informes.

1. hacer una encuesta de los votantes (*voters*)
2. mañana
3. tener experiencia
4. no
5. algunas personas no poder votar
6. los trabajadores no declararse en huelga

4 **El noticiero** Listen to this newscast. Then read the statements in your lab manual and indicate whether they are **cierto** or **falso**.

	Cierto	Falso
1. Roberto Carmona habló de los impuestos en su discurso.	○	○
2. Nadie se sorprendió de que Carmona anunciara que no se presentaría a las elecciones.	○	○
3. Corre el rumor de que Carmona está enfermo.	○	○
4. Inés espera que el Partido Liberal encuentre otro candidato pronto.	○	○
5. Ella cree que es posible encontrar otro candidato en muy poco tiempo.	○	○

vocabulario

You will now hear the vocabulary found in your textbook on the last page of this lesson. Listen and repeat each Spanish word or phrase after the speaker.